AMERICAN MEMORY HOLE

AMERICAN MEMORY HOLE

How the Court Historians Promote Disinformation

Donald Jeffries

Foreword by Sam Tripoli

Skyhorse Publishing

Skyhorse Publishing books may be purchased in bulk at special discounts for sales promotion, corporate gifts, fund-raising, or educational purposes. Special editions can also be created to specifications. For details, contact the Special Sales Department, Skyhorse Publishing, 307 West 36th Street, 11th Floor, New York, NY 10018 or info@skyhorsepublishing.com

Skyhorse® and Skyhorse Publishing® are registered trademarks of Skyhorse Publishing, Inc.®, a Delaware corporation.

Visit our website at www.skyhorsepublishing.com.
Please follow our publisher Tony Lyons on Instagram @tonylyonsisuncertain

10 9 8 7 6 5 4 3 2 1

Library of Congress Cataloging-in-Publication Data is available on file.

Hardcover ISBN: 978-1-5107-8194-8
eBook ISBN: 978-1-5107-8195-5

Cover design by David Ter-Avanesyan

Printed in the United States of America

This book is lovingly dedicated to my parents, Richard Ellsworth Jeffries and Anna Catherine Turvey, who were obsessed with the past in different ways. They triggered my own intense interest in history.

CONTENTS

ACKNOWLEDGMENTS

First, I very much appreciate Tony Lyons and Skyhorse having the courage to publish truly controversial books. I owe a deep gratitude to Chris Graves and Peter Secosh, whose research provided a great deal of material that wound up in the text. Peter also went the extra mile and proofread the manuscript with his superb editing skills, and contributed numerous suggestions that made the book better. I would also like to thank Tony Arterburn, Billy Ray Valentine, John Barbour, J. Gary Shaw, Vince Palamara, Ann Bougher, Carolyn Rose Goyda, Devvy Kidd, Felix Caraballo, G. Edward Griffin, Joseph P. Farrell, David T. Beito, Charles Key, Phil Nelson, Richard Gage, Steven Lamb, Tivilla Dean Lamar, Charles Ragan, Buell Wesley Frazier, Doug Horne, Scott Enyart, Paul Schrade, Vince Agnelli, Richard Syrett, Tim Kelly, William Matson Law, Nicole Shelton, John A. Quinn, John Hankey, Max Good, Steve Cameron, Steve Ubaney, Laurie Dusek, Jeff Rense, Robbie Robertson, Lisa Belanger, Georgia Ann Brown, and Sharon Farley. My wife Jeanne has stood beside me as I tackled one controversial subject after another, and maintains a consistently positive attitude I deeply admire. My children John and Julianna are my greatest blessings, and they are the reason why I keep doing what I do.

FOREWORD

BY SAM TRIPOLI

It is with great enthusiasm and admiration that I introduce you to Don Jeffries's latest literary endeavor, *American Memory Hole*. I've had the privilege of knowing Don through his insightful contributions to journalism—a field where his commitment to truth-telling stands as a beacon in an often-murky landscape.

In the realm of investigative journalism, Don Jeffries is a name that resonates with authenticity and courage. His career spans decades, marked by an unwavering dedication to uncovering the hidden truths that shape our world. From clandestine operations to governmental cover-ups, Don fearlessly navigates through the labyrinth of misinformation to expose the realities obscured from public view.

I first encountered Don's work through his appearances on *Tin Foil Hat with Sam Tripoli*, where his piercing analyses of corruption, secret societies, and intelligence psyops captivated audiences worldwide. What sets Don apart is his refusal to accept the status quo; he digs deeper, asks the tough questions, and challenges the narratives designed to keep us complacent.

American Memory Hole is a testament to Don's relentless pursuit of justice and transparency. In these pages, he meticulously unravels the threads of historical amnesia that cloud our understanding of pivotal events. He invites us to peer into the recesses of our collective memory, urging us to confront uncomfortable truths that have been conveniently swept aside.

Through meticulous research and a keen investigative eye, Don sheds light on the mechanisms of power that operate beyond public scrutiny.

He reminds us that journalism is not merely a profession but a moral imperative—a call to hold power accountable and to empower the public with knowledge.

I am honored to pen this foreword for Don Jeffries's new book, as it represents not only a culmination of his life's work but also a rallying cry for all who seek a deeper understanding of our world. *American Memory Hole* is a wake-up call—a reminder that the past is not always as it seems and that our future depends on our willingness to confront uncomfortable truths.

Prepare yourself for a journey into the heart of darkness and back, guided by a journalist who has made it his mission to illuminate the shadows. Don Jeffries's *American Memory Hole* is more than a book: It is a testament to the power of investigative journalism and a testament to the courage of one man who refuses to let history be written by the victors.

—Sam Tripoli
Host of *Tin Foil Hat with Sam Tripoli*

INTRODUCTION

> *The very concept of objective truth is fading out of the world. Lies will pass into history.*
>
> —George Orwell[1]

"History is a pack of lies we play on the dead," Voltaire said. George Bernard Shaw reminded us, "History, sir, will tell lies as usual." Hitler declared, "The victor will never be asked if he told the truth." And Lenin stated, "A lie told often enough becomes the truth." All the lies we've been told *have* become truth to the masses. And it isn't Hitler behind our collection of Big Lies.

This is my third volume of "hidden" history. There is a never-ending supply of ignored, suppressed, and misrepresented information from our past. If professional journalists did their jobs, and court historians told the truth, then books like this wouldn't be possible. To quote Harry Elmer Barnes, I am attempting to bring history into accord with the facts. By far my best-selling books have been *Hidden History: An Exposé of Modern Crimes, Conspiracies, and Cover-Ups in American Politics,* and its prequel, *Crimes and Cover-Ups in American Politics: 1776–1963*. Despite the dumbing down from our state-controlled media and woeful education system, some people still have a real thirst for historical knowledge.

When *Hidden History* was published in November 2014, this was an entirely different country. "Woke" madness had yet to rear its ugly head. It's hard to believe so much has changed in such a short period of time. But the Past is Prologue, and we didn't arrive at our current situation without plenty of warning. In this volume, we will dive deeper into the JFK assassination quagmire. The research community is more dysfunctional than ever and continues to work against the common interest of exposing the impossibility of the official narrative. That dysfunction extends to the 9/11 and other conspiracy-friendly researchers, who waste far too much time on infighting and accusing each other of being disinformation agents. In this book, we'll examine in greater detail the events of 9/11, the Oklahoma City Bombing, and the death of JFK Jr. We'll also look back at the Founding of the Republic, James K. Polk, Woodrow Wilson, FDR, Joe McCarthy, and several other misrepresented historical events and personalities. We'll further scrutinize "good guys" Abraham Lincoln and Ulysses S. Grant.

It isn't easy being a historian when most of America isn't interested in the past, and is woefully uninformed or misinformed about even the most important events and personalities. A 2015 poll conducted by the American Council of Trustees and Alumni concluded that many are "alarmingly ignorant of America's history and heritage." Ten percent polled thought TV's Judge Judy was a member of the Supreme Court. Barely 20 percent could identify James Madison as the father of the US Constitution. The 40 percent that were ignorant of the fact Congress has the sole constitutional authority to declare war can't really be blamed; Congress hasn't exercised this crucial power since World War II. So in effect, this power vested in Congress by the Constitution has long become irrelevant. "When surveys repeatedly show that college graduates do not understand the fundamental processes of our government and the historical forces that shaped it, the problem is much greater than a simple lack of factual knowledge," those conducting the poll noted, "It is a dangerous sign of civic disempowerment."[2] In another poll, from NPR/PBS NewsHour/Marist in 2017, only 77 percent of Americans knew which country the colonies had broken away from to declare their independence.

This isn't a brand-new phenomenon. In a 2008 Common Core survey, fewer than half of American teenagers knew when the Civil War was fought, and 25 percent thought Columbus arrived in the New World sometime after 1750. The group lamented American youngsters' "stunning ignorance" of history and literature.[3] A 2004 poll of adult Americans found that only 43 percent could correctly identify a figure as recent as President Herbert Hoover.[4] It is hard enough to get educated people to comprehend how thoroughly they've been lied to about our history. It becomes almost impossible, when you're attempting to enlighten people who aren't even knowledgeable about the lies. If someone doesn't even know the official version of an event, how do you show that it's inaccurate?

Going against the historical grain is just as bad a career move as going against the mainstream media-driven consensus on current events. Harry Elmer Barnes was a highly respectable historian, who wrote frequently for *Foreign Affairs,* the journal of the Council on Foreign Relations, one of the foremost "insider" organizations. Barnes was so enthusiastic a supporter for World War I, his anti-German propaganda was rejected for being "too violent to be acceptable" by the National Board for Historical Service.[5] However, during the 1920s, Barnes changed views dramatically, and he came to believe America had fought on the wrong side in the war. This was a period where alternative historical views were tolerated to some degree by the mainstream. Barnes's articles that portrayed Russia and France as the aggressors in WWI were published by outlets like *The Nation.* Barnes's 1926 book *The Genesis of the World War* was the first work on the subject published using primary sources. Calling the conflict "an unjust war against Germany," Barnes urged this country to be "better prepared to be on our guard against the seductive lies and deceptions which will be put forward by similar groups when urging the necessity of another world catastrophe in order to 'crush militarism,' 'make the world safe for democracy,' put an end to all further wars, etc."[6] Among those who admired Barnes's writings were classical liberal journalist H. L. Mencken and Socialist leader Norman Thomas. Barnes officially became persona non grata with his contention that all sides were equally responsible for World War II, and that Franklin D. Roosevelt had deliberately provoked the Japanese into attacking Pearl Harbor. In a letter to his friend Oswald Garrison Villard, an early civil rights activist who was one of the founding members of the NAACP, Barnes bemoaned the fact that "I cannot fight the thirty million dollars now in the coffers of the Anti-Defamation League to be used for character assassination."[7]

In 1940, the *New York World-Telegram* dropped Barnes's weekly column. As he became increasingly controversial, Barnes was forced to self-publish most of his writings after 1945. Barnes coined the phrase "court historians," which I use regularly, and I believe perfectly describes their toadying, tenured work. In his self-published book *Perpetual War for Perpetual Peace,* Barnes wrote, "It is no exaggeration to say that the American Smearbund, operating through newspaper editors and columnists, 'hatchet-men' book reviewers, radio commentators, pressure-group intrigue and espionage, and academic pressures and fears, has accomplished about as much in the way of intimidating honest intellectuals in this country as Hitler, Goebbels, Himmler, the Gestapo, and concentration camps were able to do in Nazi Germany." Interestingly, one of the last true liberals, Gore Vidal, opted to use Barnes's exact title for his 2002 book, which included the subtitle, "How We Got to Be So Hated." Barnes, like Pulitzer Prize-winning historian John Toland, learned that the court historians brook no dissent within their midst. Criticize iconic figures like Abraham Lincoln at your own peril. Contend that "We all breathe the same air. We all cherish our children's future," as John F. Kennedy did regarding the enemies of his age, and risk what George Bernard Shaw termed, "the most extreme form of censorship."

There is one underlying narrative in our modern society: while our leaders and institutions are labeled racist, homophobic, and transphobic, to call anything they do, or anything that happens, a "conspiracy" is to "threaten our safety and democracy," to quote from a March 2019 article in *Scientific American,* titled "People Drawn to Conspiracy Theories Share a Cluster of Psychological Features." With the advent of Donald Trump, opposition to "conspiracy theories" reached new levels of hysteria. *National Geographic* invoked "science" to explain the attraction of "conspiracy theories," and bemoaned the "misinformation" behind them.[8] Everywhere, the same theme was trumpeted: "conspiracy theorists" are mentally ill, endanger freedom, and must be silenced. There is even a Conspiracy Theory Addiction Center.

Economist Adam Smith explained economic price-fixing succinctly a long time ago, when he said, "People of the same trade seldom meet together, even for merriment and diversion, but the conversation ends in a conspiracy against the public, or in some contrivance to raise prices." Leo Tolstoy excited the hearts of future anarchists when he declared, "The truth is that the State is a conspiracy designed not only to exploit, but above all to corrupt its citizens." World leaders have often acknowledged a shadowy presence behind the scenes. In a July 14, 1856, speech in the British House of Commons, Benjamin Disraeli stated, "There is in Italy a power which we seldom mention in this House. . . . I mean the secret societies. . . . It is useless to deny, because it is impossible to conceal, that a great part of Europe—the whole of Italy and France and a great portion of Germany, to say nothing of other countries—is covered with a network of these secret societies, just as the superficies of the earth is now being covered with railroads. And what are their objects? They do not attempt to conceal them. They do not want constitutional government; they do not want ameliorated institutions . . . they want to change the tenure of land, to drive out the present owners of the soil and to put an end to ecclesiastical Establishments. Some of them may go further."[9]

The Establishment view of history, where high crimes and organized conspiracies are confined to Harding's Teapot Dome and Nixon's Watergate scandals, can only be promoted by ignoring all contrary evidence, eyewitness accounts, suspicious deaths, and historical precedents. Impossibly cartoonish villains from Jefferson Davis to Hitler to Osama bin Laden are trotted out to justify one unconstitutional and unjust action after another. Mass killings, like at Hiroshima and Nagasaki, are explained with the Orwellian justification that it "saved lives." According to our government, and its sycophants in the press, America *never* starts wars. And yet we are always at war. Iran has long been demonized because they called out the United States for its aggressive "bullying."[10] In a classic demonstration of what psychologists call "deflection," right-wing media especially have ludicrously called Iran "the world's bully."[11] America continues to occupy at least seven smaller countries around the world. Iran hasn't invaded a single country in more than two hundred years. Much as Agent Orange and other horrors plagued American service members in Vietnam, millions of US veterans still suffer from the toxic effects of the "burn pits" established by the military in Iraq and Afghanistan to dispose of all kinds of waste.[12] Russia and Vladimir Putin in particular, have now become the primary targets of today's "woke" Leftist hate, superseding Iran. This is especially ironic given how liberals as recently as forty years ago were magnanimous toward a much more threatening Soviet Union, urging détente and smearing the extreme Right as "red baiters."

Thanks in large part to the diligent efforts of researchers Chris Graves and Peter Secosh, I was able to find contact information for many persons associated with the events I cover in this book. The instances where I was able to contact them, and they were willing to speak with me, are recounted in detail here. However, the vast majority never answered my emails, and almost all the phone numbers listed for them—obtained via public records—had been disconnected. The few working numbers rarely answered. Messages I left on voicemail were never responded to. There is a clear reluctance or fear out there, which I don't think can be explained away innocently. Why wouldn't you be interested in questions about your loved one's unnatural death? Why wouldn't you be willing to talk further about things you had previously talked about? Why wouldn't you want to reveal the truth about events you were associated with? And if there is "nothing to see here, move along," and those asking the questions are despicable "conspiracy theorists," what is there to fear? The nefarious forces that are merely figments of our demented imaginations?

I expressed my pessimism about America in the Introduction to *Hidden History.* In the years since then, nothing has changed to make me more optimistic. Even I didn't foresee a world-wide lockdown, small businesses destroyed, millions thrown out of work, mandatory mask wearing, and the potential of a vaccine passport. The corruption in the past was always there, but it was tempered a bit by a general competence. The trains ran on time, to use the old analogy applied to Mussolini. Now things are more corrupt than ever, and the trains don't run on time. I don't pretend to know what the end game is. I just present the information, and let the reader decide. These aren't "theories," they are data unwanted by the court historians. The "Damned," as the great iconoclast Charles Fort put it.

Orwell's protagonist Winston Smith wrote in *1984,* "I understand HOW: I do not understand WHY."[13] I haven't figured out the "why" yet, either. But it is undeniable that the past is falsified in present-day America, as it was in the fictional Oceana. Think of a long, complex mathematical equation; if even one of the numbers is off, the answer will be wrong. In the case of our history, virtually *all* of the numbers are incorrect, so the answer cannot possibly be right. Sunshine is the best disinfectant; shining light on all the real disinformation and misinformation from our past can help place the Orwellian "new normal" in the proper context. Orwell also introduced "memory hole" into the popular vernacular. It is an appropriate term to use for this book, because all of the information I write about has effectively been shoved down the memory hole.

We need not go to the extremes of an H. L. Mencken, who once wrote, "Every normal man must be tempted, at times, to spit upon his hands, hoist the black flag, and begin slitting throats." But we should at least seek the truth, about the past and the present. And the ugly truth is we have been lied to about *everything.*

CHAPTER ONE

HIDDEN GEMS FROM EARLY AMERICAN HISTORY

I know of no way of judging the future but by the past.

—Patrick Henry[1]

I fell in love with history as a child, and my favorite era was the founding of this Republic. The War for Independence, the American Revolution—call it what you will—I devoured every book imaginable on the subject as a youngster. It excited me to read about the Sons of Liberty meeting surreptitiously in taverns, or angry colonists throwing tea into the Boston Harbor. Thomas Paine's *Common Sense* made a lot of sense to this blooming young radical. Thomas Jefferson became my favorite, in large part because his surname was closest to my own. That sort of thing often causes a great impression on a child.

But the Founders weren't perfect. They were flawed like all humans. George Washington first achieved notoriety at age twenty-two when his incompetence and poor judgment led to the outbreak of the French and Indian War.[2] There is still an intelligent argument to be made that the Articles of Confederation was better than what replaced it. Some of the best minds of the time—Patrick Henry, George Mason, and others—opposed the Constitution, feeling that it gave the government too much power. Mason's significance in the founding of the Republic has been largely overlooked. He wrote the Fairfax Resolves, which questioned British authority over the colonies, and drafted both the Virginia Declaration of Rights and the Virginia Constitution. Mason memorably refused to sign the US Constitution because it didn't forbid further importation of slaves, or stop the spread of slavery to other states. Declining to become one of Virginia's two US senators, he instead retired to his Gunston Hall estate. By not signing the Constitution, he lost his long friendship with his neighbor George Washington.

Seldom reported is the fact that, as would happen during the Civil War, wealthy colonists could avoid being conscripted into the War for Independence by paying a substitute to take their place. According to Howard Zinn, this led to rioting, with one familiar cry being, "Tyranny is Tyranny let it come from whom it may." In the spring of 1774, a Virginian wrote in his diary: "The lower Class of People here are in tumult on account of Reports from Boston, many of them expect to be press'd & compell'd to go and fight the Britains!" Indeed, four days after the Declaration of Independence was first read from the town hall balcony in Boston, the Boston Committee of Correspondence ordered townsmen to show up on the Common for a military draft. Connecticut passed a law requiring military service for all males between sixteen and sixty. The typical troubling exceptions for certain government officials, ministers, and Yale students and faculty were included. Eighteen men who failed to report for military duty were jailed and had to pledge to fight in the war in order to be released. Regarding the strict discipline in George Washington's army, a Concord, Massachusetts chaplain observed, "New lords, new laws. The strictest government is taking place and great distinction is made between officers & men. Everyone is made to know his place & keep it, or be immediately tied up, and receive not one but 30 or 40 lashes."[3]

The Colonial troops weren't perfect, either. In a shocking, rarely discussed atrocity, on March 8, 1782, a Pennsylvania militia group attacked peaceful residents of a Moravian Indian village in Gnadenhutten, Ohio. These Indians were Christians, and neutral in the War for Independence. Nevertheless, the militiamen voted to execute them all. The Indians spent the night before their executions praying and singing Christian hymns.

Eighteen members of the militia were opposed to killing the Indians, and refused to participate. In a barbaric act that would become all too familiar to students of hidden history, before murdering them, the American soldiers "dragged the women and girls out into the snow and systematically raped them." The Indians were bludgeoned to death and then scalped. The Moravian Indians were perhaps the earliest historical examples of nonresistance, as they did not fight back, but begged for their lives to be spared. Ninety-six Indians were killed, and the entire village was burned down. And in another precursor to what would become standard operating procedure for Northern troops during the Civil War, all property belonging to the Indians was confiscated.[4] This atrocity, which came to be known as the Gnadenhutten Massacre, led many Indians to lose faith in the Patriots' cause and precipitated reprisals.

In the summer of 1787, less than four years after they'd won their independence from England, representatives from the thirteen original colonies assembled in Philadelphia to revise the Articles of Confederation. Setting an unfortunate precedent for politicians in the future, the delegates opted for absolute secrecy of their proceedings. They decreed that "no copy be taken of any entry on the journal during the sitting of the House without the leave of the House, that members only be permitted to inspect the journal, and that nothing spoken in the House be printed, or otherwise published, or communicated without leave." During the four months they were in conference, the closed-door sessions featured sealed windows, and there were armed sentinels stationed both inside and outside of the statehouse. This was in stark contrast to the 1776 debates, when states like Pennsylvania had published weekly accounts of the proceedings in both English and German. Even George Mason himself expressed support for the secretive nature of the constitutional convention in a June 1, 1787, letter to his son George Mason Jr. James Madison kept details of the proceedings from even his close high-profile friends like Thomas Jefferson and James Monroe. In an August 1, 1787, letter to his famous cousin and namesake, the Reverend James Madison, president of the College of William and Mary, argued, "If you cannot tell us what you are doing, you might at least give us some Information of what you are not doing." James Madison would later acknowledge that, "no Constitution would ever have been adopted by the convention if the debates had been public."[5]

During the ratification debates in New York, John Lansing Jr. accused Alexander Hamilton of wanting to literally abolish the individual states altogether; retaining them merely as parts of a powerful central government. Hamilton hotly denied this, and ironically almost became involved in a duel over it. (Hamilton would, of course, later be killed in a duel by Aaron Burr.) Surprisingly, in his defense Hamilton criticized the Madison-led secrecy of the proceedings. This was perhaps the only time he agreed with his archfoe Thomas Jefferson, who wrote in an August 30, 1787, letter to John Adams that he "was sorry they began their deliberations by so abominable a precedent as that of tying up the tongues of their members. Nothing can justify this example but the innocence of their intentions, & ignorance of the value of public discussions." Jefferson referred to it as "an assembly of demigods." George Washington, as president of the Convention, was fully on board with the secrecy. Bemoaning a document recklessly left outside the meeting room, Washington told the delegates, "Gentlemen, I am sorry to find that some one Member of this Body, has been so neglectful of the secrets of the Convention as to drop in the State House a copy of their proceedings, which by accident was picked up and delivered to me this Morning. I must entreat Gentlemen to be more careful, least our transactions get into the News Papers, and disturb the public repose by premature speculations. I know not whose Paper it is, but there it is (throwing it down on the table), let him who owns it take it."[6]

Maryland delegate Luther Martin was outraged at the lack of transparency, and was compelled to write a series of newspaper articles after the Convention was over, which were titled "Genuine Information," and published in the *Maryland Gazette* from December 28, 1787 through February 8, 1788. A fellow Anti-Federalist, known only as "Centinel," credited Martin with having "laid open the conclave, exposed the dark scene within, developed the mystery of the proceedings, and illustrated the machinations of ambition. His public spirit has drawn upon him the rage of the conspirators, for daring to remove the veil of secrecy, and announcing to the public the meditated, gilded mischief; all their powers are exerting for his destruction; the mint of calumny is acidulously engaged in coining scandal to blacken his character, and thereby to invalidate his testimony; but this illustrious patriot will rise superior to all their low arts, and be the better confirmed in the good opinion and esteem of his fellow-citizens."[7] Patrick Henry predictably agreed, arguing that government shouldn't be permitted to "carry on the most wicked and pernicious of schemes, under the dark veil of secrecy. The liberties of a people never were nor ever will be secure, when the transactions of their rulers may be concealed from them . . . to cover with the veil of secrecy, the common routine of business is an abomination in the eyes of every intelligent man, and every friend to his country."[8]

George Mason foretold the kind of southern sentiment that eventually caused states to secede from the Union. Jefferson described, in a March 4, 1800, letter to Madison, how incensed Mason had been over the northern states exerting their will over the southerners. "G. Mason's proposition in the convention was wise, that on laws regulating commerce, two-thirds of the votes should be requisite to pass them. However, it would have been trampled underfoot by a triumphant majority," Jefferson wrote. Edmund Randolph was Mason's ally, and argued against the constitutional distribution of power, which would create "monarchy, or a tyrannical aristocracy," to quote from Randolph's motion for a second constitutional convention. "This Constitution had been formed without the knowledge or idea of the people," Randolph charged. Randolph refused to sign the Constitution, and every state delegation opposed his motion. On June 16, 1788, Mason declared, "Among the enumerated powers, congress are to lay and collect taxes, duties, imposts, and excises; and to pay the debts, and provide for the general welfare and common defence; and by that clause (so often called the sweeping clause) they are to make all laws necessary to execute those laws. Now suppose oppressions should arise under this government, and any writer should dare to stand forth and expose to the community at large, the abuses of those powers. Could not congress, under the idea of providing for the general welfare, and under their own construction, say, that this was destroying the general peace, encouraging sedition, and poisoning the minds of the people?" The Father of the Bill of Rights would be mortified that, over two hundred years later, our government is indeed demonizing critics as "insurrectionists" and "domestic terrorists."

Just imagine what kind of civil liberties Americans would have ever had without that Bill of Rights. Another Virginian, Richard Henry Lee, also strongly opposed expanding upon the powers granted to the government under the Articles of Confederation.

Mystery surrounds George Mason's second wife, Sarah Brent. Upon his death, she essentially disappeared from the historical record. Sources indicate she died in 1805 or 1806 at Gunston Hall, but also say it isn't known where she was buried. Researcher Vince Agnelli claimed that she seems to have vanished right after Mason's death, which he also thinks was suspicious. On the We Relate genealogy site, Sarah is listed as being born "about 1742," with no death date listed. Her birth date curiously varies as well. Wikipedia and other mainstream sources indicate she was 51–52 when they married in 1773. This would have her born around 1720, which no source lists. I've seen her birth date listed anywhere from 1730 to 1742. The online Virginia Encyclopedia informs us that Mason married "Sarah Brent, the fifty-year-old daughter of George Brent, a family friend. It is Brent's first marriage." I find it decidedly odd that a woman of her class had never married earlier. Most sources say that upon Mason's death, Sarah "probably moved to Dumfries to live with her sister Jean." This is strange behavior, since she inherited her husband's 400-acre property. It always attracts my attention when so little is known about the death of a prominent historical figure. Sarah Brent certainly qualifies in that regard, as the wife of one of the Founding Fathers.

Thomas Jefferson Battles the Supreme Court

The great object of my fear is the Federal judiciary.

—Thomas Jefferson[9]

In an 1820 letter to W. C. Jarvis, Thomas Jefferson made his views on the power of the Supreme Court quite clear. "You seem to consider the judges as the ultimate arbiters of all constitutional questions; a very dangerous doctrine indeed, and one which would place us under the despotism of an oligarchy," Jefferson wrote. "Their power [is] the more dangerous as they are in office for life, and not responsible, as the other functionaries are, to the elective control. The Constitution has erected no such single tribunal, knowing that to whatever hands confided, with the corruptions of time and party, its members would become despots. It has more wisely made all the departments co-equal and co-sovereign within themselves." Jefferson seems to have been the last politician to understand just how thoroughly the early Supreme Court justices were usurping power, and shattering the separation of powers and checks and balances which made the Constitution a revolutionary document. The essence of populism is an opposition to excessive power concentrated anywhere. Jefferson was aghast at "Judicial Review," which basically makes these unelected judges the arbiters of all important public policy. Jefferson asked how "to check these unconstitutional invasions of state rights by the Federal judiciary? Not by impeachment in the first instance, but by a strong protestation of both houses of Congress that such and such doctrines advanced by the Supreme Court, are contrary to the Constitution: and if afterward they relapse into the same heresies, impeach and set the whole adrift. For what was the government divided into three branches, but that each should watch over the others and oppose their usurpations?"[10]

John Marshall, as the first Chief Justice of the Supreme Court, became as powerful an enemy of Jefferson as Alexander Hamilton. Responding to Jefferson's constant criticisms, Marshall declared, in a September 18, 1821, letter to Joseph Story, "A deep design to convert our government into a mere league of States has taken strong hold of a powerful & violent party in Virginia. The attack upon the judiciary is in fact an attack upon the union." Note how this reverential reference to "union" foretells what would come from the first imperial president, Abraham Lincoln. Jefferson and his fellow Democrat-Republicans (it wasn't until the election of Lincoln that those who'd previously been known as Federalists broke off to become the modern Republican Party) framed the debate as one of the People versus an unelected court tied to the old aristocratic ways the Founders had rebelled against. Jefferson wanted to take away the power of judicial review, which was not sanctioned under the Constitution, and return it to the states. When Jefferson took office as the third President of the United States, there was not a single federal judge sitting in any courtroom who was not a Federalist. Much as Hamilton and his ilk had prevailed early on in terms of establishing horrific precedents like unlimited national debt and a powerful central bank, the same forces won again with the Supreme Court's 1803 *Marbury v. Madison* decision, which established the principle of Judicial Review, whereby unelected judges were granted the power to strike down laws and statutes they deem unconstitutional. Jefferson was incensed over this usurpation of power, writing in a September 11, 1804, letter to Abigail Smith Adams, "the opinion which gives to the judges the right to decide what laws are constitutional, and what not, not only for themselves in their own sphere of action, but for the legislature & executive also in their spheres, would make the judiciary a despotic branch."

Andrew Jackson, much as he took up Jefferson's mantle in battling a central bank, followed his lead in battling the Supreme Court as well. Jackson's antagonism toward the Marshall Supreme Court was more a reflection of his combative personality, however, than any strong intellectual opposition to Judicial Review. The Marshall Court ruled against Jackson when he was attempting to force out Native Americans from Georgia. In response, Jackson supposedly declared, "John Marshall has made his decision; now let him enforce it." Some believe this quote is apocryphal and was never actually uttered by Jackson. Regardless, in this case, Jackson's defiance was hardly heroic, as it led to the devastating Trail of Tears. Jackson actually acknowledged the power of the Supreme Court in a proclamation a few years later. John Marshall mockingly referred to this, stating, "Imitating the Quaker who said the dog he wished to destroy was mad, they said Andrew Jackson had become a Federalist, even an ultra-Federalist. To have said he was ready to break down and trample on every other department of the government would not have injured him, but to say that he was a Federalist—a convert to the opinions of Washington, was a mortal blow under which he is yet staggering."[11] Jackson had sounded much more like Jefferson when he courageously vetoed a request to renew the Second National Bank's charter in 1832. Jackson commented at the time, "It is as much the duty of the House of Representatives, of the Senate, and of the president to decide upon the constitutionality of any bill or resolution which may be presented to them for passage or approval as it is of the supreme judges when it may be brought before them for judicial decision. The opinion of the judges has no more authority over

Congress than the opinion of Congress has over the judges, and on that point the president is independent of both. The authority of the Supreme Court must not, therefore, be permitted to control the Congress or the Executive when acting in their legislative capacities, but to have only such influence as the force of their reasoning may deserve."[12] Jackson proved he had a lot of typical politician in him after Marshall died, when he lauded him as a national hero.

One has only to read the words of Jefferson and Jackson to understand just how thoroughly their perspective was defeated over the course of time. In today's corrupt climate, no one bats an eye at the universal declaration "let the courts decide." Not only would the Supreme Court transform the cultural landscape with their *Roe v. Wade* 1973 decision, effectively granting rights for a procedure never imagined, let alone mentioned, in the Constitution, federal courts have overturned reform-minded voter referendums and initiatives. Judicial Review of ballot initiatives was a logical extension of the power unwisely granted to the courts to decide which laws are instituted. In the 1930s, Indiana Congressman Louis Ludlow proposed permitting a referendum following any congressional declaration of war. This sounds like an eminently sensible idea, although as noted earlier Congress last exercised its power to declare war in World War II. Needless to say, America has been perpetually involved in other wars since then. Naturally Ludlow's idea was rejected, under predictable pressure from President Franklin D. Roosevelt, as was a similar effort from Rep. John Rarick during the Vietnam War. California's Proposition 187, which would have stopped illegal immigrants from getting public services, was passed by a substantial margin in 1994. Almost immediately, a federal judge declared it "unconstitutional." Why should one unelected judge be able to thwart the will of the people? In 2021, the Mississippi Supreme Court overturned a successful ballot initiative to establish a medical marijuana program, on a minor technicality.[13]

Like Andrew Jackson, Thomas Jefferson had his flaws. His behavior in pushing the prosecution of his former Vice President Aaron Burr for "treason" was deplorable. As one of Burr's lawyers charged, some of his actions indeed resembled what one might expect from a monarch, not a champion of liberty. Burr was dubiously alleged to have plotted to take some western states out of the union, in order to wage war against the Spanish in Mexico. Jefferson also publicly accused Burr of treason, before he went to trial, in the manner that other presidents like Richard Nixon, Barack Obama, and Joe Biden would employ in later high-profile trials. The motivations of the author of the Declaration of Independence were undoubtedly personal. Jefferson still smarted over the extremely close 1800 presidential election, which initially saw Burr tie him in electoral votes. Even when Burr killed his archenemy Alexander Hamilton in an 1804 duel, Jefferson remained bitter at him. Burr was acquitted of "treason," and when John Marshall, who was involved here as well, directed that he be brought before another grand jury in Ohio, Burr simply never showed up, and efforts at further prosecution were dropped. In one of those ironic quirks of history, when Burr's much younger wife sought to divorce him years later, she chose Alexander Hamilton Jr. as her lawyer.

Despite his human imperfections, the author of the Declaration of Independence was a true Renaissance man, and in my view *the* classical liberal of the era. I wrote extensively about the slandering of Thomas Jefferson in *Crimes and Cover-Ups in American Politics: 1776–1963.* This true man of the Enlightenment has been denigrated by the court historians, and in popular culture, to the extent that he is now crudely dismissed as a "racist." It's not widely publicized, but Jefferson's Monticello estate was declared a UNESCO World Heritage Site in 1987. The United Nations did recognize that Monticello, which the architect Jefferson designed himself, represents "a masterpiece of human creative genius."[14] They also noted that his unique design was based on ancient and Renaissance models. But despite this acknowledgment, those who run Monticello continue to stress the unfounded Sally Hemings nonsense, over the myriad of astonishing real accomplishments of Jefferson. Has there ever been another instance of a historical foundation denigrating the memory of the individual they are ostensibly honoring? In 2018, a new exhibit opened at Monticello, celebrating Sally Hemings, and matter-of-factly referred to her as mother of Jefferson's "other" children.[15] In fact, the DNA evidence, if it proved anything at all, completely eliminated Jefferson as the father of any of Hemings's children except one, and even that was unlikely.[16]

Most offensive of all to Jefferson's legacy was Lin-Manuel Miranda's hit Broadway musical *Hamilton.* The play, using a largely nonwhite cast, chronicles the life of Alexander Hamilton, who was the bankers' favorite Founder, and the father of our national debt, utilizing rap and hip-hop. This anti-libertarian elitist has been rebranded as extremely "cool" in the eyes of impressionable younger audiences. He and Jefferson were staunch political enemies. We can judge the effectiveness of this kind of absolutely inaccurate historical propaganda by the fact that Barack Obama told leftist comedian and talk show host Jon Stewart that he found the play "phenomenal." Miranda's Jefferson is an effeminate coward who doesn't appear until the War for Independence is over, with the opening line, "What'd I miss?" One would think his authorship of the Declaration of Independence alone might warrant some kind of mention. Jefferson and Madison are cast as dirty tricksters scheming to ruin the virtuous Hamilton. Establishment mouthpiece Conor Cruise O'Brien foretold the shifting political landscape in a biased and unfair 1996 article attacking Jefferson. "I believe that in the next century, as blacks and Hispanics and Asians acquire increasing influence in American society," O'Brien declared, "the Jeffersonian liberal tradition, which is already intellectually untenable, will become socially and politically untenable as well."[17] Presumably, the same "blacks and Hispanics and Asians" who were persuaded to turn on Jefferson somehow became entranced enough with another dead White male, Alexander Hamilton, to plunk down exorbitant money on wildly overpriced tickets for the play celebrating him.

As an illustration of the differences between the intellectual giant Thomas Jefferson and his foe (now a modern-day pop culture icon) Alexander Hamilton, consider this excerpt from Jefferson's January 16, 1811, letter to Benjamin Rush. Describing a meeting during the Washington administration between himself, Hamilton, and John Adams, Jefferson wrote, "Another incident took place on the same occasion, which will further delineate Mr. Hamilton's political principles. The room being hung around with a collection of the portraits of remarkable men, among them were those of Bacon, Newton and Locke, Hamilton asked me who they were. I told him they were my trinity of the three greatest men the world had ever produced, naming them. He paused for some time: 'the greatest man,' said he, 'that ever lived, was Julius Cæsar.' Mr. Adams was honest as a politician, as well as a man; Hamilton honest as a man, but, as a politician, believing in the necessity of either force or corruption to govern men."

In October 2021, New York City Mayor Bill de Blasio followed the recommendation of the Commission on Racial Justice and Reconciliation, which was chaired by his Black wife Chirlane McCray, to remove the statue of Jefferson which had stood in City Hall for 187 years. This was all to be done without any debate permitted. Democratic Councilman I. Daneek Miller, exemplifying the kind of "representation" Americans are being accorded in the twenty-first century, explained, "There's so much about Thomas Jefferson and his own personal writings, memoirs about how he treated his slaves, his family members and things of that nature and how he perceived African Americans and slaves—that they lacked intelligence, that they were not to assimilate into society. For us to really highlight such an individual is really not who we are as a council." Yes, Thomas Jefferson is most definitely not "who we are" at this point. In a June 1, 2020 letter, de Blasio had written, "The statue of Thomas Jefferson in the City Council Chambers is inappropriate and serves as a constant reminder of the injustices that have plagued communities of color since the inception of our country. Jefferson is America's most noted slave holder . . . and a scholar who maintained that Blacks were inferior to whites." Another statue of Jefferson, which stood outside a high school named for him, was toppled by Black Lives Matter protesters on June 14, 2020, in Portland, Oregon.[18]

Former New York Mayor Bill de Blasio epitomizes the authoritarian nature of the "woke" Left. Born Warren Wilhelm Jr., he changed his name to Warren de Blasio-Wilhelm in 1983, and didn't adopt his current moniker until 2002. Despite fawning press coverage, de Blasio has been awash in campaign finance scandals, and gave himself a hefty pay raise as mayor in 2016. Reflecting the connections we see invariably in these putrid public officials, de Blasio's uncle was a CIA official who ghostwrote the memoir of Mohammed Reva Pahlavi, the shah of Iran.[19] His mother, whose attendance at the prestigious Smith College is an indication of her impressive pedigree, served in the Office of War Information during World War

II, while his father graduated from Yale, and held top level positions like contributing editor at *Time Magazine* and Texaco's chief international economist. Both his parents were accused of being "communist sympathizers" in the 1950s. It is a severe indictment of present-day America that an entitled, lightweight, hack party politician like this could oversee the removal of a statue honoring perhaps the greatest statesman in the history of this country.

As I detailed in *Crimes and Cover-Ups in American Politics: 1776–1963,* Abraham Lincoln despised Thomas Jefferson, according to his former law partner, William Herndon. "Mr. Lincoln hated Thomas Jefferson as a man and as a politician," Herndon wrote. Lincoln particularly disliked Jefferson's "moral character" after reading Theodore F. Dwight's 1839 hit piece of a biography on the Founding Father. Modern stories dealing with this topic allege that Lincoln knew about the Sally Hemings allegations, which is frankly absurd. These lurid accusations simply were not talked about in that time period. There is no record of, and certainly no direct quotes from Lincoln, regarding Hemings beyond the dubious inferences in a 2015 *New York Times* article. The contrast couldn't be starker between the two; while Jefferson loved farmers and common people, even his associates admitted that Lincoln was never "unwilling to appear in behalf of a great soulless corporation." Huey Long loved to boast that he'd never taken a case against a poor man. It could fairly be said that Lincoln never took a case *for* a poor man. Lincoln, the Great Emancipator, supported the Fugitive Slave Law and actually represented two masters seeking the return of their runaway slaves. Lincoln also had no qualms about evicting squatters who were farming land owned by his beloved big railroads.[20] Jefferson would probably have become a leader of the Confederacy if he'd been alive in 1860. His descendant Thomas Garland Jefferson was a VMI cadet who was killed by federal soldiers at the Battle of New Market. While Lincoln became the first president to install a mandatory draft during the Civil War, states had conscripted soldiers during the War for Independence, as noted previously. Jefferson, however, was strongly opposed to a military draft, calling it "the last of all oppressions."[21] Like many of the other Founders, Jefferson was also appalled at the prospect of a large standing army, and could never have pictured our monstrous military-industrial complex. "A standing army," Jefferson wrote in a 1789 letter to David Humphreys, is one of those "instruments so dangerous to the rights of the nation." In a letter to Madison dated December 20, 1787, Jefferson had declared, "I do not like [in the proposed Constitution] the omission of a Bill of Rights providing clearly and without the aid of sophisms for . . . protection against standing armies." Jefferson reiterated this theme in a February 28, 1807, letter to Chandler Price, writing, "The spirit of this country is totally adverse to a large military force."

Consider just where Thomas Jefferson would be if he were alive today. His fervent opposition to excessive judicial power would put him on the outskirts of the political spectrum. He would undoubtedly despise the Federal Reserve, having spent so many years battling the idea of a national bank. And his warnings against a standing army, which obviously went unheeded, would not have prepared him for the leviathan that is the military-industrial complex, let alone the corrupt intelligence agencies associated with it. Who was the last politician to oppose the very concept of judicial review, which has become the foundation of our entire unfair and unjust legal system? Eisenhower warned against the military-industrial complex in his farewell address, but he spent his entire career serving it. Kennedy certainly challenged it, but after his assassination no one has followed in his footsteps. Jefferson would be so out of step with the times, he'd be relegated to appearing on "conspiracy" shows like mine. He'd be lucky to find any publishers. He would need his inherited wealth, because his job prospects in this rigged marketplace would be bleak. The University of Virginia, which he founded, probably wouldn't let him teach there. Jefferson, like George Mason, Patrick Henry, Thomas Paine, and most of the other Founding Fathers, reminds us of what great leaders can be, and were once like. It's no wonder that our cowardly court historians and state-controlled media give him such bad press.

Andrew Jackson continued Jefferson's battle against a national bank, and his successor in the oval office, Martin Van Buren, also refused to renew the bank's charter in 1837. Senator John Tyler criticized Jackson for his "abuse of executive power"[22] in opposing the bank. However, after switching to the Whig party and attaining the presidency following the abrupt death of President William Henry Harrison, Tyler shocked everyone by vetoing Henry Clay's proposal for a new Bank of the United States, calling it an infringement of state's rights. In his veto, Tyler wrote, "Before entering upon the duties of that office I took an oath that I would 'preserve, protect, and defend the Constitution of the United States.' Entertaining the opinions alluded to and having taken this oath, the Senate and the country will see that I could not give my sanction to a measure of the character described without surrendering all claim to the respect of honorable men, all confidence on the part of the people, all self-respect, all regard for moral and religious obligations, without an observance of which no government can be prosperous and no people can be happy. It would be to commit a crime which I would not willfully commit to gain any earthly reward, and which would justly subject me to the ridicule and scorn of all virtuous men."[23]

According to the court historians, the public responded with the largest protest ever assembled in front of the White House, which included a burning in effigy of President Tyler.[24] As researcher Peter Secosh noted to me, "This story has always intrigued me. It's got the *fingerprints of a manufactured event*. For one thing, what kind of a 'mob' protests the veto of a bank?" Supposedly, a large drunken group showed up outside the White House at 2 a.m. on the morning of August 18, 1841, blowing horns, beating drums, throwing rocks and firing guns, waking up the Tyler family. Some of the protesters were arrested, but Tyler interceded against them being prosecuted, being a firm believer in their right to self-expression.[25] It's instructive to reflect upon that, given the "cancel culture" authoritarians presently wielding power in this country. Tyler would also veto a revised bill to recharter a national bank, describing it as having "all the abuses of a private banking monopoly." Tyler was excoriated in the Whig press. "If a God-directed thunderbolt were to strike and annihilate the traitor," the *Lexington Intelligencer* wrote, "all would say that 'Heaven is just.'" Tyler was lambasted as "His Accidency"; the "Executive A**"; and "base, selfish, and perfidious."[26] There were numerous anti-Tyler rallies and demonstrations everywhere and other burnings in effigy. The White House received many letters threatening Tyler's life. Most incredibly, for the first and only time in history, the president's entire cabinet, except for Secretary of State Daniel Webster, resigned in protest.[27]

John Tyler was excommunicated from the Whig party. Henry Clay declared that Tyler was "a President without a party." He faced the genuine prospect of becoming the first president to be impeached. Tyler was included in a 2014 *Time Magazine* piece on the "Top 10 Forgettable Presidents." While it has always been controversial to oppose the banks, Tyler's presidential ranking is also unquestionably influenced by the fact he later supported secession, and shortly before his death won a seat in the Confederate House of Representatives.

James K. Polk: First Forays into Expansionism

The world has nothing to fear from military ambition in our Government.

—James K. Polk[28]

The first ten presidents of the United States, both Democrat-Republicans and Federalists, pretty much stayed within their constitutional boundaries, despite differing philosophies. The eleventh president, James K. Polk, came to power behind a pledge to expand America's borders westward. He was part of a group called the War Hawks, who advocated taking Mexico's northern territories and England's Oregon Territory, by force if necessary. The concept of Manifest Destiny was being promulgated by expansionists, which held that America had a God-given right to all land stretching to the Pacific Ocean. Manifest Destiny was the early precursor of American Exceptionalism, which fuels our present disastrous foreign policy.

Although Polk was a slave owner (he even brought his slaves to the White House), he is ranked in the upper tier of presidents by most court historians. Presiding over a war is always worth innumerable bonus points. His reputation, like Woodrow Wilson's, has fallen some in the past quarter-century, due to the pervasive influence of identity politics. No one objects to his expansionist impulses, however. By the time he succeeded John Tyler as president, the country was already close to war with Mexico. Texas had notably declared its independence, and Polk supported annexing it. According to historian Howard Zinn, Polk confided his goal of acquiring California to his Secretary of the Navy on the night of his inauguration. Zinn wrote, "His order to General Taylor to move troops to the Rio Grande was a challenge to the Mexicans. It was not at all clear that the Rio Grande was the southern boundary of Texas, although Texas had forced the defeated Mexican general Santa Anna to say so when he was a prisoner. The traditional border between Texas and Mexico had been the Nueces River, about 150 miles to the north, and both Mexico and the United States had recognized that as the border. . . . Ordering troops to the Rio Grande, into territory inhabited by Mexicans, was clearly a provocation. Taylor had once denounced the idea of the annexation of Texas. But now that he had his marching orders, his attitude seemed to change." Zinn goes on to quote from the diary of Zachary Taylor's aide Ethan Allen Hitchcock: "He seems to have lost all respect for Mexican rights and is willing to be an instrument of Mr. Polk for pushing our boundary as far west as possible. When I told him that, if he suggested a movement (which he told me he intended), Mr. Polk would seize upon it and throw the responsibility on him, he at once said he would take it, and added that if the President instructed him to use his discretion, he would ask no orders, but would go upon the Rio Grande as soon as he could get transportation. I think the General wants an additional brevet, and would strain a point to get it."

Zinn described how an early version of a false flag precipitated the unnecessary war: "All that was needed in the spring of 1846 was a military incident to begin the war that Polk wanted. It came in April, when General Taylor's quartermaster, Colonel Cross, while riding up the Rio Grande, disappeared. His body was found eleven days later, his skull *smashed by a heavy blow* (Emphasis original). It was assumed he had been killed by Mexican guerrillas crossing the river. In a solemn military ceremony visible to the Mexicans of Matamoros crowding onto the roofs of their houses across the Rio Grande, Cross was buried with a religious service and three volleys of rifle fire. The next day (April 25), a patrol of Taylor's soldiers was surrounded and attacked by Mexicans, and wiped out: sixteen dead, others wounded, the rest captured. Taylor sent a message to the governors of Texas and Louisiana asking them to recruit five thousand volunteers; he had been authorized to do this by the White House before he left for Texas. And he sent a dispatch to Polk: 'Hostilities may now be considered as commenced.' The Mexicans had fired the first shot. But they had done what the American government wanted, according to Colonel Hitchcock." Zinn shared another relevant part of Hitchcock's diary: "I have said from the first that the United States are the aggressors. . . . We have not one particle of right to be here. . . . It looks as if the government sent a small force on purpose to bring on a war, so as to have a pretext for taking California and as much of this country as it chooses, for, whatever becomes of this army, there is no doubt of a war between the United States and Mexico. . . . My heart is not in this business . . . but, as a military man, I am bound to execute orders." Polk had proposed declaring war on Mexico to his cabinet, before he knew of any hostilities taking place. Polk wrote in his diary, "I stated . . . that up to this time, as we knew, we had heard of no open act of aggression by the Mexican army, but that the danger was imminent that such acts would be committed. I said that in my opinion we had ample cause of war, and that it was impossible . . . that I could remain silent much longer . . . that the country was excited and impatient on the subject." Polk unquestionably incited the conflict by sending troops into disputed territory that had been historically controlled by Mexico. Like Lincoln would fifteen years later, and Franklin Roosevelt would do on December 7, 1941, Polk maneuvered the enemy into firing the first shot, then waxed indignant about it.[29]

The few Americans who know any history at all, even if they recognize that writer Henry David Thoreau was the actual originator of nonviolent protest, believe he was jailed over his refusal to pay taxes to support slavery. In reality, Thoreau was put behind bars in 1846, after he denounced the war with Mexico. His friend and fellow author Ralph Waldo Emerson is said to have visited him in jail and asked, "What are you doing in there?" To which Thoreau supposedly responded, "What are you doing out there?"[30] Posters advertising for volunteer soldiers in Massachusetts promised to pay $7 to $10 per month, as well as a federal bounty of $24 and 160 acres of land. One young man replied anonymously in the *Cambridge Chronicle,* "Neither have I the least idea of 'joining' you, or in any way assisting the unjust war waging against Mexico. I have no wish to participate in such 'glorious' butcheries of women and children as were displayed in the capture of Monterey, etc. Neither have I any desire to place myself under the dictation of a petty military tyrant, to every caprice of whose will I must yield implicit obedience. No sir-ee! As long as I can work, beg, or go to the poor house, I won't go to Mexico, to be lodged on the damp ground, half starved, half roasted, bitten by mosquitoes and centipedes, stung by scorpions and tarantulas-marched, drilled, and flogged, and then stuck up to be shot at, for eight dollars a month and putrid rations. . . . Human butchery has had its day. . . . And the time is rapidly approaching when the professional soldier will be placed on the same level as a bandit, the Bedouin, and the Thug."

There were reports of forced "volunteerism." James Miller of Norfolk, Virginia, protested that he'd been provided with "the influence of an unusual quantity of ardent spirits" before signing up for military service. "Next morning, I was dragged aboard of a boat landed at Fort Monroe, and closely immured in the guard house for sixteen days." The author of a history of the New York Volunteers wrote, "If it is cruel to drag black men from their homes, how much more cruel it is to drag white men from their homes under false inducements, and compelling them to leave their wives and children, without leaving a cent or any protection, in the coldest season of the year, to die in a foreign and sickly climate! . . . Many enlisted for the sake of their families, having no employment, and having been offered 'three months' advance,' and were promised that they could leave part of their pay for their families to draw in their absence. . . . I boldly pronounce, that the whole Regiment was got up by fraud—a fraud on the soldier, a fraud on the City of New York, and a fraud on the Government of the United States." . . . When recruits fell off by late 1846, the government paid those bringing them in $2 a head. Congress later promised regular regiments 100 acres of public land after honorable discharge.[31]

13,000 Americans died in order for the United States to increase its land base. Polk had solicited a curious ally in Santa Anna, the Mexican general who was defeated by Sam Houston after the battle of the Alamo. He naively believed the retired military officer would assist him in Mexico. Not surprisingly, Santa Anna turned on Polk and helped lead an unsuccessful Mexican resistance. The Mexican War, in many respects, resembled the kind of bullying America has become renowned for, particularly since the first Gulf "War." Mexico, like Iraq, Afghanistan, Yemen and others more than 150 years later, was a much smaller nation invaded by a great military power. American victory was a foregone conclusion, and nothing to brag about. General Winfield Scott wrote the Secretary of War in 1847, charging that "Our militia & volunteers, if a tenth of what is said to be true, have committed atrocities—horrors—in Mexico, sufficient to make Heaven weep, & every American, of Christian morals, blush for his country." In newly acquired California, during the first ten years of American rule, the Native American population plummeted from 150,000 to 50,000.[32]

A Santa Fe resistance group consisting mostly of Catholic clergymen and Pueblo Indians reacted to the military occupation of Taos, New Mexico. They rose up, killing the American provisional governor and several soldiers. Author Jolie Gallagher, described what happened when a Colonel Price marched into Taos to suppress the uprising: "They laid siege to the village, where terrified citizens took refuge in a church. Not swayed by the sanctity of the church, Price bombarded it with cannon fire. When all was done, 150 Taos villagers lay dead. Price gathered captured rebels and immediately put them on trial for murder and treason. The jury composed entirely of Americans and their sympathizers sentenced the men to hang." One American witness was appalled, writing, "It certainly did appear to be a great assumption on the part of the Americans to conquer a country, and then arraign the revolting inhabitants for treason. . . . Treason, indeed! What did the poor devil know about his new allegiance? But so it was; and, as the jail was overstocked with others awaiting trial, it was deemed expedient to hasten the execution. . . . I left the room, sick at heart. Justice! Out upon the word, when its distorted meaning is the warrant for murdering those who defend to the last their country and their homes."[33] The existing populations of New Mexico and California were disgusted at the Yankee invaders, and their brutal intimidation tactics, which included rape and robbery. Our "good guys" ethnically cleansed the enormous Native American population of California. Most of the atrocities were committed by the volunteer soldiers, who came largely from the upper and middle classes, and looked down upon the professional troops, 35 percent of whom were unable to write their own name. One private in the Army wrote to his father, "The majority of the Volunteers sent here are a disgrace to the nation; think of one of them shooting a woman washing on the bank of the river—merely to test his rifle; another tore forcibly from a Mexican woman the rings from her ears." Ulysses S. Grant wrote to his wife: "And how much they seem to enjoy acts of violence too! I would not pretend to guess the number of murders that have been committed upon the persons of poor Mexicans and the soldiers, since we have been here, but the number would startle you."[34] The Mexican War also produced the first instance of media consolidation, as five New York newspapers combined to form the Associated Press, in order to save expenses on firsthand news coverage of the conflict. Future prominent Civil War figures like Grant, Robert E. Lee, Stonewall Jackson, and Jefferson Davis were all combat veterans of the Mexican War.

The assault on Vera Cruz was especially barbaric. One Mexican observer described it: "The surgical hospital, which was situated in the Convent of Santo Domingo, suffered from the fire, and several of the inmates were killed by fragments of bombs bursting at that point. While an operation was being performed on a wounded man, the explosion of a shell extinguished the lights, and when other illumination was brought, the patient was found torn in pieces, and many others dead and wounded." A *New Orleans Delta* reporter wrote, "The Mexicans variously estimate their loss at from 500 to 1000 killed and wounded, but all agree that the loss among the soldiery is comparatively small and the destruction among the women and children is very great." The aforementioned Colonel Ethan Allen Hitchcock stated: "I shall never forget the horrible fire of our mortars . . . going with dreadful certainty and bursting with sepulchral tones often in the centre of private dwellings—it was awful. I shudder to think of it." Yet the faithful soldier Hitchcock produced "a sort of address to the Mexican people" at the behest of General Winfield Scott, in which it was claimed, "we have not a particle of ill-will towards you—we treat you with all civility—we are not in fact your enemies; we do not plunder your people or insult your women or your religion . . . we are here for no earthly purpose except the hope of obtaining a peace." A Mexican merchant detailed the bombardment of Mexico City: "In some cases whole blocks were destroyed and a great number of men, women and children killed and wounded." One lieutenant wrote to his parents about what happened after an officer named Walker was killed in battle:

"General Lane . . . told us to 'avenge the death of the gallant Walker, to . . . take all we could lay hands on'. And well and fearfully was his mandate obeyed. Grog shops were broken open first, and then, maddened with liquor, every species of outrage was committed. Old women and girls were stripped of their clothing—and many suffered still greater outrages. Men were shot by dozens . . . their property, churches, stores and dwelling houses ransacked. . . . Dead horses and men lay about pretty thick, while drunken soldiers, yelling and screeching, were breaking open houses or chasing some poor Mexicans who had abandoned their houses and fled for light. Such a scene I never hope to see again. It gave me a lamentable view of human nature . . . and made me for the first time ashamed of my country."[35] I still believe that Lincoln's army set the standard for egregious misconduct in war, but this kind of shocking testimony, along with the even earlier Gnadenhutten Massacre, indicates that the horrid instinct for mischief was already there.

Setting yet another precedent that would eventually produce the Marshall Plan after World War II, the United States paid Mexico $15 million after wreaking such destruction upon them. As for the lucrative financial promises made to soldiers, many were victimized by con artists and speculators, who appeared on the scene to try and buy the land warrants given to them by the government. Some soldiers were so desperate for money, that they sold their 160 acres for less than $50. The *New York Commercial Advertiser* reported in June 1847: "It is a well-known fact that immense fortunes were made out of the poor soldiers who shed their blood in the revolutionary war by speculators who preyed upon their distresses. A similar system of depredation was practiced upon the soldiers of the last war."[36] The profitable nature of all these perpetual wars was described brilliantly by the great General Smedley Butler, as he recounted all the fortunes that came out of World War I. While the promises to the soldiers here appear not to have been literally broken, as they were with the Indians, or the emancipated slaves ("forty acres and a mule"), or the World War I veterans, who never got their bonus, the Mexican American War veterans were still taken advantage of, victims of a rigged system still in its infancy.

Among the loudest voices against the war with Mexico was former President John Quincy Adams. Serving as a congressman from

Massachusetts, Adams was one of the few members who voted against the war; as usual, the side advocating conflict won handily, by a 174–14 margin. On February 21, 1848, the Speaker of the House called for a routine vote to bestow medals and adulation on the victorious generals of the Mexican-American War. The eighty-year-old former president bellowed out a "No!" vote, and after rising in an apparent effort to expound further on his opposition, he collapsed. Adams would remain unconscious and die two days later. To be mortally stricken in the act of opposing a typically senseless war was a fitting way for this brilliant man to end his long and illustrious career.[37]

Polk was a complex man. He voluntarily limited himself to a single presidential term. He was a staunch ally of Andrew Jackson in his battle against the Second Bank of the United States. Henry Clay, who lost the 1844 presidential election to Polk, had been one of the leaders in the Senate censure of President Jackson. Polk himself became the first of the twelve presidents in history at that point to be censured in 1848, for "a war unnecessarily and unconstitutionally begun by the President of the United States."[38] Undoubtedly inspired by the fact Andrew Jackson had won the popular vote in 1824, but because he didn't receive the required electoral votes, lost the election when the House chose John Quincy Adams, Polk was one of the first politicians to push for the elimination of the Electoral College. Although a southerner, he was also an early opponent of secession. Polk died shortly after leaving office, supposedly from cholera, and was buried with what seems to have been undue haste.

CHAPTER TWO

SCORCHED EARTH AND OTHER PRECEDENTS

Father Abraham: A Short Redux of Lincoln

Lincoln was a master politician, which means that he was a consummate conniver, manipulator, and liar.

—Murray Rothbard[1]

I covered the unrecognized crimes and tyranny of Abraham Lincoln about as thoroughly as can be in my previous book *Crimes and Cover-Ups in American Politics: 1776–1963*. The fact that almost everyone in our society continues to revere him above all other historical figures goes a long way toward explaining how we arrived at our particular present Orwellian point.

The mythology of Lincoln is built around the notion that he was a kind man leading benevolent troops, whose primary purpose was to free the slaves. Nothing could be further from the truth, as my previous book demonstrated very clearly. Whatever one can say about the average Southerner of that era, the average Northerner was certainly not supportive of the notion that Blacks were the equal of Whites. As Alexis de Tocqueville observed, "the prejudice of race appears to be stronger in the states that have abolished slavery than in those where it still exists; and nowhere is it so intolerant as in those states where servitude has never been known."[2] As I've noted before, even if the Confederates were fighting to keep slavery intact (and I think the evidence suggests otherwise), the Union Army was certainly not fighting for abolition. Lincoln's most aggressive general, the psychopathic William T. Sherman, exemplified how northerners really felt toward Blacks. In an April 26, 1863, letter to his brother, Senator John Sherman, the general wrote, "I won't trust n—s to fight yet, but don't object to the (Federal) government taking them from the enemy & making such use of them as experience may suggest." Despite the mythology that Sherman "freed" the slaves as he destroyed southern civilization, he actively discouraged them from joining his army, going to the lengths of burning bridges to stop them. Like the rest of the Southern population in the way of Sherman's troops, the slaves were often left without any food or provisions. Sherman's July 31, 1862, letter to his wife delineated the Union's purpose in the war: "Extermination, not of soldiers alone, that is the least part of the trouble, but the [Southern] people." His wife Ellen, showing the same compassion and tenderness, replied that she hoped for a war "of extermination and that all [Southerners] would be driven like the Swine into the sea."

Lincoln expounded upon his pragmatic views in a speech in Peoria, Illinois, on October 16, 1854, declaring, "Whether slavery shall go into Nebraska, or other new territories, is not a matter of exclusive concern to the people who may go there. The whole nation is interested that the best use shall be made of these territories. We want them for the homes of free white people. This they cannot be, to any considerable extent, if slavery shall be planted with them. Slave states are the places for poor white people to move from. . . . New free states are the places for poor people to go and better their condition."[3] Radical Republican and Lincoln Secretary of State William Seward explained, "The motive of those who protested against the extension of slavery had always really been concern for the welfare of the white man, and not an unnatural sympathy for the Negro."[4] In a February 27, 1860, speech at New York's Cooper Institute, Lincoln showed that his views hadn't changed on the subject when he reiterated his support for the peaceful deportation of Blacks so that "their places be . . . filled up by free white laborers."[5]

True abolitionist Lysander Spooner saw Lincoln for what he really was. "All these cries of having 'abolished slavery,' of having 'saved the country,' of having 'preserved the union,' of establishing a 'government of consent,' and of 'maintaining the national honor' are all gross, shameless, transparent cheats—so transparent that they ought to deceive no one," Spooner wrote.[6] As noted earlier, Lincoln never defended a runaway slave, but did represent their masters in court. He was also a supporter of the Fugitive Slave Law. Not exactly the stuff of a "Great Emancipator." One of his wealthy clients was an Illinois farmer named Robert Matson who brought slaves into Illinois from Kentucky to work part of the year on his farm. When Matson's freed Black overseer smuggled the slaves away, Matson brought suit to have his slaves returned. Naturally, Lincoln defended Matson before the Illinois Supreme Court. Lincoln argued that the Illinois Constitution did not apply because the slaves were only seasonal workers and did not reside in the free state of Illinois the entire year. The Court ultimately ruled against Lincoln and emancipated Matson's slaves.[7] Regarding the Fugitive Slave Act, Lincoln confided to a friend, "I confess I hate to see the poor creatures hunted down . . . but I bite my lips and keep quiet." When he proposed a resolution as a Congressman in 1849, to abolish slavery in the District of Columbia, he included a caveat requiring local authorities to arrest and return fugitive slaves coming into Washington. Wendell Phillips, an abolitionist from Boston, derisively referred to Lincoln as "that slave hound from Illinois."[8] In the first 1858 debate with Stephen Douglas, Lincoln declared, "When they remind us of their constitutional rights [to own slaves], I acknowledge them, not grudgingly but fully and fairly; and I would give them any legislation for the reclaiming of their fugitives."[9] Also in 1858, Lincoln said that if Illinois decided to offer citizenship to Blacks, he would oppose it.[10] Even in southern states that had seceded from the Union, Lincoln's federal marshals enforced the Fugitive Slave Law.[11] That's an odd policy for "good guys" fighting to free the slaves.

Lincoln didn't treat the Native American population any better than most other White leaders of the era. The Sand Creek Massacre of 1864 happened under his watch. The 3rd Colorado Calvary, under the command of Major John Chivington, had been formed exclusively to hunt down Indians. An 1851 treaty recognizing land as territory belonging to the Cheyenne and Arapaho people, was broken like so many other treaties. Gold being discovered in nearby Pike's Peak Country undoubtedly had a lot to do with that. First, a new treaty in 1861 "redefined" the Indian land to a fraction of its original size. The majority of tribal leaders refused to accept this land grab, and remained there. Not surprisingly, fighting between Indians and White settlers seeking gold soon followed. On November 29, 1864, Chivington's troops launched a surprise attack on the Indian encampment. The soldiers slaughtered between 150 and 500 Arapaho and Cheyenne. Adhering to the pattern of "total war" instituted by the Union Army, most of the victims were unarmed women, children, and elderly men. Eyewitness accounts by the soldiers themselves revealed brutalities like sabering young children, or using them for target practice, mutilating the dead by cutting off ears, noses, or fingers as "souvenirs," removing the genitals of both males and females to use as tobacco pouches or saddle decorations, and as seen in the earlier Gnadenhutten Massacre, the scalping of victims. Captain Silas Soule, who refrained from participating, reported that women were killed as they begged for their lives, and cut their own children's throats to save them from torture. "It was hard to see little children on their knees have their brains beat out by men professing to be civilized . . . there was no organization among our troops. They were a perfect mob," Soule stated. Soule would be shot and killed a few weeks after testifying against Chivington and the others, almost certainly in retribution. Foreshadowing the practice of World War II soldiers stealing Japanese skulls as gruesome trophies, the human artifacts from the Sand Creek Massacre would be displayed proudly in some Denver saloons. Chivington resigned his commission before he could be court-martialed, and the government failed to prosecute anyone involved.

This underreported atrocity was similar to other ugly vestiges of the "scorched earth" policy of generals like Sherman and Sheridan. In 1865, John S. Smith told Congress, "I saw the bodies of those lying there cut all to pieces, worse mutilated than any I ever saw before; the women cut all to pieces. . . . With knives; scalped; their brains knocked out; children two or three months old; all ages lying there, from sucking infants up to warriors. . . . By whom were they mutilated? By the United States troops" Robert Bent told the *New York Tribune* in 1879, "I saw one squaw lying on the bank, whose leg had been broken. A soldier came up to her with a drawn sabre. She raised her arm to protect herself; he struck, breaking her arm. She rolled over, and raised her other arm; he struck, breaking that, and then left her without killing her. I saw one squaw cut open, with an unborn child lying by her side."[12] A Major Anthony reported seeing a soldier shoot and kill a naked three-year-old. The legendary Kit Carson was repulsed as well, telling Col. James Rusling, "Jis' to think of that dog Chivington and his dirty hounds, up thar at Sand Creek. His men shot down squaws, and blew the brains out of little innocent children. You call sich soldiers Christians, do ye? And Indians savages? What der yer s'pose our Heavenly Father, who made both them and us, thinks of these things? I tell you what, I don't like a hostile red skin any more than you do. And when they are hostile, I've fought 'em, hard as any man. But I never yet drew a bead on a squaw or papoose, and I despise the man who would."[13] *This* is exactly the kind of criminal behavior Lincoln sanctioned in his generals, and set a precedent that we still see today in the conduct of US troops in our pointless foreign escapades.

Republican Senator John Sherman explained Lincoln's presidential platform in 1861: "Those who elected Mr. Lincoln expect him to secure to free labor its just right to the territories . . . to protect by wise revenue laws, the labor of our people; to secure the public lands to actual settlers . . . to develop the internal resources of the country by opening new means of communications between the Atlantic and Pacific." [14] Notice the word "slavery," the alleged reason why Lincoln pushed such a bloody conflict, is not mentioned. In his first inaugural address, Lincoln stated, "The power confided in me, will be used to hold, occupy and possess the property and places belonging to the government, and to collect the duties and imposts. But beyond what may be necessary for these objects, there will be no invasion, no using force against or among the people anywhere."[15] Has there ever been a more glaring misrepresentation of someone's political goals? In this address, the word "slavery" appears four times, and Lincoln made it clear that "I have no purpose, directly or indirectly, to interfere with the institution of slavery in the States where it exists. I believe I have no lawful right to do so, and I have no inclination to do so."[16] Lincoln was not a passionate abolitionist. He was a pragmatic politician who had been in the hip pockets of powerful interests his entire political career. I recounted in my previous book how Lincoln invoked slavery as a rationale for the war out of pure political expediency. Lincoln admitted that as a result of the Emancipation Proclamation, "The character of the war will be changed. It will be one of subjugation. . . . The South is to be destroyed and replaced by new propositions and ideas."[17] Not exactly the "malice towards none" we all learned about in school.

The insidious Rothschild banking titans were deeply immersed in American society by the time of the Civil War. As biographer Derek Wilson noted, Nathan Rothschild had "made loans to various states of the Union, had been, for a time, the official European banker for the US government and was a pledged supporter of the Bank of the United States."[18] The shadowy banking family has long been rumored to be in the center of dark conspiratorial activity. As another Rothschild biographer revealed, the correspondence for the London Rothschilds was "destroyed at the orders of successive senior partners" during the Civil War era.[19] Quoting author Jim Marrs, "In the middle of this immense flow of money was Rothschild agent Belmont, financing both sides. He strongly influenced bankers in both England and France to support the Union war effort by the purchase of government bonds. In 1863 the Chicago Tribune assailed 'Belmont, the Rothschilds, and the whole tribe of Jews, who have been buying up Confederate bonds.' Much later, this charge was styled a 'libel' by those who could not understand the duplicity of Belmont and his employers with their public pro-North sentiments. One of the younger Rothschilds visited America at the onset of the war and was as openly pro-Confederate as their agent Belmont was pro-Union. Concerning Lincoln, Salomon Rothschild wrote, 'He rejects all forms of compromise and thinks only of repression by force of arms. He has the appearance of a peasant and can only tell barroom stories.' The Rothschilds played both sides and apparently felt little compassion for the American tragedy. Baron Jacob Rothschild rationalized the carnage by telling US minister to Brussels Henry Sanford, 'When your patient is desperately sick, you try desperate measures, even to blood-letting.'"[20] As author G. Edward Griffin concluded, "The boot print of the Rothschild formula is unmistakable across the graves of American soldiers on both sides,"[21] *Salon* ridiculed this entire subject with a predictable June 2, 2011, piece headlined, "Was Abe Lincoln a Jewish Pawn of the Rothschilds?"

While such polls were not taken at the time, many historians admit that for much of the War Between the States, Lincoln's approval ratings with the public were probably lower than for any other president in history. The midterm 1862 elections were seen as a severe repudiation of him, and his reelection in 1864 was considered to be unlikely. Some didn't even want Lincoln as the 1864 nominee. Attorney General Edward Bates wrote in his diary, "The Baltimore Convention . . . has surprised and mortified me greatly. It did indeed nominate Mr. Lincoln, but . . . as if the object were to defeat their own nomination. They were all (nearly) instructed to vote for Mr. Lincoln, but many of them hated to do it." The Radical Republicans turned against him to such an extent that their Wade-Davis Manifesto accused him of "grave Executive usurpation" and "a studied outrage on the legislative authority." Court historians generally credit Lincoln's implausible reelection to William Sherman's vicious conquering of Georgia in early September 1864. Lincoln's friend A. K. McClure observed, "There was no time between January of 1864 and September 3 of the same year when McClellan would not have defeated Lincoln for President."[22] McClellan's "The War is a Failure. Peace Now!" platform was smashed, as notions of peace have always been in this country, by a major military victory.

Lincoln's vote total went down from 1860 in several states, and he was crushed by McClellan in New York City. Despite this, the results showed Lincoln somehow winning New York State. In response to the overt electoral fraud in the 2020 presidential elections, mainstream media outlets had the audacity to claim that Democrats had attempted to subvert the electoral process in 1864 by blocking mail-in ballots, much as modern Democrats would allege modern Republicans did in 2020. In reality, as I have noted many times, Lincoln instructed his commanders not to furlough soldiers who were suspected of being McClellan supporters.[23] In a November 9, 2020, piece for the Mises Daily, Thomas DiLorenzo wrote, "In border states like Maryland, where there was powerful opposition to the war, federal soldiers flooded the cities on election days and were instructed to vote, even though they were not residents of those states." Lincoln is lauded by the court historians simply for permitting an election during the war, and if there was any fraud in their eyes, it was on the part of Lincoln's opponents. Officially, we are told that Lincoln crushed McClellan in the Electoral College, despite his obvious unpopularity and the distrust of his own party. Lincoln has the reputation of the kindly peacemaker, while he tenaciously pushed war, and McClellan, who alone among the Union generals wanted no part of Grant's ghastly attrition strategy, is portrayed as a coward. History is written by the victors.

The outright thievery practiced by Lincoln's troops, which I described in detail in *Crimes and Cover-Ups in American Politics: 1776–1963*, continued immediately after Lee surrendered to Grant at Appomattox. Wilmer McLean had moved his family from their Manassas farm after both armies began converging on his property in 1861, and a union shell exploded in his kitchen. He hoped that the Appomattox Courthouse was far enough removed from the madness to keep his family safe. As the owner of the house where the surrender took place, McLean would later claim that Union soldiers immediately began *stealing* his furniture. Union Gen. Philip H. Sheridan was said to have purchased the table that the surrender agreement was signed on for $20 in gold. McLean insisted that the furnishings were stolen, while the soldiers claimed they paid for the items. Eyewitness *New York Herald* reporter Sylvanus Cadwallader stated that Gen. George Custer paid McLean $25 for one of the tables used during the signing. "Officers then began forcing money into McLean's hands, but McLean threw it back. Suddenly there was a rush, and the furniture was gone. Cane-bottomed chairs were ruthlessly cut to pieces, the cane splits broken into pieces a few inches long, and parceled out among those who swarmed around. Haircloth upholstery was cut from chairs, and sofas were also cut into strips and patches carried away." Wilmer McLean's son-in-law reported, "I have heard Mrs. McLean say frequently that the Union troops not only stole the tables and chairs besides other small furniture, but even took the children's playthings." Some young officers grabbed a rag doll, "lovingly handmade by a doting mother," belonging to seven-year-old Lula McLean, and "tossed [it] from one to the other, and called [it] the 'Silent Witness.'"[24]

As we have shown, horrible atrocities were committed by American military troops going back to the War for Independence. Certainly, the unconstitutional war with Mexico produced a bunch of them. The treatment of American Indians was often disgraceful. Women and children were targeted. Rape was rampant. Widespread theft of property occurred. But it took Lincoln and his bloodthirsty generals to refine such cruelty to an ugly art, and justify it as "total war."

I had a nice phone conversation with rumored George McClellan descendent Charles Ragan on April 18, 2022. Ragan was unsure of his exact relation to McClellan, but it could not have been a direct one since McClellan's son and daughter died without having children. Ragan would subsequently tell me his aunt, who had done research on the family, had determined they weren't related to McClellan. I dug deeper into George McClellan's roots, and was astonished at how many of his siblings, nieces, and nephews went childless. Still others strangely listed "private" instead of their offspring's names, and in a few instances, even kept their spouse's name as "private." I couldn't escape the notion that perhaps McClellan's descendants were, and are, ashamed to publicize their relationship with such an unfairly maligned historical figure.

Ulysses S. Grant: The Butcher

> *He is a butcher and is not fit to be at the head of an army. Yes, he generally manages to claim a victory, but such a victory! He loses two men to the enemy's one. He has no management, no regard for life.*
>
> —Mary Todd Lincoln[25]

Despite his earlier proclaimed distaste for the atrocities of the Mexican War, Ulysses S. Grant's record during the Civil War wasn't pretty. Grant was not an impressive military man. Like the other northern generals, he consistently lost battles to the plucky undermanned Confederate forces, who were led by far superior strategists. As the quote from Mary Todd Lincoln, who has been treated much more harshly than her husband by the court historians, indicates, Grant earned the ugly sobriquet of "Butcher" due to his proclivity for sacrificing his troops in a war of attrition. Even

Grant came to regret his most inexcusable move in this regard, writing in the memoir he wrote at the end of his life, "I have always regretted that the very last assault at Cold Harbor was ever made. No advantage whatever was gained to compensate for the heavy loss we sustained." Grant's staff officer Horace Porter would recount, thirty years later, "As I came near one of the regiments which was making preparations for the next morning's assault, I noticed that many of the soldiers had taken off their coats, and seemed to be engaged in sewing up rents in them. The exhibition of tailoring seemed rather peculiar at such a moment, but upon closer examination it was found that the men were calmly writing their names and home addresses on slips of paper, and pinning them on the backs of their coats, so that their dead bodies might be recognized upon the field, and their fate known to their families at home." It is estimated that some 7,000 Union soldiers died in this single, absolutely pointless charge.[26] Porter would also describe Grant's unemotional response to a particularly bloody attack on his forces, noting that upon receiving the news, he went to Grant's tent "and found him sleeping as soundly and peacefully as an infant." When Porter explained the situation, Grant's "military instincts convinced him that it was a gross exaggeration, and as he had already made every provision for meeting any renewed attempts against the right, he turned over in his bed, and immediately went to sleep again."

While Lincoln belittled Grant's predecessor George McClellan for his cautiousness and continually questioned his strategy, he trusted Grant to such an extent that he wrote, "The particulars of your plan I neither know or seek to know. You are vigilant and self-reliant; and, pleased with this, I wish not to obtrude any restraints or constraints upon you."[27] Grant had, up until the Civil War, been what most people would have called a disappointment in life, if not a failure. He wasn't helped by being a heavy drinker. Grant's other nickname was "Unconditional Surrender," due to his steadfast refusal to negotiate with the enemy. He also was irrationally proud and stubborn. After the disastrous last charge at Cold Harbor, Grant let his men's corpses lay out in the sun for four days before asking for a truce, as military tradition decreed that the one asking for a truce was admitting defeat. He lied about the massive casualties at Cold Harbor, telling the War Office that the losses were "not severe." Sixty-five thousand of Grant's men were killed, wounded, or went missing during the Overland Campaign in 1864. The damning portrayals of Grant and other Union generals by southern sympathizers in the years following the war have been dismissed by the court historians as white supremacist and racist drivel. Again, the constant reminder that history is written by the victors. One of the most popular of these revisionist views of the war was Edward Pollard's 1867 book *The Lost Cause.* Pollard charged that Grant "contained no spark of military genius; his idea of war was to the last degree rude—no strategy, the mere application of the vis inertia . . . the momentum of numbers." Over a hundred years later, biographer William McFeeley echoed this assessment, describing the Overland Campaign as "a nightmare of inhumanity and inept military strategy that ranks with the worst such episodes in the history of warfare."[28]

Grant was an integral part of the "total war" strategy of the Union army during the Civil War, which held that basically "all was fair" in defeating the enemy. While ancient wars had been full of atrocities, the Enlightenment "stressed that violence against non-combatants was barbaric and unworthy of modern military forces."[29] I provided countless examples of the horrors inflicted upon the civilian population of the South by generals like Sherman, Sheridan, and Grant in my book *Crimes and Cover-Ups in American Politics: 1776–1963.* The United States under Lincoln opted not to sign the Geneva Convention of 1862, which was an outgrowth of the Crimean War and was signed by ten European nations. Lincoln overturned the long-standing American tradition of following the international law code of Swiss jurist Emmerich de Vattel's Law of Nations. Because the law emphasized the protection of noncombatants, Lincoln replaced it with his General Orders no. 100, known as the Lieber Code of 1863. The Prussian-born Francis Lieber was, like Lincoln, no fan of our Constitution. He scoffed at the American system as "confederacies of petty sovereigns" which were based on the "obsolete ideas" of Thomas Jefferson. Lincoln, as noted earlier, despised Jefferson. The Lieber Code gave the president broad wartime authority to deny or suspend constitutional rights. In 1904, the new Geneva Convention adopted the Lieber Code almost word for word. The Code permitted "destruction of property" out of "military necessity." Obviously, this covered the tremendous crimes of generals like Sherman and Sheridan quite nicely. The Lieber Code, with its myriad of restrictions based on "military necessity," has even trickled down to our militarized police forces today, with corrupt law enforcement officials justifying the most outrageous conduct because of concerns for the police officers' safety. Lincoln's early blockade of southern ports on April 19, 1861, set yet another dangerous precedent; that withholding food and medicine from civilians is an acceptable aspect of war. Some 500,000 children died during the diabolical American embargo, or as it was typically phrased, "sanctions," against Iraq from 1990 to 2003, to cite just one horrific example.

Lincoln was quite open in his ruthless views about the South. To an Illinois congressman who requested that he "maul" the southerners, Lincoln replied, "Tell the people of Illinois that I'll do it."[30] Grant, like Sherman, Sheridan and others, was on board with Lincoln's desires. During the ferocious battle of Shiloh in April 1862, Grant vowed to "consume everything (of civilian property) that could be used to support or supply the armies."[31] General Pope's order No. 11, issued a few months later, authorized the Union Army to "proceed immediately to arrest all disloyal male citizens within their lines or within their reach in rear of their respective stations." If they refused to swear an oath of allegiance to the US government, they were to be thrown from their homes, and if they tried to return, they would be shot as spies. As an unnamed Union general noted, "our men . . . now believe they have a perfect right to rob, tyrannize, threaten and maltreat any one they please, under the orders of Gen. Pope."[32] By contrast, Robert E. Lee's General Order 73, issued in 1863, stated, "The commanding general considers that no greater disgrace could befall the army, and through it our whole people, than the perpetration of the barbarous outrages upon the unarmed, and defenseless [sic] and the wanton destruction of private property that have marked the course of the enemy in our own country." Lee went on to say, "It must be remembered that we make war only upon armed men, and that we cannot take vengeance for the wrongs our people have suffered without lowering ourselves in the eyes of all whose abhorrence has been excited by the atrocities of our enemies, and offending against Him to whom vengeance belongeth." As I stated in my previous book on the subject, the real historical record does undeniably reveal the "good guys" and "bad guys" to have been wildly misrepresented by the court historians. Court historian Jay Winik acknowledged Lee's principles, but criticized him for them, writing in his book *April 1865: The Month That Saved America*, which was lauded by Establishment figures like Doris Kearns Goodwin, "But as great a fighting man as he was, Lee had had his flaws, with many of the virtues of a man becoming vices as a commander . . . he was not stern enough with his men . . . Nor was he cruel enough. In contrast to a Sherman or a Sheridan, he refused to burn or plunder enemy property, or engage in selective assassination, declaring it 'Unchristian' and "atrocious,' even though the South could have greatly benefited from such tactics."

During Grant's bombardment and pillaging of the town of Vicksburg, the famished civilian population had to resort to eating all their horses and mules, and finally rats. When Grant ordered Sherman to take the state capital of Jackson, Mississippi, the city was evacuated by the Confederate Army, in order to avoid civilian casualties and property destruction. Despite this, Sherman's troops destroyed the town anyhow, and were rewarded with a banquet in the governor's mansion. Grant's inexcusable refusal not only to exchange emaciated prisoners of war with the Confederates, but to even permit the Confederates to release Union prisoners without exchange, was seen for what it was even by Lincoln's Secretary of War Charles A. Dana. Dana wrote, "We think after testimony given that the Confederate authorities and especially Mr. Davis ought not to be held responsible for the terrible privations, suffering, and injuries which our men had to endure while kept in Confederate Military Prisons, the fact is unquestionable that while Confederates desired to exchange prisoners, to send our men home, and to get back their own men, General Grant steadily and strenuously resisted such an exchange."[33] Despite the court historians' claim that southern prisons like Andersonville were singularly awful, Secretary of War Edwin Stanton's own statistics showed that even with 50,000 more prisoners in southern than northern prisons, the mortality rate for southern prisoners in northern prisons was much higher.

Lincoln and Grant's "scorched earth" strategy enabled the most egregious conduct imaginable. Gen. Eleazer A. Paine is not a household name today, but his brutal reputation was well known at the time.

Paine's troops held civilian hostages in Fayetteville and murdered three of them in the town square. However, Paine was not punished either for this incident or for the many allegations of a similar nature made against him. He was reputed to have hanged so many uniformed Confederate prisoners that he earned the nickname 'The Hanging General."[34] After his troops had burned several cotton mills, Gen. Kenner Garrard notified Sherman that hundreds of women and children who'd worked in them were under his control. Sherman ordered the arrest of the mill owners, and approved hanging them without trial, should "the impulse of anger" strike Garrard. As Sherman wrote to Garrard, "I repeat my orders that you arrest all the people, male and female, connected with those factories, no matter what the clamor, and let them foot it, under guard, to Marrietta, whence I will send them by (railroad) cars to the North . . . the poor women will make a howl. Let them take along their children and clothing, providing they have the means of hauling or you can spare them."[35] The list of atrocities committed by Union troops is endless. Their modus operandi was consistent: burning homes and crops, random hangings, rampant theft of personal property, and indiscriminate rape. And they were eager to brag about it; after his devastation of the Shenandoah Valley, Philip Sheridan boasted, "I have destroyed over 2000 barns, filled with wheat, hay, and farming implements . . . over 70 mills, filled with flour and wheat."[36] As the Commanding General of the Union Army, Grant bore ultimate responsibility for the outrageous conduct of Sherman, Sheridan, and others. There is nothing in the historical record to indicate a single instance where he condemned them in the slightest.

Grant's hypocrisy was most evident in his desire, after the Civil War had ended, to invade Mexico. Apparently, he'd changed his perspective significantly on the subject, since the days of President Polk. Only a month after Lee's surrender at Appomattox, Grant ordered General Philip Sheridan to Texas with instructions to "assemble a large force on the Rio Grande" for a possible invasion of Mexico to expel the French who were there. Fortunately, the invasion never took place. President Grant would propose the annexation of Santo Domingo, but again this never materialized.[37] As author Thomas DiLorenzo wrote,

> Ulysses S. Grant was notorious for using the expanded powers of government to employ almost all of his relatives, even including former Confederate General James Longstreet, whom he appointed federal railroad commissioner. (Grant and Longstreet were best friends as students at West Point. It was Longstreet who introduced Grant to his future wife, Longstreet's cousin. General Longstreet had no particular qualifications that were specific to the railroad business other than that he enjoyed riding on trains and was one of President Grant's oldest friends.) The very term 'lobbyist' was coined by Ulysses S. Grant, who used it to refer to the men who spent their days in the lobby of the Capitol building in Washington waiting their turn to bribe senators and congressmen. Such bribery was always a part of politics, of course, but with an expanded federal government came expanded lobbying and bribery."[38]

But Grant didn't stop there. There was a seldom mentioned invasion of Korea in 1871. What information is available sheds little light on the motivation, but as many as 350 Koreans were killed, including civilians. It appears to have been a very early example of the interventionist mindset that came to dominate American foreign policy.[39]

While Grant is still ranked as one of the worst presidents, his scandal-plagued administration has always been attributed to those he unwisely surrounded himself with, never to his own corruption. During his second inaugural address, Grant himself remarked in a self-pitying tone, "I have been the subject of abuse and slander scarcely ever equaled in political history, which today I feel that I can afford to disregard in view of your verdict." If only the court historians had treated Harding and Nixon with such understanding. His untrustworthy friends must have been the ones who forced Grant to secretly double his salary and accept extravagant gifts from Wall Street. Yet, when he died, his funeral attracted 1.5 million people to New York City. When Grant's Tomb was completed in 1897, a million more came to the dedication ceremonies. Frederick Douglass cast Grant in a Lincolnian light, eulogizing the former general and president as "a man too broad for prejudice, too humane to despise the humblest, too great to be small at any point. In him the Negro found a protector, the Indian a friend, a vanquished foe a brother, an imperiled nation a savior."

Evidently, Frederick Douglass wasn't aware of Grant's illegal war against the Plains Indians. In 1874, President Grant authorized the military expedition led by General George Armstrong Custer, into the Black Hills of South Dakota, rumored to be rich in gold. The Black Hills belonged to the Lakota Indians, who had signed a treaty with the US government guaranteeing their regional rights. Grant had campaigned on a peace platform with the Indians and had no legal right to the land. But as *Smithsonian* magazine put it, "Four documents, held at the Library of Congress and the United States Military Academy Library, leave no doubt: The Grant administration launched an illegal war and then lied to Congress and the American people about it." This statement is shocking, given the court historians' steadfast attempts to deflect any blame for the Indian Wars away from Grant, as they have refused to hold him responsible for the corruption of his administration. The influence of the powerful railroads, and their toady politicians like Abraham Lincoln and Ulysses S. Grant, came into play here as well. Indigenous peoples and their land had to be cleared in order for the transcontinental system to be built.

The Plains Wars symbolized the treatment of Native Americans. As the Lakota Chief Red Cloud was quoted as having said, the White man broke every promise but one: "They promised to take our land, and they took it."[40] Despite publicly remaining committed to a peace policy, in private Grant schemed to make war with his generals, including bloodthirsty Civil War commander Philip Sheridan. An aide left the following incriminating entry in a diary held at the West Point Library: "General Crook said that at the council General Grant had decided that the Northern Sioux [i.e., the Lakotas] should go upon their reservation or be whipped." Grant got a corrupt Indian Bureau inspector to manufacture transgressions against the "wild and hostile bands of Sioux Indians" that "richly merit punishment for their incessant warfare, and their numerous murders of settlers and their families." Custer's last stand at Little Big Horn came out of all this treachery. The US military responded with great force, and the Lakotas were totally routed. In 1980, long after everyone involved was gone, the Supreme Court ruled that the Lakotas were entitled to compensation for the theft of their land. That uncollected sum was over $1 billion.[41] In 1870, the Supreme Court would rule that Congress had the power to "supersede or even annul treaties" with Indian tribes. Soon afterward Congress would make any future treaty-making with the Indians illegal. The legislation decreed that Native Americans were not "to be acknowledged or recognized as an independent nation, tribe, or power." In 1876, the Grant administration, under a ludicrously termed "Peace Policy," ordered that all Great Plains tribes and bands move onto the truncated reservations outlined by his government or be considered "hostile."[42]

Should there be any doubt as to the intention behind these wars, William Sherman, whose enthusiasm for killing hadn't waned, confided to Grant, "We must act with vindictive earnestness against the Sioux, even to their extermination, men, women and children." Later, when Grant was president, Sherman's view was that "all the Indians will have to be killed or be maintained as a species of paupers."[43] This great "war hero" openly advocated a "racial cleansing of the land." A year before his death, an unrepentant Sherman stated that if not for "civilian interference" his troops would have "gotten rid of them all."[44] As Michael Fellman noted in his book *Citizen Sherman,* "The great triumvirate of the Union Civil War effort [Grant, Sherman, and Sheridan] formulated and enacted military Indian policy until reaching, by the 1880s, what Sherman sometimes referred to as 'the final solution of the Indian problem,' which Sherman defined as killing hostile Indians and segregating their pauperized survivors in remote places."[45] Does any court historian dismiss Grant as a racist?

Extending and Institutionalizing "Total War" Strategy

The diabolical "scorched earth" policy of the northern troops in the War Between the States set the tone for American military conduct in the future. The Spanish-American War represented America's first foray into foreign intervention, triggered by the sinking of the USS *Maine*, which was the first modern false flag. As historian Stephen Kinzer noted, President McKinley "became the first American president to threaten war against another country because it was mistreating its own subjects."[46] Blue Blood Senator Henry Cabot Lodge wrote to a friend, just *two weeks prior* to the *Maine* going down: "There may be an explosion any day in Cuba which would settle a great many things."[47] This foreshadowed the Project for a New American Century's desire for "a new Pearl Harbor," expressed in a paper the year before 9/11.[48] Less known is the suggestion in the declassified March 13, 1962, CIA memo on "Operation Northwoods" about arranging a "Remember the Maine" incident.[49] The Spanish-American War featured the now familiar atrocious conduct of US troops. In this case, the soldiers targeted their own Black brethren, who comprised nearly a quarter of the expeditionary force. The Black soldiers were kept out of bars and hotels in Florida. Evoking memories of the Sand Creek Massacre, drunken soldiers from Ohio snatched a black two-year-old from his mother and used him as target practice, to see how close they could shoot without killing the toddler. Both mother and child survived, but outraged black soldiers reacted by rampaging through Tampa, triggering an ugly race riot that wasn't reported by the mainstream media. The chaplain of a black regiment in Tampa wrote to the *Cleveland Gazette*: "Is America any better than Spain? Has she not subjects in her very midst who are murdered daily without a trial of judge or jury? Has she not subjects in her own borders whose children are half-fed and half-clothed, because their father's skin is black. . . . Yet the Negro is loyal to his country's flag."[50] The Supreme Court opened the door to the interventionist foreign policy that has become America's staple, with a 1901 ruling that "the Constitution does not apply" to US territories because they were "inhabited by alien races."[51]

The Philippine-American War, which began in February 1899, was pushed hardest by budding imperialist Theodore Roosevelt, who was then William McKinley's assistant secretary of the Navy. Roosevelt badly wanted to keep the Philippines, which had been ceded to the United States by Spain at the end of the Spanish-American War, as a colony. Most on both the Left and Right continue to extol Teddy Roosevelt's virtues, when in fact he probably left as many bigoted comments on the public record as any historical figure ever has. He reacted to a New Orleans mob lynching a number of Italian immigrants by writing his sister that he thought it was "rather a good thing" and referenced a recent dinner with "various dago diplomats . . . all wrought up by the lynching."[52] Teddy's commitment to war was perhaps most clearly expressed in an 1889 letter to British diplomat Cecil Spring Rice, where he declared, "Frankly, I don't know that I should be sorry to see a bit of a spar with Germany; the burning of New York and a few other seacoast cities would be a good object lesson on the need of an adequate system of coastal defenses."[53] "TR" unsuccessfully charged the *New York World* with seditious libel over their claims of his conduct during the Panamanian revolution. TR sent Marines into Colombia in 1903, and contemplated seizing Panama. Roosevelt blasted the Colombians, who had the audacity to object to being militarily occupied, as "blackmailers," "homicidal corruptionists," and "cut throats." He declared, "You could no more make an agreement with the Colombian rulers then you could nail currant jelly to a wall." Roosevelt's Secretary of State, Lincoln's former secretary John Hay, threatened to have the U.S. Navy prevent the landing of Colombian troops in the event of a revolt in Panama.[54] Panama would declare independence from Colombia with the backing of the American government. Uncharacteristically, TR's Secretary of War Elihu Root was a sole voice of reason. He recognized that the building of the Panama Canal marked a new step in America's blossoming imperialism. Root declared, "The South Americans now hate us, largely because they think we despise them and try to bully them."[55]

Theodore Roosevelt should not only be reviled by those opposed to real racism, but also by animal rights activists. In addition to being a proud big game hunter, as a young man he actually shot and killed a neighbor's dog that barked at him, after nearly riding his horse to death following a quarrel with a girlfriend.[56] On Kettle Hill in Cuba, near the fabled San Juan Hill, TR almost certainly killed a Spanish soldier as he was running away. According to podcaster Dan Carlin, Roosevelt's political opponents would later chant, "Hey hey Teddy Roosevelt, who shot a Spaniard in the back?"[57] Regarding the legendary rush up San Juan Hill, former West Point instructor Maj. Danny Sjursen wrote, "Old Teddy was as giddy as a schoolboy, shouting at the height of the battle: 'Holy Godfrey, what fun!' He would later call the battle 'the great day of my life.' After the battle, Roosevelt annoyed his professional military peers by shamelessly (and uncouthly) lobbying for a Medal of Honor for himself (President Bill Clinton would eventually bestow the award 80 years after Roosevelt's death)." Secretary of State John Hay called it "a splendid little war."[58] Such sentiments were understandable, considering Hay, as mentioned previously, had been Abraham Lincoln's personal secretary. Teddy passed his lust for war onto his son Archie, who would later revel in the giddy sensation he felt after shooting a German on the battlefield. Archie, in a violent rage, went on to stomp on the German's face, leaving his boot stained with blood. He would describe feeling like a creature "of the Stone Age."[59] According to the court historians, Teddy Roosevelt was a "progressive," dedicated to imaginary trust busting, when in fact he was a tool of Wall Street. He'd fit right into today's political world, as a Lindsey Graham–style foreign interventionist.

In 1901, a young Woodrow Wilson reacted to the invasion of the Philippines by stating, "Our interest must be marching further, though we are altruistic; other nations must stop and see this; they must not seek to stop us."[60] It was during this conflict that Americans first began the brutal practice of "Waterboarding," which was referred to then as the "water cure." This was a routine torture tactic used on Filipinos, a century before it burst into the news when our government was revealed to have utilized it against suspected "terrorists." The brave Filipinos continued to fight for some years after Roosevelt simply declared that "the insurrection against the authority and sovereignty of the United States is now at an end" on July 4, 1902.[61] Harvard philosopher William James was an outspoken critic of this hideous new interventionist foreign policy. James claimed that America's actions "reeked of the infernal adroitness of the great department store, which has reached perfect expertness in the art of killing silently, and with no public squalling or commotion, the neighboring small concerns." James was one of those who formed the Anti-Imperialist League in 1898. James summed things up succinctly: "God damn the US for its vile conduct in the Philippine Isles."[62]

In 1902, Senator George Frisbie Hoar gave a passionate speech on the floor of the Senate, in which he railed against "the attempt to subjugate a people striving for freedom" and bemoaned the "cruelties in the Philippine Islands." Hoar charged that "You have devastated provinces. You have slain uncounted thousands of peoples you desire to benefit. You have established reconcentration camps. . . . You make the American flag in the eyes of a numerous people the emblem of sacrilege in Christian churches, and of the burning of human dwellings, and of the horror of the water torture." Hoar castigated the troops for "the shooting of captives, the torture of prisoners and of unarmed and peaceful citizens . . . the hanging men up by the thumbs."[63] The Anti-Imperialist League published the letters of US soldiers serving in the Philippines. A captain from Kansas wrote: "Caloocan was supposed to contain 17,000 inhabitants. The Twentieth Kansas swept through it, and now Caloocan contains not one living native." A private in his outfit admitted that he had "with my own hand set fire to over fifty houses of Filipinos after the victory at Caloocan. Women and children were wounded by our fire." A volunteer from Washington State bragged: "Our fighting blood was up, and we all wanted to kill 'niggers.' . . . This shooting human beings beats rabbit hunting all to pieces." The Manila correspondent for the *Philadelphia Ledger* reported in November 1901, "The present war is no bloodless, opera bouffe engagement; our men have been relentless, have killed to exterminate men, women, children, prisoners and captives, active insurgents and suspected people from lads of ten up, the idea prevailing that the Filipino as such was little better than a dog. . . . Our soldiers have pumped salt water into men to make them talk, and have taken prisoner people who held up their hands and peacefully surrendered, and an hour later, without an atom of evidence to show that they were even insurrectos, stood them on a bridge and shot them down one by one, to drop into the water below and float down, as examples to those who found their bullet-loaded corpses." That same year, a returning American general revealed, "One-sixth of the natives of Luzon have either been killed or have died of the dengue fever in the last few years. The loss of life by killing alone has been very great, but I think not one man has been slain except where his death has served the legitimate purposes of war. It has been necessary to adopt what in other countries would probably be thought harsh measures."[64]

Secretary of War Elihu Root, reverting to form, responded to charges of brutality by stating, "The war in the Philippines has been conducted by the American army with scrupulous regard for the rules of civilized warfare . . . with self-restraint and with humanity never surpassed." Mark Twain commented, "We have pacified some thousands of the islanders and buried them; destroyed their fields; burned their villages, and turned their widows and orphans out-of-doors; furnished heartbreak by exile to some dozens of disagreeable patriots; subjugated the remaining ten millions by Benevolent Assimilation, which is the pious new name of the musket; we have acquired property in the three hundred concubines and other slaves of our business partner, the Sultan of Sulu, and hoisted our protecting flag over that swag." One British witness said: "This is not war; it is simply massacre and murderous butchery."[65] Historian Howard Zinn wrote, "American firepower was overwhelmingly superior to anything the Filipino rebels could put together. In the very first battle, Admiral Dewey steamed up the Pasig River and fired 500-pound shells into the Filipino trenches. Dead Filipinos were piled so high that the Americans used their bodies for breastworks."[66]

Many of the commanding officers in the Philippine War, who presided over these atrocities, were old hands at "scorched earth" techniques, being veterans of the Indian Wars. One such veteran, Brigadier General "Hell-Roaring Jake" Smith, notably issued orders to kill "everything over ten." Smith would later admit to what would certainly qualify as war crimes. He was court-martialed but served no time in prison. He was shown leniency on the grounds that he'd been driven to his actions by "cruel and barbarous savages." Another general, Frederick Funston, didn't even receive the meaningless reprimand Smith did. Funston had admitted in a speech that he had "personally strung up 35 Filipinos without trial, so what's all the fuss over [Smith] dispatching a few treacherous savages?" Funston proclaimed that anti-imperialists opposed to these horrors "should be dragged out of their homes and lynched." Upon hearing this, avowed anti-imperialist Mark Twain volunteered to be the first man lynched.[67]

The final cost of the pointless war in the Philippines was shocking. During one three-month period, 50,000 local residents of southern Luzon alone were killed. The Americans decreed that it was "a crime for any Filipino to advocate independence." Unknown hundreds of thousands of Filipinos died. The water buffalo was made nearly extinct, its numbers falling by a staggering 90 percent. Historian Stephen Kinzer charged, "Far more Filipinos were killed or died as a result of mistreatment [over four years] than in three-and-a-half centuries of Spanish rule."[68]

While not completely unprecedented, the reprehensible tactics of Lincoln's Union boys clearly established the template that the troops in the Spanish-American War, and in the Philippine-American War, followed. The odious "scorched earth" strategy of Lincoln's "total war" became standard operating procedure for the American military, with the familiar barbarity showing up everywhere from the jungles of Vietnam to the deserts of Iraq.

CHAPTER THREE

WOODROW WILSON: ONE WORLDER EUGENICIST

Neutrality is a negative word. It does not express what America ought to feel.

—Woodrow Wilson[1]

Woodrow Wilson was the first true globalist to occupy the White House. His dream of a League of Nations eventually culminated in the creation of the United Nations. If he were alive today, he'd undoubtedly be a member of the Council on Foreign Relations, and would happily attend the secretive yearly meetings of the Bilderbergers.

The son of a Confederate slave owner, Wilson became a college professor, the field to which so many future social justice warriors would flock. He openly advocated a parliamentary form of government while lecturing at Princeton, and voiced his disdain for the Constitution he would later swear to uphold. As governor of New Jersey, Wilson signed into law an odious 1911 act that approved the forcible sterilization of "the hopelessly defective and criminal classes," including those who were labeled "feeble minded."[2] The law was promoted as "An Act to authorize and provide for the sterilization of feeble-minded (including idiots, imbeciles, and morons), epileptics, rapists, certain criminals and other defectives." The law established a Eugenics board, and Governor Wilson appointed the members. The board determined who was to be sterilized, based on particular alleged physical and/or mental defects. In a precedent that would be utilized later for vaccine makers, the legislation shielded the doctors who performed sterilization procedures from any criminal liability. The author of this odious bill was Edwin Katzen-Ellenbogen, who went on to work for the Eugenics Research Association, at the Carnegie Institution's Cold Springs Harbor Lab complex. This organization campaigned across the country for the creation of a master Nordic race, and the forced sterilization of all those deemed to be unfit for procreation. Katzen-Ellenbogen left America for good in 1915, and resurfaced decades later in German-occupied France, where he was arrested by the Gestapo in 1943. Despite being a Polish Jew, his medical knowledge and affinity for eugenics resulted in him being given the position of camp physician at Buchenwald. After the war, his sentence of life imprisonment was modified to only fifteen years.[3]

Like Abraham Lincoln, by whom he was deeply influenced, Wilson had little regard for the Founding Fathers or the system of government they created. In a 1911 speech, Wilson declared, "If you want to understand the real Declaration of Independence, do not repeat the preface." He had centered his gubernatorial campaign in New Jersey around a pledge to become an "unconstitutional governor.[4] Wilson particularly disliked our Constitutional system of checks and balances, believing like his imperial predecessors Abraham Lincoln and Teddy Roosevelt that the chief executive should not be hindered by the separation of powers. Wilson and today's "woke" Democrats would be in perfect accord regarding the Senate Filibuster rule. Wilson bemoaned how a "little group of willful men, representing no opinion but their own, have rendered the great government of the United States helpless and contemptible."[5] Wilson made his views on the Founders' vision quite clear in a September 1907 speech: "We are not bound to adhere to the doctrines held by the signers of the Declaration of Independence: we are as free as they were to make and unmake governments. We are not here to worship men or a document. . . . Every Fourth of July should be a time for examining our standards, our purposes, for determining afresh what principles and what forms of power we think most likely to effect our safety and happiness. That and that alone is the obligation the Declaration lays upon us." Randolph J. May expounded upon the incompatibility between Wilson's progressivism and individual liberty, which was of paramount importance to the Founders, in a May 31, 2018, essay published in the *Washington Times,* titled "Woodrow Wilson's Case Against the Constitution." Wilson, in fact, seems to have been the first to refer to the Constitution as a "living" document, a view now embraced by virtually everyone on the Left.

Wilson only won the 1912 presidential election because the Republicans split the vote between former President Teddy Roosevelt, running on the new Bull Moose Party ticket, and incumbent William Howard Taft. As Wilson's ubiquitous aide Edward Mandell House would say, "Wilson was elected by Teddy Roosevelt." In a 1913 presidential address, Wilson declared, "the whole nation has awakened to and recognizes the extraordinary importance of the science of human heredity." Eugenics came directly from Darwin's theory of evolution. The "fittest" clearly didn't apply to many different categories of people. Most of the leading "liberals" of the day were fervent believers not only in evolution, but also eugenics. H. G. Wells, Margaret Sanger (founder of Planned Parenthood), Clarence Darrow, George Bernard Shaw, Alexander Graham Bell, and Theodore Roosevelt were just some examples of prominent eugenicists. The idea of weeding out the "bad genes" and promoting the "good" ones is now associated exclusively with Adolf Hitler's Nazi regime, but it was a popular perspective among progressives in this country well before he came to power, and continues to be a religious belief among modern figures like Bill Gates, Ted Turner, and many others.

President Wilson relied heavily upon the advice of the aforementioned Edward Mandell House, absurdly nicknamed "Colonel" despite no military background. House's Marxist beliefs were evident in his fiction. In 1912, House's novel *Philip Dru: Administrator: A Story of Tomorrow, 1920–1935* was published, incorporating his leftist mindset to such an extent that Senator Lawrence Y. Sherman would state, "Philip Dru is an autobiography of the colonel himself and solves the Conundrum how to get rid of the Constitution."[6] House's Marxist-slanted writings were initially written under a pen name, and were only revealed to be his work years later. Although Abraham Lincoln actually levied the first federal income tax in 1861, a graduated income tax (which critics have pointed out was one of the ten planks of the Communist Manifesto), was first established during the Wilson administration. The same year, 1913, saw the birth of the nefarious Federal Reserve System. *The Intimate Papers of Colonel House* revealed that House met with the Warburgs and other powerful bankers throughout 1913. Wilson's affinity for a central bank was first made evident during the Panic of 1907, when he stated, "All this trouble could be averted if we appointed a committee of six or seven public-spirited men like J. P. Morgan to handle the affairs of our country." House would also be instrumental in pushing the United States into World War I. In early 1916, the Germans attempted a serious peace overture to the Americans. This is something ignored by the court historians, but fortunately the man who received the overture, American Ambassador to Germany James W. Gerard, recounted it in his autobiography, *My First Eighty Three Years in America.* Gerard wrote, "In addition to the cable which I had already received informing me that Colonel House was 'fully commissioned to act' he himself reminded me of my duty in his February 16 postscript. In his own handwriting these were the words from House. 'The President has just repeated to me your cablegram to him and says he has asked you to communicate directly with me in future. . . .' All authority, therefore had been vested in Colonel House direct, the President ceased to be even a conduit of communications. . . . He, who had never been appointed to any position, and who had never been passed by the Senate, was 'fully instructed and commissioned' to act in the most grave situation. I have never ceased to wonder how he had managed to attain such power and influence."[7]

The one anti-war voice in the Wilson administration, Secretary of State William Jennings Bryan, had his authority basically usurped by "Colonel" House. As was noted in Bryan's memoirs, "While Secretary Bryan was bearing the heavy responsibility of the Department of State, there arose the curious conditions surrounding Mr. E. M. House's unofficial connection with the President and his voyages abroad on affairs of State, which were not communicated to Secretary Bryan. . . . The President was unofficially dealing with foreign governments."[8] The US Congress never even knew of, let alone approved, the secret treaty subsequently brokered by House, with England and France. Wilson would write to House, "England and France have not the same views with regard to peace as we have by any means. When the war is over, we can force them to our way of thinking, because by that time they will among other things be financially in our hands."[9]

The false flag that triggered America's entrance into the war was the sinking of the *Lusitania*. As always, the elite proved to have a keen sense of prophecy. "Colonel" House was in England at the time, scheduled to meet with King George V. Sir Edward Grey, who was accompanying House, asked him at one point, "What will America do if the Germans sink an ocean liner with American passengers on board?" In his diaries, House recorded that he replied, "I told him if this were done, a flame of indignation would sweep America, which would in itself probably carry us into the war." Even odder, at Buckingham Palace, King George also brought up the subject and was shockingly precise, remarking, "Suppose they should sink the Lusitania with American passengers on board."[10] In a May 9, 1915, note to Wilson, William Jennings Bryan commented, "Germany has a right to prevent contraband going to the Allies, and a ship carrying contraband should not rely upon passengers to protect her from attack—it would be like putting women and children in front of an army." During a June 1 cabinet meeting where Wilson discussed entering the war, Secretary of the Treasury William McAdoo reported, "I remember that Bryan had little to say at this meeting; he sat throughout the proceedings with his eyes half closed most of the time. After the meeting he told the President, as I learned later, that he could not sign the note. . . . Bryan went on to say that he thought his usefulness as Secretary of State was over, and he proposed to resign."[11]

The eventual inquiry into the incident, overseen by Lord Mersey,[12] would conclude, "I am directed by the board of Admiralty to inform you that it is considered politically expedient that Captain Turner, the master of the Lusitania, be prominently blamed for the disaster." Two days after that, Mersey wrote to Prime Minister Asquith and turned down his fee for services, adding, "I must request that henceforth I be excused from administering His Majesty's Justice." In later years, he would state, "The Lusitania case was damn dirty business."[13]

Wilson built upon the awful precedents sent by Lincoln, and added a few of his own. In a startling foretelling of the "Freedom Fries" nonsense decades later during the Gulf War, sauerkraut was rechristened "Liberty cabbage" during World War I. The timeless music of Beethoven was banned in many places. The teaching of the German language in public schools was discouraged, and prohibited in some cases. "Patriots" were urged to spy on suspected "disloyal" neighbors. Wilson's Committee on Public Information overtly attempted to manipulate public opinion, which was initially overwhelmingly opposed to entering the war. The introduction of Liberty Bonds in 1917 would be refined to precision during World War II. Socialist leader Eugene Debs was only one of thousands of war critics to be jailed. The great classical liberal H. L. Mencken satirized how the civil libertarians of his day were being demonized, writing that they were "the same fanatics who shake the air with sobs every time the Postmaster-General of the United States bars a periodical from the mails because its ideas do not please him, and every time some poor Russian is deported for reading Karl Marx, and every time a Prohibition enforcement officer murders a bootlegger who resists his levies, and every time agents of the Department of Justice throw an Italian out of the window."[14] The reference to periodicals being banned from the mails was related to the very real censorship the Wilson administration imposed. In this regard, again he was emulating Lincoln, who shut down hundreds of newspapers during the Civil War. Mencken scoffed at all the worship of Wilson, claiming he was becoming a candidate "for the first vacancy in the Trinity."[15] The great Murray Rothbard summed up the era perfectly, writing, "The period of the First World War was a watershed in the evolution of the corporate-liberal warfare state. It saw the burgeoning not only of the government-business alliance in industry, and American militarism and globalism, but also of the ideology and apparatus of the national security state."[16]

Wilson not only engineered American entrance into the European conflict, he set the template for our disastrous meddlesome foreign policy in the future, by interfering in Vera Cruz in 1914, and ordering an occupation of Haiti in 1915. U.S. Marines invaded Haiti in 1915, and, foreshadowing what would happen repeatedly later in the century under the auspices of the CIA, forced the Haitian legislature to install America's preferred candidate as president. When Haiti refused to declare war on Germany after the United States did, the Wilson government simply dissolved the Haitian legislature. Then the United States engineered a kangaroo pseudo-referendum, which instituted a new, less democratic Haitian constitution. The "vote" was an absurd 98,225 to 768. As foreign policy professor Piero Gleijesus put it, "It is not that Wilson failed in his earnest efforts to bring democracy to these little countries. He never tried. He intervened to impose hegemony, not democracy." The United States also converted Haiti's traditional individual ownership of modest properties into large plantations. Our troops forced shackled peasants to work on road construction. Fed up, the Haitians revolted in 1919, in a guerrilla war that killed more than three thousand. Exemplifying the atrocities that mirrored those of northern troops during the Civil War, and would be revisited in countless wars to come, US marine general George Barnett complained to his commander that, "Practically indiscriminate killing of natives has gone on for some time." Barnett would describe it as "the most startling thing of its kind that has ever taken place in the Marine Corps."[17] Barnett went on to say in a public letter, "that he was shocked beyond expression to hear of such things and to know that it was at all possible that duty could be so badly performed by marines of any class."[18]

Some sources credit then–Assistant Secretary of the Navy Franklin D. Roosevelt with actually writing the new Haitian constitution. Other sources have him overseeing the writing and approving it. Regardless, FDR would later brag about writing it. Under the constitution, Haiti explicitly allowed foreigners to control Haitian land for the first time. While serving in the New York State Senate, the iconic "liberal" Roosevelt wrote a note in the margin of a 1911 speech that stated, "story of n***er." He was also instrumental in establishing segregated restrooms in government buildings while serving in the Wilson administration.[19] It is known that FDR was even interested in setting up a *plantation* in Haiti, along with businessman John McIlhenny, who was the highest-ranking US civilian official in Haiti, and his distant cousin Major Henry L. Roosevelt, later to become assistant secretary of the navy during FDR's presidency. McIlhenny was quoted as making a terribly offensive remark about the Haitian Minister of Agriculture, and how "that man would have brought $1,500 at auction in New Orleans in 1860 for stud purposes." FDR remembered the remark favorably enough to retell it to American Minister Norman Armour during his visit as President in 1934.[20]

Wilson declared, "I am going to teach the Latin American republics to elect good men." A man of his word on this issue, Wilson intervened in Latin America more frequently than any presidential administration in history. He sent troops to Mexico in 1914, Haiti in 1915, the Dominican Republic in 1916, Mexico again in 1916 and then *nine more times* before he left office, Cuba in 1917, and Panama in 1918. Wilson also maintained a military presence in Nicaragua, to help sway the presidential election and force the passage of a favorable treaty. His pre-CIA intervention paved the way for dictators like Batista, Trujillo, the Duvaliers, and the Somozas. Wilson's persistent invasions of smaller countries, seldom touched upon by generally adoring historians, were unpopular in this country and provoked much criticism abroad.[21] Populist Senator Thomas Gore, grandfather of writer Gore Vidal, probably had good reason to state, "Woodrow Wilson had no friends, only slaves and enemies."[22] Wilson famously told the Foreign Trade Convention in 1914 that "There is nothing in which I am more interested than the fullest development of the trade of this country and its righteous conquest of foreign markets." Wilson was particularly interested in Mexico. US business investment had doubled between 1900 and 1910, giving Americans ownership of approximately 43 percent of Mexican property values. This was 10 percent more than Mexicans themselves owned. William Randolph Hearst alone held over 17 million acres. Wilson, going further than anyone else had in opposing the revolutionary forces of Francisco Madero, sent thousands of troops to the Mexican border and warships to the oil fields near Tampico and the port of Veracruz in April 1914. Over the objections of Secretary of State William Jennings Bryan, and with the hearty approval of Congress, Wilson sent a force of seven battleships, four fully manned marine troop transports, and numerous destroyers to Mexico. Over 150 Mexicans were killed at Veracruz, where six thousand marines remained in occupation for seven months.[23] Incredibly, Wilson's petty justification for invading Mexico was that they had refused to obey an order for a twenty-one-gun salute to the American flag. Wilson would have the audacity to wax rhapsodic about "the sacredness of the right of self-determination,"[24] again setting a precedent for hypocritical, interventionist politicians to come.

Wilson's rationale that World War I would "make the world safe for Democracy" has been echoed by imperialistic politicians ever since. Presently, the "liberals" of our era are saber-rattling for our involvement in the Russia-Ukraine situation, with the exact same justification—to "defend Democracy." The fact Ukraine is not a democracy doesn't deter them. Our state- controlled media and clueless celebrities converted former actor/comedian-turned-president Volodymyr Zelenskyy into a rock star, even after he summarily shut down all political opposition parties in March 2022. After being reelected to the presidency on the platform that he kept us out of the war, Wilson began indirectly involving the United States. He supported the harsh British blockade of Germany, which a young Winston Churchill, then–First Lord of the Admiralty, freely admitted was designed to "starve the whole population—men, women, and children, old and young, wounded and sound—into submission."[25] During World War II, it would be the American government that officially schemed to starve Germany.

More than 117,000 Americans died in World War I, for absolutely no discernable reason. Overall, an astounding *forty million* people perished in "The War to End All Wars." The war not only helped spawn Bolshevism, which morphed into Soviet communism, but eventually fascism in Italy and National Socialism (Nazism) in Germany. It also paved the way for Zionism. By the time America foolishly entered the European conflict, the war had already been raging for three years. There was no obvious "good guy" for this country to back; no American interest at all was at stake. To paraphrase Germany's "Iron Chancellor" Otto von Bismarck, the results weren't worth the blood of a single American infantryman. Former three-time Democratic Party presidential nominee William Jennings Bryan resigned as Secretary of State after Wilson declared his support for England thusly: "England is fighting our fight, and you may well understand that I shall not, in the present state of the world's affairs, place obstacles in her way when she is fighting for her life—and the life of the world."[26] Genuine progressive and populist Wisconsin Sen. Robert La Follette was among the loudest voices against our involvement. Huge American corporations benefited shamefully from the conflict.

The yearly profits for gun manufacturer, the Du Ponts, skyrocketed from $6 million in 1914 to $58 million by 1918. US Steel's annual earnings more than doubled, going from $105 million in the five years before the war to $240 million during 1914–1918. Profits for the International Nickel Company went from a paltry $4 million a year to $73.5 million by 1918, an increase of more than 1,700 percent. In his classic 1935 book *War is a Racket,* Smedley Butler wrote, "Take the shoe people . . . For instance, they sold Uncle Sam 35,000,000 pairs of hobnailed service shoes. There were 4,000,000 [US] soldiers. Eight pairs, and more, to the soldier. My regiment during the war had only a pair to a soldier. . . . There was still lots of leather left. So the leather people sold your Uncle Sam hundreds of thousands of McClellan saddles for the cavalry. But there wasn't any American cavalry overseas! . . . They sold your Uncle Sam 20,000,000 mosquito nets for the use of the soldiers overseas. . . . Well, not one of these mosquito nets ever got to France! . . . Some 6,000 buckboards [horse-drawn wagons] were sold to Uncle Sam for the use of colonels! Not one of them was used. But the buckboard manufacturer got his war profit."[27] As Butler said, war is always about opportunities for profit.

On February 9, 1917, Rep. Francis Oscar Callaway remarked on the floor of Congress: "In March, 1915, the J.P. Morgan interests . . . got together 12 men high up in the newspaper world and employed them to select the most influential newspapers in the United States and [the] sufficient number of them to control generally the policy of the daily press. . . . They found it was only necessary to purchase the control of 25 of the greatest papers. An agreement was reached; the policy of the papers was bought, to be paid for by the month; an editor was furnished for each paper to properly supervise and edit information regarding the questions of preparedness, militarism, financial policies, and other things of national and international nature considered vital to the interests of the purchasers."[28] Callaway's controversial comments, which led to his defeat for reelection and his retirement from politics, were recorded in the Congressional Record. We can look at today's media, with its universal themes and promotion of narratives, and see just how successful this campaign was. Callaway's sentiments were echoed during a March 1917 anti-war demonstration in the Wall Street district. Benjamin C. Marsh and other pacifists told the crowd that J.P. Morgan & Co. and others were behind a "go-to-war" agenda. Marsh declared, "I am engaged in a fight against surrendering the Government to Wall Street. If the privileged class and their wealth were to be conscripted in case of war there would be no possibility of this country becoming involved." The mayor, meanwhile, called the protesters "traitors."[29]

After the war ended, the peace conference in France made things even worse. As French military commander Ferdinand Foch presciently described the Treaty of Versailles, "This is not peace. It is an armistice for 20 years."[30] Indeed, with its unprecedented plundering of a defeated foe, the agreement guaranteed that there would be a World War II. A financially ruined Germany would turn to the rabble-rousing painter Adolf Hitler, who was the beneficiary of powerful forces himself, as Antony Sutton recounted in his book *Wall Street and the Rise of Hitler.* The concept of forcing the loser in a war to pay reparations to the victors had never been heard of before. The Treaty reassigned German geographical boundaries, providing Hitler with an early rationale that he was merely reclaiming German land. Most astoundingly of all, Germans themselves weren't allowed to participate in the Paris conference.

The international bankers would dominate the Paris conference that produced the Treaty of Versailles. Leading the American delegation was Paul Warburg, who was in the center of establishing the Federal Reserve System. An accompanying agenda, which would ultimately result in the creation of the nation state of Israel, was spurred by the Mandate of Palestine. It was drafted by Felix Frankfurter, who became a top adviser to FDR and then a Supreme Court Justice. Winston Churchill had expressed a strong resolve to create Israel during a 1921 visit to Palestine. A delegation of Muslim leaders objected to giving land to Jews that Arabs had occupied for over a thousand years. Churchill assured them that it was the best arrangement for all, and vowed, "We intend it to be so."[31] Albert Einstein was even too much of a radical Zionist for Frankfurter and his mentor, Supreme Court Justice Louis Brandeis. Einstein, who has become the scientific world's version of Lincoln in terms of irrational idolatry, turned off many with his outrageous financial demands for lectures, which were frequently brokered by his banker friends Paul and Max Warburg.[32] The great Nikola Tesla had the courage to call Einstein out for what he was, declaring, "Einstein's relativity work is a magnificent mathematical garb which fascinates, dazzles and makes people blind to the underlying errors."[33]

The Council on Foreign Relations was born during a series of meetings held during World War I. Wilson's right-hand man Colonel House assembled about one hundred prominent individuals to discuss the postwar world. They called themselves "the Inquiry," and their plans eventually evolved into Wilson's famous "Fourteen Points," which he presented to Congress on January 8, 1918. Wilson's "Points" constituted one of the first overtly globalist proposals, as it called for the removal of "all economic barriers" between nations, "equality of trade conditions," and the formation of "a general association of nations." Nearly two dozen members of "the Inquiry" attended the Paris Peace Conference. Colonel House met with both British and American peace conference delegates, at Paris's Majestic Hotel on May 30, 1919, where they resolved to form an "Institute of International Affairs," with one branch in the United States and one in England. The English branch became the Royal Institute of International Affairs, and the US branch became the Council on Foreign Relations on July 21, 1921. The mainstream media, many of whose most high-profile figures were CFR members themselves, have seen to it that very little publicity is given to this extremely important organization. Article II of the CFR's bylaws stated that revealing details of CFR meetings could result in a loss of membership, inviting comparisons to the Freemasonic oaths of secrecy.[34]

The disinformation from court historians is so intense that they routinely invent impossible timelines. And in many cases, it's for irrelevant purposes. For instance, on the September 8, 2013, broadcast of *CBS Sunday Morning,* there was a story extolling the "romantic" nature of seemingly uptight and aloof Woodrow Wilson. Author A. Scott Berg, who had just written the biography *Wilson,* was quoted as saying, "It's quite amazing: I mean, here's Woodrow Wilson at nine years old drafting a constitution for his Little League baseball team! It's got to be the only Little League team, to this day, with its own constitution." How ironic that little Woodrow would be so enamored of Constitutions, yet later as president be so unsupportive of the one he swore to uphold. More significantly though, the Little League reference is ridiculous. Little League Baseball wasn't established until 1939. Wilson died in 1924. I must remind the venerable Mr. Berg that there certainly were no Little Leagues in the 1860s, when Wilson was a boy. Sandlot baseball would still have been in its infancy. There was no need to make up this touching anecdote about Wilson, but still Berg did. And just what kind of "constitution" would a Little League Baseball team have? This respected historian's other books include a revealing look at his twenty-year friendship with actress Katharine Hepburn.

Unlike Thomas Jefferson and other historical figures unfairly smeared as "racists," there is a documented record of Wilson implementing truly racist policies. Most people don't realize that segregation didn't officially exist within the federal government until the Wilson administration, when Black and White federal employees were first required to eat separately and use separate bathrooms. W. E. B. Du Bois wrote an open letter to President Wilson in 1913 to explain his concerns with this new arrangement. "In the Treasury and Post Office Departments colored clerks have been herded to themselves as though they were not human beings. We are told that one colored clerk who could not actually be segregated on account of the nature of his work has consequently had a cage built around him to separate him from his white companions of many years." Du Bois declared. "Mr. Wilson, do you know these things? Are you responsible for them? Did you advise them? Do you not know that no other group of American citizens has ever been treated in this way and that no President of the United States ever dared to propose such treatment? Here is a plain, flat, disgraceful spitting in the face of people whose darkened countenances are already dark with the slime of insult. Do you consent to this, President Wilson? Do you believe in it? Have you been able to persuade yourself that national insult is best for a people struggling into self-respect?"[35]

The Wilson administration wasn't exactly known for its enlightened attitude toward the early women voting rights activists, either. When suffragette leader Alice Paul led a protest of 5,000 at Wilson's 1913 inaugural, the few police there allowed men to violently beat the women. Paul and hundreds of her supporters were sent to jail, where they were *stripped naked and thrown into cells with prostitutes.* The suffragettes were charged with "obstructing traffic," and when they refused to pay the fine, they were taken to the rat-infested Occoquan Workhouse, a prison in Virginia. Alice Paul and her comrade Rose Winslow staged a hunger strike in protest. Supporters telegrammed prison authorities and prominent physicians regarding the prison's threat of force-feeding them. Regardless, a feeding tube was forced down their throats. "Yesterday was a bad day for me," Rose Winslow wrote, in a letter smuggled out of jail by friends. "I was vomiting continuously during the process. The tube had developed an irritation somewhere that was painful. Don't let them tell you we take this well. Miss Paul vomits much, I do too." Fourteen other imprisoned women, at both the Occoquan Workhouse and the District Jail, went on hunger strikes. "Dr. Gannon then forced the tube through my lips and down my throat, I gasping and suffocating with the agony of it," one woman recounted. "I didn't know where to breathe from and everything turned black when the liquid began pouring in. Food dumped directly into the stomach feels like a ball of lead." Alice Paul was subjected to force-feedings three times a day. Despite her poor health and deteriorating condition, she refused to stop her hunger strike. After three weeks prison authorities transferred her to the psychiatric ward. Paul would align her forces with the radical National Women's Party.[36] When the United States entered World War I in April 1917, Paul and her followers picketed the White House. Public outrage over the abusive treatment of women suffrage militants spurred the House of Representatives to propose a woman suffrage amendment in 1918.[37] Few Americans probably realize that women weren't enfranchised until nearly sixty years after Black men were given the right to vote.

There was strong opposition to American entrance into the European War. A group of socialists and labor activists formed an organization they called the Working Class, and they planned a march on Washington, dubbed the Green Corn Rebellion because they planned to openly eat green corn, to protest the draft. However, group members were rounded up and arrested before they could march anywhere. 450 of them were accused of rebellion and sent to the state penitentiary. Union leaders were given *three to ten years* in jail, while others received sentences of sixty days to two years. Radicals paraded in Boston on July 1, 1917, carrying banners which proclaimed, "Is This a Popular War? Why Conscriptions? Who Stole Panama? Who Crushed Haiti? We Demand Peace." The protesters were attacked by soldiers and sailors. Mailing privileges of newspapers and magazines that printed anti-war articles were taken away by the government. One socialist magazine, *The Masses*, was banned entirely, rekindling memories of the hundreds of newspapers shut down by Abraham Lincoln. The magazine's offense was publishing an editorial by Max Eastman which asked, "For what specific purposes are you shipping our bodies, and the bodies of our sons, to Europe? For my part, I do not recognize the right of a government to draft me to a war whose purposes I do not believe in."

On August 1, 1917, the *New York Herald* reported that in New York City, ninety of the first hundred draftees claimed an exemption. Headlines in the *Minneapolis Journal State* on August 6 and 7 read: "Draft Opposition Fast Spreading in State," and "Conscripts Give False Addresses." Two Black farmhands in Florida mutilated themselves to avoid the draft: one shot off four fingers of his hand; the other blew off his arm below the elbow. Senator Thomas Hardwick of Georgia remarked, "There was undoubtedly general and widespread opposition on the part of many thousands . . . to the enactment of the draft law. Numerous and largely attended mass meetings held in every part of the State protested against it." Over 330,000 men in total were classified as draft evaders. The estimated 65,000 conscientious objectors who performed noncombat duty were often treated brutally at Army bases. Three men who were at Fort Riley, Kansas refused any duties, and after they were jailed, "a hemp rope slung over the railing of the upper tier was put about their necks, hoisting them off their feet until they were at the point of collapse. Meanwhile the officers punched them on their ankles and shins. They were then lowered and the rope was tied to their arms, and again they were hoisted off their feet. This time a garden hose was played on their faces with a nozzle about six inches from them, until they collapsed completely."[38] Benjamin C. Marsh told fellow pacifists during a 1917 anti-war rally, "I am engaged in a fight against surrendering the Government to Wall Street. If the privileged class and their wealth were to be conscripted in case of war there would be no possibility of this country becoming involved."[39]

Wilson suffered a debilitating stroke in 1919, and the consensus among all historians is that his second wife, Edith Bolling Galt Wilson, basically ran the country for the last two years of his presidency. While this is seen as a bit scandalous, as are the increasing indications of Wilson's racism, most of the court historians continue to rank him highly, albeit not quite as highly as before everything became subverted to political correctness. However, real or imagined racism will always be outweighed by the general adoration for war. There's a reason why everyone loves to refer to a president as "Commander in Chief." Wilson's name may be removed from some schools or buildings, but he'll never join the James Buchanans and Franklin Pierces at the bottom of the court historians' lists. Wilson died at home on February 3, 1924. Mrs. Wilson ordered a simple and private ceremony, and he was buried two days after he died, even quicker than FDR would be. In a lengthy, emotionally charged article at the time, there was no mention of an autopsy.[40] I could find no clarification on the matter of a Wilson autopsy anywhere. It is a pretty good bet that Wilson, like Harding, Coolidge, and FDR, did not have an autopsy. As I have noted in previous books, this pattern of no autopsies for prominent individuals, who often die under unclear circumstances, is exceedingly strange.

Woodrow Wilson would inexplicably win the Nobel Peace Prize in 1919. This set yet another ugly precedent, of rewarding the most bloodthirsty warmongers for advocating "peace." In decades to come, unworthy recipients of the honor would include Henry Kissinger and Barack Obama. Kissinger once notably said, "Wilson's principles have remained the bedrock of American foreign-policy thinking."[41] Considering this country's despicable foreign policy record, and Kissinger's own shameful role, that is quite a revealing statement, as well as quite a dubious honor.

The Bolshevik Revolution

You will have a revolution, a terrible revolution. What course it takes will depend much on what Mr. Rockefeller tells Mr. Hague (New Jersey politician) to do. Mr. Rockefeller is a symbol of the American ruling class and Mr. Hague is a symbol of its political tools.

—Leon Trotsky, in the *New York Times*, December 13, 1938

In 1917, a year before World War I ended, the Bolshevik Revolution deposed the old ruling order in Russia. Portrayed by the court historians as an organic uprising by radical Russian citizens, in fact it was exactly the opposite; financed and controlled by powerful outside interests. "One of the greatest myths of contemporary history is that the Bolshevik Revolution in Russia was a popular uprising of the downtrodden masses against the hated ruling class of the Czars," wrote author G. Edward Griffin, who traced the planning and funding for the revolution to financiers in Germany, Britain, and the United States.[42] As 1917 began, revolutionary leader Leon Trotsky, whose real name was Lev Bronstein and who had lived outside of Russia for most of his life, was working in New York City as a reporter for the communist newspaper *The New World.* All that would be needed was to have added "Order" to the masthead, and you'd have the most popular slogan of elitists for the next century. According to Antony Sutton, despite having very little income, Trotsky's family was regularly transported by chauffeured limousine.[43] Trotsky's passport was authorized by the Wilson administration, as he journeyed to Russia with Wall Street funding.[44] Author Jennings C. Wise wrote, "Historians must never forget that Woodrow Wilson, despite the efforts of the British police, made it possible for Leon Trotsky to enter Russia with an American passport."[45]

A shocking interview with oil baron E. H. Doheny, which appeared in the February 1, 1919, edition of *Barron,* quoted Doheny as saying, "The worst Bolshevists in the United States are not only college professors, of whom President Wilson is one, but capitalists and the wives of capitalists and neither seem to know what they are talking about. William Boyce Thompson is teaching Bolshevism and he may yet convert Lamont of J.P. Morgan & Company. Vanderlip is a Bolshevist, so is Charles R. Crane." As Gary Allen, author of the classic *None Dare Call it Conspiracy,* put it, "In the Bolshevik Revolution we have some of the world's richest and most powerful men financing a movement which claims its very existence is based on the concept of stripping of their wealth, men like the Rothschilds, Rockefellers, Schiffs, Warburgs, Morgans, Harrimans, and Milners. But obviously these men have no fear of international communism. It is only logical to assume that if they financed it and do not fear it, it must be because they control it. Can there be any other explanation that makes sense?"[46] In one of those bizarre connections, the Foreword to Allen's book was written by Congressman John G. Schmitz, who also was the 1972 presidential candidate for the American Independent Party. One of Schmitz's daughters was schoolteacher Mary Kay Letourneau, whose incomprehensible affair with and later marriage to one of her students, which began when he was *twelve* years old, introduced a litany of similar head-scratching cases of female teachers having sex with their students. Two of Schmitz's sons became advisors to both Bush presidents, indicating an entirely different political mindset from their father.

Two years after the publication of Allen's book, Professor Antony Sutton produced the seminal work on this subject, *Wall Street and the Bolshevik Revolution.* The names connected to this "radical" revolution read like a Who's Who of International Banking, including Jacob Schiff, and Elihu Root, attorney for Paul Warburg's Kuhn, Loeb, & Company, among others. According to the *New York Journal-American*, "It is estimated by Jacob's grandson, John Schiff, that the old man sank about $20 million for the final triumph of Bolshevism in Russia."[47] Schiff's financing the Bolsheviks was mentioned in a March 24, 1917, article in the *New York Times.*[48] Root, who was also a member of the Council on Foreign Relations (CFR), contributed yet another $20 million, according to the Congressional Record of September 2, 1919.[49] Root first rose to prominence as part of notoriously corrupt William "Boss" Tweed's legal team, and was the quintessential adviser behind the scenes for decades, serving in the cabinets of Presidents McKinley and Teddy Roosevelt, and responsible for overseeing the earlier described atrocities in the Philippines and elsewhere, for which he was rewarded with yet another undeserved Nobel Peace Prize. Closely allied to financier Andrew Carnegie, Root also was the president of the Carnegie Foundation for International Peace, which as I revealed in my book *Crimes and Cover-Ups in American Politics: 1776–1963,* has in actuality always served as a proponent of perpetual war. Arsene de Goulevitch, who was president during the early days of the Bolsheviks, later stated, "In private interviews, I have been told that over 21 million rubles were spent by Lord Milner in financing the Russian Revolution."[50] David Icke wrote, "In 1915, the American International Corporation was formed to fund the Russian Revolution. Its directors represented the interests of the Rockefeller, Rothschilds, Du Pont, Kuhn, Loeb, Harriman, and the Federal Reserve. They included Frank Vanderlip (one of the Jekyll Island group which created the Federal Reserve) and George Herbert Walker, the grandfather of President George Bush."[51]

In *Wall Street and the Bolshevik Revolution,* Antony Sutton went deeper into the role that the American International Corporation played in the 1917 Bolshevik Revolution. The group's executive secretary William Franklin Sands was asked for his opinion of the Bolshevik Revolution by the State Department in November 1917, and expressed his strong support for it. Other information Sutton uncovered included a memorandum to David Lloyd George, Prime Minister of England, from J. P. Morgan partner Dwight Morrow, which also supported the Bolshevik revolutionaries. In yet another of those endless elite connections, Morrow's daughter Anne would marry famed aviator Charles Lindbergh. The Federal Reserve's William Boyce Thompson personally intervened with Lloyd George on behalf of the Soviets. As Sutton described it, "In brief, we found an identifiable pattern of pro-Bolshevik activity by influential members of Wall Street concentrated in the Federal Reserve Bank of New York and the American International Corporation, both at 120 Broadway."[52]

While many well-intentioned labor activists and anarchists were targeted and persecuted by the US government during this period, there were also some prominent figures who had very suspicious connections. While *St. Louis Post-Dispatch* cartoonist Robert Minor's reputation was strangely not impacted by the fact he was also a Bolshevik revolutionary, he would be fired from the newspaper for opposing World War I. Minor was arrested in Russia in 1915 for alleged subversion, two years before the Bolshevik Revolution began. He was bankrolled by the usual Wall Street financiers who should have been mortified by his activities. Anthony Sutton used one of Minor's cartoons as the frontispiece for his book *Wall Street and the Bolshevik Revolution.* It portrays a beaming Karl Marx standing on Wall Street with a book titled "Socialism" tucked under his arm, as he accepts congratulations from the likes of J. P. Morgan, Morgan partner George W. Perkins, John D. Rockefeller, John D. Ryan of National City Bank, and Teddy Roosevelt. Wall Street is decorated with Red flags. This odd coalition between the lords of capitalism and radical revolutionaries was a very real one. As American International Corporation director Otto H. Kahn, who was also a partner in Kuhn, Loeb, & Co., explained to the League For Industrial Democracy, in New York, on December 30, 1924, "What you Radicals and we who hold opposing views differ about, is not so much the end as the means, not so much what should be brought about as how it should, and can, be brought about." This was an international affiliation. For example, Lord Milner, member of the British War Cabinet, 1917, and director of the London Joint Stock Bank, once declared, "Marx's great book Das Kapital is at once a monument of reasoning and a storehouse of facts."[53] One of the most curious figures to be on-site in Russia at the outset of the Bolshevik Revolution was the aforementioned William Boyce Thompson, who was not only the first full-term director of New York's Federal Reserve Bank, but director of two large railroads and Metropolitan Life Insurance Company. Why would anyone with such a background be literally in the middle of a revolution supposedly sworn to destroy men like him? Thompson, through his assistant, and in conjunction with the American Red Cross, "organized Russian revolutionaries," to quote Sutton. The *Washington Post* would report, on February 2, 1918, that "William B. Thompson, who was in Petrograd from July until November last, has made a personal contribution of $1,000,000 to the Bolsheviki for the purpose of spreading their doctrine in Germany and Austria."

John Reed, who would be extolled decades later by Warren Beatty in the 1981 film *Reds,* was perfectly described by Antony Sutton as an "Establishment revolutionary." One of the periodicals Reed regularly contributed to was the *Metropolitan,* which was controlled by the Morgan interests. His account of the Bolshevik Revolution, *Ten Days That Shook the World,* featured an Introduction by Nikolai Lenin. Sutton charged that Reed was "a puppet under the 'control' of the Morgan financial interests through the American International Corporation."[54] Nikolai Lenin told the Tenth Congress of the Russian Communist Party, "Without the assistance of capital it will be impossible for us to retain proletarian power in an incredibly ruined country in which the peasantry, also ruined, constitutes the overwhelming majority—and, of course, for this assistance capital will squeeze hundreds per cent out of us. This is what we have to understand. Hence, either this type of economic relations or nothing." Trotsky was even more obvious, declaring, "What we need here is an organizer like Bernard M. Baruch."[55] And, while backing the Bolsheviks, the same kinds of Wall Street forces also supported fascism. For instance, according to John P. Diggins, "Of all American business leaders, the one who most vigorously patronized the cause of Fascism was Thomas W. Lamont. Head of the powerful J.P. Morgan banking network, Lamont served as something of a business consultant for the government of Fascist Italy."[56]

Among the decidedly capitalist dignitaries traveling with Trotsky to Russia, to ignite what was actually an overthrow of socialist Alexander Kerensky's revolution earlier that year, was Charles Crane, who had established the Westinghouse plant in Russia. When the Soviets formed their first international bank in 1922, the director of the Foreign Division was Max May, Vice President of J.P. Morgan's Guaranty Trust Company. The Bolsheviks drained the Tsarist's substantial supply of gold and funneled it to American and British banks. The shipments were coordinated by Jacob Schiff's Kuhn, Loeb & Company. Standard Oil and General Electric supplied the Soviet Union with $37 million of machinery. Banker and railroad magnate Averill Harriman, whom we will examine more closely later in this book, came to monopolize Soviet manganese production for twenty years.[57]

In 1931, the State Department published a three-volume report on US external relations, which included information that highlighted the documented links between German high finance and the funding of Nikolai Lenin. In a letter dated June 18, 1917, the commercial company Waldemar Hansen & Co announced that "315,000 marks have been transferred to Mr. Lenin's account in Kronstadt as per order of syndicate." Also in the State Department volumes is a letter dated September 8, 1917, that proclaims, "Carried out your commission: passports and the indicated sum of 207,000 marks as per order of your Mr. Lenin have been handed to persons mentioned in your letter. The selection met with approval of his Excellency the ambassador." Yet another document reveals, "Dear Comrade, the office of the banking house M. Warburg has opened, in accordance with a telegram from the Rhenish Westphalian Syndicate, an account of the undertaking of Comrade Trotsky. The attorney [?] purchased arms and has organized their transportation and delivery track. Lulea and Vardo to the office of Essen & Son in the name Lulea receivers and a person authorized to receive the money demanded by Comrade Trotsky." As early as February 1914, a circular sent to all German banks urged, "Make provisions for very close and absolutely secret relations being established with Finnish and American banks." The big banks in Germany, like the biggest ones in America, are international, and not national, in nature. In the same manner, Trotsky was not American, or German, or Russian. He considered himself an internationalist, much as Woodrow Wilson did. The era that featured the creation of the Federal Reserve and World War I, formally introduced Americans to globalism and leaders whose avowed goal was establishing a "New World Order."

The great G. Edward Griffin detailed just one of the financial crimes of the "War to end all Wars," writing, "In payment for these contracts and to return the "loans" of the financiers, the Bolsheviks all but drained their country of its gold—which included the Tsarist government's sizable reserve—and shipped it primarily to American and British banks. In 1920 39,000,000 Swedish kroner; three shipments came direct involving 540 boxes of gold valued at 97,200,000 gold roubles; plus at least one other direct shipment bringing the total to about $20 million. (Remember, these are 1920 values!) The arrival of these shipments was coordinated by Jacob Schiff's Kuhn, Loeb & Company and deposited by Morgan's Guaranty Trust."[58]

Coming full circle and exemplifying how the same bloodlines perpetuate themselves in power, Trotsky's great-granddaughter Nora Volkow, is currently the head of the National Institute on Drug Abuse, which is a part of the National Institutes of Health. Volkow in fact grew up in the same Mexican house where her great-grandfather was murdered with an ice pick. She has routinely made all the mainstream media lists of "most powerful women," etc. Volkow has spoken out against the legalization of marijuana. In a 2012 interview with *60 Minutes,* Volkow stated, "We all have this sense of public service, social consciousness, responsibility toward not only yourself as individual, but for your society." Lev Bronstein couldn't have said it any better.

CHAPTER FOUR

FDR: CORRUPT FOE OF THE PEOPLE

The only difference between Hoover and Roosevelt is that Hoover is a hoot owl and Roosevelt is a scrootch owl. A hoot owl bangs into the roost and knocks the hen clean off, and catches her while she's falling. But a scrootch owl slips into the roost and talks softly to her. And she just falls in love with him, and the first thing you know, there ain't no hen.

—Huey Long[1]

Next to Abraham Lincoln, no other American president is as revered by the court historians and in popular culture as Franklin D. Roosevelt. FDR's rhetoric about helping those in need was in complete contrast to the reality of his blue-blood, patrician pedigree. Professor Antony Sutton produced the essential work on the real Roosevelt, *Wall Street and FDR.* Sutton wrote, "Franklin D. Roosevelt was, at one time or another during the 1920s, a vice president of the Fidelity & Deposit Company (120 Broadway); the president of an industry trade association, the American Construction Council (29 West 44th Street); a partner in Roosevelt & O'Conner (120 Broadway); a partner in Marvin, Hooker & Roosevelt (52 Wall Street); the president of United European Investors, Ltd. (7 Pine Street); a director of International Germanic Trust, Inc. (in the Standard

Oil Building at 26 Broadway); a director of Consolidated Automatic Merchandising Corporation, a paper organization; a trustee of Georgia Warm Springs Foundation (120 Broadway); a director of American Investigation Corporation (37–39 Pine Street); a director of Sanitary Postage Service Corporation (285 Madison Avenue); the chairman of the General Trust Company (15 Broad Street); a director of Photomaton (551 Fifth Avenue); a director of Mantacal Oil Corporation (Rock Springs, Wyoming); and an incorporator of the Federal International Investment Trust."[2] That's quite a list of connections for someone whom the court historians tell us was despised as "a traitor to his class."

FDR, like the vast majority of our leaders, was born with the proverbial silver spoon in his mouth. And that spoon was certainly tainted. His maternal grandfather, Warren Delano Jr., was chief of operations for a Boston trading firm that was deeply immersed in the Chinese opium trade. Delano first went to China at age twenty-four, and after a decade or so of dealing in drugs, returned to New York as a much wealthier man. His involvement in the drug trade was admitted in his personal letters, but he defended it as akin to importing wine and other alcohol.[3] Eventually, Delano's daughter Sara would marry a wealthy neighbor, James Roosevelt, father of Franklin Delano.

FDR became heavily involved in what alternative historians like Antony Sutton call "the pre-war Rape of Germany." German hyperinflation of the 1920s permitted a person with just a few American dollars to live like a millionaire. Foreigners swarmed into the country, buying up family treasures, estates, jewelry, and art works at unbelievably low prices. Roosevelt was connected to United European Investors, Ltd (UEI), as well as the International Germanic Trust Company, Inc., both of which capitalized on the devastated post–World War I German economy by financial speculation and manipulation of the German Reichsmark.[4] This was a parasitic effort to profit from the German economy failing. To quote Anthony Sutton, "if the exchange quotation [of German marks] should approach the vanishing point, there would be nothing tangible left for the holders of marks or drafts. The capital of the company [UEI] will be invested in improved real estate, mortgages, financing of goods in transit and participation in profitable industrial and commercial enterprises."[5] To emphasize the "inside" nature of this, two German Senators and the Reich president Wilhelm Cuno, sat on UEI's advisory board.[6] Curiously enough, Reich president Cuno just happened to be the one who oversaw the policy of German hyperinflation to begin with![7] As Sutton put it, "From at least Clinton Roosevelt in 1841 to Franklin D. Roosevelt, the political power accumulated by the Roosevelt clan has been used on the side of regulating business in the interests of restricting competition, encouraging monopoly, and so bleeding the consumer in the interests of a financial elite."[8]

President Herbert Hoover, stuck presiding over the disastrous stock market collapse and birth of the Great Depression,[9] recognized the predicament he was in. Hoover refused to accept the Swope Plan, proposed by the president of General Electric, Gerald Swope. Still misrepresented as an altruistic effort to reorganize industries into trade associations, Hoover called it a "fascist plan" in his memoirs and revealed that Wall Street had given him an ultimatum; support the Swope Plan or they would back FDR's candidacy. The rest is history; the so-called enemy of big business was enthusiastically backed by them. Sutton found that 78 percent of Roosevelt's early campaign contributions came from the scions of Wall Street. Swope was the driving force behind what developed into FDR's National Industry Recovery Act of 1933. Hoover explained, "During the campaign of 1932, Henry J. Harriman, president of that body, urged that I agree to support these proposals, informing me that Mr. Roosevelt had agreed to do so. I tried to show him that this stuff was pure fascism; that it was merely a remaking of Mussolini's 'corporate state' and refused to agree to any of it. He informed me that in view of my attitude, the business world would support Roosevelt with money and influence. That for the most part, proved true."[10]

Continuing the interventionist policies established under Wilson, prior to orchestrating America's entrance into World War II, FDR supported the coup that installed Fulgencio Batista as president of Cuba in 1934. The primary impetus for American support was the Cuban sugar industry; Americans owned some two-thirds of the sugar in Cuba. The Roosevelts, coincidentally enough, just happened to be heavily invested themselves in Cuban sugar.[11] Even disregarding the often absurd standards set by our present "woke" era, there is quite a bit of documentation indicating FDR was a genuine racist. Roosevelt alphabet agencies like the TVA and the CCC were racially segregated. FDR never supported an anti-lynching law or the abolition of the poll tax. In an attempt to gain the support of southern Democrats, Roosevelt agreed to exclude labor and domestic workers, two areas where Blacks were disproportionately employed, from New Deal programs. They were also excluded from legislation that created labor unions, minimum wage laws and work hours, and 65 percent of the Black workforce was excluded from Social Security.[12] Roosevelt appointed Klansman Hugo Black to the Supreme Court,[13] where he would later simply declare Lyndon Johnson the winner in a thoroughly corrupt 1948 Senate primary election. One would think that, with a legacy like that, FDR would be demonized along with Thomas Jefferson and the other Founding Fathers (except, of course, Alexander Hamilton). But instead, he continues to be depicted as some kind of early civil rights hero.

LBJ was such a close protégé of FDR's that he was regularly invited to breakfast in the White House, where the president enjoyed his meal in bed. As Roosevelt's aide James H. Rowe described their close relationship, "You've got to remember that these were two great political geniuses."[14] It is no accident that the thoroughly corrupt FDR despised Joe Kennedy Sr., while fawning over the sickeningly sycophantic young Johnson. A bizarre and almost certainly fictional story appeared in the 2014 book *The Sphinx: Franklin Roosevelt, the Isolationists and the Road to World War II,* by Nicholas Wapshott. Supposedly, FDR asked Kennedy to drop his pants during a 1937 Oval Office meeting, to verify if he indeed had bowlegs.

Roosevelt's laughable image as someone who "betrayed" his fellow elitists is simply contradicted by every fact that can be found. In the early 1920s, the great foe of Wall Street had an office at 120 Broadway. At the time, FDR was vice president of the Fidelity and Deposit Company. 120 Broadway hosted an assortment of interesting characters. Bernard Baruch's office was also at 120 Broadway, where future NRA administrator Hugh Johnson worked as Baruch's research assistant. The executive offices of General Electric and its president Gerard Swope, who authored the aforementioned Swope Plan that became Roosevelt's NRA, were also there. The Bankers Club was on the top floor.[15] This same Equitable Office Building, located at 120 Broadway, was the headquarters of the No. 2 District of the Federal Reserve System, the most important of all the Federal Reserve districts. The general offices of the American International Corporation, founded in 1915 by J. P. Morgan, along with the Rockefellers, were at 120 Broadway. Young Franklin D. Roosevelt was right in the middle of all this and would later stock his administration with these same kinds of Wall Street figures.

The Roosevelt administration's Blue Eagle symbol was perhaps an even more egregious example of forced compliance than the Uncle Sam character had been during World War I. As author Wolfgang Schivelbusch noted, "The Blue Eagle campaign was an initiative undertaken by the National Recovery Administration to bring the free-falling economy under control. Its centerpiece was a symbol to be displayed by producers and retailers who complied with NRA standards, and the public, in turn, was encouraged to buy only from those outlets out of a sense of patriotic duty. The campaign began in July 1933 . . . Every employer in the United States—from the owner of a drugstore to Henry Ford—received a document entitled 'President's Re-Employment Agreement,' which asked the recipient to personally promise Roosevelt his support for certain guidelines." Schivelbusch quoted FDR as declaring, "Those who cooperate in this program must know each other at a glance. That is why we have provided a badge of honor for this purpose, a simple design with a legend, 'We do our part,' and I ask that all those who join with me shall display that badge prominently." This Orwellian campaign also included pins, posters, and statuettes of that Blue Eagle, framed by the NRA logo, and wearing or displaying them instantly designated the citizen as patriotic and trustworthy.[16] And while FDR continues to be depicted by court historians as a "trust buster," much like his similarly mischaracterized cousin Teddy Roosevelt, his record was entirely different. Hugh Johnson's first draft of the NRA, for example, literally called for the suspension of all anti-trust laws.[17]

Schivelbush went into more detail, writing, "A corresponding poster, hung in shop windows or on factory gates, made it publicly known that a business had accepted NRA guidelines and was working to ensure that they were enforced. Conversely, the absence of a Blue Eagle emblem suggested that a person or business did not support Roosevelt and did not belong to the national army fighting the Depression, and that therefore that person or business was to be treated as an enemy. NRA head Hugh Johnson left no doubt as to the symbol's polarizing intention, proclaiming, 'Those who are not with us are against us.'"[18] Johnson was merely echoing the pathfinding sentiments of the tyrannical Abraham Lincoln during the War Between the States, and foretelling almost the exact words of George W. Bush during the "War on Terror." Schivelbush continued,

> The Blue Eagle campaign followed and intensified the bellicose line that had been part of Roosevelt's earliest New Deal rhetoric and strategy. It made explicit reference to the United States' wartime mobilization of 1917–18 and the measures that accompanied it: state control and direction of both the economy and the press; criminalization and prosecution of war critics; and the Creel Committee's restrictions on free speech—in short, the entire battery of compulsory and voluntary means with which American society had been brought into line with the government's wartime efforts. A number of experts from that period were enlisted to run the Blue Eagle campaign. Bernard Baruch, the finance magnate who had organized state-control of American industry's wartime production, put forward his former assistant Hugh Johnson to run the NRA."[19]

Johnson would call the Blue Eagle campaign "the greatest peace-time assault on a national enemy this country has ever seen." The frightening question here would be; just *who* was this national enemy?

The great populist Huey Long, who would be shot and killed under still murky circumstances in 1935, shortly after announcing his own presidential candidacy (and predicting his assassination in speeches on the Senate floor), was a fierce opponent of the NRA. "I come here now and I complain. I complain in the name of the people of my country, of the sovereign State I represent." Long protested. "I complain in the name of the people wherever else it may be known. I complain if it be true, as I am informed by Senators on this floor, that under this act Mr. Johnson, a former employee of Mr. Baruch, has been put in charge of the administration of the Act, and has already called as his aides the head of the Standard

Oil Co., the head of General Motors, and the head of the General Electric Co. I complain if Mr. Peek, who is an employee of Mr. Baruch, or has been, as I have been informed on the floor of the Senate, has been placed in charge of administering the Farm Act, however good a man he may be and whatever his ideas may be. I complain if Mr. Brown, who, I am informed on the floor of the Senate, has been made an influential manipulator of the office of the Bureau of the Director of the Budget, has been an employee of Mr. Baruch, and is now given this authority. I complain because, on the 12th day of May 1932, before we went to Chicago to nominate a President of the United States, I stood in this very place on this floor and told the people of this country that we were not going to have the Baruch influence, at that time so potent with Hoover, manipulating the Democratic Party before nomination, after nomination, or after election."[20] One of Johnson's so-called "Three Musketeers" of the NRA was Walter Teagle, president of the Rockefeller-controlled Standard Oil of New Jersey. Standard Oil was one of Long's many powerful foes.

In one of many disturbing parallels to the absurd mandates and unconstitutional lockdowns we've experienced recently, the Roosevelt administration pressured Chambers of Commerce—supposedly his enemies—all across the country, to get on board with the Blue Eagle and other New Deal proposals. Those who joined up with the "President's Re-Employment Agreement" were given a prominent Blue Eagle to display, and their names were hung on the wall of the local post office. The *New York Herald Tribune* described the Blue Eagle campaign as "a coercive force of the first magnitude and one likely to be no more reasonable than a lynching party." Hugh Johnson was a typical Roosevelt-style "liberal," and his comment that opponents of the Blue Eagle should be accorded "a sock right on the nose" was a predecessor to today's Left demanding the right to "punch a Nazi in the face." He also, like any good "woke" social justice warrior, justified all the constitutional overreach by saying, "this law stuff doesn't matter." Johnson, a heavy drinker, was fired by Roosevelt in 1934. The campaign would eventually collapse when, "people began to see it was a scheme to permit business men to combine to put up prices and keep them up by direct decree or through other devious devices. . . . Bitter slurs were flung at the Blue Eagle as a fascist symbol. A senator called it the 'Soviet duck.' Silk workers on strike stoned the Blue Eagle in the shop windows. Labor suddenly discovered it was getting mostly fine phrases. A wave of strikes swept the country."[21] The NRA would finally be abolished following a 1935 Supreme Court ruling. Johnson eventually turned on FDR, and became an opponent of our entrance into World War II. Roosevelt retaliated in his customary manner, resulting in Johnson being fired as a radio commentator.[22]

Author Amity Shlaes, a conservative enamored of the rigged marketplace, gently but effectively criticized some aspects of FDR's rule in her 2007 book *The Forgotten Man,* which was widely praised by leading neocons like Newt Gingrich, Rudy Giuliani, and Mike Pence. Shlaes wrote the following: "A report submitted to the fifty-seventh annual meeting of the American Bar Association noted that by June 25 of 1934, some 485 codes and 95 supplements had been approved by the president and 242 more by the Administrator for Industrial Recovery. In the period of a year, 10,000 pages of law had been created, a figure that one had to compare with the mere 2,735 pages that constituted federal statute law. In twelve months, the NRA had generated more paper than the entire legislative output of the federal government since 1789."[23] Shlaes's book is about as tough a look at the New Deal as any major publisher would buy. Shlaes noted, "Roosevelt cared little for constitutional niceties and believed they blocked progress. His remedies were on a greater scale and often inspired by socialist or fascist models abroad. A number of New Dealers, Tugwell included, had been profoundly shaped by Mussolini's Italy and, especially, Soviet Russia."[24] She quotes FDR as saying, "We are fashioning an instrument of unimagined power for the establishment of a morally better world." At another point, she reveals that Roosevelt repeatedly uttered the conspiratorial chestnut that "We are bringing order out of chaos."[25] Shlaes is a bastion of the Establishment, most obvious by her decade-long tenure as a senior fellow at the Council on Foreign Relations. Shlaes remarked on yet another ugly precedent set during this era: "critics on the left pointed out that the NRA helped big business at a cost to smaller businesses. This argument was valid. A price set to suit a big firm, with its economies of scale, was low enough to drive a smaller firm out of business; a wage set high enough to meet Washington's goals might be tolerated by a larger firm, but it killed off a smaller one. The NRA institutionalized cartels. And cartels were perceived by most citizens as one of the principal reasons the average fellow now had so much trouble."[26]

One contemporary critic of the New Deal described how the Roosevelt administration achieved industry compliance with its "compassionate" plans to help producers: "The NRA was discovering it could not enforce its rules. Black markets grew up. Only the most violent police methods could procure enforcement. In Sidney Hillman's garment industry the code authority employed enforcement police. They roamed through the garment district like storm troopers. They could enter a man's factory, send him out, line up his employees, subject them to minute interrogation, take over his books on the instant. Night work was forbidden. Flying squadrons of these private coat-and-suit police went through the district at night, battering down doors with axes looking for men who were committing the crime of sewing together a pair of pants at night. But without these harsh methods many code authorities said there could be no compliance because the public was not back of it."[27] There was also clear political favoritism involved with the Works Progress Administration (WPA). At a June 1938 WPA conference, chief deputy administrator Aubrey Williams had stated, "We've got to stick together; we've got to keep our friends in power." Some WPA workers complained about being transferred to other projects, which were a considerable distance from their homes, just because they were Republicans. A white-collar WPA worker was punished by being banished to literally working on a rock pile. He discovered others there who, like him, had refused to change their Republican registration. Some were asked for contributions or tributes, because of their political "disloyalty." When one individual rebelled against being extorted a third time, he was told, "You don't have to pay, but if you don't you'll have a hell of a time getting on the WPA."[28]

FDR's justice department foretold what would come in future administrations with their overly politicized prosecutions. One of the "crimes" committed by the Schechters, a family of Jewish poultry dealers who'd been targeted, was "competing too hard."[29] Invoking comparisons to Lincoln's onerous roundup of northern naysayers, an unfortunate tailor,

Jack Magid, was imprisoned by the "code police" because he pressed a suit of clothes for thirty-five cents, when the Tailors' Code had fixed the price at forty cents. Alabama lumberman William I. Grubb allowed his employees to work more than forty hours a week, and was indicted for code violations.[30] When the Supreme Court struck down the NRA in the Schechter case, five hundred other cases of alleged "code violations" were dropped. Shlaes described another victim: "A lady who had placed her pension in utilities had written Mrs. Roosevelt earlier that year: 'Personally, I had my savings so invested that I would have had a satisfactory provision for old age. Now thanks to his desire to 'get' the utilities I cannot be sure of anything, being a stockholder, as after business has survived his merciless attacks (if it does) insurance will probably be no good either. . . . I am not an 'economic royalist' just an ordinary white collar worker at $1,600 per [year]. Please show this to the president and ask him to remember the wishes of the forgotten man.'"[31] Enforcement of NRA regulations was predictably inconsistent. FDR reacted to a possible move against motion picture corporations by asking, "Do you really need to sue these men?"[32]

FDR also not only turned the IRS against his political enemies, but unleashed it against average citizens. Shlaes wrote, "Panicked for cash, Morgenthau now had his Treasury set about trying to create dozens of Mellons.[33] Roswell Magill of the department audited individual returns in New York and found, according to Morgenthau's diary, that citizens were using old tax breaks—legally, mostly. But Roosevelt was now set on erasing the old distinction between evasion and avoidance that the Treasury had danced around so long. Roosevelt also set out to prove that the intention of taxpayers who failed to complete complex returns correctly was malign: where there was ambiguity, taxpayers ought to be presumed guilty." Shlaes cites the fact that Roosevelt himself filed a dubious tax return in 1937, offering the lame excuse, "I am wholly unable to figure out the amount of the tax for the following reason. . . . As this is a problem of higher mathematics, may I ask that the Bureau let me know the balance due?"[34] Former attorney general, Supreme Court Justice James McReynolds summed up FDR thusly: "This is Nero at his worst. As for the Constitution, it does not seem much to say that it is gone."[35] One of those targeted by Morgenthau was Senator Huey Long.

FDR for all intents and purposes set the precedent for the ugly cancel culture which has become so predominant in present-day America. His pettiness was on full display when an anarchist journal pointed out his hypocrisy in supporting compulsory military service, despite having avoided military service himself. FDR responded by demanding that the Department of Justice initiate a prosecution that would "send the writer and his whole plant to [the federal penitentiary in] Atlanta for the rest of their natural lives." Assistant Attorney General Charles Warren reminded Roosevelt that the department had no basis for taking legal action.[36] In the June 23, 1938 edition of the *Chicago Daily News,* publisher Frank Knox, who would later become secretary of the navy, wrote, "Let a person of prominence speak up in criticism [against the president's policies] and any one of three things—or, all three! –is likely to happen to him. 1. In due time he will find himself before a legislative committee in Washington. 2. He will be publicly castigated by a federal officeholder; or 3. He will be put on the calling list of the Internal Revenue Department." During World War II, this kind of obliteration of free speech became shockingly common. In just one case, Walter Trohan, Washington, D.C., editor of the anti-Roosevelt-leaning *Chicago Daily Tribune* had four different taps on his telephone, from naval intelligence, military intelligence, the FBI, and interestingly enough the Anti-Defamation League. While the Roosevelt administration closely monitored the *Tribune*'s conservative publisher Robert R. McCormick's taxes, his chief newspaper rival, the pro–New Deal Marshall Field III, publisher of the *Chicago Sun*, was left alone.

Author David T. Beito exposed FDR's astonishing propensity to trample on American's constitutional rights in his book *The New Deal's War on the Bill of Rights.* He described how a unit in the Department of the Treasury was set up to go over the tax returns of those associated with the America First movement, but also targeted John L. Lewis, head of the United Mine Workers.[37] FDR ordered J. Edgar Hoover to closely monitor both the America First Committee, and troublesome individuals like Gerald L. K. Smith, who took over Huey Long's Share the Wealth movement after his assassination, and Senators Gerald Nye and Burton K. Wheeler.[38] In 1935, six years before Pearl Harbor, Senator Hugo Black, a viciously anti-Catholic former member of the Ku Klux

Klan, chaired the Black Committee, the most notable of the several congressional investigations of New Deal critics launched during the 1930s. Black would be rewarded with a seat on the Supreme Court, where he served for decades as a loyal "liberal." The Black Committee was granted access to millions of private telegrams sent to or from opponents of the Roosevelt administration, but also to and from every member of Congress. The Committee's tactics were described as "terroristic" and "inquisitorial."[39] Black's successor Senator Sherman Minton went even further, and his proposed legislation to criminalize the publishing of any article "known to be false" was an early effort to combat "misinformation" or "disinformation." Minton's bill would have made it a felony punishable by up to two years in prison and a $10,000 fine.[40] Even much of the friendly Roosevelt press understood how over the line this was. This included *Philadelphia Inquirer* publisher Moses "Moe" Annenberg, who broke with FDR over his outrageous scheme to "pack" the Supreme Court. Annenberg blasted FDR for attempting to "punish, muzzle, and coerce the press." The *San Francisco Chronicle* accused the administration of trying to stop the press "from printing things displeasing to the Administration. This is fascism."[41]

FDR was particularly incensed at popular columnist and radio commentator Boake Carter. A February 1938 diary entry from Secretary of the Interior Harold Ickes noted the "President told [Secretary of Labor] Miss [Frances] Perkins that he would be happy if she could discover that Boake Carter, the columnist and radio commentator, who had been so unfair and pestiferous, was not entitled to be in this country. It appears that an investigation of his record is being made." Several powerful officials in the Department of State met in New York City to discuss strategies to muzzle the commentator for his attacks on US foreign policy. Longtime Roosevelt critic Representative Martin L. Sweeney responded by proposing a resolution to investigate whether Davis and his cohorts were interfering "with the constitutional right of any American citizen in the exercise of free speech." Coincidentally or not, Carter began to tone down his commentary. During one dinner conversation, FDR was quoted by author Jerre Mangione as vowing to "put an end" to Carter's career." Mangione was devastated "That Roosevelt, the statesman I had admired, should admit to such vindictiveness came as the greatest jolt of all." FDR succeeded in getting CBS to cancel Carter's program. On his last broadcast, Carter read from John Stuart Mill's defense of free speech in *On Liberty*. In a lecture tour later that year, he accused the "Great White Father in Washington" (Roosevelt) of bullying station owners and intimidating CBS into firing him.[42]

The Federal Communications Commission was just one of many unconstitutional agencies established by the Roosevelt administration, in 1934. In response to all the heavy-handed attempts at controlling discourse by the Roosevelt White House, the National Association of Broadcasters adopted a troubling "voluntary code" in July 1939. The primary impetus appeared to be to force the popular radio host Father Charles Coughlin off the air. The code included a dangerous ban on selling commercial time for the purpose of discussing "controversial issues." Presidential press secretary Steven Early warned that, in the event of war, radio must prove itself a "good child" or the government might have to teach it "manners."[43] FDR instructed his attorney general Francis Biddle "to personally admonish black editors to cease 'their subversive language.'"[44] Biddle would inform several leading Black newspapers that the government was "going to shut them all up."[45] Columnist for the *New York Daily News* John O'Donnell covered a 1942 meeting of the Overseas Writers Association in Washington, D.C., where one of three speakers was future author of the best-selling book *Rise and Fall of the Third Reich* William L. Shirer. Later commenting on the event in his column, O'Donnell recounted, "Roosevelt advisors . . . applauded lustily such declarations as: The American Senate must be taught the facts of life. . . . The important thing is to put an end (to criticism of the Roosevelt administration) by whatever means may be necessary—be as ruthless as the enemy. . . . Get him on his income tax or the Mann Act. . . . Hang him, shoot him or lock him up in a concentration camp."[46]

While ignoring the Constitution on the domestic front, FDR's lust for war caused him to create the first peacetime draft in American history, on September 16, 1940, over a year before the Japanese "sneak" attack on Pearl Harbor. There were contentious hearings in the Senate over this Compulsory Military Training and Service bill. James Conant, president of Harvard, warned, "The country is gravely threatened. It seems to me a law should be enacted as soon as possible providing for the building up at once of our armed forces." William J. "Wild Bill" Donovan, one of the founders of our odious intelligence network, declared, "If you want to fight you have got to be strong; but if you want to have peace you have got to be stronger; and it is because I believe in peace that I am for this bill." Among those opposed to the bill were socialist leader Norman Thomas, who observed, "Military conscription is not freedom but serfdom; its equality is the equality of slaves. Conscription, whatever may be the hopes and intentions of some of its present supporters, in a nation potentially as powerful and aggressive as ours, is a road leading straight to militarism, imperialism, and ultimately to American fascism and war."[47] "Combat service will fall most heavily upon the unemployed, unskilled workers and low-income groups," said John Nevin Sayre of the Fellowship of Reconciliation. Burton Rascoe, an editor and literary critic, remarked, "The truth is that the agitation for peacetime conscription is not what youth thinks it is at all. It is a ruse of warmongers and politicians to rush this country into war as soon as they can."[48] After the bill passed, the great "liberal" warrior FDR waxed triumphant, stating, "We cannot remain indifferent to the philosophy of force now rampant in the world. The terrible fate of nations whose weakness invited attack is too well known to us all. Our young men will come from the factories and the fields, the cities and the towns, to enroll their names on registration day." FDR failed to brag about the fact that anyone who didn't enroll, or "knowingly counsels, aids, or abets another to evade registration or service in the land or naval forces," would be subject to jail or a ten-thousand-dollar fine or both.[49] Then, as now, most Americans were far more disposed toward war than peace, and they laughed at protesters from the War Resisters League, who marched down Fifth Avenue carrying signs like DOES ANYONE WIN AT WAR?

To the reasonable charges that he was covertly gearing up to enter the European war, FDR laughably declared, "To Republicans and Democrats, to every man, woman and child in the nation I say this: Your President and your Secretary of State are following the road to peace. We are arming ourselves not for any foreign war." He pledged that the United States would not send troops abroad unless we were attacked. "It is for peace that I have labored, and it is for peace that I shall labor all the days of my life."[50] The so-called Union Eight who refused to register for the draft pled guilty in court and made the statement, "War consists of mass murder, deliberate starvation, vandalism, and similar evils. Physical destruction and moral disintegration are the inevitable result. The war method perpetuates and compounds the evils it purports to overcome." Judge Samuel Mandelbaum wasn't moved, and sentenced them each to a year and a day in prison. "This is a national emergency, where the very life, liberty and defense of our country are at stake," Mandelbaum commented, "and I have no alternative but to enforce the law."[51] A divinity student at Temple University, Ernest J. Kirkjian, was sent to jail on January 6, 1941, after explaining, "In registering I would have only dropped incense on the fire now burning on the altar of hate."[52] Draft resister Albert Herling told the judge: "I do not have any right to take part in any legislation the result of which would be a sacrifice of life. One of the things I do not want to see is for the United States of America to become a totalitarian country." He was sentenced to two years in prison.[53] In New York, another draft resister went before a judge. His name was Lowell Naeve. "If everybody did what I did," he said, "there would be no wars." The judge sent him to jail for a year.[54] Two Quaker students in Philadelphia, Arnold Satterthwait and Frederick Richards, were charged with refusing to register for the draft. Richards said, "For a man eager to work towards the alleviation of human suffering, conscription leaves no freedom of conscience." Satterthwait argued that kindness and forgiveness were supple enough to cope with man's mistakes, whereas violence was not. "I cannot understand how a life such as all of us desire can possibly be attained by spreading hate, death, chaos throughout the world," he said. The judge sentenced them to a year and a day in federal prison.[55] Howard Schoenfeld and others detained in a Connecticut prison were thrown in solitary confinement (demurely referred to as "constructive meditation" by the warden), for attempting to stage a demonstration for Student Peace Day.[56]

In July 1941, Members of the Socialist Workers Party were arrested under the revived Alien and Sedition Act, which had first been instituted by President John Adams in 1798. Thomas Jefferson and the

Democrat-Republicans were strongly opposed to these unconstitutional acts, which resulted in publishers being sent to prison for opposing the Adams administration. The Socialist Workers Party members were charged with supporting an "armed revolution against the Government of the United States." Journalist I. F. Stone, years before he sadly became an apologist for the Warren Report, confronted Attorney General Francis Biddle's office and asked, "What did these people do? What were they about to do? In what way did they menace Minneapolis?" Biddle claimed ignorance of the case, but he nevertheless attempted a rationalization. "If I understood Mr. Biddle rightly," Stone wrote in *The Nation*, "he thinks a government need not wait for an overt act but can punish men for the probable consequences which would result if they tried to put their ideas into action. This reasoning is no different from that on which Trotskyists are jailed in the Third Reich or the Soviet Union. On this basis Thoreau could have been kept in jail for life."[57] Keep in mind all of these prosecutions were taking place months *before* America entered the war. Is there any wonder where the present concept of "insurrectionists" came from?

Once the country entered World War II, the president used both the 1917 Espionage Act and the Smith Act of 1940 to target citizens who had opposed American involvement. In 1944, thirty-three defendants were charged in the largest sedition trial in American history. Accused were an assortment of alleged Nazi sympathizers, anti-Semites, and reporters like William Griffin, who had editorialized before 1941 against participation in the war, but like many changed his position after Pearl Harbor.[58] Among the charges were referring to the United Nations as "ineffectual" and of waging "a systematic campaign of personal vilification and defamation of the public officials of the United States government."[59] *Pittsburgh Courier* reporter George S. Schuyler, despite being investigated by the FBI for his anti-FDR writings, charged that the defendants were being persecuted for what they'd "said and wrote." He admonished Americans to consider just "who is safe?" in such a climate.[60] Eventually, the judge died and a mistrial was declared. *The Saturday Evening Post* editorialized, "only the death of Judge Eicher availed to release American justice from an exhibition far more appropriate to the court rooms of Berlin and Moscow than to those of the United States."[61]

By war's end, the federal government counted the total number of draft resisters—violators of the Selective Service Act taken into custody — to be nearly 16,000. In 1947, after being pressured by a large contingent of clergy and other activists, President Truman pardoned 1,523 of the young men still lingering in prison. As convicted felons, the remaining 90 percent lost their voting rights and remained barred from holding certain jobs, even after having served out their sentences. Truman declared that he had little sympathy for conscientious objectors, viewing them with contempt, and believed them to be "just plain cowards or shirkers" who were using their religion as an excuse to avoid service.[62]

In June 1941, 11,000 workers went on strike at a Los Angeles airplane factory, where fighters, bombers, and training aircraft were made. They were striking for higher pay. FDR, usurping authority he didn't constitutionally have once again, ordered the War Department to take over the North American Aviation plant. "Our country is in danger," the president warned, "and the men and women who are now making airplanes play an indispensable part in its defense." Again, this was six months *before* Pearl Harbor. Army soldiers subdued the strikers, with the *New York Times* reporting, "Slowly they moved along, the hot early morning sun glinting on their bayonets," one of which caused a gash in the thigh of a striking worker. A lieutenant colonel took a microphone and announced that the Army Air Corps had taken over the factory in the name of the United States government. Secretary of the Navy Frank Knox gloated that the introduction of the military into the affairs of a private company "has had a profound psychological effect. From now on I think our troubles from that source will grow less."[63]

In my book *Crimes and Cover-Ups in American Politics: 1776–1963,* I covered all the numerous Allied atrocities from World War II that have been glossed over by the court historians. However, all the atrocities didn't occur in Germany or Japan. There was an unconscionable theft of personal property by the "good guys" running our own concentration camps. In the book *Years of Infamy: The Untold Story of America's Concentration Camps,"* author Michi Nishiura Weglyn revealed that an astounding *80 percent* of the goods and property of Japanese and German detainees were stolen and sold after the war by those who interned them in *this* country. In early

1942, FDR signed an executive order which resulted in some 120,000 Japanese Americans being summarily marched off to internment camps. There was very little advance notice given to these hapless souls, making it easy for the vast majority of their homes and other possessions to be confiscated by the government. Subsequent orders from Roosevelt rounded up German Americans as well, and their often valuable businesses wound up in the government's hands, too. The Feds would eventually accumulate a half-million acres of prime California farmland, and over 1,200 Japanese-owned hotels alone, just in California. It's been estimated that the value of the property stolen from Japanese Americans would amount to about $3 billion today. The property seizures from German Americans amounted to more billions. Organized crime was front and center in reaping the profits, with the result that Los Angeles journalist Art White would write, "During these years some hundreds of associates of Greenberg, Evans, and others of the Capone crime syndicate, and of Arvey and Ziffren, poured hundreds of millions of dollars into California. They bought real estate, including hotel chains through apparently unrelated corporations from San Diego to Sacramento. They invested in vast tracts of land, built or bought motels, giant office buildings, and other commercial properties."[64] It is a certainty that a significant chunk of this property came from those who'd been interned in camps. Future Supreme Court Chief Justice Earl Warren, whose name will forever be connected with massive suppression of the truth, was deeply involved in this outright theft. Warren, like most of our leaders a passionate eugenicist, supported the forced sterilization of Japanese, and was a member of the racist, anti-Asian group Native Sons of the Golden West. The chief architect of the property theft was David L. Bazelton, a mob-connected Democratic Party loyalist, who would go on to become a Circuit Judge of the United States Court of Appeals for the District of Columbia. Weglyn's book was instrumental in getting the Japanese victims redress through the Civil Liberties Act of 1988. Nothing for German Americans or Italian Americans, however.[65]

What happened in those internment camps has been largely overlooked. FDR's bigotry was evident in several private conversations he had, which indicated he believed that the Japanese were inferior to Whites.[66] Often depicted in textbooks on American history as giving in to public pressure,

Roosevelt, in reality, was the driving force behind the roundup and internment of citizens. Among those in opposition were J. Edgar Hoover and Attorney General Francis Biddle. Japanese children were removed from orphanages and sent to the camps. The pets belonging to Japanese families that were interned were often killed by the government.[67] The Works Progress Administration constructed the camps and was involved in overseeing them, along with the military. Seven inmates were shot and killed for such transgressions as failing to stay ten feet away from the fence or walking on a sidewalk. The concentration camps became the single biggest project of the WPA. Jason Scott Smith remarked, "The eagerness of many WPA administrators to place their organization in the forefront of this wartime enterprise is striking."[68]

The Roosevelt administration's actions in Puerto Rico were ugly as well.[69] Puerto Rico became a US territory in 1917, but although its people became American citizens, they didn't enjoy full rights. In 1934, separatist leader Pedro Albizu Campos led a Puerto Rican agricultural strike which impacted the profits of the US sugar corporations and resulted in a significant pay increase for sugar cane workers. Campos was thereafter subjected to arson and bomb threats on his home, the FBI tapped his phone, read his mail, and followed him everywhere. In 1936, he would be imprisoned along with several other Puerto Rican nationalists for "advocating the overthrow of the US government." US congressman Vito Marcantonio blasted their trial as a "frame-up," and called it "one of the blackest pages in the history of American jurisprudence." Marcantonio would charge that the prosecutor had been allowed to hand pick a jury, and they all "had expressed publicly bias and hatred for the defendants." He alleged that the prosecutor had been assured that "the Department of Justice would back him until he did get a conviction."[70] Campos would be arrested and thrown in prison two more times. All told, he served over twenty years behind bars. Interestingly, Campos would allege that during his incarceration, he was subjected to human radiation experiments. When the president of the Cuban Cancer Association verified his claims, J. Edgar Hoover would issue instructions in an FBI memo regarding one doctor visiting Campos in prison, that agents "furnish any subversive information concerning him."[71]

FDR's administration desperately tried to foil efforts at nationalism in Puerto Rico. In 1936, the Senate passed the Tydings Bill (courtesy of Millard Tydings, who would become one of Joe McCarthy's many foes). The proposal was hardly a gift to the Nationalist movement. If granted independence, their products would face a steadily increased US tariff, up to 25 percent. As Luis Munoz Marin observed: "The bill gives Puerto Ricans a very clear impression of being designed to obtain the mandate for independence from the Puerto Rican people under threat of literal starvation or a continuance of the present colonial status." New Deal officials indicted Puerto Rican Nationalist leaders on charges of "political sedition." On Palm Sunday, March 21, 1937, a peaceful march was organized in support of the imprisoned Pedro Albizu Campos. Puerto Rico's Governor, retired US General Blanton Winship, ordered police to open fire on the unarmed demonstrators, killing twenty-one and wounding some two hundred. One woman killed was carrying a palm leaf crucifix. A boy riding a bicycle was shot, and a seven-year-old girl was shot as she ran toward a church for safety. The police clubbed numerous men, women, and children. One woman was beaten so severely her brain matter spilled out onto the street and people repeatedly slipped on it. Cadet Bolivar Márquez Telechea was shot, and before dying, managed to scrawl on a wall, using his own blood and three crucifixes to write, "Long live the Republic, Down with the Murderers." No arms were found on any of the victims. Governor Winship was blamed for the entire event, and under pressure from Congress, FDR removed him from his position in 1939. However, as is typical in such cases, neither Winship nor anyone else was ever prosecuted for what became known as the Ponce Massacre. The American Civil Liberties Union would declare that the US government had been guilty of "gross violation of civil rights and incredible police brutality."[72] The government covered this incident up, even to the extent of re-creating "live" shootings using corpses, in an effort to show that police were firing back in defense.[73] In light of all this, the November 1, 1950, attempted assassination of President Truman by Puerto Rican nationalists should be assessed in a broader context.

Shadowy financier Bernard Baruch was the kind of Establishment figure that characterized the Roosevelt administration. Baruch explained how our state-controlled media works perfectly when he said, "The best method of enforcement lies in the power of public opinion. If it is completely understood that those who are cooperating are soldiers against the common enemy within, and those who omit to act are on the other side, there will be little hanging back."[74] After amassing a fortune in the stock market, Baruch managed Woodrow Wilson's War Industries Board. In the aftermath of World War II, he developed the Baruch Plan for international control of atomic energy. His personal friend Winston Churchill often stayed in Baruch's New York home when visiting America. He lived to the ripe old age of ninety-four.

The death of Franklin Roosevelt, allegedly from a cerebral hemorrhage, on April 12, 1945, in Warm Springs, Georgia, was exceedingly suspicious. As author Stephen B. Ubaney documented in his 2016 book *Who Murdered FDR?,* the president had obviously been declining for the past year, losing significant weight and appearing shockingly gaunt and sickly in his few public appearances. Considering the questionable circumstances around his sudden death, the fact that there wasn't an autopsy performed certainly ought to have raised, and should still raise, some eyebrows. As if that wasn't enough, FDR's medical records disappeared from Bethesda Naval Hospital, scene of the world's worst autopsy in JFK's death, and the facility where both James Forrestal and Sen. Joe McCarthy met their demises in highly questionable fashion. This is no "conspiracy theory." It has been openly discussed in the mainstream media. Professor Harry S. Goldsmith wrote about his quest to find out what happened to these records, in his book *A Conspiracy of Silence: The Health and Death of Franklin D. Roosevelt.* As Goldsmith told *Newsweek* in a 2008 interview, "It's very rare, and especially for somebody of the stature of Franklin Roosevelt—his records disappearing, that is absolutely strange. Somebody had to suppress those records and for some reason, and that's what intrigued me. We know these records were kept in the safe at Bethesda Naval Hospital, and I've been told that 48 hours after Roosevelt's death they disappeared."[75]

Author Steve Ubaney discovered that there was at least one related death here which should arouse our curiosity. Major General Edwin Watson, one of FDR's closest friends and military advisors, as well as his appointments secretary, died a few months before the president, on

February 20, also supposedly from a cerebral hemorrhage. As was the case with FDR, there was no autopsy or embalming for Watson. Author Emanuel Josephson was actually the first to express skepticism about Watson's death in his book *The Strange Death of Franklin D. Roosevelt.* Ubaney raised the very intriguing question about the unlikelihood of FDR, Benito Mussolini, and Adolf Hitler all dying in a span of a little over two weeks. Ubaney noted that FDR was buried less than sixty-nine hours after his death, an incredibly short period of time for such a dignitary. No witnesses were questioned, not a single fingerprint was taken. He also wondered why FDR's widow Eleanor hired a private investigator to look back into her husband's death, in 1957. What was she expecting to find? And why did she wait so many years? Ubaney maintained that FDR was poisoned by someone in his inner circle. I won't write a spoiler here; those interested can check out Ubaney's book for full details.

Like so many other influential Democrats at the time, Eleanor Roosevelt had no love for then Senator John F. Kennedy. "I did not feel I could support him because he had avoided taking a position during the controversy over Senator Joseph McCarthy's methods of investigation," she told a Kennedy representative in rejecting a plea to endorse JFK for vice president during the contentious 1956 Democratic convention. Kennedy aide and speechwriter Ted Sorensen would declare that Eleanor "used the occasion to chastise the Senator in a roomful of people for being insufficiently anti-McCarthy."A bitter JFK would remark that Eleanor "hated my father and can't stand it that his children turned out so much better than hers." When it became clear by 1958 that Kennedy would be seeking the presidency, Eleanor commented on the Sunday-afternoon ABC program *College News Conference* that her sources told her, "Senator Kennedy›s father has been spending oodles of money all over the country and probably has a paid representative in every state by now." JFK openly challenged her on this "misinformation," and demanded "concrete evidence" of what he termed "gossip and speculation." Eleanor failed to respond to Kennedy's request that she acknowledge there was no evidence for such an accusation, but she resorted to a passive-aggressive telegram, which read, "My dear boy, I only say these things for your own good.

I have found, in a lifetime of adversity, that when blows are rained on one, it is advisable to turn the other profile." Using the word "profile" in this context was hardly accidental, and was an obvious reference to JFK's best-selling book *Profiles in Courage.*[76] Just as her husband had disliked Joseph Kennedy Sr., Eleanor clearly didn't like or trust his charming and charismatic son.

The Morgenthau Plan: Advocating Mass Starvation

Enforced poverty . . . destroys the spirit not only of the victim but debases the victor.

—Henry L. Stimson[77]

Henry Morgenthau Jr. was Roosevelt's Secretary of Treasury. His top assistant, by the way, was alleged Soviet agent Harry Dexter White, who apparently held a good deal of influence with him. It seems exceedingly strange that a Treasury official would be so intimately involved in the treatment of postwar Germany. And yet it was Morgenthau, who was known to "have the ear" of Eleanor Roosevelt, who pushed for a proposal that exceeded even the Treaty of Versailles in terms of unreasonable vengeance. Morgenthau basically wanted *all* Germans punished for the worst transgressions of the Nazis, by deindustrializing and disarming them. "I am for destroying it first and we will worry about the population second. . . . I am not going to budge an inch. . . . The President is adamant on this thing. Sure, it is a terrific problem. Let the *Germans solve it!* Why the hell should *I worry abou*t what happens to their people?" Morgenthau declared.[78] When FDR sent Morgenthau a report from OSS chief William Donovan, explaining that this policy might cause all Europeans to starve, since Germany produced most of the farm machinery for Europe, the Treasury Secretary replied, "I would like to say in the words of your son Johnny, 'So what?'"[79] Keep in mind, the source for these quotes, Michael Beschloss, is a preeminent court historian and transparently committed to presenting Morgenthau and the Roosevelt administration in the best possible light. The Morgenthau Plan was first published in the press on September 21, 1944, by reliable Establishment toady Drew Pearson, who of course supported it. The Germans reacted predictably, with one headline proclaiming, "Roosevelt and Churchill Agree to Jewish Murder Plan."[80]

FDR, sometimes portrayed as advocating a more lenient approach to postwar Germany (much as Lincoln is said to have been in favor of leniency for the South), revealed his true feelings in the following hateful quote, which was in response to the more measured policy proposed in the 1944 *Handbook of Military Government in Germany*: "Too many people here and in England hold the view that the German people as a whole are not responsible for what has taken place—that only a few Nazis are responsible. That unfortunately is not based on fact. The German people must have it driven home to them that the whole nation has been engaged in a lawless conspiracy against the decencies of modern civilization." The whole nation? How about the infants and toddlers? Why weren't all Japanese or Italians responsible? Morgenthau would detail his hideous plan in the 1945 book *Germany is our Problem.* Winston Churchill would say, at the Second Quebec Conference, "the German working man should be allowed sufficient food for his bare need, and work, but no more." FDR's pre-conference comments were even harsher, as he exclaimed that "you either have to castrate the German people or you have got to treat them in such a manner that they can't just go on reproducing people who want to continue the way they have in the past."[81] There's that eugenicist mindset again, castration and sterilization being interchangeable terms. Roosevelt would later deny he'd ever supported the plan, which he unquestionably had. General Dwight Eisenhower approved the distribution of 1,000 copies of the book to American military officials in occupied Germany. Eisenhower not only favored this draconian plan, he had provided Morgenthau with his personal, decidedly anti-German input.

While the *New York Times* and most other huge news outlets were sympathetic to the Morgenthau Plan, there were a few dissenting voices. In an October 2, 1944, article titled "The Policy of Hate," *Time* magazine reported, "The plan that had been put forward, by Treasury Secretary Henry Morgenthau, had roused the violent objections of Secretaries Cordell Hull and Henry Stimson. The President was said to be leaning toward the Morgenthau side. . . . Far & away the most drastic yet proposed for the future of Germany, it was just barely above the level of 'sterilize all Germans.' It would reduce Germany from a prewar industrial giant to a fourth-rate nation of small farms." This diabolical plan called for the elimination of all German industrial machinery and all German mines. As happened with the Treaty of Versailles after World War I, it would take German lands and cede it to nations like France and Poland. Most cruelly, it would withhold all financial aid to Germany, including food and clothing for the devastated civilian population. The quickly fading German resistance reacted to the plan on radio by charging, "Morgenthau wants to see 43,000,000 Germans exterminated." Herbert Hoover led an investigation that concluded the Morgenthau Plan would result in up to twenty-five million Germans dying from starvation. Cordell Hull, in his 1948 diaries, quoted Morgenthau as saying that the Germans should be "fed three times a day with soup from Army soup kitchens," so "they will remember that experience the rest of their lives." Senator Robert Taft astutely assessed our disastrous postwar foreign policy, stating, "We created an impossible situation in which freedom is suppressed throughout large sections of Europe and Asia. In Germany our policy has been dominated by the harsh and impractical Morgenthau plan, even though the Government pretended to repudiate it. Our German policy has wrecked the economy of Europe and now we are called upon for cash from our taxpayers to remedy the breakdown."[82]

In the minds of Holocaust-obsessed court historians, the Morgenthau Plan, and FDR's military actions, are analyzed exclusively from the viewpoint that those fighting the Nazis actually did far too little to help the Jews. Some of the more extreme ones name Roosevelt and Churchill as accomplices to the Nazis because of their supposed inaction. They hold a generally favorable view of a devious plan that would have turned Germany into a purely agrarian state, setting it back a thousand years. This virulent anti-German bias now permeates academia and the world of the court historians. It was inevitable that a book like Daniel Goldhagen's *Hitler's Willing Executioners: Ordinary Germans and the Holocaust*, published in 1996, would appear. Goldhagen argued that something he fancifully dubbed "eliminationist anti-Semitism" was in fact the cornerstone of German national identity. The book essentially blames every German citizen for every atrocity committed by the Nazis. I cannot help but think of the parallels to the "blood libel" held against the Jews for centuries, wherein every Jew was blamed for the crucifixion of Christ. Even most court historians blasted the book for its broad accusations of guilt against an entire population. Nevertheless, Goldhagen's book was an international award-winning bestseller. The *Harvard Gazette* declared that it had "helped sharpen public understanding about the past during a period of radical change in Germany."[83] Goldhagen asserted that it was wrong to treat Germans as "more or less like us," in other words as flesh-and-blood human beings, with values approximating our own. This kind of bigotry is, of course, at the heart of all prejudice, whether it stems from the KKK or "liberal" eugenicists.

During World War II, Morgenthau presided over the marketing of War Bonds, utilizing popular cultural figures like cartoon star Bugs Bunny. Although the Morgenthau Plan was never literally implemented, its influence was obvious in President Truman's May 10, 1945, approval of the Joint Chiefs of Staff's policy for American occupying forces to "take no steps looking toward the economic rehabilitation of Germany [nor steps] designed to maintain or strengthen the German economy." Truman would rescind this order on grounds of "national security" two years later. Morgenthau, interestingly, was married to the granddaughter of one of the founders of the giant banking firm Lehman Brothers. Devoting his final years to Jewish causes, Morgenthau would work closely with the United Jewish Appeal and the creation of the state of Israel. He would later become a financial advisor to Israel. He helped establish the dominance of the World Bank and International Monetary Fund in the postwar world.

CHAPTER FIVE

JOE McCARTHY: UNFAIRLY MALIGNED AND MISREPRESENTED

How can we account for our present situation, unless we believe that men high in this government are concerting to deliver us to disaster? This must be the product of a great conspiracy, a conspiracy on a scale so immense as to dwarf any such previous venture in the history of man.

—Sen. Joseph McCarthy[1]

Senator Joseph McCarthy continues to be smeared as the ultimate political bad guy, by both the Left and the Right. As I noted in my earlier book *Crimes and Cover-Ups in American Politics: 1776–1963,* McCarthy was not associated with the House Un-American Activities Committee (HUAC), since he was a member of the US Senate. It was the HUAC that "canceled" alleged "communists" in Hollywood and elsewhere, not McCarthy's committee. McCarthy's 1950 Wheeling, West Virginia speech, in which he held up a list of names he claimed were tied to the communist party, immediately garnered him some powerful enemies. His critics quickly focused on the fact that there appeared to be fluctuation in McCarthy's numbers. Was he talking about 300 security risks, or 205, or 57? Senator William Benton responded by summarily introducing a motion to expel McCarthy from the Senate. Even if McCarthy had given different numbers, *that* was a transgression worthy of being removed from office? Compare this to then–Secretary of State Hillary Clinton getting rid of over 30,000 emails, to cite just one example of high corruption that went entirely unpunished.[2]

The hearings McCarthy presided over in 1953, which delved into security lapses in the US military, and more particularly alleged Soviet sympathizers in the Army, were not declassified until 2003. An examination of these transcripts reveals some "high strangeness," to use researcher Peter Secosh's term. For instance, McCarthy's committee's chief counsel, the notoriously controversial Roy Cohn, brought up the Rothschild banking family several times during the questioning of Abraham Chasanow, on November 3, 1953. Chasanow was a veteran employee with the U.S. Navy's Hydrographic Office. Cohn asked Chasanow twice if he knew the Rothschilds. Chasanow denied knowing them, but admitted, "I may have seen them at a public meeting."[3] There is no explanation or context to Cohn's sudden reference to the world's allegedly wealthiest bankers, and they weren't mentioned again. Was this simply a clumsy attempt to connect the shadowy world of international finance to alleged subversion within the American military?

During their investigation of lapsed security at Fort Monmouth, New Jersey, McCarthy's Permanent Subcommittee on Investigations found that over fifty classified documents were missing, and that three top-secret document registers—lists of the titles of documents—had been destroyed.[4] Interestingly, McCarthy himself would cite the time period of July 1947 during the testimony of "missing document" witness Harry J. Donohue.[5] McCarthy's reference to the month when the infamous Roswell, New Mexico, incident took place seems to have been more than coincidental, especially considering that in several instances, "July 1947" was mentioned in connection with New Mexico.[6] As Joseph P. Farrell, author of the book *McCarthy, Monmouth, and the Deep State* noted, "The Roswell Incident involved the US Army Air Force, as the US Air Force had not yet been spun out of the Army. It was the army itself, and security risks, that McCarthy's committee was investigating in the Monmouth hearings, and hence, the subject of crashed UFOs and security risks and espionage would have been of interest to McCarthy's committee. Thus, I believe McCarthy's reference to July 1947 is deliberate 'message sending,' a way of bringing up the UFO subject without explicitly mentioning it." This indirect UFO connection was also found in the testimony of witness Allen Sterling Gross, who stated that the security regulations at Fort Monmouth were amplified by "the Blue Book."[7] Project Blue Book was the name for the Air Force's UFO investigative unit, which served to debunk reports of "flying saucers." Farrell discovered many other Committee references to the month of July 1947,[8] as well as to US planes being shot down—but that those planes ceased being shot down once special equipment was installed in 1947.[9] One of the witnesses before the committee, engineer Dr. Fred Daniels, testified that areas of investigation for him were "optical telephony," a subject oddly mentioned in aspects of German wartime research; and "compressional waves," which happened to be something worked on by the great Nikola Tesla. Tesla's invaluable papers were confiscated for the government and inspected by John Trump,[10] an MIT engineering professor and uncle of Donald Trump.[11] Daniels explained that some of his research was so highly classified he could not discuss it before the committee; but that this highly classified research also began in 1947.[12]

Another crucial area McCarthy was probing concerned the information disclosed in the private diaries of Lend-Lease liaison officer Major George Racey Jordan.[13] Jordan had written about the highly suspicious transfers of American technology to the Soviets during World War II. Jordan's testimony was the subject of an earlier investigation by the House Un-American Activities Committee (HUAC). Involved in these shipments was not only nuclear technology—including uranium and refined aluminum tubes (the kind used to cook uranium into plutonium)—but also the printing plates for the "occupation money" that Allied armies distributed and used in postwar Germany.[14] Jordan had learned that the approval of the transfer for the plates came from high-ranking Roosevelt Administration advisor, Harry Dexter White of the US Treasury, and Roosevelt Treasury Secretary Henry Morgenthau. The reason for the Soviets' interest in these plates was obvious; the Soviets could simply print any amount they wanted, and convert them into American dollars—which they did, to the tune of some $250,000,000.[15]

Were these plate transfers the subject of international finance, and might it explain the earlier noted, "cameo appearance" of the Rothschilds in the testimony of Abraham Chasaow? When McCarthy headed his later Senate investigation, he was keenly interested in investigating the transfer of these money plates. Senator Karl Mundt—who as a congressman sat on the House Un-American Activities committee, with Richard Nixon incidentally—would preside over the testimony of one William Taylor, when he broached the subject of "our loan of money plates to the Russians in the concluding days of the War." Interestingly during this discussion, Taylor, the assistant director of the Middle East division of the International Monetary Fund (IMF) explained that while serving in French North Africa, "I had my first experience with invasion currency. The invasion currency used at that time was what the army called yellow seal dollar. That invasion currency was withdrawn from troop circulation shortly after the opening days in [French] North Africa and we went on a franc basis. It was in Africa that it was first called to my attention that some of the finance officers were receiving back more francs in exchange for the dollar method than paid out." (Taylor's reference to a "yellow seal" here is significant. That can only refer to gold certificates, which mostly disappeared from circulation following FDR's 1933 executive order confiscating gold from American citizens.) This seems to imply that these yellow seal dollars were fetching a higher exchange rate, way out of proportion to the actual exchange rate at the time. Taylor alluded to this later in his testimony, stating, "In Italy some of the GI's and military personnel sent back sums vastly in excess of what they had received in pay."[16] In other words, occupation money in the form of yellow seal dollars was flowing *out* (along with the gold that it may have represented), and paper occupation currency was flowing *in* to the occupied countries. So much occupation currency was printed up in fact—for France, Italy, the Netherlands, Austria, Belgium, Denmark, and Germany—that the United States had to outsource this whole printing scheme to the private, Forbes Company in Boston.[17] Additionally, Taylor testified that currency plates for a special currency that was *not* denominated in any unit—not Italian lira, not French francs, not German marks, not dollars, not pounds—had been drawn up. This special currency that was printed was to be used as a basis for other currencies to be drawn from. Had McCarthy's committee bumped into the earliest formation of a hidden system of finance? Was this a precursor to a global currency; an early version of the International Monetary Fund's Special Drawing Rights (SDRs), being used to "reset" the exchange rate of existing national currencies? Author Joseph Farrell noted, "money is being *laundered* and gold and exchange rate manipulation *is* the mechanism. . . . There is one additional implication of this: the War is being used *as a mechanism of financial consolidation.*"[18] Asked who he was reporting to at the time, Taylor responded, "Mr. Harry Dexter White."

One wouldn't have to have been a right-wing extremist to understand how much smoke there was in McCarthy's general charge that there were communists infiltrating the US government. Senior Treasury Department official Harry Dexter White was proven, to most people's satisfaction, to have been a Soviet agent in FDR's White House. Despite all the allegations swirling around White, President Harry Truman nominated him to be the American director of the IMF in 1946, and the Senate confirmed him. Truman would later lie about this, claiming that White had been terminated from government employ once he'd received information about his suspect status from the FBI, when in fact he chose White for the IMF position after he'd been informed of White's situation by the FBI.[19]

Near the end of World War II, a German Panzer division was accused of murdering over eighty American POWs in what came to be called the "Malmedy Massacre." When the German officers and soldiers allegedly involved were put on trial after the war, they maintained that their confessions had been coerced "by beatings and torture." Joe McCarthy pressured the Senate Armed Services Committee, chaired by his arch-nemesis Millard Tydings (father of later longtime US Senator Joe Tydings), to investigate the German defendants' claims. A subcommittee was formed, and while all Senators were invited to participate in the proceedings, McCarthy was the only one who accepted. Author Daniel Oshinsky described the kind of mindset that came to rule postwar American defense policy: "The Armed Services Committee . . . existed mainly to support the whims of the Pentagon and to uphold the military's popular image.

Its role in the Malmedy investigation would be predictable enough: play up the German atrocities, ignore the American abuses, protect the Army's good name. Anyone who took the opposition position was bound to upset the Senate leadership and to make a few headlines." While McCarthy has been demonized like few other political figures, Oshinsky asked, "Is it possible, just possible, that the senator came to the defense of those soldiers because he believed they were being denied due process? Is there a chance that his motives were in the best tradition of American justice?"

Oshinsky, on the surface a typical McCarthy critic, goes on to lambast the Wisconsin senator as a bully, but again relates how, "When the war ended, the Army rounded up as many First S.S. Panzer Division soldiers as it could and charged them indiscriminately with taking part in the massacre. Confessions were obtained through force: Jaws and teeth were broken by rifle butts, men were permanently disabled by kicks to the groin, and mock trials were held in a style reminiscent of the Ku Klux Klan. This was hardly surprising, since most of the prosecutors attached to the case were '39ers,' Jewish refugees who had fled the Nazis and who intensely hated the German people as a race. Those prosecutors were not the real villains, however. They were men with overwhelming grievances against the men whose bitter memories had been shamefully exploited by their military superiors. Needless to say, the confessions obtained were worthless. 'I assume that you and I would agree,' Joe lectured one witness, 'that an innocent man will scream about as loudly as a guilty man if you are kicking him in the testicles, and an innocent man will perhaps sign the same confession that a guilty man will if you kick him long enough and hard enough.'"[20] McCarthy would eventually storm out of the proceedings after declaring, "I accuse the subcommittee of being afraid of the facts. I accuse it of attempting to whitewash a shameful episode in the history of our glorious armed forces."[21]

McCarthy's countless critics have used this incident to ludicrously smear him as an anti-Semite. The soon-to-be beleaguered senator had addressed his concerns about possible torture of prisoners before he held up that paper in Wheeling, West Virginia, and became a legendary villain to the court historians. Unlike many "chicken hawk" warmongers then, and now, McCarthy was a genuine war hero, winning eleven medals, commendations, and ribbons, and indeed rode his war record as "Tail Gunner Joe" into Congress. McCarthy had risked the wrath of the public before: during his 1946 Senate campaign, he bemoaned the horrific conditions in postwar Germany, alleging that more than 100,000 German POWs had died from "ill treatment and lack of food." McCarthy's wartime diaries would reveal his disdain for US military brass, which he referred to as "mental midgets." McCarthy's widow Jean would write in her unpublished memoir, "Joe felt this was a brand of 'justice' that could be turned against us in the future. This was not a popular opinion to hold." She confessed that his willingness to take unpopular stands was what made her fall in love with him. Ironically, the same kind of guilt by association that leftists attribute to "McCarthyism" has been used against his legacy, regarding all the supposed "Jew haters" who supported him. "There was scarcely a professional American anti-Semite who had not publicly endorsed the senator," charged Arnold Forster, general counsel for the Anti-Defamation League. The Anti-Defamation League continues, to this day, to be the loudest voice for censorship, and against free speech, in this country. One article alleging that the Wisconsin senator was anti-Semitic noted that forty-one out of forty-five civilians suspended by Fort Monmouth as possible security risks, during McCarthy's investigation were Jews. In reality, McCarthy was a supporter of Israel, and some on the extreme Right even ridiculed him as a "Crypto Jew."[22]

In later years, McCarthy's widow, now remarried as Jean Minetti, refused to discuss her husband with researchers. As of 1977, she was living in "relative seclusion" in Maryland. His many siblings were just as close-lipped. While they seem to have thought the venomous media coverage of Joe McCarthy was unfair and untrue, they never went public to set the record straight. Although almost no information can be found about it, McCarthy's younger brother Howard "died suddenly the day after his divorce became final in 1960."[23] McCarthy and his wife adopted an infant daughter, whom they named Tierney, and the adoption papers hadn't been finalized at the time of his death. When a museum exhibit on McCarthy opened in his hometown of Appleton, Wisconsin, in 2002, his daughter, Tierney Grinavic, who "reportedly lives in the Washington, D.C. area," ignored entreaties from the museum.[24] Later reports had her living in Huntingtown, Maryland, where she was known to refuse to discuss anything about her adopted father. According to a GoFundMe posted by a man who claimed he had been her boyfriend, Tierney died of cancer on November 11, 2020. Rumors persist that Joe McCarthy became a morphine addict, and that the FBI paid for his drugs. There were also lurid allegations that McCarthy was a homosexual who preyed on young males. All these accusations, in addition to the insinuations that he was a hopeless alcoholic, must be viewed in context with the unprecedented mainstream media assault upon him.

In his 1970 book *The Assassination of Joe McCarthy*, Medford Evans wrote, "Fanatical Zionists would begin with a no doubt insuperable hostility toward McCarthy, if for no other reason than that he was in some sense a protégé of and successor to the late James Forrestal, whose position on Palestine in the late 1940s was anything but satisfactory to the Zionists. It is doubtful, however, whether McCarthy even knew what Forrestal's position on Palestine was, though he was perfectly clear as to the position of the first Secretary of Defense on Communism and Soviet Russia. The main reason for widespread Jewish hostility toward McCarthy was the misplaced respect for the professional intelligentsia which is all too common among Jews, and which culminates in acceptance of the canonicity of the *New York Times*. . . . As can hardly be overemphasized, one of the key figures in the career of Joe McCarthy was Alfred Kohlberg, the New York importer of Irish-linen handkerchiefs from China (where the ornamental work was done). Kohlberg was one of the most intensely patriotic Americans—without being fanatical about patriotism or any other subject—of whom I know. Alfred Kohlberg and his wife Ida were among the last close personal friends to see McCarthy alive and in good spirits. It was just a week before he was to make his last trip to Bethesda that the Kohlbergs called on him at his Washington home. Mrs. Kohlberg . . . thought the Senator looked well. And he might have been. If all his friends had been as loyal as Kohlberg, he might have stayed that way."[25] McCarthy's death was extremely suspicious, to put it mildly. His scurrilous critics in the press, led by Jack Anderson's mentor Drew Pearson, insinuated that he died from cirrhosis of the liver, caused by alcoholism. Or was it hepatitis, which killed a very small minority of those who contracted it? As I noted while exploring this subject in my previous book, incomprehensibly there was no autopsy performed. Author Evans discovered that "McCarthy's hospital records are unavailable to scholars" while researching his book.

The Army has been cast in the role of "good guy" in its battle with ultimate "bad guy" Joe McCarthy. As always, the facts contradict the court historians. Unscrupulous Army officials went to the lengths of attempting to expose McCarthy's Senate committee chief counsel Roy Cohn, and his young aide David Schine (both Jewish, by the way) as homosexual lovers. "I'm getting fed up with the way the Army is trying to use Dave as a hostage to pressure us to stop our hearings," an exasperated McCarthy exclaimed. The court historian's "McCarthyism" narrative holds that the evil ogre's demise can be summed up in Army special counsel Joseph Welch's sanctimonious barb to the Wisconsin Senator, "Have you left no sense of decency, sir, at long last?" This related to McCarthy's perceived smearing of Fred Fisher, who was a young attorney on Welch's staff. Welch's moral outrage, however, was pure theater, much like the scripted nonsense that propels politics these days. As author Victor Herman wrote, "No other episode is more important to the McCarthy myth: how McCarthy needlessly maligned an innocent lawyer on Welch's staff in order to wound his chief antagonist, and how Welch rose up in indignation and shamed him on national television. However, the real encounter took place long before the television cameras were turned on. Two days earlier, Joseph Welch and Roy Cohn had reached a deal: Welch would not mention Cohn's avoidance of the draft during his testimony if Cohn did not bring up Fred Fisher's brief membership as a law student with the National Lawyers' Guild, a Communist front. That dirty little secret had already been published in the *New York Times* two weeks earlier. Welch had decided to relieve Fisher as his assistant in the hearings; otherwise, he told Cohn, 'we would all end up looking like Communist sympathizers.' He wanted to make sure the McCarthy team did not bring it up. Cohn told McCarthy; McCarthy agreed."[26] Welch's dramatic confrontation with McCarthy moved him to tears, but once he was out of sight of the press and television cameras, Joseph Farrell reported, "Welch turned to his colleague, the tears still staining his face, and said without changing expression, 'Well, how did it go'?"[27]

David Schine became a noted film and record producer. In an odd move for a homosexual, he married Miss Universe and had six children with her. He would die in a 1996 plane crash along with his wife and son. Joseph Welch, meanwhile, was rewarded by fellow Leftist, director Otto Preminger, with being cast as the judge in his 1959 film *Anatomy of a Murder*. He was nominated for a Golden Globe as Best Supporting Actor. Perhaps he honed those skills with the crocodile tears he shed after his famous confrontation with McCarthy. Roy Cohn became a power behind the scenes in Republican politics, and grew close to New York's Cardinal Spellman, the subject of gay rumors himself. He also was something of a mentor to then young business titan Donald Trump. Cohn died of AIDS in 1986. New York attorney John Klotz would allege that Cohn provided protection for "a ring of pedophiles" operating out of the Plaza Hotel, who had "connections to the intelligence community."[28]

Joe McCarthy wasn't involved with the blacklisting of the "Hollywood Ten" or any other private sector individuals. The communist witch hunt that has been compared to the Salem witch hysteria, was propelled by the House Un-American Activities Committee, with which McCarthy had no connection. And yet his name is firmly associated with blacklisting in the public mind. "Red Scare" articles appeared throughout the Cold War-era mainstream media, in publications like *The Hollywood Reporter*, which excoriated Dalton Trumbo and the other members of the "Hollywood Ten" in a July 29, 1946, column headlined "A Vote for Joe Stalin." Trumbo would be blacklisted in the film industry for a decade, until writing the 1960 screenplay for *Exodus* under a pseudonym. That movie was a glorification of the creation of the modern state of Israel, and is diametrically different from the perspective now almost universally shared by leftists in regard to the displacement and mistreatment of Palestinians. Does anyone remember the name of the chairman of HUAC during the infamous 1947 hearings, which drew testimony from many of the biggest stars in Hollywood? That would be J. Parnell Thomas, a Republican from New Jersey. I guess "Thomasism" just doesn't have that ring to it.

McCarthy wasn't interested in "canceling" individuals in the film colony, or outside the world of politics. He was looking at internal subversion in government, and this included poking around the issue of what appears to have been the theft of $100 billion of Chinese Nationalist gold in Chiang Kai-shek-run China. In 1934, American officials had struck a deal with China, whereby they would physically store their gold in return for securities which included Federal Reserve bonds. Of course, only the U.S. Treasury normally issues bonds. Harry Dexter White, the suspected Communist in FDR's administration, was in the center of the deal with China, and would later personally obstruct delivery of Chiang's gold, "because the money is being badly used." In other words, the gold was *simply stolen*, and support for his government allowed to lapse, in hopes that if his government fell, there would be no reason to return the gold.[29] This area of inquiry was only one of those where McCarthy threatened to expose Deep State secrets that would tar both FDR's and Truman's legacies.

The United States has an unfortunate history in this regard, having been prone to looting their enemies since the Civil War, when William Sherman and his troops stole gratuitously from the defeated southern population. Near the end of World War II, the Americans found a trove of gold and other treasure in the Philippines, which had been confiscated by the Japanese from their opponents over thousands of years. This war booty was hidden in numerous caves throughout the islands, but their locations were revealed to the Americans after the torture of a Japanese general's driver—most notably by a young Ed Lansdale and his assistant.[30] Former Joint Chiefs of Staff officer L. Fletcher Prouty would maintain that Lansdale was in Dealey Plaza on the day of the JFK assassination. For the next 2 years, the Americans worked to recover hundreds of billions of dollars worth of treasure from the tunnels in the Philippines[31] When informed of this, President Truman decided to keep secret this war loot. Meanwhile, John Foster Dulles—who alone wrote and negotiated the 1951 Peace Treaty—forced through a clause that exempted Japan and its corporations from paying compensation to POWs and civilian victims, and told the world Japan was broke.[32] In a September 5, 1951 speech before the San Francisco Peace Conference, Dulles stated, "Reparation is usually the most controversial aspect of peacemaking. . . . Japan's aggression caused tremendous cost, losses and suffering. Governments represented here have claims which total many billions of dollars, and China could plausibly claim as much again. One hundred thousand million dollars would be a modest estimate of the whole. On the other hand, to meet these claims, there stands a Japan presently reduced to four home islands which are unable to produce the food its people need to live, or the raw materials they need to work. Since the surrender, Japan has been 2 billion dollars short of the money required to pay for the food and raw materials she had to import for survival on a minimum basis."[33]

Since Japan negotiated its treaty with the Medal of Freedom recipient Dulles, the Department of State and Department of Justice have used a clause in the Treaty of 1951 to prevent POW victims from suing for compensation. Sterling and Peggy Seagrave, in their book *Gold Warriors: America's Secret Recovery of Yamashita's Gold,* write, "Despite such impassioned appeals, on September 21, 2000, U.S. District Court Judge Vaughn Walker ruled against American POWs and other slave laborers. Walker dismissed their suits, saying that, 'it was dangerous to upset the diplomatic alliance that existed between America and Japan since the end of the war.'"[34]

All this was connected to the wildly inconsistent nature of postwar reparations. As noted, following World War I, Germany became the first loser in a conflict to be forced to pay the winner money. But after World War II, theoretically, the reparations levied upon the Axis powers should have been uniform. Germany didn't pay off its "debt" from World War I until 2010! It's hard to find an accurate figure for World War II reparations, but it seems that Germany was compelled to pay some $14 billion to Israel alone, until 1987.[35] A figure between $22.5 and $33 billion to be paid by Germany to the victorious Allied powers was set by the Paris Reparations Conference of 1946, but some claim all of it was never paid. One online source had Russia still getting $12 billion in 2022, while another source claimed they were paid $3.5 billion altogether. Japan, however, wasn't held to the same harsh standard. Japan fared much better at Nuremberg, where the vanquished was tried in court by the victors for the first time in history, and they certainly fared much better in terms of reparations. Essentially, we confiscated Japan's own stolen property, and then claimed they couldn't afford to pay reparations after the war. If Japan actually paid anything, it was $6.67 million to the International Red Cross.

McCarthy seems to have been one of the first "conspiracy theorists" in regards to the "surprise" attack by the Japanese on Pearl Harbor. In his own book which excoriated Gen. George C. Marshall, McCarthy quoted from George Morgenstern's 1947 exposé, *Pearl Harbor: The Story of the Secret War*: "The 'winds' message was a Japanese coded message as to the time and target of their attack. . . . Despite all this pressure upon him, Safford, when he was called as a witness before the congressional committee on February 1, 1946, opened his statement with the flat assertion: 'There was a 'winds' message . . . and we knew it meant war.'" McCarthy continued to quote Morgenstern: "Safford testified that he had been told by W. F. Friedman, chief Army cryptanalyst, that the 'winds' message had been destroyed prior to the Pearl Harbor investigation 'on direct orders from Chief of Staff Marshall.'"[36] The Captain Laurance Safford referenced was a Navy cryptologist who had declared that the 'winds' message had been intercepted on December 4, 1941—just more evidence of the FDR administration's foreknowledge. Peter Secosh, in paraphrasing Joseph P. Farrell, observed, "Why is this significant? Consider when McCarthy published his book: at the height of the Army-McCarthy Hearings. In his speech (and subsequent book), he indicts not only Harry Hopkins and George Marshall, but through them, he is *implicating the Administration of Franklin Roosevelt* in, at the minimum, gross incompetence and corruption. Consider, the outcome of the Army-McCarthy Hearings was by no means certain until McCarthy had his career-ending showdown with Army special counsel Joseph Welch, which everyone saw on television. But had he won, or at least, stalemated the Army in the hearings, the movement for censure may not have been successful, and he may have therefore retained his chairmanship over the US Senate Government Operations Committee, and thus have been able to subpoena General Marshall and the other witnesses named for an investigation of the whole Pearl Harbor foreknowledge matter in conjunction with his investigation of Communist subversion."[37]

McCarthy also pointed out the curious fact that George C. Marshall appeared not to recall what he was doing at the time Pearl Harbor was attacked. This brings to mind Richard Nixon's conflicting accounts of where he was when JFK was assassinated. Marshall's and Nixon's faulty memories contradict the accepted consensus that "everyone remembers where they were" when they heard about Pearl Harbor, or that JFK had been shot. McCarthy wrote, "Originally, Marshall testified that he was out horseback riding and for that reason could not be contacted. Later, he testified his memory had been refreshed and that he actually had not been horseback riding but was at home with his wife. The third version of where the Army Chief of Staff was on that fateful morning is contained in Arthur Upton Pope's book *Litvinoff*, in which the diary account of [Soviet Ambassador] Litvinoff's trip from Russia to the United States shows that Marshall was meeting Litvinoff at the airport on Pearl Harbor morning." As I wrote in *Crimes and Cover-Ups in American Politics: 1776–1963,* Republican presidential nominee Thomas Dewey was planning to use Pearl Harbor subterfuge as a campaign issue against Roosevelt. However, McCarthy notes, "Another interesting point brought out by Morgenstern on pages 201 and 202 was that Marshall, fearing that Thomas E. Dewey, in the 1944 (presidential) campaign, was about to expose Marshall's part in the Pearl Harbor disaster, sent to him a staff officer with letters from Marshall, and persuaded Dewey that such an exposure would thereby inform Japan that we had broken her code and would thereby impair our military efforts. Dewey was apparently convinced and, being a loyal American, did not mention this matter during the campaign."[38]

The 2002 Hollywood hit piece *Good Night and Good Luck* presented the familiar, poisonous Establishment view of McCarthy as clearly as anything ever has. As the subject of unfiltered vitriol, McCarthy is barely depicted as human. There is no nuance or subtlety in these demonic characterizations, and McCarthy is second to no other historical figure other than Hitler, and now perhaps Donald Trump, in this regard. To anyone assessing historical events in an independent manner, Joe McCarthy had the right friends, men like the almost certainly murdered Secretary of Defense James Forrestal (who, by the way, was friendly enough with a young John F. Kennedy to tour the ruins of postwar Germany with him[39]), and Joseph P. Kennedy Sr. He certainly had the right enemies: most of the US Senate, the Army leadership, Presidents Truman and Eisenhower, and virtually the entire mainstream media. Court historians love to pare complex events and personalities down to sound bites that can be easily digested in our social media–dominated era. I don't care what the court historians conclude about anything. Their conclusions are inexorably based on biased and flawed research, if they conduct any research at all. The record shows that Joe McCarthy was a naïve but well-meaning man who honestly sought to root out what he believed was corruption in our government. He was despised by the horrific figures of the era, and died two days after entering infamous Bethesda Naval Hospital complaining of knee pain.

Korean War Atrocities

I have seen, I guess, as much blood and disaster as any living man, and it just curdled my stomach.

—Gen. Douglas MacArthur[40]

Rarely reported is the ugly fact that the US military wiped out nearly every city in North Korea, killing over a million civilians, during the Korean War. The bombing included napalm, and was worse than what Germany had been subjected to during World War II. Koreans were reduced to living in tunnels to escape the relentless bombardment. General Douglas MacArthur himself, as the above quote illustrates, claimed to have been sickened by the devastation. Both North Korea and China would allege that by early 1952, the United States was using biological or germ warfare weapons against them, a charge vehemently denied by our government. Captured US pilots supposedly told their captors about the use of such weapons. Later, these prisoners were interrogated by counterintelligence experts and psychiatrists, and threatened with court-martial if they didn't renounce their revelations about germ warfare. They all did recant their confessions. The International Scientific Commission, or ISC, led by one of the foremost British scientists of his time, Joseph Needham, traveled to China and North Korea in the summer of 1952 to investigate these claims. They produced the "Report of International Scientific Commission for the Investigation of the Facts Concerning Bacterial Warfare in Korea and China," which corroborated the charges of the Chinese and North Koreans. Jeffrey S. Kaye published explosive details from the ISC Report in a 2018 article. The ISC found that the United States had used biological weapons in an experimental fashion on civilian populations. The report produced over six hundred pages of documentation, including statements from witnesses, doctors, autopsy reports and lab tests, photos, and other materials. The ISC Report, naturally, wasn't widely disseminated in this country. Among the biological weapons used by the Americans were anthrax, plague, and cholera.

The United States granted amnesty to Japanese doctors who performed hideous experiments on human beings during World War II, including vivisection. They killed thousands of Chinese with biological weapons. The amnesty was in return for providing their research to the American government. Much of the questioning of the Japanese involved in the biological warfare took place at Maryland's notorious Fort Detrick. The CIA would counter with a 1951 report, "Communist Propaganda Charging United States with the Use of BW in Korea." The CIA's report noted that the North Koreans claimed the South Koreans were planning to infect rivers and reservoirs with bacteria. The "capsules of bacilli" were said to have come "from American Camp Detrick or from Japanese stocks." Foretelling modern-day claims about US biolabs in Ukraine, a *Pravda* report, run by Associated Press on January 7, 1951, alleged that the Americans had "established a bacteriological warfare center in Japan under the direction of former Japanese Lt. Gen. Shiro Ishii." AP also quoted *Pravda* as saying Ishii's work was being sent from Japan "to an American bacteriological warfare research center at Camp Dietrich [sic], Md." A British sergeant described seeing American military police, in unmarked vehicles, and wearing helmets, parkas, gloves, and masks, entering houses in a North Korean village in November 1950. He witnessed them spreading "feathers" among all the homes. The sergeant testified, "They were holding the feathers at a distance from their bodies, not in the normal way . . . they had no identifying insignia. . . . It was all very fishy. They were very surprised and unhappy to see us. It was obvious that something suspicious was going on, and that it was a clandestine affair." In their book, *Unit 731: The Japanese Army's Secret of Secrets,* authors Peter Williams and David Wallace noted, "it is known from declassified documents that the Biological Department of the US Chemical Corps was at this time experimenting with feathers as carriers of biological agents."[41]

Echoing what was reported decades earlier in places like the Philippines and Haiti, American troops in Korea adhered to the Northern Civil War "Total War" policy. In July 1950, as many as three hundred South Korean refugees were indiscriminately murdered by weaponry and air assault, on a bridge near the No Gun Ri village. The United States initially denied any culpability in what became known as the No Gun Ri Massacre, but the horrifying details emerged years later, from eyewitness accounts of both survivors and perpetrators. One US veteran admitted, "There was a lieutenant screaming like a madman, 'fire on everything, kill 'em all. . .' Kids, there were kids out there, it didn't matter what it was, eight to 80, blind, crippled or crazy, they shot 'em all." Declassified documents in the National Archives revealed instructions from late July 1950, to shoot refugees approaching their position. Major General William B. Kean advised that civilians found in the area should be considered enemies and "treated accordingly."[42] This was only one of several such atrocities, which are war crimes by any definition. Only one individual faced charges for this mass murder, Captain Ernest Medina, who was court-martialed but acquitted. CBS News would report on a U.S. Air Force memo, dated July 25, 1950, which explained how the U.S. Army had *requested* that civilians be attacked, and "to date, we have complied with the army's request."[43] In response to the Associated Press report, the U.S. Army launched an "investigation" which not surprisingly attributed the deaths, which it now acknowledged, to "an unfortunate tragedy inherent to war and not a deliberate killing." President Clinton admitted that "things happened that were wrong," but didn't apologize. The No Gun Ri survivors' committee dubbed the Army report a "whitewash." Among those critical of the Army report was Rep. Pete McCloskey, who would be hounded out of Congress by the Anti-Defamation League, for his criticism of Israeli treatment of Palestinians.[44]

As I have commented regarding my work on atrocities committed by Northern troops in the Civil War, or by the Allies in World War II, I am perfectly aware that atrocities were committed by the Confederates and the Nazis. They've all been thoroughly publicized, by the court historians and in Hollywood. Michigan Senator Charles E. Potter produced a report alleging more than 1,800 atrocities had been committed by the

Communists during the Korean War. I'm trying to show that there are allegations against the winners in these conflicts by the hapless losers who don't get to write the history books. History is always written by the victors.

CHAPTER SIX

THE KENNEDYS: WE HARDLY KNEW YE

For all those whose cares have been our concern, the work goes on, the cause endures, the hope still lives, and the dream shall never die.

—Senator Edward Kennedy[1]

No prominent family in the history of this country, we have been reminded by reporters and court historians alike many times, has ever endured so much tragedy and triumph as the Kennedy clan from Dunganstown, Ireland. They dominated the 1960s like no other family ever has, and were on the cusp of a presidential dynasty that might have lasted into the twenty-first century.

In my first nonfiction book, *Hidden History: An Exposé of Modern Crimes, Conspiracies, and Cover-Ups in American Politics,* I delved deeply into the deaths of President John F. Kennedy, Senator Robert F. Kennedy, and John F. Kennedy Jr. I also covered the tragedy at Chappaquiddick, which I believe was the political assassination of Senator Edward Kennedy. I covered some other deaths in less detail, such as the mysterious airplane crash that ended the life of young Joseph Kennedy Jr., who was on a path to become the nation's first Catholic president before his younger brother John was pressured into picking up the fallen mantle and entering politics.

I also provided many examples in *Hidden History* of prominent "liberals" who despised the Kennedys. Saul Alinsky's famous credo, "There are no enemies on the Left" doesn't seem to apply to the Kennedy clan. Dan Rostenkowski, a corrupt hack party Democrat who "served" in Congress for far too long, reflected upon President Kennedy's legacy not long before his own death. Regarding JFK's chances for reelection in 1964, Rostenkowski declared, "I think he would have had a problem. Jack Kennedy took his wife to Dallas [on November 22, 1963, when he was assassinated] because they were having a problem with support. College campuses were really turning conservative. I don't think Illinois would have gone for Jack Kennedy the second time. . . . Aside from Camelot and a wonderfully delicate, beautiful wife, tell me what else he did."[2] 1960s College campuses were turning conservative? You would never hear any high-profile Democrat say something like that about any other Democratic president. Rostenkowski was a quintessential Establishment stooge; he was deeply involved in Ronald Reagan's disastrous commingling of Social Security funds with the general revenue, and helped pass the terrible 1986 tax "reform" act. After eighteen terms in office, he was finally convicted of misusing office funds for personal use, and actually went to federal prison. Bernie Sanders once proclaimed that he became "physically nauseated" by a speech President Kennedy made, and lamented JFK's "hatred for the Cuban revolution." Far leftist philosopher Bertrand Russell, who ironically became one of the first high-profile figures to doubt the official JFK assassination narrative, once famously called JFK "much more wicked than Hitler."[3]

From a seeming political dynasty, the large Kennedy family has been largely weeded out of the political world by a series of mostly unnatural deaths, negative press, and overt disinterest. Only the increasingly bold Robert F. Kennedy Jr. is carrying on the family legacy. Massachusetts Rep. Joseph Kennedy III, who appeared to be an unthreatening mainstream liberal, lost the Democratic Senate primary to longtime party hack Sen. Edward Markey in 2020. Caroline Kennedy's son Jack Schlossberg seems to be even more Establishment-minded, as evident by his hosting the 2014 Profile in Courage Award ceremony, where he proudly bestowed the honor upon former President George H. W. Bush.[4] Unlike his cousin

RFK Jr., Schlossberg is not exactly courting controversy. The young Yale graduate wrote an op-ed for *Time* in 2017, which excoriated "conspiracy theories" about his grandfather's death. He called media coverage of the potential release of the remaining JFK files (which Donald Trump, naturally didn't release after vowing to), a "distraction." Schlossberg, one Kennedy who is still popular in the state-controlled media, wrote, "For decades, conspiracies surrounding his death have shifted focus away from the important lessons of his life and the critical issues of the moment. They continue to do so today. . . . The extent to which the release has been made into a drama, first about the potential release of these files, then the release itself, then a recounting of the most popular conspiracy theories, is one example of how impulsive and frenetic our public dialogue has become." Displaying the "right stuff" for a future political career, young Schlossberg urged Americans to concentrate on truly important issues, like climate change and "systemic racism."[5]

The personal diaries of Robert F. Kennedy Jr. provided an extremely interesting glimpse into dysfunctional family dynamics. Intriguingly, the diaries were discovered and shared with the *New York Post* by his ex-wife Mary, who would later be found, hanged in a barn on her Bedford, New York property. The diaries showed that RFK Jr. clearly didn't hold a high opinion of Caroline's husband Ed Schlossberg. At one point, he describes how Schlossberg "bullied, bullied, bullied the shattered grieving mother," referring to Ann Freeman, whose daughters Carolyn and Lauren Bessette perished along with John F. Kennedy Jr. in a highly suspicious 1999 plane crash. The Kennedys, via spokesman Schlossberg, told Freeman that JFK Jr. was going to be buried in the family's Brookline, Massachusetts burial plot, and "that they could do with Carolyn as they pleased." Freeman preferred that her daughters be buried near their Greenwich, Connecticut home. RFK Jr. charged that "All the Bessette family knows that Ed hated Carolyn and did everything in his power to make her life miserable." Apparently, there was no love lost between Carolyn Bessette and Caroline Kennedy Schlossberg, either. Of course, left unanswered here, by RFK Jr. or anyone else, was exactly why the bodies of all three victims were subsequently cremated, when both families had clearly expressed wishes for them to be buried. The Bessette family would settle a wrongful death claim against JFK Jr.'s estate for a reported $15 million in 2001.[6] RFK Jr. portrayed Ed Schlossberg as a dictator, who even refused to allow him to deliver a eulogy for John and Carolyn. "Kennedys don't eulogize non-Kennedys," he was quoted as telling Carolyn and Lauren's surviving sister Lisa. RFK Jr. related how Carole Radziwill, the wife of JFK Jr.'s cousin and best friend Anthony Radziwill, had recounted even more of Schlossberg's bad behavior. "She says she wants to start an 'I hate Ed Club.'" RFK Jr. wrote. "There would be many, many members. John & Carolyn would have certainly applied."[7]

The diaries also alluded to contention existing between JFK's children. JFK Jr. expressed to RFK Jr. "how hurt he was by Caroline's actions."[8] Schlossberg obviously wasn't well-liked by the Kennedy family. Jackie Kennedy was quoted as calling her son-in-law an "egghead" and a "boring old fogey." Jackie mistrusted Schlossberg to such an extent that a rift developed between mother and daughter. Caroline eventually threatened to cut Jackie off from her grandchildren, as recounted by singer Carly Simon in her 2019 book *Touched by the Sun: My Friendship with Jackie.*[9] John Jr. was appalled when Caroline began selling family possessions at auction. "The whole sale process is causing him a lot of anxiety," an anonymous family source said.[10] Despite the friction between himself and his sister, John Jr. left the largest portion of his significant estate to Caroline's children.[11] Another book, written by JFK Jr.'s supposed close friend Steven M. Gillon, *America's Reluctant Prince: The Life of John F. Kennedy Jr.,* claimed JFK Jr. was barely talking to his sister in his final days, because she and her husband had treated him like "shit." Caroline was allegedly hypercritical of her brother and called him and his friends "potheads." He, meanwhile, supposedly considered her and her crowd to be "entitled snobs."[12] The book also contended JFK Jr. was so estranged from his wife that he was considering divorce. Gillon, who went on to become the Scholar-in-Residence at the History Channel, made some wildly inaccurate comments in other regards in the book, which will be examined here in the updated section on the death of JFK Jr. Thus, his comments about the family relationships should be taken with a huge grain of salt.

The RFK Jr. diaries also displayed his independent streak, as he pulled no punches in criticizing untouchable modern icons of the Left. Of then brother-in-law and future New York Governor Andrew Cuomo, Kennedy said "he lacks humanity and doesn't love people." RFK Jr. served a month in a Puerto Rican prison in July 2001. He'd been arrested, along with Al Sharpton and Jesse Jackson's wife Jacqueline, for protesting the U.S. Navy using an island as a bombing range. In one entry, RFK Jr. stated that Sharpton and Jesse Jackson "give me the creeps." "Al Sharpton has done more damage to the black cause than [segregationist Alabama Gov.] George Wallace. He has suffocated the decent black leaders in New York," RFK Jr. declared. "His transparent venal blackmail and extortion schemes taint all black leadership." He called Sharpton a "buffoon," who was still drenched in the "stench" of the Tawana Brawley hoax. Of Jesse Jackson, RFK Jr. wrote, "I feel dirty around him, and I feel like I'm being used. I feel like with Jesse, it's all about Jesse." He alleged that at labor leader Cesar Chavez's funeral, Jackson had pushed "Cesar's friends and family out of the way to make himself lead pall bearer." The son of JFK's attorney general called George W. Bush "an idiot and a puppet," and remarked that "it's painful watching him on TV."[13]

RFK Jr. delved into many of the slanderous myths about the Kennedys in his 2018 book *American Values: Lessons I Learned from My Family*. In covering the bitter feud between President Kennedy and the CIA, RFK Jr. revealed that the animosity the Agency held toward his family actually began with Joseph P. Kennedy's work on the President's Board of Consultants on Foreign Intelligence Activities in the 1950s, which was tasked to investigate covert CIA activities. Kennedy and the commission determined that the Agency had been responsible for many "dirty tricks," including regime change operations in Iran and Guatemala. Kennedy recommended that the CIA's power be severely curtailed, leaving it to only collect intelligence. As RFK Jr. put it in a 2020 interview with Ron Paul, "Allen Dulles never forgave him—never forgave my family—for that." As we all know, Dulles became perhaps the most active and influential member of the Warren Commission.

David Kaiser craftily demeaned Robert F. Kennedy in an article on the fiftieth anniversary of his assassination. Kaiser is the author of one of many absurd books on the JFK assassination, *The Road to Dallas*. Kaiser claimed that RFK would never have been able to win the 1968

Democratic Party presidential nomination, a favorite mantra from anti-Kennedy historians, which is at odds with the evidence.[14] A typically scurrilous 2016 book on the family, *Bobby Kennedy: The Making of a Liberal Icon,* by Larry Tye, pushed the sensationalist claim that RFK was a "serial cheater." Ethel Kennedy, the book declares, understood "there was no monogamy in the Kennedy clan." Sinking deep into a fantasy tabloid world, the book describes RFK's first sexual encounter as having been with a black prostitute, paid for by Old Joe. It also repeats the C. David Heymann slander that RFK had an affair with his brother's widow Jackie. Longtime Kennedy aide Richard Goodwin was on hand to note that it was a "Kennedy family tradition" to sleep around.[15] Goodwin was married for over forty years to Doris Kearns Goodwin, a preeminent court historian who was widely believed to have slept with Lyndon Johnson. Michael Reagan would allege, without citing any evidence, that Attorney General Kennedy somehow got his father fired as host of CBS's *GE Theatre* program.

While the mainstream media and court historians stayed away from the topic of Chappaquiddick, until Ted Kennedy finally decided to belatedly run for president in 1980, in the years just prior to his falling gravely ill, he became a target of their ridicule. By 2007, the then-seventy-three-year-old youngest son of Joe Kennedy was regularly being lambasted on Comedy Central's *The Daily Show.* One powerful reason for the media, at least, to hate the Kennedys is Joe Kennedy's purportedly overt anti-Jewish comments. The late Michael Collins Piper, whose book *Final Judgment* was the first to expose JFK's behind-the-scenes battle with Israeli prime minister David Ben-Gurion, detailed conversations Old Joe supposedly had over the years with model, Hollywood agent, and television executive DeWest Hooker. Hooker told Piper that Kennedy lamented the stranglehold Jews held over the media, especially in Hollywood, and is once said to have remarked, "We lost World War Two, and the Jews won." While a student at Harvard, a young JFK reacted to one of his father's passionate anti-war speeches by writing, "while it seemed to be unpopular with the Jews, etc., it was considered to be very good by everyone who wasn't bitterly anti-fascist." The desire to depict Joe Kennedy as anti-Semitic was strong; in 1938, the *New York Times* reported the fantasy that the then-Ambassador to England had worked out a plan with his friend Neville Chamberlain to ship all German Jews to Africa and other locations.[16]

Less than a year after the death of RFK's granddaughter Saoirse Rosin Hill (daughter of Courtney Kennedy), from an overdose of alcohol and drugs, the Kennedys added another in their incomprehensibly long list of unnatural deaths on April 2, 2020. On that day, RFK Jr.'s niece (daughter of his sister Kathleen Kennedy Townsend, RFK's oldest child), forty-year-old Maeve McKean, drowned, along with her eight-year-old son. Reports claimed that McKean took off in a canoe, on the choppy waters of Maryland's Chesapeake Bay, in order to retrieve a ball that had been kicked into the water. Making things more perplexing, she took her eight-year-old son on this dangerous mission with her. I wasn't the only one to question why anyone, let alone someone from such a wealthy family, would take such risks for an easily replaceable ball. Of course, any speculation was instantly diverted into the "Kennedys are reckless" realm. A few hinted at that legendary Kennedy "curse." I was the only one who mentioned McKean's intriguing job, as executive director of Georgetown University's Global Health Initiative, which was funded by the Bill & Melinda Gates Foundation. McKean was staunchly pro-vaccine, and had publicly denounced her uncle, in an article that was oddly published a month after her mysterious death. McKean's name appeared alongside her mother Kathleen Kennedy Townsend, and RFK Jr.'s older brother Joseph P. Kennedy II, under the headline, "RFK Jr. Is Our Brother and Uncle. He's Tragically Wrong About Vaccines."[17]

RFK Jr., coincidentally or not, really stepped up his radical stance on COVID, the lockdown, and vaccines in general, following the death of his niece. Less than a week after McKean's death, on April 8, Kennedy blasted Bill Gates with a shocking ferocity on Instagram. "Promising to eradicate polio with $1.2 billion, Gates took control of India's National Advisory Board (NAB) and mandated 50 polio vaccines (up from five) to every child before age five," Kennedy charged. "Indian doctors blame the Gates campaign for a devastating vaccine-strain polio epidemic that paralyzed 496,000 children. . . . In 2017, the Indian government dialed back Gates's vaccine regimen and evicted Gates and his cronies from the NAB. Polio paralysis rates dropped precipitously. In 2017, the

World Health Organization reluctantly admitted that the global polio explosion is predominantly a vaccine strain, meaning it is coming from Gates's vaccine program." In another Instagram post, on May 6, RFK Jr. declared, "Bill Gates Wants to Chip Us and Not Only for Vaccines—for Surveillance and Transhumanism Using #5G."[18] Through the organization he founded, Children's Health Defense, RFK Jr. launched a petition which was sent to the White House, calling for "Investigations into the Bill and Melinda Gates Foundation for Medical Malpractice and Crimes against Humanity."

In August 2020, RFK Jr. delivered a revolutionary address in Berlin, site of one of his uncle's most famous speeches. Despite the historical significance alone, the mainstream media almost entirely ignored the event. Perhaps this was because of what Kennedy said. Summoning up all the best memories of his father, RFK Jr. proclaimed, "Humanity cannot and will no longer be ruled by a model based on threat and control. Right here, right now, we can all refuse this. Right here, right now, we can change the 'narrative'. We can create 'OUR new normal.' We keep hearing the words 'Solidarity,' compassion, and equal rights in the mouths of politicians who try to separate and divide us. People who order fines, isolation, experiment on our health, and restrict all our freedoms. Those people are not philanthropists. They ask us to believe in a new religion called 'the scientific consensus,' a fabricated dogma used by a corrupt cast called 'experts' who serve no other than their own interest. . . . Tracking and tracing are the tools of this inquisition. We know where this ultimately leads us to: Isolation, punishment, and slavery." Kennedy also regularly lambasted Dr. Anthony Fauci, as "an absolute dictator" whose promotion of "deadly" vaccines was motivated by personal profit. Kennedy was one of the more prominent victims of the draconian online censorship, when he was banned from Instagram for promoting "misinformation." RFK Jr. hasn't allowed a rare condition, spasmodic dysphonia, which causes his voice to sound hoarse and raspy, to slow him down. In April 2023, following in his uncle's and father's footsteps, he announced his own run for the 2024 Democratic Party presidential nomination. He was attacked relentlessly as an "anti-vaxxer" and "conspiracy theorist" by virtually the entire Establishment press.

This would follow the predictable pattern of what Jim DiEugenio has called "The Posthumous War" on the Kennedys. In August 2021, an alleged "secret" mistress of John F. Kennedy "broke her silence" over sixty years later. Diana de Vegh claimed that she'd had an affair with the married JFK, starting in 1958, when she was a twenty-year-old Radcliffe student. The affair would last until 1962. She stated she'd decided to "go public" to expose, "The whole idea of conferred specialness—'You go to bed with me, I'll make you special'—we've seen a lot of that with Harvey Weinstein, Roger Ailes, show business." Shockingly, she didn't use Bill Clinton, Bill Cosby, or Joe Biden and his son Hunter as recent examples of male predatory behavior. In an article about her "revelations," the writer referred to JFK's "carnal Camelot marathon."[19] The double standard the mainstream media deploys here is overt. Any woman stepping forward and claiming an affair with a Kennedy is instantly believed, by the same "journalists" who refuse to even look at any witness hinting at a conspiracy behind the assassinations. Juanita Broderick and others accusing Bill Clinton of forcible rape were treated far differently than Judith Campbell Exner, Mimi Alford, and other supposed Kennedy conquests; none of whom, of course, claimed to have been raped. The mainstream narrative of JFK now is that of a serial adulterer, having nearly nonstop sex with a plethora of women. But the same narrative accuses the Kennedy family of covering up JFK's serious physical ailments, which it is insinuated should have left him unqualified for office. Thus, John F. Kennedy has been transformed into the ultimate rarity: a deathly sick man who was nevertheless an insatiable sexual dynamo.

As the sole Kennedy attempting to carry on the legacy of his fallen predecessors, Robert F. Kennedy Jr. became a favorite whipping boy of the mainstream media, even before announcing his presidential run. A remarkably vicious article in the September 23, 2021 *New York Post* was headlined, "Anti-vax, conspiracy theorist, collector of dead animals—RFK Jr. is the dumbest Kennedy." Reporter Maureen Callahan charged, "The only thing RFK Jr. is successful at, it seems, is lowering the bar for atrocious behavior and the deliberate spread of misinformation." Displaying the standard animus toward the entire family, Callahan declared, "Even Bobby's own family members have called him out publicly—something

Kennedys almost never do, especially if you are a sexual assaulter or rapist or have left a young woman paralyzed for life or to die alone in a shallow body of water." While referencing Chappaquiddick and Joe Kennedy II's 1973 auto accident which left a passenger paralyzed, Callahan didn't reveal just which Kennedy had been a "sexual assaulter" or "rapist." She blasted RFK Jr. for his position on vaccines, definitively referred to Sirhan Sirhan as "his father's assassin," mocked his latest book's lack of advance reviews or blurbs, and ridiculed Skyhorse—my primary publisher—for publishing the book. Callahan's vitriol went out of control with "He does crazy things like pick up dead road kill out of compassion for animals and keep rotting carcasses in the family minivan for days or weeks—a minivan he never cleans! What a wild and zany guy. . . . Conspiracy theories, paranoia, the denial of empirical facts, hoarding dead animals: Does this not sound like mental illness to you? No? How about comparing oneself to Jesus Christ?" Callahan went on to issue a plea to "cancel" RFK Jr. in the best "new normal" tradition, stating, "Should these points fail to convince publishers, parole boards and anyone in power from giving this guy a platform, may I submit: Robert F. Kennedy Jr., in a speech to protesters in Berlin last August, compared Dr. Anthony Fauci, vaccines and the CDC to Nazi Germany." This "journalist" closed with another stab at the family, "No matter how much trouble they cause, how carelessly they move through the world, imposing what little they think they know, the lack of education jaw-dropping." Callahan must have become apoplectic when RFK Jr's 2021 book *The Real Anthony Fauci: Bill Gates, Big Pharma, and the Global War on Democracy and Public Health,* became the best-selling book in the country.

Joseph P. Kennedy Jr.

His worldly success was so assured and inevitable that his death seems to have cut into the natural order of things.

—John F. Kennedy, from *As We Remember Joe*[20]

As the eldest of Joe and Rose Kennedy's nine children, Joseph P. Kennedy was the apple of his father's eye. Early on, he dreamed that his oldest son would become the first Catholic president of the United States. Young Joe was tragically killed on August 12, 1944, at just twenty-nine years of age, when his plane exploded during a secret bombing mission for Operation Aphrodite.

In 1986, a story in the West German newspaper *Bild am Sonntag* maintained that Kennedy Jr. had been captured by Nazi SS troops in July 1944, and shot to death as he tried to escape. In an interview with the paper, former German antiaircraft officer Karl Heinz Wehn claimed to have interrogated Kennedy after his plane was shot down and he was captured. Wehn stated that Kennedy had parachuted to safety some 11 miles southwest of the French city of Caen. However, Elliot Roosevelt, son of President Franklin D. Roosevelt, who had reported seeing Kennedy's plane explode, while flying closely by in a reconnaissance aircraft, hotly disputed this. "If he (Wehn) says he interrogated Joe Kennedy Jr., I think he's dreaming," Roosevelt told the *Boston Herald*. "(It's) an absolutely cockamamie story. . . . He never was shot down. The plane exploded before it left the English coast."[21] As I noted in *Crimes and Cover-Ups in American Politics: 1776–1963*, it is quite convenient that the primary witness to what supposedly occurred just happened to be the son of one of history's all-time great conspirators. Not to mention one who had despised Joe's father and namesake. Roosevelt's eyewitness account essentially established the official narrative here, and over forty years later, it was obvious from his comments that he wasn't going to entertain any suggestion that might contradict that narrative. Largely overlooked was a reference to combat cameraman Lt. David J. McCarthy filming from the nose of the backup aircraft. Presumably, he would have captured the explosion, or whatever happened to Kennedy's plane, but if so there is nothing to indicate that in the record.[22] Operation Aphrodite was the brainchild of Major General Jimmy Doolittle (famous for his bombing raid on the Japanese homeland during the World War II, and author of the "Doolittle Report," which called for more aggressive CIA covert activities during the Cold War). Doolittle would write the telegram first reporting on Kennedy's death during Aphrodite's initial mission.[23] Curiously enough, in later years Doolittle, a close friend of David Harold Byrd, owner of the Texas School Book Depository where Lee Harvey Oswald was working on November 22, 1963 (more about him later), would be involved in investigating reports of unidentified aerial phenomena known as "Ghost Rockets" in Sweden.[24]

The ignored but important book *Aphrodite: Desperate Mission* by Jack Olsen, argued that the mission was a fraud from the beginning. The Kennedy family had been assuaged, as so many grieving families of fallen soldiers have been, by assurances that the death was heroic and a posthumously awarded Navy Cross. In fact, Olsen claimed that the electrical system aboard the plane was known to be faulty, to such an extent that a Navy ground officer had tried to get the mission canceled. The mission's target was a German rocket site in France, which according to Olsen had been abandoned by the Nazis three months earlier. Exactly why would the US military waste time and money, not to mention potential lives, on a site that had been abandoned? What military purpose would have been served? "The exact details of the death of the 29-year-old 'star of our family,' as his father once described him, were kept secret from the family." Olsen wrote. "The Kennedy family comforted itself with a letter from a naval officer who had gone to college with Joe Jr. 'As you no doubt are aware,' the young lieutenant wrote to Joseph P. Kennedy Sr., 'the mission was an extremely important one of an experimental nature and exceedingly dangerous. . . . You may not have heard that he was successful and that through Joe's courage and devotion to what he thought was right, a great many lives have been saved.'"[25] What "success" could possibly have come from, and what lives were saved, by a senseless bombing of what was akin to an open field? Joe Jr. had already started out on his political path, as a delegate to the 1940 Democratic convention. Plans were in the works for a congressional run once he'd completed his military service.

As Olsen wrote: "One day in the early 1960s a Navy captain called on Earl P. Olsen of the Systems Integration Laboratory at the Navy Missile Center, Point Mugu, California. 'Earl,' he said, 'President Kennedy's flying here for a visit, and I'm gonna get the two of you together for a long talk.' 'Why?' Olsen asked. 'So you can talk over old times about his big brother Joe! Weren't you on that secret mission with Joe in World War II?' The usually relaxed Olsen became excited. 'For God's sake, Captain,' he said, 'don't do that! I don't want to talk to the President about that mission.' 'Why not?' 'I don't want to have to tell him the truth.'" Col. Roy

Forrest, a descendant of Confederate legend Nathan Bedford Forrest, was given strict orders not to discuss anything about the death of two men on what seemed to be a nonsensical mission never tried before, and never tried again. A project officer supposedly took Joe Kennedy Jr. aside just before the flight, and told him he'd heard rumors that the plane's arming system wasn't safe, but Kennedy laughed it off. Earl Olsen recounted telling Kennedy that "I'm sure the plane'll malfunction before it gets to the target."[26] Jack Olsen documented the incredible sloppiness of the operation (one officer scoffed at a piece of equipment that looked like it had been "built with an Erector Set") and the cover-up that ensued following the needless death of Kennedy and fellow Lt. Wilford John "Bud" Willy. The Kennedy family kept up a lifelong correspondence with Willy's widow and paid for their children to go to the college of their choice.[27] President Kennedy would invite the Willy family to breakfast with him at the Hotel Texas in Fort Worth, on the morning of November 22, 1963. It's just another astounding tidbit to learn that JFK would tell Willy's daughter how brave her father was only a few hours before being assassinated himself.[28]

In a shockingly underpublicized story, a report into the death of Joe Kennedy Jr. was released during the presidential administration of his brother. An article encapsulating this report appeared in *Look* magazine, with much of the information supposedly provided by President Kennedy himself. However, there were strange mistakes, including the wrong crash site and the wrong target. The claim was made that Kennedy's plane was shot down. In a video about this report, an odd anomaly is that the *Look* magazine cover shown was from December 1963. So was the story not published until after JFK was assassinated?

Some have actually accused Elliot Roosevelt of shooting down Kennedy's plane. "Alert Reader" on the Public Intelligence Blog noted, "Joe had enough missions to return stateside, but volunteered for Operation Aphrodite as drone take off pilot to two thousand feet, bail out, a following 'recon' would then fly autopilot remote and kamikaze into target. Elliot was recon (and trigger) pilot. Joe Sr. was ambassador to UK from 1938, anti-war and openly stated his ambition for a Kennedy POTUS dynasty. Mostly circumstantial evidence, but motives, methods, means. . . . Elliot Roosevelt was the trigger puller in the chase plane." Researcher Ann Bougher told me she'd seen a documentary online that directly accused Elliott Roosevelt of triggering the explosion, but she cannot find it. Perhaps it became another victim of the onerous censorship on the internet. The website for the John F. Kennedy Library quotes a "fellow officer" as declaring, "No final conclusions as to the cause of the explosions has ever been reached."

A convicted stock swindler would accuse Elliott Roosevelt of offering him $100,000 to assassinate Prime Minister of the Bahamas Lynden O. Pindling in 1968. He was also accused of dealing in stolen securities. Roosevelt angrily reacted, calling the charges "vicious lies." He would tell a Senate subcommittee, "I completely and categorically deny each and every charge made before this subcommittee." Louis P. Mastriana claimed that Pindling had reneged on granting a gambling license to Michael McLaney, rumored to be associated with both Roosevelt and notorious Mafia kingpin Meyer Lansky, which was to be a reward for a $1 million contribution to Pindling's campaign. Both Mastriana and Patsy A. Lepera, who described himself as a "middleman" between organized crime and brokerages, claimed that Roosevelt had "dealt in stolen securities" in 1969 and 1970. Roosevelt demanded that the men be prosecuted for perpetrating "a hoax." A copy of a check from McLaney to Roosevelt was entered into the record. According to one article, "A subcommittee investigation showed that Mr. Roosevelt had been associated with a number of persons who have been involved in fraudulent security transactions." Roosevelt explained this by declaring, "a tremendous number of freaks and strange characters came through my office" in Miami Beach, Fla., where he had worked as a public relations consultant.[29] This was not Roosevelt's first allegation of wrongdoing. In 1943, he'd become embroiled in a warplanes purchasing scandal. There is nothing in the record to indicate what happened regarding these charges, which is typical in such cases, but it seems a certainty that FDR's boy wasn't held accountable. In an interesting sidebar, Attorney General Robert F. Kennedy is said to have confronted McLaney in 1961, and angrily jabbed his finger into his chest, over a supposed plot to bomb oil refineries in Cuba.

Joseph P. Kennedy had been an outspoken opponent of American involvement in World War II. During his 2024 presidential campaign, RFK Jr. pointed out that his grandfather was also a World War I protester. In a line from a speech that Roosevelt censored, JFK's father had stated, "I should like to ask you all if you know of any dispute or controversy existing in the world which is worth the life of your son?" Joe Jr.'s death further fueled his anger at FDR for entangling America in the European war. As if that wasn't enough tragedy for anyone, his oldest daughter, Kathleen, perished in a separate plane crash in 1948. Kathleen, nicknamed "Kick" for her outgoing, rebellious personality, scandalized the family with her romances with married Protestants. Her father was the only family member to attend her funeral.[30] JFK couldn't bring himself to visit her grave in Chatsworth, Ireland, until he stopped there during his visit to the Emerald Isle in June 1963.[31]

Kennedy's parents established the Joseph P. Kennedy Jr. Foundation in 1946, to help people with intellectual disabilities. This was a clear forerunner to the magnificent work led by Eunice Kennedy Shriver, which would result in the creation of the Special Olympics. For decades, details about young Kennedy's mission were strangely classified. His death remains suspicious in my eyes, given what happened to his younger brothers after they entered the political world, not to mention the myriad of unnatural family deaths that followed, defying every actuarial table imaginable.

LBJ: No Love Lost with the Kennedys

He's mean, bitter, vicious—an animal in many ways.

—Robert F. Kennedy describing Lyndon B. Johnson[32]

Jacqueline Kennedy never liked Lyndon Johnson. When her oral history was examined in 2011, the former First Lady revealed that John F. Kennedy feared an LBJ presidency. "Bobby told me this later, and I know Jack said it to me sometimes. He said, 'Oh, God, can you ever imagine what would happen to the country if Lyndon was president?'" Jackie remarked. "He didn't like that idea that Lyndon would go on and be president because he was worried for the country," Jackie stated. "Bobby told me that he'd had some discussions with him. I forget exactly how they were planning or who they had in mind. It wasn't Bobby, but somebody. Do something to name someone else in '68." Jackie also mentioned LBJ being close to FBI Director J. Edgar Hoover,[33] whom she said JFK was planning to force out after the 1964 election. Jackie characterized Lady Bird Johnson as being akin to "a trained hunting dog."[34] JFK's loyal secretary Evelyn Lincoln claimed that, during her last conversation with President Kennedy, he'd discussed replacing LBJ on the '64 ticket with Florida Senator George Smathers.

LBJ's entourage seemed to reflect the abominable personality of Johnson himself. Evelyn Lincoln told Penn Jones about their behavior on the trip back from Dallas to Washington, D.C. on Air Force One. Air Force One steward Doyle Whitehead, who was on the plane when they brought JFK's body onboard, corroborated this. Whitehead told James Jenkins, a medical technology student at Bethesda Naval Hospital who was asked to assist with JFK's autopsy, that he watched LBJ get roaring drunk, consuming an entire bottle of Cutty Sark. LBJ and his entourage were "whooping it up" and making so much noise that Whitehead had to shut the doors so Jacqueline Kennedy wouldn't be disturbed by the partying. Whitehead made this shocking revelation when Jenkins was trying to talk him into doing a book with author and researcher William Matson Law. Whitehead explained that he was reluctant to tell his story for fear of reprisals from the Johnson family.

While the notorious feud between LBJ and Robert F. Kennedy became far more pronounced starting on November 22, 1963, RFK always seems to have held an antipathy for the crude Texan. During a late-night dinner at the White House in 1961, Johnson confronted Bobby Kennedy in front of all in attendance. "Bobby, you do not like me," LBJ declared. "Your brother likes me. Your sister-in-law likes me. Your daddy likes me. But you don't like me. Now, why? Why don't you like me?" RFK refused to respond, which obviously made LBJ even angrier. RFK had never forgotten how Johnson raised the Catholic issue and questioned JFK's health during the 1960 presidential campaign. Even mainstream sources acknowledge that the younger Kennedy "despised Johnson with a ferocity that startled many observers." RFK was once given a Johnson voodoo doll during a gathering at his Virginia estate. One witness to this noted, "The merriment was overwhelming." When RFK was shot following his victory in the 1968 California primary, LBJ was reported to have called the Secret Service incessantly to see if his nemesis had died. He was described as pacing around the White House, phone in hand, while repeating, "I've got to know. Is he dead? Is he dead yet?"[35] One vindictive measure of Johnson's was to sign legislation that banned future presidents from naming relatives to their cabinets. This was clearly in reference to JFK appointing his brother Bobby as Attorney General.

LBJ was hardly alone in his hatred for Bobby Kennedy. RFK probably accumulated even more powerful enemies than his brother, to a great degree because of his less amiable personality. Actor Robert Vaughn, best remembered for his starring role in television's *The Man from U.N.C.L.E.,* wrote a fascinating article which appeared in the January 12, 2009, *U.K. Daily Mail,* headlined, "I Know Who Was Behind Bobby Kennedy's Murder." Vaughn charged that the mastermind of the RFK assassination was none other than the soon-to-be husband of former First Lady Jackie Kennedy, Greek shipping magnate Aristotle Onassis. Vaughn, who was an astute student of the RFK assassination and had performed independent research, claimed that Aristotle's hatred for RFK started in 1953, when Kennedy, then counsel to Senator Joe McCarthy, found that more than three hundred Greek shipping families in New York were trading regularly with China. Vaughn interviewed Helene Gaillet, who'd worked as a photographer for the *New York Times,* among other places. Gaillet claimed that, during a 1973 stay at his Greek island estate, Onassis had referred to Bobby Kennedy as "that little runt." He then confessed to her, "You know, Hélène, I put up the money for Bobby Kennedy's murder."

In an FBI document finally released through the ARRB, it was revealed that the Soviets had a chief suspect in JFK's assassination. The report states, "Our source added that in the instructions from Moscow, it was indicated that 'now' the KGB was in possession of data purporting to indicate President Johnson was responsible for the assassination of the late President John F. Kennedy."[36] Despite appointing the Warren Commission, which never honestly investigated a single aspect of the JFK assassination, LBJ laughably boasted, "I'm going to make sure there isn't one damn question or one damn mystery that isn't solved about this thing."[37]

I covered LBJ's impressive Body Count in *Hidden History.* As I noted, some believe he actually ordered the murder of his own sister. One of the most important victims of LBJ's Body Count was Henry Marshall, an investigator for the Agriculture Department who was looking into the shady dealings of Johnson's crony Billie Sol Estes. Marshall's body was found June 3, 1961, on his family farm north of Bryan, Texas. He had been shot five times in the abdomen with a .22-caliber rifle. In 1985, a Texas state judge ordered the official cause of death to be changed from suicide to homicide. Clint Peoples was a Texas Ranger who worked hard on the Marshall case for years and never bought the official story. "My opinion from the investigation prior and after is that someone went out there to make it look like a suicide," Peoples said in response to the judge's ruling.[38] By 1992, Peoples had become a U.S. Marshal. Peoples discovered new evidence in the Marshall case, including a fingerprint found on the sixth floor of the Texas School Book Depository matching that of Mac Wallace, thought by many to be LBJ's personal hit man. Peoples's assistant, referred to only as "Georgia," because she feared being identified, cooperated with French researcher William Reymond for his 2003 book *JFK le Dernier Témoin: Assassinat de Kennedy, enfin la vérité,* written with LBJ associate Billie Sol Estes. Peoples died in a suspicious car accident, on June 22, 1992, just prior to a planned press conference to announce his new findings. According to author Philip Nelson, Georgia "stated that when she went to the funeral home for the viewing, a woman came up to her and told her not to tell anyone else, but that she had witnessed the entire incident; she said it was no 'accident,' because Clint's car was pushed off the road from behind by a 'big red truck' and the weather was clear, the road was dry. The driver of the truck did it intentionally, she said, and then left the scene." Georgia told Reymond that she was hesitant to get involved because "Too many people have been killed."[39] Peoples died twenty years after Johnson. These Body Counts live longer than those who directly benefit from them.

Perhaps the most intriguing unnatural death associated with LBJ was that of his lookalike cousin, Jay Bert Peck. Peck was a deputy sheriff and a part-time security guard for the Dallas Cowboys. LBJ also secretly employed him as a stand-in on several occasions. Peck even appeared on

The Tonight Show to talk about his experiences as LBJ's double, and played the president in a few scenes in the 1969 movie *The Wrecking Crew.* His scenes would later be mostly deleted. According to Billie Sol Estes, Peck stood in for LBJ on November 21, 1963, so that Johnson could attend a party at oilman Clint Murchison's house, where some believe that the final "go" for the assassination was given. Estes claimed that LBJ eventually grew paranoid about Peck keeping his mouth shut, and ordered him murdered. Peck was found shot in his home on the evening of July 4, 1969, and died the next day. Billie Sol Estes would finger the killer as mortician John M. Liggett, who had curious connections, and was allegedly responsible for the deaths of several other people, some of them JFK assassination witnesses. After his death, LBJ toady Jack Valenti, then-president of the Motion Picture Association of America, helped to purge Peck from the record. Peck is not listed among all the guests who ever appeared on *The Tonight Show.* Five years after Peck's murder, his wife Dorothy Peck was beaten with a hammer and left for dead. Fortunately, she survived, and was able to identify her attacker as the same John M. Liggett. Liggett would be shot and killed by a prison guard in 1975, after supposedly trying to escape. All of this research was produced by Phillip F. Nelson, who wrote the important books *LBJ: The Mastermind of the JFK Assassination,* and *LBJ: From Mastermind to "The Colossus."*

In a March 3, 2012, post on The Education Forum, Douglas Caddy, an attorney connected to Watergate and later Johnson's old crony Billie Sol Estes, described what happened when he confronted LBJ biographer Robert Caro at an event in the mid-1980s, and asked him if he planned to cover LBJ's reputed personal hit man Mac Wallace in his book. Caddy wrote, "Caro looked startled and shaken and grabbed me by the lapels of my business suit, saying, 'Who are you? How can I get in touch with you?'" Caddy noted that Caro never contacted him. Caddy also related how "When Barr McClellan's book *LBJ Killed JFK* was about to be released in 2003, both Barr and I independently received about a half dozen phone calls from someone who was vitally intent in stopping its publication or limiting its impact." Author Phil Nelson confirmed this with McClellan, who acknowledged receiving such calls, which took place right before The History Channel aired Episode 9 of Nigel Turner's *The*

Men Who Killed Kennedy documentary series. That episode mentioned Mac Wallace's fingerprint being found on the sixth floor of the Texas School Book Depository and touched on other ugly rumors about LBJ. "The Guilty Men" would be quickly flushed down the memory hole, when Jack Valenti, Lady Bird Johnson, and other Johnson loyalists threatened to sue.

Phil Nelson unearthed yet another important victim of LBJ's Body Count, which he detailed in a June 26, 2022, article on his "LBJ: Master of Deceit" blog. Nelson recounted how RFK had sent a special investigative team of Texas Rangers to Southwest Texas, just prior to the 1960 Democratic convention. Their task was not only to investigate LBJ's sordid activities with Billie Sol Estes, but also look into the stolen 1948 Senate election, which garnered Johnson the ugly epithet "Landslide Lyndon." One member of RFK's volunteer team, Milt Good, a former rodeo star who served years in prison for murder, would die from a supposed accident, when his car inadvertently went into reverse and ran into him outside a cattle gate on July 3, 1960, only one week prior to the start of the convention. In Nelson's words: "everyone with any knowledge about it whatsoever were all threatened and sworn to secrecy, precisely as so many other witnesses were treated throughout LBJ's reign of terror: They were forcefully warned about never revealing the truth about Milt's murder, else their own lives and those of their families would be put into jeopardy." Nelson talked about Chad Mills, the great-grand nephew of Good, who was writing a book about him tentatively titled "Good & Evil." Regarding Mills, Nelson wrote, "the matter of his continuing ability to pursue related truths may be jeopardized by a mysterious disease that has heretofore never been diagnosed. He is not able to pay the travel expenses to go see the specialist doctors at the Mayo Clinic in Rochester, Minnesota and is appealing for help to secure that financing." In an August 29, 2023, email, Nelson informed me that, "Chad is continuing to work on his manuscript and I believe he will get it done, just can't say when."

In his 2000 biography of the former Secretary of Defense, *Driven Patriot, the Life and Times of James Forrestal,* author Townsend Hoopes revealed that during his fateful stay at the notorious Bethesda Naval Hospital, Forrestal would be denied most normal visitation rights. While he would see his wife, two sons, and a handful of government colleagues,

Forrestal was not permitted to see several people he continually asked for: his brother, a friend, and two priests. (Only after threatening to go to the press and suing the hospital would his brother, Henry, be permitted to visit; the others, however, would be denied.) One of the visitors to successfully bull his way into Forrestal's hospital room would be none other than a young congressman, Lyndon Baines Johnson. Top Forrestal aide Marx Leva would recount that Johnson, "managed to gain entrance to the suite against Forrestal's wishes."[40] One must truly wonder why Johnson, a supporter of the fledgling state of Israel, would have wanted to visit Forrestal in his hospital room and what on earth the two adversaries might have said to one another.

There was an odd connection between the family of Lee Harvey Oswald and two different Secretaries of the Navy. Most researchers are aware that Oswald wrote to John Connally in January of 1962, asking for his help in changing his dishonorable military discharge status. Oswald evidently didn't know that Connally had left his position in December 1961. Oswald's letter was forwarded to Kennedy's new Secretary of the Navy, Fred Korth. Korth, like Connally, was considered a staunch Johnson man. In one of those head-scratching coincidences, Korth had represented Oswald's mother Marguerite in a divorce proceeding years earlier.[41]

Stories about LBJ's hatred for the Kennedys are legion. After attaining the presidency, he once supposedly saw a Secret Service agent wearing a PT-109 tie clip, and tore it off in anger and threw it in the trash, then reassigned the agent. After LBJ died, Secret Service agents guarding Lady Bird Johnson were astonished to find that of all the many photographs in the Johnson home with notable persons, not a single one pictured him with President Kennedy.

Ted Kennedy: The Lone Survivor

> *I have fallen short in my life, but my faith has always brought me home.*
>
> —Edward Kennedy[42]

Ted Kennedy was the youngest of Joseph P. Kennedy's expansive clan. The bar was set tremendously high for him, and he almost certainly must have felt overwhelmed by the legacies of his martyred older brothers. The record seems to indicate Teddy was a pleasant, affable fellow, but unfortunately, he wasn't up to the task of filling the shoes of John or Bobby (not to mention Joe Jr.).

In June of 1964, Edward Kennedy became the third of Joseph Kennedy's children to be involved in a plane crash. Unlike his older siblings Joe Jr. and Kathleen, he survived. The pilot and another passenger died in the crash, and young Senator Kennedy's serious injuries required a long recuperation in the hospital of some five months. When older brother Bobby joined him in the Senate, the two formed a close bond, very much like the one Bobby had shared with Jack. While Bobby's brief political career would end, like Jack's, in assassination while running for president in 1968, Teddy would become the third longest-serving member of the Senate in American history.

Ted's own presidential aspirations were shattered forever by the death of RFK's former campaign worker Mary Jo Kopechne on Chappaquiddick Island on July 19, 1969. I covered the many questions surrounding this incident in *Hidden History*. In short, I don't believe Kennedy was in the car, and was in fact the victim of a setup that took an innocent woman's life and became in effect his political assassination in terms of any hopes for the presidency. Kopechne's surviving family members received a letter in 2018, which was titled "The Untold Story of Chappaquiddick." The unidentified writer spoke of a lunch he'd shared years earlier with a woman who had been at the party with Mary Jo, Teddy, and the others on the night in question. She was referred to in the letter by the pseudonym "Betty." She claimed Mary Jo had too much to drink that night, and passed out in the back seat of Kennedy's car, where she was unseen by the senator and another woman who later left the party for a drive. When the car went over the bridge, they escaped but never realized they left Mary Joe behind. I find this story implausible, for the very reason Kennedy's ridiculous claims were: he had almost certainly been drinking, was a big man, and suffered from a bad back. He wouldn't have been able to get out of that car, when the younger, athletic Mary Jo couldn't.

Kopechne's aunt Georgetta Potoski continues to seek the truth about the incident. In a March 28, 2018, article, she told *People* magazine that

Mary Jo's parents "loved the Kennedys. Everyone did. But later on, they started to question what happened. . . . The longer it went on, more and more inconsistencies were discovered and he wasn't telling Gwen and Joe anything. . . . Gwen and Joe never had the last hours of their daughter's life explained to them." Literary agent Esther Newberg, like Mary Jo one of the "Boiler Room Girls" who was on Chappaquiddick Island, told *People* that the others had maintained their silence "Because it's tasteless and in America, everyone thinks that anything is fair game for conversation and I didn't feel that way and neither did my friends." A year later, in another *People* magazine story, Potoski declared, "I'm not convinced the mystery has been solved. I know there are things that we do not know about what happened that night. The truth, even if it's not what you want to hear, at least has some dignity around it. . . . There was such a cover-up and such disregard for Mary Jo when she died. I don't think there will ever be justice for the loss of her life. [But] I think the truth would make our hearts rest easier."[43] On the fiftieth anniversary of the Chappaquiddick incident, the Kopechne family released a letter boxer Muhammad Ali had written to them shortly after Mary Jo's death. Ali urged the Kopechnes to sue Kennedy "for everything he's got." The prizefighter also expressed his view that Mary Jo had died in suspicious circumstances and that there had been "an illicit sexual encounter" between the victim and Ted Kennedy.[44]

During his strange, belated run for the White House in 1980, when he challenged sitting President Jimmy Carter for the Democratic Party nomination, Senator Edward Kennedy's campaign was rife with rumors of assassination. In 2010 more than 2,300 pages of the Senator's FBI file were released. In one 1968 report, just three weeks after his brother, Robert Kennedy was shot dead in Los Angeles, Albert "Sonny" Capone, son of the legendary mobster Al Capone, was overheard making a call from a public phone in Florida. At one point in the conversation, witnesses claimed to have overheard Capone say, "If Edward Kennedy keeps fooling around, he was going to get it too."[45] In another instance, a tipster in North Carolina told police he'd overheard a conversation in a movie theater about killing Kennedy in Pittsburgh. Behind the scenes, Teddy was very much aware of the threats. He'd once notably declared, on an airplane, that "They're going to shoot my ass off the way they shot Bobby." Patrick Kennedy, Teddy's youngest son, recalled in his 2015 book, *A Common Struggle: A Personal Journey Through the Past and Future of Mental Illness and Addiction*, how his father had written him a letter at the beginning of the 1980 campaign. "In it, he talked about how much he loved me, and how I had given him so much love. He said he would never forget the times we went fishing and sailing," Patrick Kennedy stated. An even more bizarre rumor involved Anton LaVey of the Church of Satan. During that 1980 presidential bid, an informant contacted the Chicago FBI office, regarding a plot to kill Ted Kennedy. The informant said he'd received a phone call on October 20, from a man identifying himself as LaVey, requesting his help to murder Kennedy. Anton LaVey was known to possess weapons, and FBI files showed he once tried to join the National Socialist White People's Party. The FBI inexplicably is still keeping the identity of this informant secret. He told agents that LaVey had pressured him by saying he needed to return a favor. He was told that he'd receive a package, which he was to deliver to a mob boss on the South Side of Chicago. The mob was supposedly going to "hit" Ted Kennedy. After talking to LaVey on the phone, the informant was visited by someone from the Church of Satan. FBI records state that the visit "was specifically to discuss the satanic cult and the plot against Senator Kennedy." LaVey denied everything; according to the FBI, "LaVey advised that of any political official, he has the highest regard for Senator Kennedy and his family."[46]

Ted Kennedy's extraordinarily long Senate career was largely disappointing. He often advocated for disastrous policies, like the 1965 Immigration "Reform" Act. But at times, he would display a spark of courage and independence, which served as a reminder that he was the brother of John and Robert Kennedy. In a 1977 speech on the floor of the Senate, Teddy stated, "The Deputy Director of the CIA revealed that over thirty universities and institutions were involved in an 'extensive testing and experimentation' program which included covert drug tests on unwitting citizens 'at all social levels, high and low, native Americans and foreign.' Several of these tests involved the administration of LSD to 'unwitting subjects in social situations.' At least one death, that of Dr. (Frank) Olson, resulted from these activities. The Agency itself acknowledged that these tests made little scientific sense. The agents doing the monitoring were not qualified scientific observers."

The eulogy Ted Kennedy gave for his brother Robert after his assassination was one of the most beautiful I've ever heard. Real human emotion caused his voice to crack as he said, "My brother need not be idealized, or enlarged in death beyond what he was in life, to be remembered simply as a good and decent man, who saw wrong and tried to right it, saw suffering and tried to heal it, saw war and tried to stop it. Those of us who loved him and who take him to his rest today, pray that what he was to us and what he wished for others will someday come to pass for all the world. As he said many times, in many parts of this nation, to those he touched and who sought to touch him: 'Some men see things as they are and say, 'Why?' I dream things that never were and say, 'Why not?'"

One of the few phone numbers I found for people I wanted to talk with, that actually worked, was that of Joan Kennedy, Teddy's former wife. We had the briefest of conversations on March 30, 2022. Joan kept saying she couldn't hear me, and the person who answered the phone at the residence had a limited grasp of English. I didn't get to ask her any questions, but it was highly unlikely she would have discussed anything controversial anyhow. It was rather amazing that she even agreed to talk with me, given how reluctant most others connected to the subjects I write about invariably are. I had the impression that maybe she isn't contacted much by reporters now, and hoped she might want to go on the record. Alas, it wasn't to be.

CHAPTER SEVEN

THE KENNEDY ASSASSINATIONS

I shouted out, "Who killed the Kennedys?"

—The Rolling Stones[1]

The JFK Assassination: My Never-Ending Obsession

If somebody wants to shoot me from a window with a rifle, nobody can stop it, so why worry about it?

—John F. Kennedy, the morning of November 22, 1963[2]

My research into the assassination of President John F. Kennedy began when I read an excerpt from George O'Toole's *The Assassination Tapes,* which was published in the April 1975 issue of *Penthouse* magazine. My mother then gave me a copy of Robert Sam Anson's *They've Killed the President!* for Christmas, and the rest is history. I couldn't get enough of the subject. I could become absorbed in the minutiae of any number of aspects of the case. Most people quickly learned not to bring the subject up around me, unless they were prepared to hear a long and detailed lecture about how impossible the official story was.

As I mentioned in my book *Hidden History: An Exposé of Modern Crimes, Conspiracies, and Cover-Ups in American Politics,* my first foray into the political world was as a teenage volunteer for my hero Mark Lane's group Citizens Committee of Inquiry. Meeting Lane was one of the greatest thrills of my young life, and I was fortunate enough to meet another of my idols, Harold Weisberg, in the early 1980s. Weisberg hated Lane, and pretty much the rest of the critical community. He was as cranky as I'd heard he was; a stereotypical curmudgeon. But he asked me to have dinner with him and his quiet, patient wife, and that was a real highlight for me. He actually wanted to talk more about Big Band music than the JFK assassination, and played some of his favorites for me after dinner. But as the 1980s wore on, my obsession became a bit muted, until it exploded again upon the release of Oliver Stone's epic film *JFK.* A few decades later, I would teach a course on Stone's great movie for my county's adult education program. Once I went online, and experienced the heady Wild West world of the internet in the 1990s, I immediately sought out the JFK assassination forums.

The late Rich Dellarosa ran the first and best forum on the subject, in my view. Names I had long admired, like the late Jack White, and the late Gary Mack, posted regularly there. I quickly discovered how Mack had turned from the guy who co-discovered "Badgeman" on the Grassy Knoll and wrote many good pieces for Penn Jones's *The Continuing Inquiry*, into what I termed a "neocon," or neo believer in conspiracy. "Neocons" claim to doubt the official story, but focus almost all of their attention on discrediting evidence, witnesses and researchers that strongly support conspiracy. Once Mack was hired by the Sixth Floor Museum, he began appearing regularly on a series of awful cable documentaries, and in each he touted the official party line. White, on the other hand, grew more radical as he aged. We had begun corresponding and were kindred spirits. I regret that he died before my first *Hidden History* was published. I'm certain he would have loved it. On Dellarosa's forum I really saw how prevalent the petty infighting was. Seemingly respectable researchers resorted to childish name-calling very easily. Later, as a moderator on London's Spartacus Education Forum, which became the most popular place on the internet to discuss the assassination, I clashed with the huge egos and difficult personalities that continue to dominate the critical community. I made a lot of enemies, and when *Hidden History* became a surprising best-seller, it wasn't because of any support from my fellow researchers. The forums and community at large have become infested with, and largely dominated by, these "neocons."

The "neocons" have given ground on many of the most critical points that led people like me to question the official story in the first place. They dismiss all the "mysterious deaths." *Six Seconds in Dallas* author Josiah Thompson argued with me on a forum some years ago, that the Umbrella Man really was Steven Witt, the belatedly produced House Select Committee on Assassinations witness who laughably explained he'd been wielding an open umbrella on a sunny day to protest JFK's father's early opposition to our entrance into World War II. Thompson maintained that the Umbrella Man never "pumped" the umbrella. Thompson and others accept Witt's ridiculous account, which included his claim that he didn't see the assassination because his close view was blocked by his open umbrella. No one "questioning" him during his HSCA testimony bothered to refer to any of the many photos and still frames which show clearly that he was standing with the umbrella over his head at the time. Thompson poked fun of himself at ever believing that the Umbrella Man was a possible conspirator in the short film *The Umbrella Man,* released in 2011. Sounding far different from the author of *Six Seconds in Dallas,* Thompson addressed Witt's ludicrous alleged motivation by saying, "I read that and I thought this is just wacky enough it has to be true. And I take it to be true. What it means is, that if you have any fact which you think is really sinister, right? Is really obviously a fact which can only point to some sinister underpinning. Hey, forget it man, because you can never on your own think up all the non-sinister, perfectly valid explanations for that fact." The film was directed by Errol Morris, who like Brad Meltzer "investigates" those dreaded "conspiracy theories," but invariably rejects them. Morris revealed his bias by saying in an interview, "Conspiracies tell you that there's a kind of easy way to grasp the idea of evil. It's those bad guys rubbing their hands together."[3]

Thompson also argued with me about the hole in the limousine's windshield—which several unconnected witnesses reported seeing. There are some more extreme "neocons" out there who seem to particularly dislike me, but I won't give them the satisfaction of naming them. Virtually everything they post online is an attempt to diminish the case for conspiracy. Some of them angrily refute that there were any legitimate Oswald impersonator sightings in the weeks leading up to the assassination. They are venomous toward Ralph Leon Yates, a refrigerator mechanic who claimed to have picked up a hitchhiker who strongly resembled Lee Harvey Oswald in Oak Cliff on November 20, 1963. The man was carrying a package that he told Yates contained curtain rods. Buell Wesley Frazier, who rode Oswald to work on the morning of November 22, 1963, reported seeing him carry a similar brown paper bag which he claimed contained curtain rods. Yates and "Oswald" discussed the upcoming presidential visit, and "Oswald" asked him if he thought a man could assassinate a president, from a window in a high-rise building. "Oswald" pulled out a picture of a man with a rifle, and wondered if it could be done with such a weapon, but Yates kept his eyes on the road and didn't get a good look at the photo. Could this have been one of the "backyard photos?" Yates told a coworker about his experience with the odd hitchhiker after he returned to work. Remember, this was *before* the assassination. Yates talked to the FBI multiple times, and as the father of five children, was reluctant to draw much publicity. Incredibly, after his last meeting with the FBI on January 4, 1964, Yates was ordered to turn himself in for evaluation at a Dallas mental hospital. Yates spent the remaining eleven years of his life in and out of mental facilities. He told his wife Dorothy that he feared she and the children were in danger because of his encounter with "Oswald." He died in one of these hospitals at only thirty-nine years old. But in the eyes of many "neocons," Yates was just a mentally disturbed guy making up a story.

Ruth Paine has also been the recipient of a historical facelift by many of the "neocons." To most serious researchers, Ruth and her husband Michael Paine were supremely suspect characters, who certainly appear to have played some kind of "handling" role with Oswald. The Paines just happened to move from Pennsylvania to Irving, Texas, home of Marguerite Oswald, in September 1959, during the same week that her son Lee defected to the Soviet Union. Ruth returned a book to Lee Harvey Oswald's wife Marina after the assassination, and was subsequently confronted by government agents with a note that had been found in the book, supposedly written by Oswald, which incriminated him in the shooting attempt of General Edwin Walker. Marina would be cut off from contact with Ruth a few days after the assassination, and was told by the Secret Service to stay away from her because "she was sympathizing with the CIA." In her New Orleans grand jury testimony, Marina stated, "Seems like she (Ruth) had friends over there and it would be bad for me if people find out a connection between me and Ruth and CIA." Ruth and Michael Paine, whom we are told by officials had no connection to the assassination, were asked six thousand questions between them by the Warren Commission, by far the most of any witnesses. In 1997, researcher Steve Jones had some intriguing conversations with a friend of Ruth Paine's, who very adamantly requested to remain unidentified for fear of repercussions. She had been with Ruth in Nicaragua in the early '90s, working with the group Pro-Nica. She stated that everyone in the group thought that Ruth was there working for some intelligence outfit. Ruth wrote copious notes, asked personal questions, and took inappropriate photos. She was asked to take a leave of absence, and went to Costa Rica, where she was asked to leave as well after being suspected of the same thing. Ruth would admit to her friend that her father had indeed worked for the CIA as an "executive agent." It was already known that Ruth's sister had been a psychologist for the CIA. Jones was among the many researchers who beseeched the Assassinations Record and Review Board (ARRB) to depose the Paines, but they were never questioned by the ARRB, just as they had not testified before the HSCA.[4]

Michael Paine, whom Ruth was separated from but still friendly with, worked for Bell Helicopter, where the supervisor of his classified projects division was Walter Dornberger. Dornberger had been the head of the Nazi Peenemünde rocket center. At the end of the war, Wernher von Braun and his superior Dornberger turned themselves in to the American military unit of General Charles O. Thrasher, where Major Clay Shaw was serving as Thrasher's aide-de-camp.[5] Dornberger was, incredibly enough, also connected to Guy Banister. Although most of Banister's files were destroyed after his 1964 death, some file names did survive. One of the file names listed below "Assassination of President Kennedy" was titled "Dyna-Soar Space Warcraft," which just happened to be a project run by Dornberger: a space plane, the Boeing X-20 Dyna-Soar[6] After Dornberger was arrested by the Allies, instead of being prosecuted at Nuremberg, he entered Operation Paperclip, like Wernher von Braun and other more fortunate ex-Nazis. Dornberger became chief of the US Army's Weapons Department, and was placed in charge of America's V-2 missile development program. He spent 15 years as director of Research and Development at Bell Aircraft Corporation, helped develop the world's first air-to-surface nuclear missile, and played a role in creating the space shuttle. Meanwhile, Michael's mother, Ruth Forbes Paine, was associated with the shadowy Round Table Foundation, also referred to as "The Council of Nine," whose backers included FDR's second vice-president, Henry Wallace. Israeli psychic Uri Geller was a member, as was *Star Trek* creator Gene Roddenberry. The group, which believed it was channeling entities from another world, was later revealed to have been funded by the U.S. Army.[7]

The 2022 film *The Assassination and Mrs. Paine* tells Ruth's story objectively. I interviewed the filmmaker, Max Good, on my *I Protest* show. Ruth notably declares, at one point in the film, that Oswald "did not live at my house—he was not invited to—it was a very small house." Apparently, it wasn't too small to accommodate Oswald on weekends. In an early interview, when the results of any "investigation" were largely unknown, Ruth was asked if she thought there had been some kind of conspiracy, and she replied, "No, I think there certainly was not." Priscilla Johnson McMillan, the intelligence-connected author who became very close to Marina Oswald for a while, appears in the film to state that the "conspiracy theories" about the assassination "did more harm to the nation" than the assassination itself! An elderly Michael Paine is adamant onscreen that Oswald shot the president saying, "I think that Oswald did it, and I don't happen to know anything else." Ruth's sister Sylvia Hoke, a psychologist whose association with the CIA was obvious enough that Ruth, in this film, more than once acknowledges it being "possible," refused to talk to Max Good. Ruth completely contradicted Marguerite's account of the *Life* magazine photographer who took photos of her, Marina, and Ruth the night of the assassination at the Paine residence. While Marguerite had claimed she didn't want the photographer there, Ruth would tell Good that Marguerite "sort of negotiated a chance to stay with me overnight, and, unbeknownst to me, invited some *Life* people to come along." Even more incredibly, Ruth informed Good that when she told Marguerite that Lee had called, and wanted to talk with Marina, Oswald's mother replied, "Well, we can't be too concerned with what Lee wants at this point, can we?"

The dysfunction in the critical community goes back to the very beginning. It became especially pronounced when New Orleans District Attorney Jim Garrison began his investigation. Sylvia Meagher, whose essential book *Accessories After the Fact* remains perhaps the finest overview of the case, became estranged from Garrison when he didn't answer a letter she wrote him, which had pointed out an error. Harold Weisberg, whose book *Oswald in New Orleans* is essential to understanding the basis of Garrison's case, broke with him for typically unclear reasons. While Mark Lane, Vincent Salandria, and many other critics remained faithful supporters of the embattled New Orleans' District Attorney, Josiah Thompson, Peter Dale Scott, and Anthony Summers were among those who followed Meagher's lead in opposing him. I would characterize pretty much all of Garrison's present critics in the research community as "neocons." One of Garrison's top aides, Tom Bethell, openly admitted to researchers that he initially was scouring the National Archives "to see if he could prove there was no conspiracy." In a Qanon, Trumpian type of 4D chess logic, he claimed that this would somehow lead him to evidence of conspiracy. Bethell would turn on Garrison, and gave all his files to Clay Shaw's lawyers. It is logical to speculate that the CIA or some other agency inserted him onto Garrison's staff, or bought his loyalty early on.[8]

Jim Garrison believed, as I do, that Lee Harvey Oswald was on assignment for some intelligence agency at the time of the assassination, to infiltrate a potential plot to kill JFK. The characters in this plot would have included Clay Shaw, David Ferrie, and Jack Ruby. In my view, these were ground-level conspirators who seem to have been government assets themselves, and were probably all being manipulated like Oswald. More documentation for this can be found in my book *Pipe the Bimbo in Red: Dean Andrews, Jim Garrison, and the Conspiracy to Kill JFK*, which was co-written with the underrated researcher William Matson Law.

Researcher James Gochenaur gave a signed affidavit to the Senate Intelligence Committee in 1975, which maintained that Oswald had been reporting to FBI agent James P. Hosty and possibly others in the Bureau about "his infiltration of a group that was planning to kill the president." Gochenaur's source for this was a retired FBI agent in Seattle, who was questioned early on by the HSCA, which was initially doing good work under chief counsel Richard A. Sprague. Hosty visited the Irving, Texas, home where Marina was staying with Ruth and Michael Paine, on November 1, 1963, because he hadn't received his regular update from Oswald. Hosty's name and license plate number were found in Oswald's personal notebook. Hosty wasn't called to testify before the HSCA, and was quoted as telling the *Dallas Morning News* that the committee—now run by G. Robert Blakey—feared he would "drop bombs" to them. One of Sprague's former investigators (the HSCA staff was cut significantly once Blakey took over) quoted the retired FBI agent in Seattle as saying Hosty "would be willing to tell whomever might be interested in this, the whole story. If there was some way he could be granted immunity and given protection."[9]

Many have wondered why Oswald appeared so confused at his midnight press conference on the night of the assassination. To a reporter's question about shooting the president, Oswald answered "No, I have not been charged with that. In fact, nobody has said that to me yet. The first thing I heard about it was when the newspaper reporters in the hall asked me that question." At first glance, this seems like a bit of an awkward, odd response. However, I was aware that Harold Weisberg insisted repeatedly that Oswald had never been officially charged with murdering Kennedy. A little-known FBI document, dated November 25, 1963, the day after Oswald himself was shot and killed by Jack Ruby, makes his comments more understandable. The document notes that "The following information was obtained by SA (Special Agent) James F. Hosty Jr., from the office of Captain Will Fritz, Dallas Police Department, on November 25, 1963. . . . No arraignment on the murder charges in connection with the death of President Kennedy was held inasmuch as such arraignment was not necessary in view of the previous charges filed against Oswald and for which he was arraigned."

In this book, we'll cover more of what I consider to be the best evidence of conspiracy in greater detail. Some "neocon" JFK assassination researchers have added the aborted phone call Oswald attempted on November 23, to a man many assume was his handler, to the list of conspiratorial evidence they claim is bogus. Michael Canfield and A. J. Weberman, in their 1975 book *Coup D'etat in America,* were the first to write about this strange incident, although neocon author and researcher Anthony Summers is usually given credit since it appeared in his 1980 book *Conspiracy.* Alveeta Treon was the switchboard operator on duty at the Dallas Police Department on November 23, 1963. When Treon arrived at work somewhere around 10 p.m., her coworker Louise Swinney informed her that their supervisor had asked them to assist law enforcement with listening in to a call that Lee Harvey Oswald would be making. Two men, whom Treon guessed were Secret Service agents, went to a room where they could monitor the call in privacy. Oswald's call came through at approximately 10:45 p.m., and Swinney wrote the information down and notified the men in the room. Treon would tell researcher Bernard Fensterwald in 1968 that "I was dumbfounded at what happened next. Mrs. Swinney opened the key to Oswald and told him, 'I'm sorry, the number doesn't answer.' She then unplugged and disconnected Oswald without ever really trying to put the call through. A few moments later, Mrs. Swinney tore the page off her notation pad and threw it into the wastepaper basket." After Swinney left work, Treon retrieved the note from the trash and copied it down, to keep as a "souvenir." That note would finally be released in 1970, thanks to a Freedom of Information Act suit by the indefatigable Sherman Skolnick. It revealed that the attempted collect call was to a John Hurt, with two phone numbers, both with Raleigh, North Carolina area codes, listed. One was a John David Hurt, the other John William Hurt. Researcher Grover Proctor called one of the numbers, and spoke with John David Hurt, who claimed to have never heard of Oswald prior to the assassination. Hurt was known to have been a U.S. Army Counterintelligence Special Agent during World War II. The other John Hurt was contacted as well, and also denied any connection. Sknolick discovered, from sworn statements in his lawsuit, that the Secret Service took a sudden interest in someone named Hurt on November 23, 1963. Former Secret Service agent Abraham Bolden claimed that he was contacted by the Dallas Secret Service late on November 23rd, and asked about any phonetic spelling of the name "Hurt" or "Heard."[10]

Treon would tell the House Select Committee on Assassinations (HSCA) that Swinney seemed very anxious, and she suspected that the agents had pressured her to stop the call and inform Oswald there had been no answer. Immediately after the call was disconnected, the agents exited the listening room and left. Both Treon and Swinney testified before the HSCA in 1978. Some researchers, like former CIA agent Victor Marchetti, believed Oswald was attempting to contact his intelligence "cutout" to help him. Marchetti also revealed that a false defector program was being run by the CIA/ONI out of Nags Head, North Carolina at the time, which obviously could have involved Oswald and his highly questionable defection to and return from Russia. Rather unexpectedly, Robert Blakey also insisted the phone call had been attempted. Oswald was complaining about not having an attorney, and almost certainly was beginning to understand that he'd been set up. An internal HSCA report, written by senior staff counsel Surrell Brady, concluded, "The information provided by Mrs. Treon, her daughter, and Louise Swinney all indicate that Oswald did in fact attempt to place a call from the Dallas City Hall Jail on the night of November 23, 1963. Ms. Kovac and Mrs. Swinney also confirm Mrs. Treon's allegation that 'law enforcement' officials came into the switchboard room at the time of Oswald's call. The Committee has been unable to identify those men or the agency for which they worked." Brady went on, "Mrs. Treon's account would indicate also that Mrs. Swinney deceived Oswald and did not put his call through as requested. If believed, that may indicate there was some agreement between Mrs. Swinney and the law enforcement officials to thwart Oswald's attempt to place a call from the jail. It is known that Oswald never reached Attorney John Abt in New York City to represent him after his arrest. If the law enforcement officials did in fact interfere with Oswald's attempt to contact an attorney, the committee recognizes that that would have been a serious violation of his constitutional rights, in view of how long he had been in custody at that point and the extensive interrogation to which he had been subjected. The Committee also notes that Mrs. Swinney appeared nervous when contacted by Committee investigators to discuss the incident. While that may indicate some concern on the part of Mrs. Swinney that she had been involved in something devious, the Committee is not able to conclude as a fact based on what has been presented that there was actually interference with Oswald's call by Mrs. Swinney." HSCA staff investigator Harold Rose corroborated this about Swinney, stating, "The only thing I can tell you is the lady in Dallas I interviewed was very, very nervous. She was very upset that I had discovered her. She didn't want to get involved." Greene County, Missouri Sheriff Arnold Mickey Owen, recalled how Treon acted when she told him about the incident, "She gave me the impression she was scared to death. Absolutely afraid, period. In my opinion, she thought she was telling the truth." Swinney would tell researcher J. G. Harris, "Treon wasn't there. It wasn't that area code. It wasn't that city (Raleigh), it wasn't that name (Hurt)." As Rose put it, "I think it could have stood quite a bit more looking into."[11]

Another underreported tidbit from this case is the April 9, 1964, FBI report which noted that military cryptographic code operator Eugene B. Dinkin had predicted, "that a conspiracy was in the making for the 'military' of the United States, perhaps combined with an 'ultra right-wing economic group'" to assassinate President Kennedy. Dinkin claimed to have processed messages between plotters like the CIA's William Harvey, Guy Banister, and the French mob hitman QJ/WIN. Dinkin talked too much, telling some fellow soldiers about his story, and hearing rumors he was going to be sent to a mental health facility, went AWOL. Arriving in Geneva, Switzerland on November 6,1963, Dinkin shared his account with reporters in a United Nations pressroom. He then went to Germany, where he was coerced into turning himself in to authorities. On December 5, 1963, he was returned to the United States and committed to Walter Reed Hospital. Powerful psychotropic drugs and shock treatment forced him to pretend to be afflicted with the Orwellian malady "schizo-assassination prognostication." Dinkin's concerned mother wrote Robert F. Kennedy on December 20, 1963, in which she said her son "claims this to be a frame up." The CIA's James J. Angleton apparently intercepted the letter, and Richard Helms wrote, in a classified memo, "All aspects of this story were known, as reported above, by US military authorities and have been reported by military attaché cable through military channels." Dinkin, somewhat surprisingly, lived on until 2012. An article from that year on the Kennedys and King website adds the intriguing detail that Dinkin himself had sent a registered letter to Robert F. Kennedy about the brewing plot, before going AWOL, but received no reply. Among the files released in 2017 and 2018 by the Trump administration, was a CIA cable about Dinkin arriving in Geneva, in which it was noted, "Neither the FBI nor the Warren Commission ever investigated the Dinkin case." Seemingly supporting Dinkin's contentions was another CIA document, released in 2018, detailing how Air Force Sergeant David Christensen had intercepted a communication just before November 1963, about an assassination attempt to be made on JFK. The document reports that, predictably, Christensen was "committed to a mental institution." Christensen died in 2008.

Seldom mentioned by researchers is the special unit of six high-ranking Dallas Police officers, headed by Captain Orville Aubrey "O.A." Jones, who were assigned by Chief Jesse Curry to conduct an in-house probe, shortly after Jack Ruby killed Lee Harvey Oswald. Notably missing from this unit was Captain Will Fritz. Jones told *Dallas Morning News* reporter Earl Golz in 1978 that all tapes, documents and other material from their several-months-long investigation had been turned over to Curry, whom he assumed passed them on to the Warren Commission. However, there is no mention of this internal Dallas Police investigation in the Commission's records. Curry reacted by telling Golz, "I don't remember what all was sent up there now." In the same story, Golz reported on a box of evidence which seemingly came from this police inquiry, which was in the possession of former Dallas Police Captain Paul McCaghren. Investigators for the House Select Committee on Assassinations examined the material. "They asked me why I sat on this stuff all these years," McCaghren, who had become a private investigator, explained. "And I told them no one ever asked me." The HSCA investigators were described as "ecstatic" over the find. Captain Jack Reville was the only other member of the internal Dallas Police unit mentioned. He was quoted as saying he was "surprised" the records hadn't been turned over to the Warren Commission, and claimed he'd spoken to HSCA investigators three times, but told them, "I have nothing to support or disprove your allegations or whatever you are thinking."[12] However ecstatic they might have been, there are no further reports on this mysterious box, and what it contained.

Texas state highway patrolman Charles W. Harbison, who guarded Governor John Connally's Parkland Hospital room after the assassination, years later recalled turning over more bullet fragments than the three the Warren Commission reported came from the governor's wounds. Harbison's testimony corroborates that of Audrey N. Bell, supervisor of Parkland's operating room, who stated she was given four or five additional fragments taken from Connally. This would add up to eight fragments from the nearly pristine CE399, the so-called "magic bullet." In an April 1977 article about this, HSCA investigators were said to have interviewed Bell and believed her account could topple "the very cornerstone and basis of the entire Warren Commission report."[13] Bell's HSCA testimony is not readily available, but she told Doug Horne of the ARRB that Dr. Malcolm Perry, who initially identified JFK's throat wound as one of entry, had recounted to her that officials in Washington, D.C. kept him up all night trying to get him to change his description of the hole in the throat. In Horne's words, Perry was "tormented" because, as he told Bell, "my professional credibility is at stake." That same month, Connally surgeon Dr. Robert Shaw declared that the bullet "was not consistent with the appearance of the bullet that was found on the governor's stretcher." Shaw observed that the bullet "just didn't seem to have lost enough of its metallic substance" for the absurd single-bullet theory to work.[14] Like so many other witnesses, Audrey Bell would tell the ARRB that her initial FBI report was not recorded accurately. Reporter Martin Steadman would corroborate Bell's testimony about Malcolm Perry. In his diary, Steadman recollected being in Perry's home, along with a few other journalists, about a week after the assassination. Perry assured them that it had been an entrance wound in JFK's throat, and talked about the doctors at Bethesda calling him that night, and badgering him. He claimed that they warned him if he continued to insist it was an entrance wound, he would be brought before a medical board. He said they threatened to take away his license. In the documentary *The Parkland Doctors,* narrated by former HSCA deputy counsel Robert Tannenbaum, Parkland Dr. Robert

McClelland described seeing a man in a suit and tie forcefully grab Dr. Perry about ninety minutes after JFK was pronounced dead, and advise him, "Don't you ever say that again!" The aforementioned researcher James Gochenaur told both the Senate Church Committee and the HSCA that Secret Service agent Elmer Moore had confessed to him in 1970 that he had "leaned on Dr. Perry" to get him to change his description of the bullet wound, shortly after the autopsy at Bethesda Naval Hospital. Moore admitted that the Secret Service had to support the official story or "get their heads chopped off." Researcher Vince Palamara has found that there was a real hostility toward Kennedy on the part of some agents, which was exemplified by Moore's comment to Gochenaur that JFK was a "traitor" who was "giving things away to the Russians."[15] Moore seemed to be attempting to justify his actions to Gochenaur, who admitted to being frightened and intimidated by him.

Another little-followed-up story appeared in the July 22, 1981, issue of *The Continuing Inquiry*. It was written by Gary Mack, who hadn't converted to quasi-lone nutter or started working at the Sixth Floor Museum yet. Mack quoted a former Dallas Police officer who didn't want to be identified, regarding yet another unseen film taken at the time of the assassination. According to the ex-cop, an anonymous cameraman, who Mack claimed was still working for the same local Dallas television station (and thus withheld his name), was assigned to get sound film of the motorcade in downtown Dallas. He supposedly set up very near witness Howard Brennan's position opposite the Texas School Book Depository, started recording, and then raced off to film the motorcade. According to Mack, the unidentified reporter "won't say" what happened to his film. The sound tape, meanwhile, was conveniently erased, but he didn't know who did it or why. Mack, interestingly enough, in this article expressed my exact sentiments when he wrote, "I've long been puzzled by the lack of any professional footage of the motorcade in Dealey Plaza before or during the assassination."

Buell Wesley Frazier, the man who drove Oswald to work on November 22, 1963, has been used by both conspiracy believers and lone nutters to advance their beliefs. On page 163 of his 2021 book *Steering Truth: My Eternal Connection to JFK and Lee Harvey Oswald*, Frazier writes, "As I explained earlier, after the president's motorcade sped off, Mr. Shelley and Billy took off to the grassy knoll area. I walked down to the bottom of the steps, where I had been standing, and I looked toward the triple underpass. I figured I'd walk down to find Mr. Shelley and Billy to see if they knew anything. I walked just twenty yards before I realized there was no way I going to find them. As I paused to turn around to go back to the entrance of the Texas School Book Depository, a man walked up carrying a rifle. He wore a light-beige slacks with a white shirt and tie and light-brown shoes, and he had a brown-colored plaid tweed sports coat with a brown fedora. I think he was in his late thirties. When he walked up and I saw him with the rifle, my heart jumped into my throat. I knew the president had been shot, and I was now face-to-face with someone not in police clothing carrying a weapon. I was terrified. He bored a hole right through me with his brown eyes, and I said, 'don't worry, I didn't see anything.' Without missing a beat, he opened the trunk of his car, and I saw what happened to be a pump shotgun. He put his rifle he was carrying in the trunk and shut it. He was calm and never said a word to me, but I'll never forget his face. I turned around and headed back to the front steps of the Texas School Book Depository. At the same time, I heard the car door open and close, the car start, and him pull out of the angled parking spot. I never looked back as I walked toward the entrance of the building and then to the corner of Houston and Elm, where a couple was standing."

Frazier also claims in his book that he saw another man with a rifle the next day, outside his home. It is noteworthy that Frazier was at one point close to, and probably influenced by, lone nutters Gus Russo and Dave Perry. It is certainly interesting that TSBD employee Roy Lewis stated, in a 2017 interview, that Oswald rode with Frazier every day and usually parked on the curve of Houston St. at the rear of the TSBD. I have commented on this before: the Oswalds' living arrangement has never made sense to me. On his minimum-wage salary, why would he rent a room? Wouldn't Ruth Paine have let him stay there with his wife and child (soon to be children)? Wouldn't Frazier have been willing to drive him to work every day? In the book *The Lone Star Speaks: Untold Texas Stories about the JFK Assassination*, authors K.W. Zachry and Sara Peterson write, "Recently, Frazier shared a detail he had forgotten for decades. As he stood at the corner of Elm and Houston, he glanced up and saw Oswald walk from behind the Depository, cross Houston Street, and proceed south." Why didn't Frazier ever mention the ominous armed man who stared him down and put a gun in the trunk of his car, or the man with a gun outside his home, or Oswald walking from behind the Depository, to the authorities or researchers before? Frazier is the witness whose testimony about Oswald carrying a package of "curtain rods," and uncharacteristically wanting a ride home the night before (which was a Thursday), supposedly breaking his pattern of only riding home with Frazier on Fridays, fueled an essential part of the lone assassin narrative. But his description of the package worked against it having been a rifle, and he spoke positively of Oswald loving his children. He was still reiterating in 2013, "It wasn't long enough to put that type of rifle in that bag. There is no way it would fit in that package." And Frazier may have actually been a backup "patsy" in the assassination; police arrested and fingerprinted him, then forced him to take a polygraph test. Captain Will Fritz tried to pressure him into signing a typed confession. "This was ridiculous," Frazier declared. "Captain Fritz got very red-faced, and he put up his hand to hit me and I put my arm up to block. I told him we'd have a hell of a fight and I would get some good licks in on him. Then he stormed out the door." Following the assassination, Frazier remained suspect in the eyes of his community and claimed he had trouble finding work.[16]

I became friends with Buell Frazier during the course of writing this book. Buell is one of the nicest people I've ever had the pleasure of talking with. He appeared on *The Donald Jeffries Show* on September 15, 2021. In my view, Buell is essentially accommodating with everyone because of his incredibly polite nature. On my radio show, Buell came down strongly on the side of conspiracy, and reiterated, "I've said from Day One that I didn't think he did it." He spoke in more detail about the man with a gun outside his home the day after the assassination. He and his sister called the Irving Police, who came and talked to the man outside, then left. When they called the police station to ask what happened, they were told that no call had been placed, and no officer had come to their property. Buell also informed me that there is no record of his having been questioned, fingerprinted and polygraphed by the Dallas Police on November 22nd.

He revealed that his sister, Linnie Mae Randle, shared his conviction that Oswald hadn't been the assassin, and spoke of how they'd been frightened for years. He also assured me that he would have been willing to drive Oswald to work every day, telling him, "You can have a ride whenever you want to." He agreed with my suspicions regarding the Oswalds' living arrangements, declaring, "I did think that was strange at the time." Frazier doubled down on his past comments regarding Oswald's love for his children, and emphasized how his little nieces and all the other neighborhood children would become very excited whenever Lee came to the Paines. He recalled how they loved the games he'd play with them around the big oak tree in the front yard. He also related that, in addition to frightening him into the early morning hours of November 23, the police had also trashed his car. Frazier vehemently expressed his disbelief that Oswald could have hidden the rifle and exited down the stairs so quickly. "No one heard him," he noted that someone running down those wooden stairs would have made a great deal of noise. Frazier also mentioned that when officer Marion Baker and Roy Truly supposedly encountered Oswald in the lunchroom only ninety seconds or so after shots had been fired, that there was a half-eaten apple and cheese sandwich found there, which might imply that he was indeed eating his lunch there. Frazier closed with stronger comments than he had ever made, saying, "I've always said there was a huge conspiracy here in this JFK assassination and I don't think the real true story's ever been told."

Frazier continues to be misrepresented by the critical community. After my interview with him, a Facebook post stated that Buell had told the HSCA that he'd been in the same lineup with Oswald, and quoted him as bragging, "I own Dallas." This sounded ridiculous to me, and totally out of character for the less-than-garrulous Oswald, but I asked Buell about it in a September 24, 2021, phone conversation. He said, "I don't know where they got that" and assured me he had never been in a lineup with Oswald, and certainly hadn't heard him say anything like that.

I had a long phone conversation with Rachel, youngest daughter of Lee Harvey Oswald, on March 15, 2021. She and I seemed to agree politically on many things, and in a few later emails, I thought she was slowly becoming interested in what I was telling her about her father. She told me she listened to my interview with Buell Frazier, and became a subscriber to my writings on Substack. She let me know that she reads them all and enjoys them. I wanted to have her on my radio show, but she is intent on maintaining a low profile, to protect her family. I respected and understood that. There was even initially a hope of perhaps getting her mother Marina to break her long silence and talk with me, but that never happened. In her last television appearance, on Jesse Ventura's *Conspiracy Theory* show, Marina had expressed fear for her children's safety. Despite being candid about Trump and politics in general, there was still a clear reluctance on Rachel's part to broach the topic of the assassination. As Rachel told me, while Lee Harvey Oswald has been a huge part of my life, he hasn't been in hers—"by design." I think Rachel knows her father didn't shoot JFK, but she feels much more comfortable talking about other subjects.

Patrick Dean

Your testimony was false, and these reports to your chief of police are false.

—Warren Commission counsel Burt Griffin to Patrick Dean[17]

I've long been interested in Dallas Police Sgt. Patrick Dean, as I alluded to in *Hidden History.* While most of the testimony in the Warren Commission's twenty-six volumes of Hearings & Exhibits is tedious and largely meaningless, I found Dean's follow-up appearance before the Commission to be second only to the beatnik-flavored testimony of New Orleans attorney Dean Andrews Jr., in terms of human interest and potential significance. Dean initially was deposed by Commission counsel Burt Griffin, but in typical Warren Commission style, that testimony (Vol. VII, p. 415) actually appears after his second appearance does (Vol. V, p. 254) in the record. After requesting to testify again, Dean was given the rare honor of appearing before Chairman Earl Warren (as well as former CIA Director Allen Dulles, fired by JFK after the Bay of Pigs), instead of the typical junior counsel who questioned almost all the witnesses. Dean charged Griffin with badgering and quasi-threatening him during one of the multitude of "Off the Record" discussions in the collected testimony. He also mentioned one of the too-many-missing films recording the events in

Dealey Plaza. This film, taken by Canadian Ralph Simpson, is a source of great mystery. Simpson, for inexplicable reasons, chose to contact Dean about this, with a middle-of-the-night phone call (variously stated to be 2 a.m. or 4 a.m.). A 1991 article by Peter Whitmey, "The Long Distance Phone Call," appeared in *The Third Decade* newsletter. Whitmey delved much deeper into this issue than critics Mark Lane and Sylvia Meagher had in earlier books. It is revealed here that the British Columbia phone operator was convinced the man had important information, and Dean stated Simpson "sounded rational." Apparently, it was Simpson's lawyer, a Mr. Batter (no first name listed), who advised him not to contact the Warren Commission directly with his information. Why he picked this particular Dallas Police sergeant is unknown. Whitmey claimed Simpson hadn't bothered to develop the film, which seems very odd, and sent only the negative to Dean.

Dean, like so many others in Dallas, was interviewed in 1978 by reporter Earl Golz. He recounted being phoned at such an unusual hour, "the night after the verdict in the Ruby trial." ABC correspondent and talk show host (among those he interviewed was Jim Garrison) Murphy Martin called Simpson, in the presence of Dean and his wife, and was told that he'd been advised by the Royal Canadian Mounted Police, the Canadian government, and the US government, not to talk about the film. In this article, Whitmey writes that it was a 1970 car accident (not 1973, as in some other reports) that left Dean with brain damage and forced his retirement. In a 1987 phone conversation with Whitmey, Dean seemed very clearheaded, refused to believe Simpson's story was a hoax, and remained particularly impressed with the Canadian's knowledge of the area where he'd filmed, and his concern that the film might get into the wrong hands. In response to whether or not the film ever arrived, Dean told Whitmey it was likely it was "intercepted by the authorities." Interestingly, the late-night phone call from Simpson to Dean had originated from the home of R. H. W. Smele. Whitmey talked with Smele's sister-in- law, who had no knowledge of the phone call. She told him Smele's first name was Ralph, and that his mother's maiden name was Simpson, leading to the logical conclusion that he'd been using an alias. Smele/Simpson died in 1982, and was known to be "somewhat of an alcoholic," and prone to playing practical jokes. Neither Smele's sister-in-law, nor his nephew, who Whitmey also talked to, had any idea that their relative's name, phone number, and address were in the Warren Commission's records. As Sylvia Meagher asked, "this is the first and last that is heard of the film: the Commission has told us nothing beyond what is contained in Dean's testimony. Was the film received? Was it viewed? What did it show?"[18] Simpson's film, if it ever existed, is not known to have been seen by anyone. As Whitmey writes, "and yet, today, Ralph Simpson's allegations, like so many others, still remain an unresolved mystery even to members of his own family."

Earl Golz interviewed Patrick Dean again the following year. The article claimed that Dean feared a "setup" by the HSCA to blame him for letting Jack Ruby into the city hall basement on Sunday, November 24, where he shot Oswald. Dean complained of being so "harassed" by committee investigators that he lost 20 pounds and wound up being hospitalized with a "nerve condition." Dean was quoted as saying, "And I don't think I've heard the last of it. I think I'll be hearing from another agency of the federal government (the U S. Department of Justice)." Dean refused to answer some fifty-three questions the Committee sent to him in November 1978, declaring that they would have to subpoena him to Washington. Dean claimed that Melvin Belli, Jack Ruby's lead attorney, had agreed to represent him if he'd been subpoenaed. HSCA investigator Albert Maxwell allegedly warned Dean: "I feel we should inform you that we have 200 pages of declassified material, all of which concerns you." "I took it as a threat," Dean said. "That's the last I heard from them." Dean had stated that Forrest Sorrels, head of the Secret Service in Dallas, also heard Ruby maintain he'd entered the basement via the Main Street ramp, which was the reason counsel Griffin had directed his anger at Dean, to insist that Ruby "did not" say such a thing. Sorrels never corroborated this, but Dean recounted how Sorrels had called him on the phone the night before his Warren Commission appearance, "pleading with me" for over an hour, wanting to know what he was going to testify to. "I told him, 'I'm not going to blow the whistle on you,'" Dean said.[19] Sorrels was perhaps more involved than anyone else in Dallas with arranging the security for JFK's visit. He rode in the car in front of the presidential limo, along with Police Chief Jesse Curry. He was the person who acquired the most famous films of the assassination: the home movies taken by Abraham Zapruder and Orville Nix, and the photos of Mary Moorman and Phil Willis, for the government.

I had a long phone conversation with Tivilla Dean Lamar, daughter of Patrick Dean, on April 14, 2021. She provided some interesting background on her father's near-fatal car crash. She remains suspicious about it and agreed with my assessment that it certainly looked like a murder attempt, putting him in the Warren Reynolds category of witnesses who were fortunate to escape the JFK assassination Body Count. Dean was the son-in-law of O. P. Wright, who as head of security at Parkland Hospital was right in the center of the CE399 "magic bullet" narrative. Wright's wife Elizabeth was also a significant figure as the head of nursing at Parkland. Patrick Dean was never the same after his car accident. Much like Deputy Seymour Weitzman, it seems that Dean was severely impacted by the assassination, even before the accident. Dr. William Hall of Dallas described Dean's "nervous irritability and insomnia and inability to perform productive labor of any sort." Hall diagnosed him with "chronic anxiety syndrome." Dean had connections to the mob and was good friends with Jack Ruby. Tivilla mentioned that she had a copy of the Warren Report, which was inscribed to her father by Ruby. She was the only one in Dean's family who had any interest in the assassination.

Tivilla sent me an email on June 13, 2022, in which she wrote, "Sgt. P.T. Dean was in charge of security of the basement on 11/24/1963. He was the key witness in the Jack Ruby trial in February of 1964, that gave the most damaging testimony, resulting in a guilty verdict. . . . He was a friend of Jack Ruby as well as many other Dallas Police Officers. Over the following 25 years until his death in August of 1988, he was plagued by his role as head of security of the basement that fateful day when Jack Ruby silenced Lee Harvey Oswald. . . . There were interviews with many Conspiracists and reputable authors that needed answers to one of the most unsolved crimes in history. My father was always accommodating with interviews and his story never changed. I, having a fascination with the JFK assassination would constantly pressure my Dad throughout the years to speak out if he indeed knew of any plot. He would always say, 'even if I did know something, I wouldn't be able to say anything.'" Tivilla went on to state, "My father was in a serious, almost fatal car accident in 1972. He was off duty on his way home from work in the very early morning around 4 a.m. He missed his exit due to heavy dense fog . . . and hit a parked caterpillar earthmover where he sustained a major head injury. . . . This forced him into early retirement from the DPD. . . . My father remembered nothing prior to the accident. My father was a plain clothed Detective at the time, no longer in uniform. At the hospital, his suit jacket and dress shirt were removed. He had just purchased a brand new pistol leather shoulder holster that was also removed. What was odd was that his suit jacket was in pristine condition. His dress shirt was tattered, dirty, and bloodied. His new leather holster had deep embedded scratches with dirt in it. What happened prior to his accident that evening has always left me bewildered."

Tivilla clarified her experiences in a July 6, 2022, email, writing, "Yes, it is correct about the bullet not seeming to be the same. It was unfortunate the bullet that was discovered by Mr. Tomlinson then turned over to my Grandfather O.P. Wright, was not allowed to be 'notched' with either of their initials which should have been protocol. As for Mr. Griffin, interrogating my father for as long as he did 'off the record' was not right. My father said he lied about so many things. When I gave you the information about my father's car accident, I fell short of saying many of us in the family highly suspected someone had attempted to cause him harm. It was nothing we could ever prove but it was always suspicious to us." She went on to say that Wright died when she was just sixteen, so she never had a chance to talk to him about it, but "there was so much chaos brought on by the Secret Service at the hospital that day, things were just awry. He was in charge of security at Parkland Hospital. . . . I believe that he lost some of his power to the 'men in black suits' in order to get JFK out of Dallas asap. I don't think that's how he wanted it but he had no choice."

Tivilla's grandmother Elizabeth Wright told the Warren Commission that both she and her husband thought shots had come from more than one direction. In an October 11, 1994, videotaped interview with researcher Mark Oakes, Elizabeth showed him a .38 special bullet which she claimed was the one her late husband had attempted in vain to give to "an FBI agent." Readers of *Hidden History* will recall that I went over the unfathomable "chain of possession" for this "magic" bullet, which no one seemed to want. Muddying the waters even further, John Connally claimed, in his autobiography, that a bullet fell to the floor when they rolled him off of a stretcher at the hospital, and "the nurse picked it up and slipped it into her pocket." A 1993 interview with District Attorney Henry Wade quoted him as saying, "Some nurse had a bullet in her hand and said this was on the gurney that Connally was on. . . . I told her to give it to the police, which she said she would. I assume that's the pristine bullet."[20] In a 2003 speech at Duquesne University, Josiah Thompson would quote a Parkland nurse who said, "I wish they would stop putting bullets on these stretchers." "Reasonable doubt" doesn't seem quite strong enough to describe the state of the "evidence" against Oswald.

Patrick Dean, as his daughter noted, was in charge of the security detail during Oswald's transfer. Dean is credited (or blamed) by almost all critics for stating that Ruby entered the Dallas Police basement via the Main Street Ramp, which was guarded by Officer Roy Vaughn. Vaughn supposedly passed three lie detector tests about this, and Dean failed his, after being allowed to write his own questions. I disagree with most critics of the Warren Report, who view Dean negatively. Gary Shaw, who knew Dean, told me that he thought he was basically good but with "a touch of larceny" about him. That would probably describe most human beings. An April 1, 1996, memo from the ARRB noted, "Dean was very bitter about his treatment by the HSCA (and the Warren Commission, too, for that matter). There was, of course, a polygraph examination in '64, which Dean asked for. He came up with a list of questions he wanted to have asked of him. Copies of these are in the collection, but the actual polygraph results themselves are not. Dean was told that he failed the polygraph, but I don't believe he ever saw the results, per se. The HSCA contacted the Dallas PD to see if they could get a hold of the polygraph test/results, but were told that they weren't around and would have been 'routinely' destroyed within a couple years of the test." It seems entirely possible then, that the much-maligned Dean may not have failed the polygraph, as has been commonly reported. Patrick Dean was the only witness the Warren Commission had who was close to being what is called in legal circles "hostile." I think Dean has been treated unfairly, by both government authorities and the research community.

On June 3, 2014, Joe Bauer commented on my blog, "I remember seeing a video clip on YouTube years ago where you clearly see and hear Sgt. Patrick Dean (head of the basement police security) being interviewed in the Dallas PD building basement by the media right after Oswald was shot there by Jack Ruby. In this he comments that when he first heard the gun shot, he gave some thought that it might have been from one of his own men shooting Oswald!" Beverly Oliver, the alleged "Babushka Woman" who can be seen filming the assassination from a plum spot, and whose footage has never publicly surfaced, claimed to have seen Patrick Dean with officer Roscoe White on the Grassy Knoll in the immediate aftermath of the shooting. White's wife Geneva (who was an employee at Ruby's Carousel Club) would later claim she'd heard her husband discussing killing Kennedy with Jack Ruby.

Roscoe White briefly caught the attention of many in the JFK assassination research community after his son Ricky came forward in 1990 to allege his father was an undercover CIA operative who had been a gunman firing from behind the picket fence on the Grassy Knoll, as well as the murderer of Dallas police officer J. D. Tippit. White was known to have served in the same Marine unit with Lee Harvey Oswald. Sam Giancana, of all people, fingered Roscoe as Tippit's killer, according to Giancana's son. Roscoe White died in a suspicious fire in 1971 at only thirty-five. The remarried Geneva Dees gave the HSCA a copy of a backyard photo her husband possessed, which was different from any in the record. According to researcher John Armstrong, "the photo had been acquired by her former husband, Roscoe White (deceased) while employed with the Dallas Police at the time of the assassination. The HSCA designated this photograph as 133-C (Dees). Mrs. Dees told the HSCA that following the assassination her husband was sent to the Oswald home in his capacity as a plainclothes detective for the photography division." Mrs. Dees is verified as having given the HSCA a "first generation print" of a backyard photograph depicting "Oswald" in a previously unseen pose, which was acquired by Roscoe White "in the course of his employment with the Dallas Police at the time of the assassination." This could very well have been the same photo of Oswald with the rifle raised above his head that Oswald's mother Marguerite would claim his widow Marina had hidden in her shoe, and then burned in an ashtray. Marguerite then testified she had flushed the remains down the toilet.[21]

The late researcher Jack White often referred to a "Roscoe White" curse. Roscoe White Jr. would shoot himself in 2013. In an early online chat room, White posted the following on October 8, 1996:

> About 6 years ago I was at the old JFK-AIC in the Dallas West End when the Roscoe White News Conference was held. At the head table in the front of the assembly space, in addition to Ricky White and Roscoe's minister, were 5 prominent JFK researchers. All were comparatively young or middle-aged and vigorous, and each presented some aspect of the Roscoe White story. These researchers were . . . Bernard "Bud" Fensterwald, Gary Shaw, Larry Howard, Joe West, Larry Ray Harris. Now, about 6 years later 4 of the 5 are dead, despite their relative youth and vigor. Coincidence? Or curse? Given their ages and good health, it would be interesting to see actuarial statistics on this, in the manner of the famed 'mysterious deaths' study. Fensterwald, who founded/funded the Washington Assassination Information Bureau and supported the AIC, became ill while dining in Dallas. He cancelled appointments and flew back to Washington, where he died of a sudden 'heart attack.' West, the Houston private investigator who later discovered the James Files story, was just fine when I talked with him on the phone on a Friday. Almost incidentally, he told me that at a recent health check-up, his doctor recommended heart by-pass surgery for the following Monday; he said he would call me after the surgery. The heart surgery was a success . . . but his breathing never resumed. He was kept alive for a while by a lung machine but died without ever regaining consciousness. Howard, the ardent JFK buff who (with Gary Shaw) co-founded the Dallas JFK Information Center, had been doing further Roscoe White research in West Texas, along with a 'former FBI agent.' While driving late at night, Larry suffered a 'stroke.' When he died, the JFK-AIC died with him. Harris,

> the young research expert on the Tippit killing, has now died in a recent auto accident (one-car?) for which we have few details as of now. Shaw, the other co-director of the AIC, is the sole survivor of this group. We hope that Gary is very very careful in the future, whether these deaths are curse, conspiracy, or coincidence. Geneva White Dees, Roscoe's widow, also died during this period. Less than a year after attending this news conference, I was attacked in my bedroom at 5 a.m. on Sunday by a nude intruder, who (unprovoked) stabbed me in the chest with an ice pick 12 times and hit me in the head, fracturing my skull and destroying my hearing (right ear) and balance (permanent vertigo). At the time I was serving as a (unpaid) photo consultant to Oliver Stone in the production of JFK. I was in the hospital for 22 days with the skull fracture and collapsed lung, for four days near death. Coincidence? Conspiracy? Or Roscoe White curse?

Geneva White Dees was only fifty when she died in 1991.

One of the more interesting JFK assassination file releases during the Trump administration was an April 6, 1977, FBI report, recounting how on March 2, 1977, Dallas IRS Intelligence Chief Robert J. Potrykus, had hand delivered a letter to Ted Gunderson, Special Agent in Charge of the Dallas FBI office. Gunderson became a real renegade in later years, and was well known to conspiracy researchers for his work on a variety of important issues. The FBI Report stated that Arlen Fuhlendorf of the Dallas Intelligence Division had received information from a confidential informant that "on the morning of the assassination, Ruby contacted him and asked if he would 'like to watch the fireworks.' He was with Jack Ruby and standing at the corner of the Postal Annex Building facing the Texas School Book Depository Building at the time of the shooting. Immediately after the shooting, Ruby left and headed back toward the area of the Dallas Morning News building." Fuhlendorf would reveal his informant to be Bob Vanderslice. After being contacted by the FBI, Vanderslice came up with a ridiculous story about bumping his lip, which was cancerous, and then didn't show up for his scheduled appointment with the Bureau. Vanderslice had also told Fuhlendorf that he'd been arrested himself at the time Ruby shot Oswald, and got to know him better in the Dallas County Jail. The report details the futile efforts of the FBI to reach Vanderslice by phone, and how when they visited his home, "no one could be located at the residence." The story appears to end there. The then seventy-eight-year-old Fuhlendorf was tracked down by a typically skeptical mainstream reporter in November 2017, after the file was released, and laughed, "At the time I wrote it, I didn't believe the information in it." The article revealingly notes, "The special agent was always a Warren Commission Report man and believed Oswald acted alone." It is also stated, without comment or explanation, that Vanderslice "died in August 1978 while out on parole."[22]

Another interesting file released in 2017 was a November 27, 1963, memo to FBI Director J. Edgar Hoover, about an anonymous call a British newspaper had received, in the moments *before* JFK was assassinated, about "some big news" from the United States. Written by notorious CIA counterintelligence chief James Jesus Angleton, the memo read, "The British Security Service (MI-5) has reported that at 1805GMT on 22 November an anonymous telephone call was made in Cambridge, England, to the senior reporter of the Cambridge News. The caller said only that the Cambridge News reporter should call the American Embassy in London for some big news and then hung up," A *Cambridge News* reporter called the memo "completely jaw-dropping," but as might be expected the paper had no record of who answered the call. The memo also noted, "The Cambridge reporter had never received a call of this kind before and MI-5 state that he is known to them as a sound and loyal person with no security record."[23]

Who really discovered CE399, the notorious "magic bullet?" Veteran researchers, including me, had long thought that Parkland Hospital orderly Darrell Tomlinson had found the bullet, when he was in the process of moving some stretchers in the emergency room. However, the record indicates this might not be true. Nathan Pool, an inspector with the Otis Elevator Company, was interviewed by the HSCA in 1978. Counsel James McDonald questioned Pool, and it evoked memories of the kind of overt padding of the record the Warren Commission employed during its "investigation." We learn here, for instance, that Security supervisor

O. P. Wright was known to all as "Pokie" and that the "boys" at Parkland were "real serious" about their ping-pong. Pool was discussing what had just happened in Dealey Plaza with his good friend Tomlinson, when one of them—Pool didn't seem to know which—leaned up against a stretcher and a bullet rolled off onto the floor. Even more oddly, Pool didn't recall whether he or Tomlinson had picked the bullet up. McDonald attempted to clarify this by asking Pool, "It's your testimony that you seem to recall that you're the one who first saw the bullet?" Pool replied, "I think so." If Pool indeed handled CE399, it makes the already confusing and undocumented chain of possession for this most crucial piece of evidence even murkier. Reading the HSCA testimony, one is struck by all the similarities to the Warren Commission. There are even those suspicious "off the record" discussions with Pool. Pool's recollection of being with Tomlinson throughout this process contradicts the orderly's Warren Commission testimony, in which he never mentioned being with Pool or anyone else. CE399, long reported to have been carried back to Washington, D.C. in the coat pocket of Secret Service agent Richard Johnsen (which I covered in more detail in *Hidden History*), was nevertheless, the record states, given to the FBI's Robert Frazier by Secret Service agent Elmer Todd, according to Frazier's Warren Commission testimony.[24] Frazier's testimony makes the chain of possession for the "magic" bullet even more dubious. When, for example, did Johnsen give it to Todd? It shouldn't surprise anyone that neither Elmer Todd, nor Richard Johnsen, nor O. P. Wright, all key figures in the bullet's laughable chain of custody, were called to testify by the Warren Commission. Even more remarkably, none of these witnesses were able to identify CE399 as the bullet they'd handled. Imagine any competent defense attorney licking their chops at the prospect of cross-examining such witnesses, and countering such evidence.

In September 2023, a new revelation from elderly Secret Service agent Paul Landis was widely publicized by the mainstream media, in conjunction with the release of his book *The Final Witness: A Kennedy Secret Service Agent Breaks his Silence after 60 Years.* Landis claimed that he found the "magic bullet" resting on top of the rear seat of the presidential limousine.[25] Instead of treating this crucial evidence appropriately—marking it with his initials and documenting the chain of possession—Landis strolled into Parkland Hospital and placed it on President Kennedy's stretcher. Recall that the official story is that CE399 wound up in John Connally's thigh and rolled out onto the stretcher at the hospital. So how did it possibly go from his thigh (Connally was in the middle seat in front of JFK) to the top of the back seat? Landis was one of the White House detail agents who were out drinking until 5 a.m. on the morning of November 22, 1963, in violation of Secret Service protocol. Landis initially testified that he thought shots had come from the front, but by the time fellow Secret Service agent Gerald Blaine published his absurd disinformation work *The Kennedy Detail* in 2010, he had learned to trust his "rational mind" and now felt he'd heard an echo. Like John Connally and several other totally uniformed witnesses, Landis didn't accept the single-bullet theory, but still nonsensically believed that Oswald acted alone.

On September 9, 2023, Robert F. Kennedy Jr. tweeted in response to Landis's severely belated disclosure: "The magic bullet theory is now dead." Oddly, ten years earlier on the fiftieth anniversary of the assassination *yet another* Secret Service agent, Sam Kinney, had also claimed to have found the "magic" bullet in the back seat of the Presidential limo, slipped it into his pocket, and put it on a stretcher, according to his neighbor, Gary Lee Loucks. On February 23, 2023, Louks passed away from unknown causes at age seventy-six. The obituary on the Johnson Arrowood Funeral Home noted that it was "sudden," but no official cause of death was listed, there or anywhere else. Landis stated, in retrospect, "There was a fear that I had done something wrong and I shouldn't talk about it." You think? I guess Landis missed any training he had on the proper handling of evidence. Landis's fellow agent Clint Hill, who has now produced a series of extremely misleading and self-serving books about that day in Dallas, tweeted out, "In my mind, there are serious inconsistencies in his various statements/stories." He was kindly asked to appear on CBS News on September 10, 2023, to further prop up the discredited Warren Report.

Vanishing Parties

Rita Musgrove was an interesting, enigmatic researcher. What happened to her is a mystery, as she literally vanished from the scene sometime in the late 1980s. In the October 22, 1982, *The Continuing Inquiry,* she described her experiences attending the exhumation and reburial at Rose Hill Cemetery of the body interred under the name Lee Harvey Oswald. A Pinkerton detective approached her and questioned her about her camera. He then offered to get close-ups of the grave from all angles for her, if she agreed to immediately leave afterward. This was fine with her. When Musgrove went to get her film developed, she discovered that the helpful detective had held his thumb over the camera lens on all the pictures he took. As Musgrove noted, "What were they trying to cover-up?" There are intriguing mentions of Musgrove in Harold Weisberg's archives at Hood College. In one document, Weisberg described getting a late-night phone call from Musgrove, who had been close to Penn Jones and Roger Craig. Weisberg writes of Musgrove's claim that she'd experienced "violence and violent talk" from Jones in the past. There is also a mention of Musgrove needing bodyguards provided by Craig on a trip to the airport, where she'd previously been "beaten up . . . losing teeth, etc." Roger Craig acknowledged Musgrove, in a January 7, 1972, letter to Penn Jones, for her "great job in editing" his manuscript *When They Kill a President.* Weisberg sent a lengthy letter to Musgrove on May 20, 1987, which revolves around the petty quarrels that have always plagued the research community. A June 14, 1987, long reply from Musgrove discusses a painful blood clot in her right hand, and she fiercely defends Ed Tatro, who Weisberg was clearly turning against in his customary fashion. In an October 7, 1991, response to Matt Flower-Smith (name is pretty illegible), Wesiberg notes, "I do not have Rita Musgrove in my Rolodex. I suppose that when she moved to Texas, I heard from her only by phone." The last word on Musgrove appears to be when Ed Tatro (evidently back in his good graces) asked Harold Weisberg, at the end of a letter dated December 20, 1993, "Do you have any addresses/phone #s, of anyone, friend, family members, daughter, of Rita Musgrove?"

In the January 1983 issue of *The Continuing Inquiry,* which happened to feature a cover story by me (my first published work), Rita Musgrove wrote an article titled "Introduction to *Diary of an ex-Dallas Deputy—Roger Craig.*" In it, she stated that this story would be told "in this newsletter over the next few months." Musgrove clarified that these were Roger Craig's words, and she was simply sharing the work in his honor. At the bottom of the article is the note, "The first segment of *Diary of an ex-Dallas Deputy—Roger Craig* to begin in the next month's issue of *The Continuing Inquiry*." There was never another installment of Craig's diary, and Rita Musgrove's name never appeared again in *The Continuing Inquiry*, which ceased publication in August 1984. Author and filmmaker Steve Cameron verified for me that this diary of Craig's, which appears to have disappeared after Rita Musgrove died (although rumors persist she might have given a copy or copies to someone in the research community) was separate from the manuscript he wrote entitled *When They Kill a President.*

I've never spoken to or communicated with Ed Tatro. But he appears to exemplify the kind of personalities that dominate the research field. No wonder he and Weisberg—arguably the king of difficult personalities—inevitably clashed. I asked two different fellow researchers to broach the subject of Rita Musgrove with Tatro, figuring he'd know what happened to her if anyone did. He told one of them, "It is not my intention to discuss Rita Musgrove with anyone." In a July 10, 2022, phone conversation with Steve Cameron, who has worked diligently with Roger Craig Jr. to expose the full extent of the horrific blowback Deputy Roger Craig received for telling the truth, he shared an illuminating incident about Tatro. During a November 2018 JFK assassination research conference in Dallas, Tatro approached Cameron and Roger Craig Jr., and exclaimed, "They murdered her!" in reference to Rita Musgrove. When Cameron asked who "they" were, Tatro replied, "Penn Jones and the others." I asked Gary Shaw about all this during a phone conversation on July 11, 2022, and he said he'd only met Rita and didn't really know her well. However, he did mention that it was his impression that Roger Craig and Rita were involved in some kind of close relationship. Gary thought that the relationship appeared to have driven a wedge between Craig and his good friend Penn Jones.

Gary Shaw, who has been very helpful to me, found the Find a Grave listing for Rita Joysette Musgrove, who died at age forty-nine on either February 15 or February 17, 1988 (the dates differed on two sources). Adding to the intrigue, her husband Robert Wayne Musgrove died a few months later, on May 31, 1988. Gary would tell me that he could find nothing more on the husband, which he found "puzzling." Digging deeper into Harold Weisberg's Hood College archives, I found Weisberg talking about Rita calling him late at night (it's unclear if this is a different call than the one mentioned previously), to complain about Penn Jones insisting she come to Dallas for a showing by Robert Groden of assassination films. Musgrove seemed frightened of Jones, and disenchanted with the research community in general. She mentioned Roger Craig's diary, which she possessed, and told Weisberg that Penn Jones "wants it." Rita also seemed especially wary of Mary Ferrell, as many have been over the years. Ferrell was in the middle of the research community, but had openly opposed John F. Kennedy. The suspicions about her and allegations against her are too numerous to cite in this book.

Finding out what happened to Rita Musgrove became something of a personal quest for me. Despite the yeoman work of Chris Graves, Gary Shaw, Steve Cameron, the Palmer, Texas Historical Association, the funeral home in Palmer, Texas that was given the records of the now defunct business that buried Rita, both the Palmer, Texas police department and sheriff's office, the caretaker for the Palmer Cemetery where both Rita and her husband are buried, the Ellis County, Texas clerk's office, an archivist with the Ellis County public library system, and several genealogy researchers, I was unable to find out anything further about the circumstances of either Rita or her husband's deaths. The difficulties involved only reinforced my suspicions that she was murdered, and that her husband's death shortly afterward was related in some way to hers.

Steve Cameron published Roger Craig's personal memoir of the assassination, *When They Kill a President,* under the new title, *The Patient Is Dying,* in July 2020. I was deeply honored to be asked to write the Preface (Steve also included Rita Musgrove's original first installment in *The Continuing Inquiry* as the Introduction.) In an April 9, 1975, letter to researcher Ed Tatro, Craig had mentioned a heretofore unknown (and still unseen) photograph of the man he, and several other disparate witnesses, saw running down the slope outside the TSBD, and entering a Rambler, shortly after the assassination. All of the witnesses claimed the man looked like Oswald. "As for the man running down the grassy knoll and the station wagon," Craig wrote, "Dick Sprague has pictures of this as well as the clock showing what time 12:44 P.M. I saw them in New York. Why he doesn't show them I will never understand." This is the only reference I know to such a tantalizing photo, which if it exists has never been published, in the record. I interviewed Steve and Roger Craig Jr. several times, and there can be no question that the senior Craig was a murder victim, like so many others connected to this case, and not a suicide (which his friend Penn Jones, oddly enough, believed). The record is replete with references to other photographs and home movies that seemingly captured crucial moments in the assassination, which have never been seen and have vanished down the memory hole. Harold Weisberg wrote an entire volume about missing film, *Photographic Whitewash.* What happened to Bob Croft's photo? Croft took three photos of the motorcade from a plum viewing point, and then snapped a fourth, "taken simultaneously with the shot that killed the president," as he told author Richard Trask. Croft dutifully gave his pictures to the FBI and the Secret Service, but when they returned them, the one taken during the shooting was a "complete blank," with the explanation being that his camera had "malfunctioned" at that moment.[26]

There are so many forgotten witnesses who once offered intriguing information. Veteran Air Force pilot Ben Phelper tried to notify the FBI that Secret Service agent Howard W. "Skip" Chilton had told him JFK was going to be killed in Dallas. The person who answered the phone for the Bureau told Phelper, "You are a kook!" According to Penn Jones, Phelper was subsequently thrown in jail for a being a subscriber to *Penthouse* magazine![27] Ruth Hallmark, who worked across the street from the TSBD, for the Miller-Randazzo Company in the then John Deere building, claimed she'd seen Lee Harvey Oswald and Jack Ruby together in her building on November 21, 1963. Her son, Milton Hallmark, called the FBI on March 11, 1967, to report this. On March 20, Mrs. Hallmark was interviewed by the FBI. In an FBI report dated March 27, 1967, it was detailed how she'd witnessed four men, none of them employees of her company, arriving separately on the third floor. The man who resembled Oswald asked to use the phone, but then left before attempting to make a call. After the assassination, with the faces of both Ruby and Oswald familiar to them, she discussed the incident with her coworker Thelma Marical, but hesitated to come forward because she was "uncertain about this." Hallmark also described seeing smoke coming out of one of the upper floor windows of the TSBD following the shots. The FBI report disclosed that Hallmark's son had contacted Jim Garrison's office, and they had promised to get back to them. The FBI also contacted Marical, who informed them she hadn't been watching the motorcade because "she was not an admirer of President Kennedy." Marical contradicted Hallmark, saying she hadn't seen any strange men, and had never discussed the matter with her. She stressed that the women had been merely coworkers, not friends.

House Select Committee on Assassinations

After talking with Sprague I was now certain he planned to conduct a strong investigation and I was never more optimistic in my life. . . . The Kennedy assassination would finally get the investigation it deserved and an honest democracy needed.

—Gaeton Fonzi[28]

Although I was still a teenager while lobbying Congress to reopen the Kennedy case, I was already becoming jaded and cynical. The aides to the "representatives" we spoke and met with (no real member of Congress was about to directly speak with radicals like us), clearly had no knowledge of, and less interest in, the assassination. When the HSCA was finally established, they didn't hire a single one of the citizen researchers who'd been responsible for raising all the public doubts, as consultants. However, I began to hear good things about the HSCA's Chief Counsel, Richard A. Sprague. Gaeton Fonzi, an HSCA staff investigator who had previously worked with renegade Senator Richard Schweiker on the Senate Select Committee on Intelligence, stated, "Sprague was known as tough, tenacious and independent. There was absolutely no doubt in my mind when I heard of Sprague's appointment that the Kennedy assassination would finally get what it needed: a no-holds-barred, honest investigation. Which just goes to show how ignorant of the ways of Washington both Sprague and I were."

The entire scope of the HSCA investigation was turned on its ear with the forced departure of Richard Sprague, and the insertion of Robert

Blakey as Chief Counsel and Staff Director. The fact that the day Sprague was pressured into resigning just happened to be the day after key witness George DeMohrenschildt was found dead in Florida is one of those cosmic "coincidences" veteran researchers are accustomed to. Blakey immediately fired Robert Tannenbaum and other Sprague loyalists. Blakey had acknowledged the failure of the Warren Commission with his comment, "To see how poor this was done . . . has been the single most soul-shattering experience that I've ever had." However, he would callously dismiss protests about the onerous fifty-year restriction on the release of HSCA files by explaining that critics would have access to them "if they are historians and if they live long enough." Blakey made no effort to hide his bias, declaring, "Look, I have no doubt that Lee Harvey Oswald killed the President. Oswald did it, it's an open-and-shut case. I should be a prosecutor with evidence like that in every case."[29] HSCA records are far more difficult to research than those of the Warren Commission. As bad as they were, the Warren Commission's testimony is all available. I have run into many examples of interesting witnesses whom reports indicate "talked" to the HSCA, but for which there are no publicly available records. What is publicly available of the HSCA's "investigation" seems almost entirely limited to Oswald's alleged associates: anti-Castro renegades, Soviet defector Yuri Nosenko, etc. Like most of the Warren Commission testimony, it is tedious and packed with irrelevant information.

Warren Commission counsel Burt Griffin testified before the HSCA. To be more accurate, he read a very long and boring statement into the record. He was served some softball questions, many by his "good friend" Chairman Louis Stokes. Naturally, he wasn't asked about Sgt. Patrick Dean's allegations that he tried to pressure him into saying that Jack Ruby didn't tell him he'd entered the basement via the Main Street ramp, or state that he'd planned the murder of Oswald in advance. He certainly wasn't grilled about Dean's claim that he subtly threatened him and advised him that he was going to need some "help." During his own lengthy follow up to Griffin's statement, Stokes mentioned that the HSCA had interviewed over 1,548 witnesses. Only a relative handful of these seem to be available for the public to read. Where are the rest? Why would Blakey's very telling secrecy agreement with the CIA result in so much witness testimony remaining classified? Another HSCA witness whose testimony is readily accessible was Warren Commission chief counsel J. Lee Rankin. Rankin came off as incredibly uninformed about the assassination in general. Warren Commission members Gerald Ford, John J. McCloy, and John Sherman Cooper gave similarly worthless, self-serving testimony before the HSCA. One of the more active counsels on the Warren Commission, David Belin, served as Ford's attorney and also sat with Cooper, in an unofficial supporting role, as he testified. Cooper, as a close friend of John Connally, like the former governor, expressed his belief that he'd been hit by a separate bullet, thus discrediting the single-bullet theory and making a lone assassin impossible (tests showed conclusively that the Mannlicher-Carcano dubiously tied to Oswald was not capable of firing fast enough to account for four shots in the allotted time frame). However, like Connally, he publicly at least continued to support the nonsensical lone assassin theory. McCloy, as a real, blue-blood Deep Stater, vigorously praised the FBI, CIA, Secret Service, Dallas Police, and all the other "trained and conscientious investigators." Nicholas Katzenbach was gently questioned about his infamous November 25, 1963, memo to Bill Moyers, which bluntly revealed the government's position that "the public must be satisfied that Oswald was the assassin." Senator Christopher Dodd challenged Katzenbach a bit on the wording of this memo, but he maintained he'd meant that, if the FBI were claiming there was no conspiracy, then the public had to be shown "the facts" to demonstrate that. He did acknowledge that he could have worded the memorandum better. Dodd, a close friend of Ted Kennedy, would dissent from the HSCA's Summary of findings, clearly dubious that Oswald could have fired all the shots.

The HSCA's overt pro–Warren Commission bias is easily discernable, in all of the available testimony. They trotted out their deputy chief researcher Jacqueline Hess as a "statistical expert" to debunk all the mysterious deaths associated with this case. Hess arrogantly declared, "Our final conclusion on the issue is that the available evidence does not establish anything about the nature of these deaths that would indicate that the deaths were in some manner, either direct or peripheral, caused by the assassination of President Kennedy or by any aspect of the subsequent investigation." Hess predictably left out most of the really suspicious deaths, and included some "natural" deaths which only gained significance in light of the myriad of unnatural ones. Most incredibly, she didn't include all the recent convenient deaths of George DeMohrenschildt and other potential HSCA witnesses. Richard Charnin convincingly refuted Hess and the HSCA in an April 19, 2013, article on Lew Rockwell's website. Hess and the HSCA even defended the absurd, inconclusive cause of high-profile columnist Dorothy Kilgallen's death. Rarely reported is the fact that her father, James Kilgallen (who lived well into his nineties) attempted to alert the HSCA about material his daughter had placed in a safe-deposit box, and his concern for his grandson Kerry Kollmar.

The HSCA simply concluded that all of the numerous Dallas doctors and nurses who reported a huge blowout in the back of JFK's head were mistaken, since that conflicted with the official autopsy photos and x-rays, which show the back of the head to be intact. This is the position that many of the "neocons" take today in the research community. Blakey and his team misrepresented what the medical witnesses told them in their final report, which was revealed when these interviews were released to the public in 1993; like the Warren Commission, the HSCA's conclusions didn't match their evidence.

One of the few interesting HSCA witnesses whose testimony is available was Ann Ruth Moore. Her October 20, 1977 testimony has been largely ignored by researchers. Moore described seeing a similar truck to the one Julia Ann Mercer had observed, but she claimed that "It was a black truck and it had lots of writing on it and the truck had 'Jack Ruby and Honest Joe' and I remember saying to one of my co-workers: 'What in the world is Honest Joe doing out in the middle of the street in a time like this?'" Moore reiterated that Ruby's name had been on the truck, and noted "Yeah, it had 'Jack Ruby' written on there and 'Honest Joe' and we thought, I said, 'Well, that must be the same person.'" Moore estimated she'd seen the truck about fifteen minutes before the arrival of the motorcade. The sloppiness of the HSCA probe is transparent here; those interrogating Moore are merely identified as Mr. Maxwell and Mr. Day. Mr. Day is so uninformed that he at first states that the assassination "took place in February," then, "no, January," before Mr. Maxwell finally corrects him. Mary Hall corroborated this to some extent. She told the HSCA that she'd seen a truck with the writing "Honest Joe" on it park next to the TSBD sometime between 9:30 and 10:30 a.m. on the morning of the assassination. She added the fascinating tidbit that a young man exited the vehicle and took a package about five feet long and 6–8 inches wide through the side door of the building. She also reported seeing smoke coming from the railroad. While Julia Ann Mercer, who went underground out of fear for her life a long time ago, had emphasized that "I clearly stated there was no printing on the truck" to Jim Garrison, several other witnesses reported seeing an "Honest Joe's" vehicle at the same time, and in the same vicinity. Reporter Tony Zoppi declared, "We all said, here comes the parade, and it was honest Joe in his station wagon about two minutes before the parade."

A. J. Millican, whose fear after the assassination I recounted in *Hidden History,* told sheriff's deputies that he'd witnessed "a truck from Honest Joe's Pawn Shop park close to the Texas School Book Depository, then drive off five-to-ten minutes before the assassination." Millican, it should be noted, also described *eight* shots coming from different directions. It's hardly surprising that he wasn't called as a witness by either the Warren Commission or the HSCA. Millican's undated statement in Sheriff Bill Decker's records also mentions another unreported oddity: "A man standing on the South side of Elm Street, was either hit in the foot, or the ankle and fell down." Like the reports of a Secret Service agent being killed, or the mysterious pool of blood on the pergola, this was seemingly consigned to the memory hole. In a 1969 letter to Harold Weisberg, researcher Richard E. Sprague described Millican as "The guy with the thick Texas accent who told me 'I can't help ya, Podner' when I asked him about what he saw. He was standing very near the man with the umbrella, and the only nearby witness to face him." Jean Hill, one of the closest eyewitnesses to the assassination, later told Jim Marrs that she'd seen a van with "Uncle Joe's Pawn Shop" written on it, which drove past police lines in front of the TSBD. In a June 19, 1964, FBI report, witness Marilyn Willis stated that only thirty seconds or so before the motorcade arrived, "there was an old loan truck called 'Honest Joe.' He was a pawn shop operator and his old black car was painted with all kinds of signs on it and it had a great big gun mounted on top of that car. And he drove up Houston towards the Depository and pulled in behind somewhere back there and turn around and came back." "Honest Joe" was Joe Goldstein, a good friend of Jack Ruby.

The HSCA looked into the Sylvia Odio incident as well, which represented one of the most credible of all the Oswald impersonator sightings. In the HSCA's Appendix to Hearings, Volume X, the Odio incident is covered. In their report, it is stated, "One of the problems faced by the committee was Odio's negative attitude toward a governmental investigation of the Kennedy assassination. Her attitude, she said, was the result of her relationship with the Warren Commission. She expressed sharp disillusionment with the Warren Commission and said that it was obvious to her that the Commission did not want to believe her story. A committee investigator noted that her whole demeanor was 'one of sharp distrust of the government's motives. She claims she feels she was just used by the Warren Commission for their own ends and she does not want to be put in the same position." However, it was noted that "after contact was established by the committee, Odio's cooperation with the committee was excellent, and she voluntarily submitted to interviews and, subsequently, sworn testimony." Odio's testimony, like the vast majority of those questioned by the HSCA, is not available to the public. This report also mentioned Odio's psychiatrist at the time (the young woman was struggling financially, and both her parents were imprisoned in Cuba, so she had good reasons to need a therapist), Dr. Burton C. Einspruch. In reference to the three men visiting her apartment, one of them introduced as Leon Oswald, "He recalled that she told him of the visit prior to the assassination." The HSCA concluded, "It appears that Sylvia Odio's testimony is essentially credible." This report was written by the most truth-seeking member of the HSCA, Gaeton Fonzi.

There can be little doubt now that Lee Harvey Oswald was some kind of American intelligence operative. In a rare example of important, publicly available testimony taken before the HSCA, CIA accountant James Wilcott stated: "Well, it was my understanding that Lee Harvey Oswald was an employee of the Agency and was an agent." Wilcott dubbed it "the Oswald Project." Wilcott claimed that records at least once existed that would have documented Oswald's employment with the Agency. He also charged that records from a particular CIA ustation (the name of the

Tokyo Station is redacted) had been "destroyed or changed." Oswald's connection to the Agency was an open secret. Wilcott declared, "From the time I left I talked at various times, especially at parties and things like that, on social occasions, with people at headquarters and with people at my station, and we would converse about it and I used to say things like, 'What do you think about Oswald being connected with the CIA?,' and things like that." To which he'd receive the response, "Oh, well, I am sure he was." Based on discussions Wilcott had with several people at the Tokyo Station, he speculated, "I believe that Oswald was a double agent, was sent over to the Soviet Union to do intelligence work, that the defection was phony and it was set up and that I believe that Marina Oswald was an agent that had been recruited sometime before and was waiting there in Tokyo for Lee Harvey Oswald." Wilcott claimed that he heard references to Oswald being an agent from "literally dozens" of CIA employees. Mainstream media accounts dutifully focused on "several discrepancies" from Wilcott and attempted to tie him to demonized former CIA case officer Philip Agee, author of the controversial 1975 best-seller *Inside the Company: CIA Diary.*[30] Wilcott's wife Elsie had also been a CIA employee. Wilcott testified that both of them left the Agency in protest in 1966, "because we became convinced that what CIA was doing couldn't be reconciled to basic principles of democracy or basic principles of humanism." The Wilcotts have been all but forgotten, but were in fact the first CIA whistleblowers to publicly criticize the Agency. The Wilcotts were retaliated against like all whistleblowers: they received threatening phone calls, frightening notes were left under their car's windshield wipers, and their car's tires were slashed. Jim Wilcott lost both his legs when a train ran over him during a protest against the Nicaraguan Contra war.

Despite later seeming to back away from his position as a Warren Commission apologist, and even criticizing the CIA, G. Robert Blakey remained a rock solid lone nutter. In a 2003 interview with ABC News, he was asked, "40 years after the fact and 25 years after your investigation, who killed John F. Kennedy?" Without hesitation, the man who sabotaged what had the potential of being the first true investigation into the assassination, responded, "Lee Harvey Oswald killed John Kennedy. Two shots from behind. The evidence is simply overwhelming. You have to be lacking in judgment and experience in dealing with the evidence to think that Lee Harvey Oswald did not kill President Kennedy." As critic Richard E. Sprague (not to be confused with original HSCA chief counsel Richard A. Sprague) noted, "Most JFK researchers feel that the American public had been deceived once again. The HSCA reaffirmed all but one of the Warren Commission's findings, including even the famed single-bullet theory. The simplified conspiracy finding is now subject to review by the Justice Department and the FBI because it is based on very questionable acoustical evidence." Sprague went on to say, "How did the CIA turn things completely around from the 1976 days when Henry Gonzalez, Thomas Downing, Richard A. Sprague, Robert Tanenbaum, Cliff Fenton and others were pursuing the truth about the assassination, to essentially the same status as when the Warren Commission finished its work?" Because Blakey emphasized that, if there was anyone "behind" Oswald, it was some shadowy Mafia force led by Carlos Marcello, once again Americans were assured that our horribly corrupt government was not involved. Blakey has belatedly stated that had he known his CIA liaison, former Agency psychological chief George Joannides, had been involved in the psyop surrounding Oswald and anti-Cuban activists, he would not have continued in his position. "If I'd known his [Joannides'] role in 1963, I would have put Joannides under oath—he would have been a witness, not a facilitator," Blakey self-righteously declared.[31] In a 2003 addendum to his statements that appeared in PBS' *Frontline*'s 1993 disinfo piece, Blakey declared, "We also now know that the Agency set up a process that could only have been designed to frustrate the ability of the committee in 1976–79 to obtain any information that might adversely affect the Agency. Many have told me that the culture of the Agency is one of prevarication and dissimulation and that you cannot trust it or its people. Period. End of story. I am now in that camp."

HSCA investigators allegedly talked to Dallas Police Captain Will Fritz, but according to Gary Mack, before he devolved into a neocon, "their report has been withheld." In an issue of his monthly newsletter *Coverups!* Mack also reported that "the wife of one of Fritz's best friends recently told researchers that Fritz had secretly recorded his Oswald interrogations." Fritz reportedly said that Oswald had admitted to being a member of the intelligence community, but feared for the safety of his family. She added that the tapes were supposedly safe.[32] This is exactly what researchers Ted Gandolfo and Robert Groden would claim in 1993. These tapes, like so many other rumored pieces of evidence, have never surfaced. While quibbling a bit about the CIA and FBI not being forthcoming with all their information on Oswald, the HSCA report concluded, "The Secret Service, the Federal Bureau of Investigation, and the Central Intelligence Agency were not involved in the assassination of President Kennedy." The HSCA, while concluding their infamous "probable conspiracy," absolved virtually every suspect ever mentioned by researchers, from the Soviet and Cuban governments, to anti-Cuban exiles, and the Mafia "as a group." The ridiculous finding of their "investigation" was that an unknown gunman fired from the Grassy Knoll, and missed. And, of course, good old Lee Harvey Oswald was still responsible for all the shots that struck Kennedy and Connally.

Richard A. Sprague famously arranged a presentation of Richard E. Sprague's impressive photo collection early on, for the HSCA staff. When he was finished word was he had convinced virtually all of the staff lawyers there that the single-bullet theory was impossible. The original chief counsel of the HSCA told those in attendance, "I don't want anyone to leave unless I leave. And I don't plan on leaving." A series of persistent disinformation pieces and attacks in the Mockingbird press had the desired effect of dividing and conquering both Sprague and Chairman Henry Gonzalez. Gonzalez and Sprague each eventually were pressed into resigning, and the rest is history. While the ARRB ordered over 2,000 of the HSCA files to be declassified in the 1990s, they were routinely stonewalled, and many remain classified. To knowledgeable researchers, the HSCA was a monumental waste of time, and as an increasingly jaded young man, I realized that expecting our "representatives" to expose the truth about one of the Deep State's most significant high-profile crimes was no more of a solution than establishing another "blue ribbon" commission.

It is instructive to look at what happened to some political figures connected to the HSCA or the Senate Committee chaired by Frank Church, which first exposed the assassination plots against Fidel Castro. The Church Committee was one of the most valuable ever established by Congress. It was 1975, and the post-Watergate ardor for reform was a dominant force in the Democratic Party. The Church Committee exposed the fact that the FBI had sent Martin Luther King a letter, basically demanding that he kill himself. They also disclosed that Black Panther Fred Hampton's bodyguard William O'Neal was an FBI undercover agent who, days before his murder, had provided the Bureau with an apartment floor plan that included an "X" to mark the location of Hampton's bedroom, where most of the shots would be fired. In an early (and seldom publicized) instance of "cancel culture," the Committee found that both the CIA and the FBI had sent anonymous letters to employers of political dissidents, urging that they be fired. A subcommittee, tasked to look into the performance of the intelligence agencies in connection with the JFK assassination, was chaired by Senators Gary Hart and Richard Schweiker. The final report of the Committee charged, "Some of the so-called security objections of the CIA were so outlandish they were dismissed out of hand. The CIA wanted to delete reference to the Bay of Pigs as a paramilitary operation, they wanted to eliminate any reference to CIA activities in Laos, and they wanted the Committee to excise testimony given in public before the television cameras. But on other more complex issues, the Committee's necessary and proper concern for caution enabled the CIA to use the clearance process to alter the Report to the point where some of its most important implications are either lost, or obscured in vague language." It is worth noting that the bulk of the Church Committee records remain unavailable to the public. Hart publicly called for a new Senate investigation into the assassination of President Kennedy. After a strong presidential run in 1984, Hart was widely considered the front runner for the 1988 Democratic presidential nomination. His campaign was famously derailed by an extramarital affair with the much younger Donna Rice. Media hit pieces included a story in the September 1987 *Vanity Fair,* which maintained that Hart was on a "collision course" to crash his own hopes with his personal behavior, which the magazine alleged had caused all of his 1984 campaign staff to turn their backs on him.

Hart's cohort Richard Schweiker memorably called the Warren Report "a house of cards," and publicly charged that the FBI, CIA, and the Johnson administration may have all been involved in a cover-up. During his nearly successful 1976 presidential run, Ronald Reagan named Schweiker as his vice-presidential nominee. Schweiker was said to be shocked at his selection, as he didn't know Reagan at all. Could the choice have been influenced by Reagan's alleged interest in the JFK assassination, which I discussed in *Hidden History*? Schweiker left the Senate in 1981, and after serving for two years as Reagan's Secretary of Health and Human Services, he largely disappeared from the political world. He died at eighty-nine in 2015. Frank Church ran for president in 1976 and won several primaries. After being defeated for reelection in 1980, Church left politics and died at only fifty-nine in 1984. Church's comments on NSA spying predated Edward Snowden by decades, when he said, "I know the capacity that is there to make tyranny total in America, and we must see to it that this agency and all agencies that possess this technology operate within the law and under proper supervision, so that we never cross over that abyss. That is the abyss from which there is no return."[33] Thomas Downing, who was one of the first voices in Congress to demand a new investigation and the brief initial Chairman of the HSCA, retired in 1976. One can only imagine how different a committee chaired by someone who said, "I am firmly convinced, I am sincerely convinced, that more than one person was shooting at President Kennedy in Dallas that day. It is so obvious to me" might have been. Inexplicably, Downing would label Oliver Stone's 1991 film *JFK* "implausible."[34]

There are some interesting items in another rarely examined document—the CIA's timeline of events for November 22, 1963. Marina Oswald is quoted as having said, on November 22, that Oswald left before she awoke that morning. The same day, Ruth Paine also testified that she'd been asleep when he left the house. On November 28, Marina contradicted herself, stating that Oswald got up at 7 a.m.; she talked to him and said "Good-bye." Two days later, Marina added the essential change that she was nursing the baby when she woke her husband up at 7 a.m. Also on November 30, Ruth Paine altered her testimony almost identically, now stating that Marina was nursing the baby when Oswald got up at 6:30 a.m. At Clay Shaw's trial, Marina's steadfastly inconsistent testimony was, "I was awake but I did not get up because he told me to stay in bed."[35]

A truly strange discrepancy is mentioned in the CIA's timeline of events, regarding Book Depository employee Frankie Kaiser. It is stated that Kaiser was "absent from the TSBD on Thursday and Friday with a toothache (At the time of the assassination he is at the Baylor Dental School). The TSBD records show that Kaiser is working 8 hours both of these days. TSBD superintendent says that Kaiser was not working either day. Kaiser is an order clerk and truck driver. He finds Oswald's jacket on the first floor and his clipboard on the sixth floor several days after the assassination." Kaiser didn't find Oswald's clipboard until December 2.

Of even greater interest is a little-quoted comment Marina provided to researcher A.J. Weberman, coauthor (with the late Michael Canfield) of the underappreciated 1975 book *Coup d'Etat in America: The CIA and the Assassination of John F. Kennedy*, in 1994. "Do you think Hemming is making these statements right now only to add some importance to himself?" Marina told Weberman. "We're all here to make ourselves look a little better than we really are. The answer to the Kennedy assassination is with the Federal Reserve Bank. Don't underestimate that. It's wrong to blame it on Angleton and CIA per se only. This is only one finger of the same hand. The people who supply the money are above the CIA. I never heard the name Gerry Patrick Hemming until Garrison [the New Orleans District Attorney who investigated the assassination of former President John Kennedy] told me. I never heard Lee mention that name. He never mentioned anything. He lived double life, know what I mean? Do you think I would be giving this interview right now if I knew? I inherited the mess, but the tragedy is not only mine, but the whole nation's." Hemming is one of several shadowy characters with an Oswald-like intriguing background. He formed the anti-Castro group Interpen (Intercontinental Penetration Force) in 1961. Interpen has been connected to the anti-Castro Cuban exiles in Florida, funded by the CIA in Florida during the early 1960s. Members included Oswald lookalike William Seymour and Loran Hall, who as one of Jim Garrison's witnesses would implicate yet another of these endless murky figures, Edgar Eugene Bradley, in the JFK assassination. Bradley was one of several people Garrison attempted unsuccessfully to extradite from other states. Beleaguered Dallas Police Deputy Roger Craig would identify the extreme right-winger Bradley as the Secret Service imposter he encountered on the Grassy Knoll shortly after shots had been fired. Bradley is often confused with the similarly named Eugene Hale Brading (aka Jim Braden), a man with an extensive criminal record for the likes of burglary and embezzlement, who was arrested for "acting suspiciously" in the Dal-Tex Building in the immediate aftermath of the assassination. Brading had links to David Ferrie among others, and was interviewed by the LAPD in 1968, about his curious presence in Los Angeles on the night Robert F. Kennedy was shot.

A Secret Service memo on "the measures employed to effect security of the President's car," signed November 27, 1963, by Charles E. Taylor and Harry W. Goiglein, details how the presidential limo was transported back to the White House garage. The report states, "What appeared to be bullet fragments were removed from the windshield and the floor rug in the rear of the car." Reflecting the thoroughness of this "investigation," the next paragraph notes, "A meticulous examination was made of the back seat of the car and the floor rug, and no evidence was found." Since the Secret Service cleaned the interior of the limousine—which was *the* crime scene—as it sat outside Parkland Hospital, such an examination was largely worthless. Most interesting was the statement, "of particular note was the small hole just left of center in the windshield from what appeared to be bullet fragments were removed." Neither the official narrative nor the neocon "researchers," acknowledge any bullet hole in the windshield, just some fragmentation. This memo supports the several credible witnesses who reported seeing a hole in the windshield.

One of the more interesting pieces of testimony before the Assassination Records Review Board (ARRB) was that of Steve Osborn, on November 18, 1994. Osborn shared the story of someone "who claimed to have been very near Dealey Plaza during the assassination." This claim is all the more compelling considering that there was no professional footage filmed of JFK's final motorcade through Dallas. Osborn testified, "The gentleman I spoke with proceeded to tell me he was in the Army Station in Fort Hood, in Clean, Texas. On the day of the assassination his group, a communications group, was assigned the task of observing and videotaping the presidential motorcade as it moved through the Plaza. This unit had no similar assignment in any other Texas city during the President's visit, and they were only to tape that portion of the motorcade as it proceeded through Dealey Plaza." The witness had promised to share his account on videotape, but backed out at the last minute. So Osborn was left to recall what the man had told him as best he could. "This military communications group had several cameras stationed around the Plaza. The signals from the cameras were sent back to a semi-tractor-trailer acting as a mobile studio parked a short distance from the Plaza. Each camera had a preview monitor and videotape machine associated with it inside the trailer recording the view of each camera. There was no sound recorded in this assignment," Osborn stated. "About 15 minutes after the assassination, a group of men appeared who identified themselves as FBI agents. These agents seized all the equipment used to videotape the motorcade. Each man was put on a bus which had been summoned to the scene and they were all driven back to their base. Upon their arrival, they were simply told to forget it."

In his invaluable book *In the Eye of History: Disclosures in the JFK Assassination Medical Evidence,* William Matson Law interviewed the leading players connected to the autopsy of the president. Dennis David recounted typing a memorandum for "a government agent," on the evening of November 22, in which he stated that four bullet fragments had been removed from Kennedy's head. Quoting Law, "After the memorandum was typed, the agent took all copies of it along with the carbon paper, removed the typewriter ribbon, and said, "Forget I was here." David held these fragments in his hand, and they weren't mentioned in the autopsy report.[36] The Warren Report describes the removal of only two fragments.

It astounds me that there is still any debate about the medical evidence in this case. The record is clear; *all* the medical personnel in Dallas described an entirely different head wound than the one which appears in the official autopsy photos and x-rays. Jerrol Custer took the x-rays at Bethesda Naval Hospital. In 1992, Custer held a news conference in Manhattan to note these differences. He pointed out that the x-rays in the record show a black hole where the right side of JFK's face should be, when in fact everyone who examined the President at Parkland Hospital testified that there was no visible damage to his face. Custer reiterated that the face was intact, as well as the forward part of his skull, which is missing in the x-rays. At the same news conference, photographer Floyd Riebe, who took the pictures of the President's body, maintained that the photos in the record do not reflect what he saw. Riebe described being sent to an admiral's office after the autopsy, where he was "warned to keep my mouth shut." He claimed, "If I were to open my mouth, I would wind up in prison." The news conference was called to rebut the recent article in the *Journal of the American Medical Association*, written by the pathologists who performed what Harold Weisberg aptly termed "an autopsy unfit for a bowery bum."[37] Custer finally opened up to researcher William Law in 1998, stating, "I realized that the government can do what they want, when they want, and as often as they want. I kept my quiet for 35 years. . . . Truthfully, the only thing I think that actually saved me was they felt that I was too low on the totem pole to worry about. . . . Later on down the line, I thought, 'Well, it's about time the truth should come out.'" Custer lost his job as an x-ray technician supervisor after the assassination, working as a security guard in Pittsburgh before dying of a heart attack in 2000.

Riebe's testimony before the ARRB was difficult to read. Basically, he took back everything he'd said at the 1992 press conference and stated that the photos represented the wounds accurately. Jeremy Gunn asked him, in very vague terms, about this discrepancy, and he replied, "Well, it was chaos in that room that night, and I just misjudged where the wounds were." Gunn, in the best Warren Commission/HSCA style, continued, "Just to make certain, has anyone asked you in any way to change your observations or to report anything different from what your recollections are?" and "Has anyone from the Review Board asked you to change your testimony or alter it?" and "Has anyone from any other Government agency asked you to change your recollections?" To each of these questions, Riebe dutifully answered, "No." Putting the exclamation point on it, Gunn summed up, "As best you understand now, that you would believe it is fair to say that the photographs accurately portray what you observed on the night of November 22nd?" Riebe meekly replied, "Yes, I would." I asked ARRB senior analyst Doug Horne about Riebe's reversal, and in an August 2, 2021, email he wrote, "Yes, I was shocked by Floyd Riebe's retraction. He ruined his own credibility, unfortunately;

that was the last thing I expected of him. There was something strange going on with him, psychologically. He overslept the day of his deposition and was not ready—either he was an alcoholic and overslept because he was stressed out and got drunk the night before, OR he was hoping to dodge it by just not showing up. We literally had to 'roust him' to get him to appear. I think he was terrified of Jeremy and I, and misinterpreted our strict neutrality in our dealings with him for 'hostility.' I think he was so scared 'of the government' that he simply flipped and denied everything he had previously said to Lifton and others, on audiotape and video. Very sad, really."

In his own quite feisty ARRB testimony, Custer described how his boss, Dr. John Ebersole, burned a paper in front of him, and replied to each of his astonished reactions to what he was seeing by admonishing him, "mind your own business." Ebersole comes off as suspect from Custer's recollections. At one point, Ebersole handed him "3 or 4" bullet fragments and instructed him to tape them to JFK's bones. When he was asked what he thought the purpose was behind this, Custer replied, "That was a good question, because I didn't understand it at the time either." Custer's testimony reminded me how, like the HSCA, the ARRB resorted to those familiar "Off the Record" intervals that the Warren Commission was famous for.

The ARRB testimony of official autopsy photographer John Stringer was interesting as well. Stringer recalled how a Secret Service agent destroyed a roll of film that the previously mentioned Floyd Riebe, who was a student assisting Stringer, had taken. Following Captain Stover's orders, Stringer gave each exposed roll of film to a waiting Secret Service agent. Stringer maintained that some of the photographs he'd taken at the autopsy were missing from the materials he viewed in 1966. He talked about giving photos of JFK's brain to the main autopsy pathologist Dr. James J. Humes, for which he didn't receive a receipt. Earl McDonald, a photographer trained by Stringer, told the ARRB that Stringer would never tell his students anything about the JFK assassination except, "They took my film away from me and I never saw it again." Stringer's recollections have been inconsistent over the years, as researchers like Doug Horne and Milicent Cranor have demonstrated. Stringer's ARRB testimony included his admission that, in reference to the autopsy being rushed and sloppy, and being asked why he didn't "object to that at all," people that object to things "don't last long." This attitude was understandable. As one of the most outspoken doctors at Parkland Hospital, Charles Crenshaw, once stated, "anyone who would go so far as to eliminate the President of the United States would surely not hesitate to kill a doctor."[38]

One of the many mysterious deaths associated with this case was that of Lt. Commander William Bruce Pitzer. Pitzer was head of the audiovisual department at Bethesda Naval Hospital. When Pitzer was called in to take film of the autopsy, he didn't return home until the following afternoon. Dennis David was close friends with Pitzer, and described dropping by his office a few days after the autopsy, where he was shown film of it. David would adamantly state that both he and Pitzer concluded, "Number one, it was our distinct impression—impression, hell, it was our opinion, actual opinion—that the shot that killed the President had to have come from the front." On October 29, 1966, Pitzer was found shot to death on the floor of the TV production studio in the National Naval Medical Center. Pitzer's family disagreed with the predictable official finding of suicide. Only a few days before his death, Pitzer told his friend Dennis David that he'd received some lucrative employment offers from major television networks. Pitzer's autopsy film, which David also viewed, has never been publicly produced and officially doesn't exist. Pitzer's wife Joyce reported being sworn to silence by Navy Intelligence officials. "They told me," she recounted to Lt. Col. Dan Marvin in a 1995 telephone conversation, "not to talk to anyone . . . the Navy intelligence [people] were here, and—at the house, and everything—and for twenty-five years, I did not really discuss it." Marvin, an elite member of the Green Berets, claimed to have been asked by the CIA to murder her husband, which he refused to do. Marvin was attacked by many neocon "researchers," who are skeptical of conspiratorial claims in any witness deaths. Pitzer's left hand was so severely mangled when his body was found, that his wedding ring could not be removed. But this claim, of course, is dismissed by neocon debunkers as well. In the eyes of the neocon researchers who now dominate the critical community, there is nothing mysterious or unexplained left in the record. And yet, they will express a belief in conspiracy.

Marvin died in 2012, while working on a book he'd titled *The Smoking Gun: The Conspiracy to Kill LCDR William Bruce Pitzer.*

Navy photographer Vincent Madonia was asked by the ARRB about White House photographer Robert L. Knudsen, who took so many iconic photos of the Kennedy White House. Madonia stated that Knudsen "may have been there that weekend (right after the assassination)." However, he seemed to instantly regret saying this, and told the interviewer, "take that out of your notes, I shouldn't have said that, I'm not sure." Knudsen's widow and adult children told the ARRB that he had received a phone call summoning him to Andrews Air Force Base, where JFK's body was arriving from Dallas, on the afternoon of the assassination. They said that Knudsen was gone for three days. When he finally returned home, he told his family that he had photographed the autopsy of President Kennedy. Like so many others, he reported being sworn to secrecy. In 1977, in an interview with *Popular Photography* magazine, Knudsen recounted photographing JFK's autopsy and called it "the hardest assignment of my life." When Knudsen testified before the HSCA, he was shown Kennedy autopsy photographs. He later told his family that these photos were fraudulent, and he wanted them to know that he'd had nothing to do with that. Strangely, despite there being no official record of Knudsen at Bethesda that night, his 1989 obituary in both the *Washington Post* and the *New York Times* mentioned him photographing the autopsy of John F. Kennedy. During their ARRB interview, the Knudsen family mentioned a publicly unknown inquiry or seminar about the assassination, which he had attended in 1988. They had the impression that it was held "on Capitol Hill." They unanimously stated that Knudsen came away from this seemingly secret event very upset, and talked about four photographs being missing, while one was "badly altered." He complained about having his first- hand recollections being challenged or contradicted. The ARRB also spoke to former government photographer Joe O'Donnell, who recalled being shown autopsy photographs of JFK by Knudsen.

Knudsen's HSCA testimony, which is actually accessible online, revealed a witness who was being as circumspect as possible. However, in detailing the metal probes he saw on Kennedy's body, depicting the bullet wounds, he testified that one of them was "right near the neck and out the back." He would clarify that the wound in the throat was "right about where the neck-tie is," while the hole in JFK's back was "six, seven inches" lower than the throat wound. This lines up perfectly with where the back wound was marked on Boswell's official autopsy face sheet, where FBI agents James Sibert and Francis O'Neill described it, where the death certificate located it, and most importantly, where the holes in Kennedy's suit and shirt reveal it to be. However, after some prodding by HSCA counsel Andy Purdy, Knudsen would state the rear wound was "about the base of the neck." Like a good soldier, Knudsen responded to Purdy's question if the photographs in evidence were inconsistent with what he saw originally, "No, not at all." Saundra Kay Spencer, who worked under Knudsen, told researcher William Law that she'd seen a photo that could only have been taken *before* any tracheotomy done in Dallas (and why would anyone take a picture at that time?) Spencer described the throat wound as "small, about thumbnail size," which is far different from the open gash seen in the official autopsy photos. Law was shocked when Spencer described seeing a photo of JFK with what appeared to be an intact brain next to him. Since much of JFK's brain was blasted out of his head, and it is *officially missing* from the official record, this is exceedingly strange.[39] Spencer, who was involved in developing the autopsy photos, flatly told the ARRB: "Between those photographs and the ones we did, there had to be some massive cosmetic things done to the President's body."

So many questions remain unanswered about one of the world's worst autopsies. On November 22, 1963, FBI agent Alan H. Belmont wrote a memo to J. Edgar Hoover's significant other Clyde Tolson, in which he noted that he'd told Special Agent Gordon Shanklin "that Secret Service had one of the bullets that struck President Kennedy and the other is lodged behind the president's ear." Like the receipt for a "missile" that FBI agents James Sibert and Francis O'Neill described in their report, this bullet cannot be accounted for in the official record. According to William C. Sullivan, the FBI official who would die in a highly suspicious hunting accident before being able to testify to the HSCA, Belmont was heavily involved in the FBI's campaign against Martin Luther King. The ARRB published the affidavit of Leonard D. Saslaw, PhD, who claimed to have overheard Dr. Pierre Finck complaining loudly, while dining with two officers in the Armed Forces Institute of Pathology lunchroom. This was during the week after the assassination. Saslaw testified that he heard Finck "complain that he had been unable to locate the handwritten notes that he had taken during the autopsy on President Kennedy." Finck declared, "with considerable irritation," that the notes had suspiciously disappeared during his post-autopsy cleanup.

Verifying what Custer, Riebe, and others have testified to over the years is a November 26, 1963, memo from Captain J. H. Stover, the Commanding Officer at U.S. Navy Medical School, to Captain John Ebersole, the radiologist mentioned so frequently in Jerrol Custer's ARRB testimony. The memo advises, "You are reminded that you are under verbal orders of the Surgeon General, United States Navy, to discuss with no one events connected with your official duties on the evening of 22 November–23 November 1963." Stover further wrote, "You are warned that infraction of these orders makes you liable to Court Martial proceedings under appropriate articles of the Uniform Code of Military Justice." All these orders of secrecy, like the classification of so many records related to the assassination, and the threats so many witnesses reported receiving, contradict the official narrative that Kennedy was killed by a lone nut. Why would anyone be sworn to secrecy, or any data withheld, or any witness threatened, if the crime was committed by an unconnected individual, who was dead himself? What "national security" interests would be associated with a "little shit," to quote best-selling author Stephen King, who was earning minimum wage stocking books?

The aborted plot to kill JFK in Chicago, only a few weeks before Dallas, featured another "three namer" patsy, Thomas Arthur Vallee. The FBI reported on a strange incident where an unnamed individual from New York was arrested by Chicago Police on November 2, 1963, for a minor traffic infraction. A December 2, 1963, FBI report noted, "A search of this individual's automobile resulted in the finding of numerous rounds of ammunition and a weapon, make and caliber unknown." This information came from Bill Corley, a news manager with NBC, who got it from "an unrecalled source." Corley's interest was aroused after the assassination, when he realized that on November 2, President Kennedy had been attending a college football game at Chicago's Soldier Field. Corley assigned reporter Len O'Connor to investigate further. Luke Hester, another NBC employee, was asked to check on the license plates. The FBI report states matter-of-factly, "inasmuch as this registration plate had some connection with LEE .HARVEY OSWALD and the assassination." Hester would inform Cooley that "the FBI in New York—had placed a 'freeze' on any information concerning this registration." By "freeze" Corley explained he meant that no information could be given out concerning this registration because "the FBI had requested New York authorities to keep the Information confidential."

Thomas Arthur Vallee was the subject of a December 4, 1963, FBI report. Vallee served in the Marines from 1949 to 1952. He reenlisted in 1955 and was discharged in 1956 with a physical disability. There are large redactions in the report. The FBI also states that Vallee's middle name is actually spelled "Auther," and his birth date should be changed from 1931 to 1933. Details of Vallee's being psychologically tested, and found to be abnormally nervous, hyperactive, and prone to paranoia are in this report. Another FBI report, dated December 20, 1963 (the date and most of the text is very difficult to read, in the tradition of too many JFK assassination-related FBI documents), mentioned that a Secret Service investigation had determined that the only arrest made on November 2 in Chicago, "regarding protection of President Kennedy," was that of Thomas Vallee. Vallee would appear in a Chicago court on January 14, 1964, on a charge of "unlawful use of weapon." Vallee was found guilty, but the FBI document is nearly illegible, making it difficult to obtain more details. A more legible FBI report, dated February 2, 1964, reveals that Vallee was "placed under local court jurisdiction, for one year and finding of guilty withdrawn." Someone from the FBI called the Secret Service in Chicago, warning of a very credible assassination plot. In writer Edwin Black's words, "This information came from an informant named Lee." Black wrote that Vallee had been declared an "extreme paranoid schizophrenic" by military doctors. Like Oswald, Vallee had been assigned by the Marines to a U-2 base in Japan. Oswald served at Atsugi; Vallee at Camp Otsu. Vallee trained an anti-Castro guerilla group in Long Island. Oswald and Vallee even bore a physical resemblance to each other. In another parallel to Oswald, Vallee had been recently hired by a warehouse—the IPP Litho-Plate at 625 West Jackson Boulevard—overlooking the motorcade route in Chicago. (In a strange turn of events following the assassination in Dallas, the stretch of freeway one block away from West Jackson would be renamed the "Kennedy Expressway.") Police had found a hunting knife in open sight on Vallee's front passenger seat, and 750 rounds of ammunition in the trunk. We learn here that the legendary Sherman Skolnick, who founded the Citizens' Committee to Clean up the Courts, had been looking into the Vallee case early on, even filing Freedom of Information Act requests, which were ignored.

In 1970, Edwin Black was commissioned by *Atlantic Monthly* to write a story about the Chicago plot to kill Kennedy. Black stated, "When I asked the wrong questions and came too close to sensitive information, I was followed and investigated by a Defense Intelligence Agency (DIA) operative . . . the harassment didn't end until after my apartment was broken into. No valuables were taken. But all my files were obviously and clumsily searched." Black's research on the plot was eventually published in the November 1975 *Chicago Independent.* Black found "strong evidence that four men were in Chicago to assassinate John F. Kennedy on November 3, 1963." In Chicago, there was even a difficult forced turn for Kennedy's limousine, much as there would be in Dallas. There was also the potential for a triangulation of gunfire. When Black talked to a few agents from the Secret Service, who had knowledge of the thwarted plot against the president, they told him they didn't recall anything about a conspiracy. Vallee was never questioned in regards to the events in Dallas.

There were other tantalizing gems, like the fact a passenger named J. Oswalt was on a November 12, 1963, flight from Mexico City to Chicago. Black would be told by Freedom of Information officer Robert Goff that the Secret Service could locate no records of any teletype sent regarding a warning about a plot to kill JFK in Chicago. They also claimed to have found no records of the surveillance and interrogation of two other suspects believed to be involved in the attempted conspiracy. Goff would eventually tell Black, "We're not going to give you this information so you may as well give up." He then spoke with FBI agent Thomas B. Coll, in charge of press relations. Coll at first refused to check on anything, blurting out, "I remember that case. Some people were picked up. And I'm telling you it wasn't ours. That was strictly a Secret Service affair, that whole Soldiers Field matter was a Secret Service affair." At length, Coll broke things off with, "You'll get no more out of me. I've said as much as I'm going to on that subject. Get the rest from the Secret Service." Black went undercover to track Thomas Vallee down in a ramshackle trailer outside of Houston. He pretended to be recruiting for a right-wing anti-Castro group. Vallee explained that, on November 2, 1963, "Soldiers Field. The plot against John F. Kennedy. I was arrested." He admitted everything about the guns in his possession, but adamantly denied any intention to harm JFK. In fact, Vallee claimed he'd been framed because of his open hostility toward Kennedy. Interestingly, the Chicago Secret Service was monitoring the movements of Eddie Brokaw, the alias Black had adopted. Afterward, Black called the agent who'd made inquiries, Tom Hampton, and demanded to know how he was aware of a fictitious person who'd only been created a few days earlier. Hampton snapped back, "Well he's been asking a lot of sensitive questions and we want to know why." Though no details about his death seem available, Vallee died at fifty-five in 1988.

Despite the formation of the Assassination Records and Review Board (ARRB), thanks to renewed interest in the subject generated by Oliver Stone's 1991 film *JFK,* many records relating to the assassination remain classified. Researcher Bill Kelly compiled a list of the most important withheld records on his blog. Kelly had asked ARRB chairman John Tunheim if anyone was looking for missing items like the Air Force One tapes from November 22, 1963, and Tunheim merely shrugged and looked at researcher John Newman, who responded. "You are." The unedited AF1 transmission tapes from the afternoon of the assassination could contain significant information. As Kelly wrote, "Two different edited versions of these tapes are available, one on cassette tapes released by the LBJ Library and a reel to reel version discovered among the personal effects of General Clifton. The White House Communications Agency (WHCA) is responsible for these tapes. As Vince Salandria has pointed out "there was a transcript of the complete AF1 radio transmissions in the LBJ White House, where two reporters—T. H. White and William Manchester were permitted to read it and quote from it. They recount conversations not on either of the extant tapes." It would be interesting to see the files of HSCA initial chief counsel Richard A. Sprague, who took them with him when he was fired. The ARRB had carelessly confused Sprague with assassination researcher/author Richard E. Sprague, who had produced extensive files of his own. Sprague's HSCA files, which belong to the public, at last report were housed in Sprague's old Philadelphia office. KGB records relating to Oswald's time in Russia were obtained by author Norman Mailer, but are now in the possession of his former associate, sensationalist lone-nutter Lawrence Schiller, who refused to turn them over to the ARRB. Perhaps most absurdly of all, the pink suit Jackie Kennedy wore on November 22, 1963, remains in an acid-free, temperature-controlled box at the National Archives, and will be unavailable for public view until at least the year 2103. Caroline Kennedy Schlossberg donated the clothing to the Archives in 2003, with the stipulation that they not "dishonor the memory" of her parents or "cause any grief or suffering to members of their family," by permitting the common riffraff to view it.[40]

Kelly also notes the startling fact that the Office of Naval Intelligence employed undercover agents working in Jack Ruby's Carousel Club. ONI Director Rufus Taylor's assassination files are not available, either. In the lone surviving document, the undercover agents reported that Oswald had been seen in the club. As if utterly failing to protect JFK in Dallas wasn't enough, Kelly points out that, "The Secret Service destroyed many records, including the Advance Reports for the Tampa trip after the JFK Act was passed by Congress." Why is Robert F. Kennedy's date book for 1963 missing from the Kennedy Library? Oswald's court records in New Orleans were "accidentally destroyed" when they were sent to be microfilmed. In a June 15, 1978, memo, we learn that the HSCA was told by Roger Denk of the Defense Intelligence Agency, that "the DIA has destroyed all its files which might relate to the assassination." The CIA destroyed a tape of a man identifying himself as Oswald, while calling the Russian Embassy in Mexico City on October 1, 1963. The tape was "routinely" erased, according to Richard Helms. In a November 23, 1963, recorded phone conversation with Lyndon Johnson, FBI Director J. Edgar Hoover said, "We have up here the tape and the photograph of the man who was at the Soviet embassy, using Oswald's name. That picture and the tape do not correspond to this man's voice, nor to his appearance." It seems likely that CIA Mexico City Station Chief Win Scott kept the tape, until his sudden death in 1971 (alleged heart attack, no autopsy performed.) As author Jefferson Morley wrote, "The CIA found material evidence related to Kennedy' assassination in Win Scott's home office, hid that evidence from all official investigations over the course of twenty four years, and then, when Michael Scott, started asking for his father's effects, destroyed it."[41]

Why does the White House Situation Room Incoming and Outgoing Message Log for November end abruptly on the morning of November 22, 1963? Records of FBI wiretaps on Oswald in custody, and on the phones of Ruth and Michael Paine, Marina and Robert Oswald, are all missing. Also unavailable are the Secret Service motorcade security radio channel tapes of the day of the assassination, which included Roy Kellerman's comments as the third shot was being fired, and the radios in LBJ's car. Researcher Peter Dale Scott writes about these tapes, "Early on November 22, at Love Field, [Secret Service agent, Winston] Lawson installed, in what would become the lead car, the base radio whose frequencies were used by all Secret Service agents on the motorcade. This radio channel, operated by the White House Communications Agency (WHCA), was used for some key decisions in Dealey Plaza before and after the assassination, yet its records, unlike those of the Dallas Police Department (DPD) Channels One and Two, were never made available to the Warren Commission, or any subsequent investigation. The tape was not withheld because it was irrelevant; on the contrary, it contained very significant information. The WHCA actually reports to this day on its website that the agency was 'a key player in documenting the assassination of President Kennedy.'[42] However it is not clear for whom this documentation was conducted, or why it was not made available to the Warren Commission, the House Select Committee on Assassinations, or the Assassination Records Review Board (AARB)."[43] According to John Armstrong, whose voluminous book *Harvey and Lee* has produced so much controversy in the research community, Oswald's employment records from Pfister Dental Lab have disappeared. The records from Stripling Junior High in Fort Worth, which Oswald attended in 1954, have vanished from the FBI. The FBI lost or buried all of Oswald's original New York City school records. Why are Oswald's mother Marguerite's employment records from 1955 to 1963 missing? A CIA memo dated April 5, 1972, addresses the subject of "Harvey Lee Oswald." It was curious enough that the authorities transposed Oswald's first and middle names more than once back in 1963, but could an intelligence agency possibly still be confusing Oswald's name a decade later? The memo bluntly states, "Today the DC/CI staff advised me that the Director had relayed via the DDP the injunction that the agency was not, under any circumstances, to make inquiries or ask questions of any source or defector about Oswald." The author of the memo isn't identified.

One largely unknown possible entry in the endless JFK assassination Body Count was that of popular country singer Jim Reeves, best remembered for the 1959 smash hit "He'll Have to Go" In the book *Jim Reeves: The Untold Story* by Larry Jordan, he quoted a Texas radio station owner's claim that Reeves, upon seeing Oswald's picture on television, told the others watching with him that he'd seen him on multiple occasions at the Longhorn Ballroom, where Reeves regularly performed. Supposedly, Reeves had seen Jack Ruby there as well. On July 31, 1964, Reeves was killed at age forty, when a small plane he was piloting crashed. According to songwriter John Loudermilk, "Music producer Chet Atkins called me and he said, 'Jim's down. He crashed last night and we need to go out and find him.' And I said, 'Why?' and he said, 'He's got a briefcase that has some important papers in it that are private, and nobody should have those.'"[44] Such a briefcase was never reported found. Then, while researching his biography of Reeves, Larry Jordan reported getting a phone call from someone claiming to be with American intelligence, who warned him not to look "too deeply" into the plane crash.

Jack Zangretti, a mobster out of Altus, Oklahoma, two hundred miles northwest of Dallas, was manager of the "Red Lobster," a gambling resort on Lake Lugert. The casino was on par with many of the hotels in Las Vegas at the time, and often served as a venue for the meetings of high-ranking mobsters. On the day following the assassination, Zangretti informed friends that "a man named Jack Ruby will kill Oswald tomorrow, and in a few days, a member of the Frank Sinatra family will be kidnapped just to take some of the attention away from the assassination." Sure enough,

Ruby did kill Oswald, and Sinatra's son was kidnapped. Zangretti would be found dead two weeks later, his body floating in Lake Lugert with multiple gunshots to the chest. His resort and restaurant were demolished, "and all traces of its existence were removed."[45]

John F. Kennedy was the only president who ever attempted to really curtail the power of the Mafia. One of his lesser-known targets was Thomas D'Alesandro Jr, father of former Speaker of the House Nancy Pelosi. D'Alesandro served in Congress from 1939 to 1947, and was mayor of Baltimore from 1947 to 1959. D'Alesandro had close ties to mobster Benjamin "Benny Trotta" Magliano. The FBI investigated Magliano in 1947, for securing a draft exemption from Selective Service for himself and prizefighters that he controlled. Magliano and his boxers were convicted for their draft-dodging scam. It was reported that these individuals had worked hard for Thomas D'Alesandro's reelection to Congress and on his campaign at that time to become Mayor of Baltimore. The FBI never investigated D'Alesandro regarding this and numerous other allegations involving associations with gangsters, or additional evidence of corruption. While in Congress, D'Alesandro sat on the powerful appropriations committee and became a friend of FBI Director J. Edgar Hoover. President Kennedy launched an investigation in 1961 into "D'Alesandro's involvement with Baltimore hoodlums; with favoritism in awarding city contracts; [and] protection for political contributors and the prosecution of local cases." Hoover counseled the FBI offices in Baltimore and Washington, D.C. that an investigation could produce "substantial derogatory information" and impact D'Alesandro's political future.[46] Much of this was revealed in an FBI report on D'Alesandro, which was belatedly released shortly after the public was distracted by the "insurrection" of January 6, 2021. Another shocking claim in this report was that Nancy Pelosi's brother Franklin D'Alesandro had once been charged in a gang rape of two underage girls. The charges were dropped against D'Alesandro, but his eleven fellow defendants were convicted in 1953. Another explosive revelation was the elder D'Alesandro's alleged connection to several suspected communist groups in the 1940s. The report alleged that D'Alesandro took payoffs from police applicants and helped hinder investigations and prosecutions.[47]

Marguerite Oswald has been treated unfairly by the mainstream media, court historians, and most assassination researchers. She was the first person to question the absurd official story, and it was more than an understandable-mother-defending-her-son kind of thing. Marguerite scoffed at the "evidence," and maintained that Lee would have had to be a "superman" to have done everything attributed to him. She made some underreported prescient comments during the Jack Ruby trial. She declared, "Lee was not the type of boy to have Mrs. Paine get the job for him," in reference to Ruth Paine's supposed arrangement of him getting hired by the Texas School Book Depository. "There are two or three stories about how he got the job. The trouble started at the Paine house." Marguerite had told the Warren Commission, "I was suspicious of Mrs. Paine from the time I entered her home," a provocative comment that predictably was ignored by chief counsel J. Lee Rankin.[48] The prosecution in the Ruby case had subpoenaed her as a witness, but neither side had any intention of calling her to the stand. They didn't want anything to do with someone who was publicly saying, "There have to be more people involved."[49] Although most critics now contend conclusively that the man resembling Oswald, standing in the TSBD doorway at the moment shots were being fired, was his fellow employee Billy Lovelady, Marguerite was one of many at the time who disagreed. Jim Marrs stated, "In the 1970s, I spent many hours with Lee's mother, Marguerite, who repeatedly brought my attention back to the Altgens photograph. She continually asserted that the man in the doorway was her son, Lee Harvey Oswald." The Altgens doorway photo is another of the issues that neocon researchers have given ground on, for no good reason. There is no more credible proof that the figure is Lovelady than there is that it's Oswald.

Marguerite was smeared by everyone from then young, future national CBS anchor Bob Schieffer (who gave her a ride to the police station on the day of the assassination, and helped establish her negative image as a whiny, greedy woman), to authors like Don DeLillo and Stephen King, who postulated an inappropriate relationship between her and Lee, based on zero evidence. Schieffer's long career at CBS hardly inspires confidence in his credibility. At the time of the assassination a typically incurious reporter for the *Fort Worth Star-Telegram,* Schieffer claimed that Marguerite hounded him for years, and he also seems to have started the "money grubbing" depiction of her. "Marguerite would call me, even when I was in Vietnam on assignment, and call my mother, saying, 'Is Bob there? I need to get ahold of him. I've got new information.'"Schieffer said. "And even after I got to CBS, she would ask, 'Do you think CBS would pay me?' 'No, Mrs. Oswald, we just don't do that. I don't think we would.' She lived out her life selling his clothes to souvenir hunters and people like that. I just came to believe she was deranged." Maybe she thought CBS might actually be interested in the countless impossibilities of the official story? I find the entire account of Schieffer riding Marguerite to be curious; he claimed that she phoned his newspaper's office asking for a lift from Fort Worth to Dallas. Why would she call a newspaper? The record is unclear in terms of whether or not Marguerite had a driver's license and/or a personal vehicle, although Ruth Paine (who else?) would tell filmmaker Max Good decades later that she "didn't drive, didn't have a car." As a woman who worked outside the home most of the time, and moved quite a bit, it would seem logical that she had a means of transportation.

Emblematic of how ironclad the "Oswald did it" mantra was in the Mockingbird media was an account written by Lloyd Grove, about visiting Marguerite's home in 1977. He was a young reporter for *Crawdaddy* magazine, which portrayed itself as representing the counterculture. Grove fixated on Marguerite's alleged demands to be paid for an interview. Grove did reveal just how serious a researcher Oswald's mother was, writing, "she showed off her library, a shelf-lined alcove off the living room, it appeared to contain every volume ever produced on the subject up till then, including the 26 volumes of the Warren Commission Report, each book carefully preserved in plastic sheathing." Marguerite informed him that "I don't just talk off the top of my head. I read every book that comes out. Sometimes I'll stay up until 3 or 4 in the morning doing research."[50] The same certainly cannot be said for Grove, Schieffer, or any other mainstream "journalist." The only truly sympathetic portrayal of Oswald's plucky mother was an article, "The Unsinkable Marguerite Oswald," written by Harold Feldman, which appeared in the September 1964 issue of *The Realist.* Feldman charged, "Now they have her on their trail, and they snarl at her from all sides with malice and menace. Their literary agents cannot write three lines about her without suggesting that the only proper place for this aging Antigone who cries for justice for her murdered son is an asylum or a grave. Yes, there is a touch of the prima donna about Marguerite Oswald as she garners some egoistic comfort from her isolation. Here and there she responds to the icy deafness of the dominations and powers with extravagant suspicion and speculation. But if Ibsen is right and the strongest is the one who stands alone for integrity and honor, then Marguerite Oswald is the strongest woman in America. One thing is sure for anyone who knows about her life and knows her—she is a brave, bold and good woman." We learn from Feldman's article that Marguerite was fired from her position as a nurse a few days after the assassination. Feldman and Marguerite went to the backyard where the dubious photos of Oswald holding a rifle, handgun, and communist newspapers were purportedly taken. She pointed out the obvious difference in the bottom of the fence, as opposed to what was depicted on the cover of *Life* magazine. They visited fanciful Tippit witness Helen Markham, who told them to come back later when she could talk. When they returned, her husband was blocking the doorway, and begged them to "Please go away and don't come back." When Marguerite asked him, "You've been threatened, haven't you?" he replied, "Yes. Please go away." Outside, Marguerite was incensed. "That poor man! . . . He was frightened to death. What right do they have to threaten him? This is still America, by God. We're going to see if they can still get away with this." After Markham's twenty-year-old son talked to them, and explained he needed money badly, and would get it one way or another, he was arrested two days later for burglary. Marguerite, who had vowed to help him, spent seven hours on the phone in Feldman's presence, trying to get young Markham a lawyer.

Feldman's portrayal of Marguerite belied the negative image of her created in the press. As he noted, she was basically unemployable now, and her income was thus entirely dependent upon selling memorabilia of her son or anything else she could. That hardly made her the money-grubber Schieffer and others painted her as. Feldman contrasted her treatment to that of Oswald's young widow Marina, who was scared into cooperating with the authorities. "The Russian girl, whom Lee married after he had already decided to return to America, has received some

$75,000 in contributions and compensation," Feldman wrote. "She is the object of every tender solicitude, public and domestic, from the Secret Service. When the Fort Worth Council of Churches started a fund for the Oswalds, they soon made it clear that none of their charity was meant for the mother who was so unmotherly as to defend her son. Checks donated for the relief of Marguerite were returned to the senders." Again demonstrating that she was indeed the first critic of the official fairy tale, Feldman quotes Marguerite as saying, "First, they took the President's body out of Texas. The Dallas doctors thought the bullets came from the front, but the Federal men had a secret autopsy in Bethesda, Maryland, when it should have been done here and become part of the court record. Then they took the President's limousine out of the state, rushed it off. This was a most important item of evidence but they dismantled it and rebuilt it before anyone here could examine it for bullet holes." Feldman's brother-in-law Vincent Salandria was also favorably impressed with Oswald's mother, recollecting, "I spent four days sleeping over at Marguerite Oswald's apartment. She told me about her visit to the State Department after Lee defected to the Soviet Union. She said that she got red-carpet treatment and was assured that she need not worry about him. She felt that her son, Lee, was a U.S. intelligence agent." In addition to being the first to charge that Oswald worked for the government, Marguerite also discovered important witnesses like Acquilla Clemons, who insisted the Tippit killer was not Oswald, and shared that information with Mark Lane. J. Edgar Hoover would charge, in regards to Marguerite, "the first indication of her emotional instability was the retaining of a lawyer that anyone would not have retained if they really were serious in trying to get down to the facts." He was speaking of Mark Lane. Being condemned by the likes of corrupt Deep State Hall of Famer Hoover should be considered a badge of honor.

Marguerite lived in great fear from the time her son was framed for the JFK assassination until her death in 1981. She became ostracized from her son Robert, over his willingness to buy the absurd official story depicting Lee as the lone assassin. Her other son, John Pic, strongly criticized her before the Warren Commission, as did her daughter-in-law Marina. Both touted the mantra that she was seeking to make money, again ignoring the fact she had no other means of income. Publishers consistently turned down her book manuscript. Joy Smith, a sympathetic woman who read about Marguerite's financial struggles, and bought her $100 worth of food, recounted how she wouldn't accept the food until it had been analyzed by the Fort Worth crime lab. "I'm very interested in everything going on in this case," Marguerite related. "I hope sometime to have an opportunity to change some of the things that have been said—an opportunity to write the truth. I don't really have to investigate any more. I'm going to defend Lee Harvey Oswald until the day I die. The Warren Commission was wrong."[51] In a June 9, 1981, phone conversation with reporter Jim Marrs, Robert Blakey responded to a question about why the HSCA didn't call Oswald's mother to testify by stating, "Marguerite was totally unreliable. Around the committee we had a saying that the best proof of Oswald's innocence was that if he had been capable of murder, he would have shot Marguerite instead of JFK." Again, Marguerite had a lot of really good enemies. A particularly odious article, startling even for our state-controlled media in its thorough inaccuracy, was written by court historian emeritus Michael Beschloss in 2014. Full of vitriolic bias, it was ludicrously titled "When Lee Harvey Oswald Shot the President, His Mother Tried to Take Center Stage." All the familiar themes are there, and it is stated that shortly after the assassination, Marina never allowed her daughters June and Rachel to see their grandmother again. Beschloss blasts her for having "no expression of remorse, no regret, only an unceasing drive to carry on, fight on, despite the abandonment of her family and friends. Her combative attitude never wavered."[52] It seems not to have occurred to him that she might have been a mother who was standing by her wrongfully accused son, who had studied the evidence, unlike well-paid puppets like Beschloss, and thus had nothing to regret or feel remorseful about. Beschloss, and his fellow sycophants, on the other hand, should be ashamed of their intellectual dishonesty. Beschloss's article was based on his ridiculous 2013 book *The Gunman and his Mother: Lee Harvey Oswald, Marguerite Oswald, and the Making of an Assassin.*

Myth is more powerful than truth, when dishonest people have the power to determine what are and aren't "facts." Marguerite has been consigned to history as an overbearing, selfish woman who was such a bad mother she raised a presidential assassin. The 2015 play *Mama's Boy* just perpetuated these damaging, inaccurate stereotypes about her. Steve North, an ABC journalist who worked with Geraldo Rivera, felt compelled to pile on Marguerite one more time, with a 2017 article titled, "Oswald's Mother was a Thoroughly Disagreeable Piece of Work." North recounted the familiar slanders from Bob Schieffer, who here calls her "a self-centered, seriously deranged person." Marguerite unwisely trusted North, and kept in contact with him over the years, once even sending him a copy of her meager Social Security receipt. But that didn't stop him, or anyone else, from blasting her for charging for autographs and anything else she could, in order to survive. When the HSCA implied that Marguerite might have had Mafia associations herself, she told North, "What they are implying is beneath contempt!" She confided to North that she had sometimes gone to her granddaughter June's elementary school, and peered through the schoolyard fence, just to catch a glimpse of her.[53] Jean Stafford, in her 1966 book, *A Mother in History*, attributes quotes to Marguerite that conflict with everything else she said multiple times, and are almost certainly contrived. Can we really picture this indefatigable defender of her son saying, "Now maybe Lee Harvey Oswald was the assassin. But does that make him a louse? No, no! You find killing in some very fine homes for one reason or another. And as we all know, President Kennedy was a dying man. So I say it is possible my son was chosen to shoot him in a mercy killing for the security of the country."[54] Marguerite sent a telegram to Coretta Scott King after her husband was assassinated in 1968, and MLK's widow regarded it as the expression of sympathy that had most touched her. When Marguerite Oswald died, the funeral home told the media that the only person to view her body had been her son Robert. Her doctor was quoted as saying, "She was alone and estranged from her family and had to make all the decisions concerning her own care and welfare." One of her last requests was to be buried next to her son Lee Harvey Oswald.[55]

Marguerite Oswald summed up the laughable official narrative succinctly when she said, "Lee was *offered* the job in the Book Depository. He didn't get it on his own. He was placed there. He was the perfect patsy. They set him up. The case against Lee Harvey Oswald is hearsay, distortion, and omission, and the FBI used wrong investigative techniques. Lee died an innocent man. He was neither tried nor convicted for his alleged crime. And history is being defamed."[56] No serious researcher could have said it any better. Marguerite's keen knowledge of the framing of her son does her credit, and in my view she comes out looking far better than any of the journalistic parasites who continue to defame her.

An article by the late Larry R. Harris (killed at a young age in a suspicious car accident), in a special supplement to the September 22, 1977, edition of *The Continuing Inquiry,* noted that some connected to the assassination were profiting financially, unlike Marguerite Oswald, whose "money grubbing" seems not to have made her wealthy. Retired Dallas Police Chief Jesse Curry was said to be demanding $50 for an interview. Laughably uncredible J. D. Tippit murder witness Helen Markham Grant was asking for a minimum of $30 in advance to talk to researchers (more for professional journalists). Officer J. D. Tippit's widow Marie was the recipient of an incredible $647,579 in donations from the public, including $25,000 from Abraham Zapruder.[57] And, of course, Zapruder himself profited handsomely by selling the rights to his little film to *Life* magazine for $150,000 (for years the smaller figure of $25,000 was reported).[58] *Life,* naturally, in the best tradition of a free press, buried the film for over a decade. In 1999, Zapruder's heirs received an incomprehensible $16 million for the slightly over 26-second-long video of the assassination.[59] The Zapruder family in turn donated the copyright to the Sixth Floor Museum in Dallas, which has become the face of the official fairy tale. Abraham Zapruder, unlike Marguerite Oswald, has never been portrayed as a "money grubber," although he certainly did become wealthy.

The owner of the Texas School Book Depository, where Lee Harvey Oswald was working at the time of the assassination, was David Harold Byrd. He was an influential figure in Texas, who could go to the likes of LBJ, Sam Rayburn, and John Connally for favors. Byrd was related to both powerful Senator Harry Byrd and famed explorer Admiral Richard E. Byrd, whose Antarctic expeditions he financed. (The grateful explorer named an Antarctic mountain range after him.)[60] At the time of the assassination, Byrd would be on an extended African safari. Byrd's host, who ran the hunting preserve "Safarilandia" in Mozambique, would be one Werner von Alvensleben, a former Nazi assassin-turned-OSS/CIA double agent, codenamed "DRAM." Alvensleben was called to Dallas by Byrd in early 1963, and both would depart for their trip shortly before Kennedy's arrival. *Dallas Morning News* in late December that year wrote: "DH Byrd just returned from a safari in Africa run by Werner Von Alvensleben. . . . Werner Von Alvensleben's favorite rifle was a big game rifle called the Mannlicher-Schonauer, a Greek version of the Mannlicher-Carcano rifle. There is a document that says the US contracted Western Cartridge Company to manufacture Mannlicher ammunition for the Greek Civil War after World War II and a report that Western Cartridge-manufactured ammunition for the Greek civil war was interchangeable between the Mannlicher-Carcano and the Mannlicher-Schonauer rifles."[61] All of this would be the subject of an August 2023 Freedom of Information Act (FOIA) lawsuit against the CIA by the Assassination Archives and Research Center (AARC). According to the lawsuit summary found online: "Multiple reports in hunting and gun publications state that Werner von Alvensleben was legendary for using a 6.5 mm Mannlicher-Schoenauer rifle for his hunting activities. The rifle found on the sixth floor of the TSBD and alleged to be connected to the assassination of President Kennedy was a 6.5 mm Mannlicher-Carcano. Warren Commissioner John McCloy questioned the FBI firearms expert who testified before the Warren Commission in 1964 as to whether the ammunition found in the Mannlicher-Carcano and on the floor at the TSBD could be fired from a Mannlicher-Schoenauer rifle (ammunition for the Mannlicher-Carcano and Mannlicher-Schoenauer are said to be virtually identical). . . . Further, Commissioner McCloy specifically questioned the FBI firearms expert as to the diameter of the bullet found in the TSBD building. FBI expert Frazier gave McCloy a diameter of 6.65 millimeters, which is too small a diameter for a Mannlicher-Carcano bullet, but is consistent with the reportedly slightly smaller Mannlicher-Schoenauer bullet."[62]

Von Alvensleben's nephew, professional photographer Christian Alvenslaben, would display his pictures from Byrd's hunting safari on his website. A caption under a photo of Byrd states, "The arrival of Colonel Byrd for his hunting expedition. On one of the days to come J.F. Kennedy will be shot from his building in Dallas, Texas." And even more curious, written below another photograph in this collection (of a dead elephant): "Colonel Byrd's trophy picture, an alibi?"[63]

President Johnson would grant a large defense contract to Byrd's experimental aerospace corporation, Ling-Temco-Vought (LTV) after the assassination, according to researcher Peter Dale Scott. Subsequently, LTV's planes (most notably, the A-7 Corsair) would be used in the Vietnam War. Writer Stan Deyo found that one of the major contractors for the secretive Pine Gap facility (known as "America's Area 51 in Australia") was LTV.[64] In 1957, Byrd organized and became board chairman of the Space Corporation, which manufactured propulsion and ground test equipment for jet engines and aerospace ground support equipment.[65] Byrd's company E-Systems was a well-known CIA contractor that would go on to purchase Air America. Byrd is rumored to have known George de Mohrenschildt, David Atlee Phillips, and George H. W. Bush, through his membership in the Dallas Petroleum Club. Researcher Richard Bartholomew claimed that Byrd, as a co-founder of the Civil Air Patrol, knew David Ferrie. The eager trophy hunter Byrd had the original "sniper" window from the sixth floor of his building removed to take home as a keepsake, where it remained prominently displayed in his banquet room until his death in 1986. His son, Caruth, kept the window out of sight, until it was dramatically unveiled at the Sixth Floor Museum on February 21, 1995.

Peter Secosh unearthed a fascinating tidbit that has heretofore never been published by any researcher to my knowledge. We all know that President Kennedy was on his way to deliver a speech at a Dallas Trade Mart luncheon, when he was shot in Dealey Plaza. What hasn't been reported is that he was scheduled to hold a press conference there with physicist Dr. Lloyd V. Berkner. According to Berkner's notes, dated November 23, 1963, on the official letterhead of the Graduate Research Center of the Southwest, the president's first words were to have been about his organization; and Kennedy was "to have made a major national and international address."[66] Berkner was a member of the 1953 Robertson Panel, which "investigated" UFO reports, and was closely aligned with Project Blue Book.[67] Berkner also had a connection with Admiral Richard E. Byrd, having worked as an engineer on his 1928 expedition. Like David Harold Byrd, Berkner too has land named after him in Antarctica.[68] Berkner was an original member of the infamous Majestic-12 and would work closely with physicist and UFO researcher James E. McDonald.[69] In a July 29,

1968, hearing before the House Committee on Science and Astronautics, McDonald accused the scientific community of "casually ignoring as nonsense a matter of extraordinary scientific importance." McDonald's 1971 alleged suicide was exceedingly strange.[70] Examined in context, Lloyd Berkner was quite a curious figure for JFK to be holding a press conference with on November 22, 1963.[71]

Following the JFK assassination, another member of the Robertson Panel, Berkley and MIT physicist Dr. Luis W. Alvarez, would be tasked by the Warren Commission with examining the Zapruder film, providing "scientific" cover, and demonstrating "that one person could have fired all the shots that hit Kennedy and Texas Governor John Connally."[72] His ridiculous "jet-effect" theory—that the backward snap of the President's head was somehow consistent with being shot from behind—was soundly criticized by critics of the lone-assassin theory.[73] In 1940, Alvarez would be involved with the secretive MIT Radiation Laboratory, and would later be credited with producing both the fuses for the plutonium bomb, and with designing the detonators used in the Trinity bomb test and the Nagasaki bomb.[74] During the dropping of the bomb on Hiroshima in August 1945, he would act as a scientific observer aboard a B-29 that flew in formation with the *Enola Gay*.[75] There were even reports that Alvarez would be part of a study into "foo fighters," mysterious glowing orbs that were able to duck and dodge World War II military flight formations at high speed, seemingly while under intelligent control.[76] He would later develop a fascination with the Pyramids of Egypt, and attempt to discover hidden chambers through the use of cosmic rays.[77] And in 1980, would be responsible for the Alvarez hypothesis, the now mainstream scientific view that an asteroid collided with the Earth leading to the extinction of the dinosaurs.[78]

The Secret Service

Kennedy was killed by a breakdown in a protective system that should have made the assassination impossible.

—Robert Groden and Harrison Livingston, *High Treason*[79]

For unknown reasons, many researchers who believe there was a conspiracy are reluctant to look critically at those who made it possible by their complete inaction: JFK's Secret Service detail. The Secret Service's conduct was reprehensible after the assassination as well. Dallas patrolman Stavis Ellis recounted one example in Larry Sneed's 1988 book *No More Silence*: "I remember a little kid I had first seen out at Love Field who had a little home camera with the old reel type of film, and he had taken some pictures there. I saw him again on Lemmon Avenue where he had taken more pictures, and again in town. Well, he also showed up at Parkland and was taking some pictures of the hearse that they had brought in. He was one of a bunch of people in the back of the hospital taking pictures. A Secret Service man ran up, grabbed that camera out of his hand, opened it up, shook the film down and gave it a kick. You know how those reels of film unroll? I'm sure it exposed everything he had. I felt sorry for him. I got into a little hassle over it and told the Secret Service man, 'I don't think that's right the way you did that. That poor kid's been taking pictures ever since we left Love Field and now you've exposed every one of them!' He made some smart comment to the effect that he didn't think it was right for me to say anything to him about it. But I didn't appreciate it a bit! I understand that they were under pressure, but they were awfully uncouth, all of them!"[80] Fellow Dallas officer James W. Courson corroborated Ellis. So we can add this unknown youngster's pictures to the Babushka Lady film, the fourth photo of Bob Croft, the films of Ralph Simpson and Norman Similas, and so many others which have never surfaced. Ellis was also one of the several witnesses to the bullet hole in the limousine's windshield. He told Sneed, "Some of the jockeys around the car were saying, 'Looky here!' What they were looking at was the windshield. To the right of where the driver was, just above the metal near the bottom of the glass there appeared to be a bullet hole. I talked to a Secret Service man about it, and he said, 'Aw, that's just a fragment!' It looked like a clean hole in the windshield to me. In fact, one of the motor jockeys, Harry Freeman, put a pencil through it, or said he could." Richard Dudman of *The St Louis Post-Dispatch* also notably claimed to have stuck a pencil through this hole. Ellis also told Sneed that Police Chief Jesse Curry wanted to transport Oswald in the middle of the night, without all the press around, but was ordered to do it "with their lights and cameras set up" by City Manager Elgin Crull and Dallas Mayor Earle Cabell, brother of the CIA's Charles

Cabell, whom JFK fired along with Allen Dulles and Richard Bissell after the Bay of Pigs fiasco. Documents released a few years ago revealed that Mayor Cabell had been a CIA asset, too.[81] Ellis's recollections were colorful; he categorized Officer Marion Baker as "slow" and said his nickname was "Momma Son."

Interestingly, General Charles P. Cabell was behind Project Grudge, which later turned into Project Blue Book. He'd been assigned as Air Force chief of the Strategy and Policy division in 1945. In December of that year, he rose to chief U.S. Air Force delegate to the United Nations Military Staff Committee. In May 1948, he became director of Air Force Intelligence. In 1949, Cabell set up Project Grudge to "make a study reviewing the UFO situation for AF HQ." Much like the Project Blue Book that would follow, Project Grudge did little real investigation into UFOs, while maintaining that all cases were being thoroughly looked into.[82]

As Donald E. Wilkes Jr. wrote, in a 2012 paper for the University of Georgia School of Law, entitled, "Intriguing Mystery—The Secret Service and the JFK Assassination," "Based on the information now available nearly 50 years after the assassination, there is a consensus among those who have investigated President Kennedy's Secret Service protection. The consensus: JFK's protection was inadequate. Or, as the HSCA would put it, 'uniquely insecure.' Indeed, the protection was so defective that it dangerously increased the likelihood that an assassination plan involving one or more concealed snipers firing into the presidential limousine would succeed. By making the murder of JFK easier and the undetected escape of the assassins more likely, this Secret Service bungling contributed to the assassination." Just prior to the assassination, the Secret Service was aware of plots against the president in Chicago, Miami, and Tampa. Combined with the violent reaction United Nations Ambassador Adlai Stevenson had recently drawn in Dallas, if anything the Secret Service should have been on a high alert status for JFK's Texas trip. Wilkes hardly fits the description of a "conspiracy theorist," but his assessment of JFK's detail was damning and accurate. "With a few exceptions, Secret Service agents in the motorcade performed poorly when the shots rang out." Wilkes charged. "The 54-year-old agent driving the presidential limousine failed to accelerate the moment the shooting began. Instead, he hesitated, applying the limousine's brakes and slowing it down to such a degree that many Dealey Plaza eyewitnesses thought the vehicle had actually stopped; he twice swiveled his head backward to look at Kennedy; and he did not put his foot on the gas and speed away until after JFK suffered the fatal headshot. . . . At the time Secret Service guidelines provided: 'The Driver of the President's car should be alert for dangers and be able to take instant action when instructed or otherwise made aware of an emergency.' In violation of other Secret Service procedures, the forty-eight-year-old agent in the right front seat made no attempt to move to the president and shield him. This, it is true, would have been difficult, because a special handlebar for the president to hold on to while standing in the limousine made it very hard for someone in the right front seat to get into the rear compartment. Nonetheless, the agent should at least have made an effort to get to the president. He should not have sat there. The agents standing on the running board of the follow-up car that trailed the limousine by five feet also seemed drugged with an elixir of sluggishness."

When the Secret Service's Protective Research Files for 1963 were computerized, the original files were inexplicably destroyed. The Secret Service infamously destroyed crucial records requested by the ARRB in 1995. Among these were protection survey reports for JFK's 1963 trips, records for the intriguing JFK November 2, 1963, visit to Chicago and a whole folder of vital data from July through November 1963. The Secret Service destroyed these records in violation of the John F. Kennedy Assassination Materials Disclosure Act of 1992, and even though they had been notified not to destroy any records by the National Archives. No one with the Secret Service was punished in 1963, or 1995. Even an article in *Vanity Fair* asked the question, "The White House Secret Service is famous for its split-second reflexes and for being trained to take a bullet for the Commander-in-chief. Why didn't that happen on November 22?" The writer, Susan Cheever, mentioned the well-known fact that nine of the agents had been out late drinking the night before, in violation of agency protocol. But she resorted to the usual methodology of blaming Kennedy himself for setting a womanizing, partying example.[83] The first Black Secret Service agent on the White House detail, Abraham Bolden, called out his colleagues for their startling incompetence. Like all high-profile whistleblowers, Bolden was retaliated against, and sent to prison on bogus bribery charges. The allegedly distraught reactions of agents like Clint Hill and Paul Landis don't seem convincing. Driver William Greer, whose failure to do anything other than slow down during the five or more seconds of shooting made Kennedy a sitting duck, told author William Manchester he'd tried to apologize to Jackie by saying, "Oh my God, oh my God. I didn't mean to do it. I didn't hear, I should have swerved the car, I couldn't help it. Oh Mrs. Kennedy . . . if only I had seen in time."[84] In his Warren Commission testimony, Greer makes an obvious effort to blame Kennedy, explaining that because of the president's affinity for crowds, he had often been instructed by him to "slow down." There is a revealing photo of Greer leaving the building after his Warren Commission testimony, with an inappropriate smile on his face.

There were attempts to debunk the story about the agents drinking the night before, which bothered even Earl Warren. The club was a "dry" place, however it was common for patrons to bring their own alcohol in, and booze was routinely provided to the police, doctors, lawyers, and other prestigious citizens. In 1984, Patrick Kirkwood, the owner of the bar in question, The Cellar Coffee House, said the agents were indeed drinking alcohol and that they'd been pressured not to say anything negative. "About 3:30," Kirkwood told reporter Jim Marrs, "these Secret Service men were sitting around giggling about how the firemen were guarding the president over at the Hotel Texas." Cellar manager Jimmy Hill recalled, "After the agents were there, we got a call from the White House asking us not to say anything about them drinking because their image had suffered enough as it was. We didn't say anything but those guys were bombed. They were drinking pure Everclear." Everclear was a very strong and popular intoxicant.[85]

A February 14, 1964, memo written by Secret Service Inspector Thomas J. Kelley has received little scrutiny from critics, despite its intriguing nature. Kelley was sent to assist Forrest Sorrels, the agent-in-charge of the Dallas office of the Secret Service, in determining what had happened in Dealey Plaza. Kelley sat in on four of Lee Harvey Oswald's unrecorded interviews with the authorities. In the memo to Chief James

Rowley, Kelley states his strong opposition to proposed legislation to make the assassination of a president a federal crime. He actually mentions the possibility of a "Seven Days in May" scenario, whereby in the future an FBI director "could bring about or allow the assassination of the president" whom he was opposed to. The memo's preference for a local investigation of such crimes to take precedence is decidedly odd, considering that JFK's Secret Service detail literally took the president's body by force from Dallas officials. Kelley reiterated to the HSCA that his "investigation" into the agents who were drinking the night before had concluded that it hadn't impacted their performance. Overall, Kelley testified that, "I felt that none of the agents could be charged with any dereliction of duty in connection with the assassination." Kelley excused even driver William Greer's complete dereliction of duty, and deflected the very mild criticism in a few questions to the "lack of resources" the Secret Service supposedly had in Dallas. Surprisingly, it was Chairman Louis Stokes who asked the hardest questions about the blatant lack of response on the part of the agents in the motorcade.

Anticipating the work of Vince Palamara, the late researcher Philip Melanson castigated JFK's Secret Service detail. "At least two agents lied to the Warren Commission." Melanson charged. "Even worse, as they created the fiction about how thorough they had been, they implicitly pinned the blame on the fallen president himself, hinting that Kennedy's recklessness or fatalism—not anything the agents had done in Dallas—ignited a tragic sequence of events. Kennedy's critics still chant the mantra that the president brought it on himself. These outright lies and half-truths cannot absolve the Secret Service for losing the life of a president for the first time in its history." While Assistant Special Agent in Charge Roy Kellerman sat motionless in the limousine's front seat, next to nonresponsive driver Greer, later at Parkland Hospital he and the other lackadaisical agents wielded guns and displayed their "toughness" in forcibly removing JFK's body from the authorities who had legal jurisdiction over the crime. The limousine, which represented the crime scene, was not only cleaned but also whisked away by the Secret Service.

As if stealing the body from its legal jurisdiction, and corrupting the crime scene, wasn't enough, the Secret Service also broke protocol at

Andrews Air Force Base, when JFK's body was flown home to Washington, D.C. Lt. Sam Bird was the platoon leader of the Honor Guard Company, and designated in-charge of the Joint Service casket teams. Bird and his team regularly drilled four times a month on how to properly receive the remains of a president. General Godfrey McHugh waved Bird and his team off, declaring that he and the Secret Service would unload JFK's bronze casket. Bird was affronted at this and watched in horror as the thuggish Secret Service agents carelessly struggled to handle the casket, bouncing it around and eventually damaging it. Researchers like David Lifton and Doug Horne have postulated that Kennedy's body wasn't in this bronze casket; were McHugh and the Secret Service agents trying to hide the fact that the casket was much lighter than it should have been?[86]

The ARRB interview with James Mastrovito, who was in charge of the JFK assassination file for the Secret Service, is noteworthy. Mastrovito, following orders from Chief Rowley, "culled" the five-or-six file cabinets of material down to one five-drawer file cabinet. What was thrown out was left entirely up to Mastrovito's discretion. Mastrovito talked about receiving a piece of President Kennedy's brain, from the Armed Forces Institute of Pathology, in a vial the size of a prescription bottle, "about 3 or 4 years" after the assassination. Mastrovito would revise this time frame to "1969 or 1970." The label only indicated that it had come from the autopsy at Bethesda, with no other details. Mastrovito subsequently destroyed the vial in a food processor. I covered this gruesome story in *Hidden History*, but reading the entire ARRB account clarifies that it was not what was left of JFK's missing brain, but only a small piece of it. That doesn't detract from the extremely bizarre nature of it. Why was a piece of Kennedy's brain preserved in some vial? Were there other pieces? In an odd aside in this account, it is noted that "After the assassination, the Secret Service recalled its criminal files from the Truman Library saying that the agency wished to review them in light of the assassination. Instead of returning these files to the Truman Library as promised, as Mastrovito put it, "the Secret Service kept the files, and we destroyed them."

Following up on the disinformation peddled in recent books by former Secret Service agents Gerald Blaine and Clint Hill was Carol Leonnig's 2021 book *Zero Fail: The Rise and Fall of the Secret Service*, which parroted their insinuation that JFK was responsible for his own death by not letting them do their jobs properly. In other words, the famous Kennedy "recklessness." Secret Service critic Vince Palamara, in a review of Leonnig's book, described the harassment he'd experienced at the hands of Blaine, Hill, and Lisa McCubbin (coauthor for both men, who went on to marry the much older Hill). Palamara wrote, "My first book *Survivor's Guilt* was due out in October of 2013. Gerald Blaine marked my book as 'to read' on Good Reads; Lisa McCubbin gave it a one-star rating on Good Reads before it even came out; and former JFK Secret Service agent Chuck Zboril gave my book a one-star review on Amazon when it did come out, which prompted a specific friend of Blaine's (whom I will not name for legal reasons and to give him any notoriety), a person formerly in military intelligence who had also worked for the United States Post Office, to begin bothering me online with many nasty comments on both Amazon and my blogs . . . not once but twice I was called to a private conference room at work, as a woman from Human Resources (HR) alerted me to the fact that the same above noted individual wrote to the CEO of my company attempting to get me fired for a) my unpatriotic attacks on Blaine and b) doing these things on company time." Palamara called *Zero Fail* "an epic professional fail when it comes to its Kennedy-era chapter."

There were numerous early references to a Secret Service agent being shot in Dallas. A curious story was published in Penn Jones's *The Continuing Inquiry* on January 22, 1977. The article quotes from a letter purportedly received by Jim Garrison during the Clay Shaw trial: "A Mr. Robertson, Assistant Director of the Dallas or Fort Worth Secret Service office, confided to [friend of writer who requested anonymity] in 1963 that a plot to kill President Kennedy was planned and he did not want any part of it. On November 22, 1963, my friend was in the office of Mr. Robertson when all phones began to ring, about the time Kennedy was arriving at Carswell Air Force Base [in Fort Worth], Mr. Robertson then said, 'Well, this is it' and left the office. Since that time Mr. Robertson's family of seven children and wife have not seen or heard from him, yet his paychecks continue to be mailed to his home." The article, written by Jones and Gary Shaw, goes on to note, "Our 1965 investigation lead us to believe Robertson was in Dallas but was posing as a POSTAL INSPECTOR, but it was reported to us that he had left Dallas. We also learned from newsmen that something unusual did happen on Harwood [street] shortly before the turn to Main Street. No one wanted credit for this, but we were told by reliable newsmen that a man jumped in front of Kennedy's car on Harwood shouting, 'Stop, I must tell you.' The man, according to the report, was promptly wrestled to the ground and hustled away."

Researcher Robert Howard delved into this further, and in a April 11, 2007 post on The Education Forum, wrote, "To my great surprise, there are FOUR reports that corroborate the above article, in conjunction with the overlooked Kantor report: The first is the actual LETTER sent to Garrison from an 'Amy Britvar' dated 2/21/68 and originating from Turtle Creek Blvd. in Dallas, TX. [thanks go to John Armstrong and Jack White for the copy of this letter]! An internet people search for Britvar drew a blank, although there ARE other Britvars in Texas (further work will be done on locating this person). The second is a Treasury Department (U.S. Customs Service) document, dated 1/17/80, from Joseph G. Forrester, U.S. Customs, to Attorney General Benjamin R. Civiletti [thanks go to John Armstrong and Ed Sherry for this document]. The letter reads in part: 'My interest in the Kennedy murder started in 1966 when I met an Air Force Master Sergeant at St. Albans Naval Hospital, Queens, New York. This sergeant, an elderly man, was suffering from terminal cancer. He stated that on November 22, 1963, he was attached to Air Force One as an electronics technician. He further stated that after the President was shot a message was received over a military frequency that multiple assassins had attacked the President . . . a Secret Service agent, Mr. Robertson, stationed in the Dallas-Fort Worth area disappeared on November 22,1963, yet his family still receives his paychecks. The disappearance of an individual is not unusual except that it has been said that Mr. Robertson became aware of an assassins plot against the president. . . . Please do not misconstrue this letter. I am not a crank; but I am sincerely interested in this crucial investigation. I am willing to join an investigative team and if that is not possible, will make myself available for an interview by investigative officers.' The third is a lengthy memorandum written by Vince Salandria, dated 1/31/67, regarding an interview with Rita Rollins, a Navy Nurse with an interesting story to tell. —the crucial part in question reads as follows: 'The name of the person in Dallas . . . is Inez Robertson. CHUCK ROBERTSON, HER HUSBAND, WORKS AT THE POST OFFICE . . . Inez Robertson, actually saw them [men with guns] make a breakdown of the rifles. This tall man with long grey or white hair—he was in the station wagon. There is a luggage rack on the station wagon. It was a Rambler station wagon. This fellow with the mixed grey hair carried them [the armed men] to the airport . . . This tall man had been around Dallas the day before the assassination . . . THIS EPISODE HAS CAUSED FRICTION BETWEEN CHUCK ROBERTSON AND INEZ ROBERTSON. HE IS NOT IN DALLAS NOW.' The fourth can be found in the WC volumes: 17 H 749 (CE 705: the DPD Channel 2 transcripts) — 'One of the SECRET SERVICE MEN ON THE FIELD—ELM AND HOUSTON; said it came over the teletype that one of the Secret Service men had been killed.'" Clearly, there are too many references to this for there not to be some validity to it.

I asked Vince Palamara, the go-to expert on the Secret Service, about the rumors regarding agent Robertson. In a June 5, 2022, email reply, he wrote, "I covered this briefly in my first book. It is a tantalizing dead end—there isn't much to go on with it. It may be true . . . it may not be true." I spoke with Gary Shaw on June 27, 2022. Gary told me he had tried to track down Amy Britvar (full name Amelia Frances Britvar), who'd sent that curious letter to Garrison, and discovered she died in 2016. As for Rita Rollins, who provided such interesting information to Vincent Salandria, he subsequently found that her real name was Lola Belle Holmes, and she had been an undercover FBI agent. Gary Shaw unearthed a story in the December 3, 1968 *Green Bay Press Gazette* where Holmes/Rollins was referred to as "A communist for seven years," doing undercover work for the Bureau, and a member of the John Birch Society. She was quoted as saying that "Martin Luther King was assassinated by a communist" and that the United States government was communist-controlled. Holmes/Rollins's reference to Robertson as a post office employee, not a Secret Service agent, corresponds with Jones and Shaw speculating that he was working undercover. But why would a Secret Service agent be doing that? What little information there is about Holmes revolves around her being a Black woman working undercover for the FBI, and then joining the John

Birch Society. It was very hard to find any mention of her connection to Garrison's case.

If there had been an honest investigation of the events in Dealey Plaza, the first ones questioned would be the members of JFK's Secret Service detail. Not only were they out drinking late the night before; not only did they fail to respond whatsoever to the sound of gunfire; not only did they illegally steal JFK's body from its legal jurisdiction, they indisputably corrupted the crime scene by cleaning the limousine. Lone nutters will still absurdly argue that this never happened; that a bucket seen in photographs outside Parkland Hospital, next to the limousine, was related to something else. A number of reporters, including well-known names like Robert MacNeil, Hugh Sidey, and Tom Wicker, testified to witnessing the cleanup. Sidey wrote, "A guard was set up around the Lincoln as Secret Service men got a pail of water and tried to wash the blood from the car."[87] White House photographer Cecil Stoughton took photos of this happening, with captions like "A bucket at his feet, an agent [Kinney] is seen leaning into the back seat of the Lincoln cleaning up some of the gore." ABC's Don Gardner reported, on the day of the assassination, "Outside the hospital, blood had to be wiped from the limousine." Echoing this, UPI would report, "Outside the hospital, blood was cleaned from the limousine." Nurse Shirley Randall was asked if she "would get someone to come and wash the blood out of the car," but was so upset she forgot about it.[88] For all intents and purposes, this cleaning made anything purportedly discovered in the limousine to be worthless in terms of evidentiary value. Destroying the crime scene after allowing the assassination to happen; it would be irresponsible and intellectually dishonest not to point the finger at the Secret Service.

One of the many, many strange deaths connected to the JFK assassination may well have taken place *before* the event. Thomas B. Shipman was one of President Kennedy's regular limo drivers. It is altogether possible that he would have been assigned the role of driving JFK on November 22, 1963. It was only with considerable digging by Secret Service expert Vince Palamara, that it was found Shipman had died suddenly of a heart attack, on October 14, 1963, while stationed at the presidential retreat Camp David. He was only fifty-one. Inexplicably, there were no news reports about this extremely rare instance of a Secret Service agent dying on duty. He was quickly buried without an autopsy or toxicology report, and there doesn't seem to be a death certificate available for him. His family was shocked, claiming he was "as fit as a fiddle."[89]

Another odd death occurred just after the assassination. Army Captain Michael D. Groves was in charge of the Honor Guard at JFK's funeral. He died of a supposed heart attack on December 3, 1963, at just *twenty-seven.* Adding to the intrigue, on December 12, a fire destroyed all his possessions. According to "JFK: The Dead Witnesses" by Craig Roberts and John Armstrong, "The Honor Guard, for some mysterious reason, had been practicing for a presidential funeral for three days before the assassination." They also categorize his death as "Unknown. Possibly poison."[90] Researcher Bill Kelly received an email from a former neighbor of Groves's parents, in which he was told that they suspected he was murdered, as did his sister (who died at only thirty-seven herself). The email also claimed that Groves had been in charge of White House communications, a duty of which he was relieved when LBJ assumed the presidency. The neighbor additionally stated that the date of death was wrong, and that Groves had died before the assassination. This might explain why Kelly had been unable to find a photo of Groves at JFK's funeral. Supporting this is the account of Bobby Lee Hayden, another member of JFK's Honor Guard, who claimed that only two hours after the burial they learned of the death of Groves.[91] The email to Kelly emphasized that "The daughter, as I stated in my conversation with you was very vocal about the 'murder' of her brother. She told me that 'they' tried to get her committed and 'they' told her if she didn't 'shut up' she'd never see her kids again. It doesn't surprise me that she died in 1978 about 5 years after her last conversation with me."

Militarycorruption.com delved into the strange death of Captain Groves in 2020. They spoke with Delano "Del" White, who had been neighbors with Groves's parents in Birmingham, Michigan. He met the Groves after seeing Don Groves passed out in his backyard, which his wife Gladys explained, "We drank a bit too much last night and he passed out in the yard. He was too heavy to move, so I just left him there to sleep it off." As they became friends, the Groves ultimately shared the sad story of their son. They showed White a letter from Mark Lane, in which he told them that he felt Michael had been murdered for something he knew. The article even used an exact quote from Michael's sister Darbea that appeared in the email to Bill Kelly. Obviously, the neighbor who'd emailed Kelly was Del White. White recalled, "Most of the neighbors on Euclid Avenue told me that it wasn't a good idea to associate with the Groves family. To my mind they were wonderful people who were terribly disappointed in the government and the powers that be. It was readily apparent to me, the Groves family was under a lot of pressure to keep quiet." The feisty website also spoke with Bobby Lee Hayden, who as noted gave November 25, 1963, as the date of Groves's mysterious death. Hayden said Groves was buried on November 28, in the same section of Arlington National Cemetery as JFK. The official White House logs and Groves's gravestone give the date of death as December 6, 1963. Why such a discrepancy? Groves and President Kennedy, who had handpicked him for his position, were said to be exceptionally close.[92]

Jack Ruby's chief attorney Clayton Fowler died at only forty-nine in 1971. There was no cause of death listed in the only report I could find about this death.[93] Fowler also represented George de Mohrenschildt. Ruby's family tried to fire Fowler, but Ruby insisted he stay on. According to the always interesting (but sometimes unreliable) Penn Jones, Fowler was involved in an illegal gold-importing scheme with Lyndon B. Johnson. Richard Kollmar, husband of columnist and television personality Dorothy Kilgallen, who as mentioned earlier was found dead under extremely suspicious circumstances while investigating the JFK assassination, either died in his sleep or killed himself, depending on the source, in 1971 at age sixty. A third death associated with Kilgallen's was that of her close friend (and, in yet another twist, former lover of John F. Kennedy) Florence Pritchett Smith, who died only two days after Kilgallen, allegedly of a cerebral hemorrhage.[94] Kilgallen had reportedly given all her notes on the assassination to Pritchett Smith. Kilgallen's father, veteran journalist Jim Kilgallen, lived on for several years after her death. According to Kilgallen's biographer Lee Israel, friends and colleagues knew not to discuss Dorothy's death with him. In fact, he informed Israel in a January 26, 1976, letter that he would not help her in any way, maintaining his commitment "not to grant interviews to anyone concerning her career." This seems especially odd given the fact that as noted earlier, he attempted to alert the HSCA to her files being locked in a safe-deposit box, and his concerns about his grandson's safety. Dorothy had supposedly confided to her hairdressers and friends that she feared someone was going to kill her. More interestingly, "Ninety-year-old Jimmy Kilgallen has made a collage of newspaper clippings from 1977–78 concerning the build-up publicity for the HSCA. He has mailed it 'special delivery' in a 9 x 12 envelope to Louis Stokes, postmarked December 3, 1978, possibly too late for the HSCA to do much with it. Jimmy wants the HSCA to know about Richard Helms denying that any anti-Castro plots had 'ever got[ten] out of the laboratory planning stage,' Jose Aleman's oft-repeated comment that Santo Trafficante said JFK would get hit with Republican votes and the two Zurich hotels where his daughter may have left her papers." Among the clippings was a story from *The New York Post* about employees at the Regency Hotel on Park Avenue, where Dorothy was last seen alive, being ordered not to talk to Lee Israel. He seems to have gone to a lot of trouble for someone who didn't want to discuss the subject. In 2017, the Manhattan District Attorney's office announced that it had found "no evidence" that Dorothy was murdered. Mark Shaw, author of the book *The Reporter Who Knew Too Much,* blasted the finding as a "miscarriage of justice."[95] Shaw, despite writing a book about Kilgallen being killed and the ensuing cover-up, incomprehensibly believes Oswald was the assassin.

Regis Kennedy was a senior FBI agent in New Orleans who interacted with Oswald, with Guy Banister crony Jack Martin, and Beverly Oliver, who claims to be the mysterious "Babushka Lady" that was filming in Dealey Plaza. Oliver identified him as the one who confiscated her film. The circumstances of Regis Kennedy's death are unclear, which is the case far too often with those connected to the events in Dallas. He died shortly after testifying before the HSCA (and ludicrously claiming Carlos Marcello was not a mob boss, but a mere tomato salesman), and some online sources say he was murdered. *Politico,* of all sources, reported the following: "Kennedy (no relation to the president) is among several witnesses connected to the events in Dallas in 1963 who died before they could be fully questioned. Kennedy reportedly suffered a heart attack the day before he was scheduled to testify before a grand jury on confiscated home movies of the assassination."[96] Many researchers cite far right-winger Joseph Milteer's eerily prophetic comments about the assassination, shortly before JFK was killed, but few mention that he died unnaturally like so many others, when a stove exploded in his home. Even those with only a seemingly minor connection to these events have been the victims of strange demises. Mona Saenz was a Texas Employment Commission clerk who interviewed Lee Harvey Oswald, and was struck and killed by a city bus in 1965.

Karen Carlin, aka "Little Lynn," was one of Jack Ruby's Carousel Club strippers. Carlin was Ruby's alibi; a witness that his shooting of Oswald had been a spontaneous act, inasmuch as he'd wired her $25 immediately beforehand. In an August 4, 1964, sworn affidavit, Secret Service agent Roger C. Warner stated, "On November 24, 1963, at the request of Inspector Thomas Kelley, U.S. Secret Service, I met with Karen Lynn Bennett Carlin at 3809 Middlebrook Drive, Ft. Worth, Texas. The time was about 11:00 PM. Also present at the interview was Bruce Ray Carlin, who was identified by Mrs. Carlin as her husband. Mrs. Carlin related to me facts regarding a $25 money order sent to her by Jack Ruby on 11-24-63. She also related to me the fact that she had learned that Mr. Dewar, once employed by Jack Ruby, had seen Lee Harvey Oswald in Ruby's night club, the Carousel. Mrs. Carlin stated that she had also vaguely remembered Oswald being at the club, but was by no means sure of that fact, nor of the fact that she had ever seen Oswald." However, as Warner went on to note, "At the beginning of the above interview Mrs. Carlin was highly agitated and was reluctant to make any statement to me. She stated to me that she was under the impression that Lee Harvey Oswald, Jack Ruby and other individuals unknown to her, were involved in a plot to assassinate President Kennedy and that she would be killed if she gave any information to the authorities. It was only through the aid of her husband that she would give any information at all. She twisted in her chair, stammered in her speech, and seemed on the point of hysteria." For years, Carlin was included in the "mysterious deaths" of witnesses, with the claim being she'd been murdered in 1966. However, in October 1992, a woman claiming to be Carlin (she'd lived under an assumed name for almost thirty years), contacted researcher Gary Shaw. She declared that she'd known about a conspiracy to kill Lee Harvey Oswald, and that Jack Ruby had instructed her to phone him Sunday morning. An hour later he would telegraph her $25, just before shooting Oswald, to establish an alibi. In 1964, Carlin told Jack Gordon of the *Fort Worth Press,* "I've had to move 12 times. Whenever a landlord found out who I was, I was asked to move. They were afraid of getting mixed up in the Ruby case." Penn Jones reported her as dead in 1966, and his widow would later claim that he'd done it in order to protect her at the urging of someone else. Carlin, apparently for real, died in 2010.[97] Another of Ruby's strippers, Janet "Jada" Conforto, in true Body Count style, was struck and killed by a bus in 1980, at age forty-four.

George de Mohrenschildt

My wife and I spent many an agonizing moment thinking of Lee, ashamed that we did not stand up more decisively in his defense. But who would have listened to us at the time and would have published anything true and favorable to him?

—George de Mohrenschildt[98]

Few persons associated with this case are more intriguing than George de Mohrenschildt. Old enough to be Oswald's father, and with class distinctions far different from the former defector turned minimum-wage earner, de Mohrenschildt and the alleged lone nut were a decidedly odd pair of friends. De Mohrenschildt is probably the only person in the world with a connection to both Jacqueline Kennedy's mother and to Lee Harvey Oswald. He would later express deep regrets about cooperating with the authorities in framing his young friend. In his manuscript, *I Am a Patsy!,* he wrote, "Our performance at the Warren Committee was very lukewarm and not decisive enough in favor of Lee. I hope he will forgive us. . . . And I hope also that Mrs. Marguerite Oswald will also forgive us." He went on to say, "I was cleverly led by the Warren Committee counsel, Albert Jenner, into saying some things I had not really wanted to say, to admit certain faults in Lee, which I wasn't sure were his. In other words, I consider myself a coward and a slob who did not stand up to defend proudly a dead friend, whatever odds were against him." After noting that counsel Albert Jenner (later to be cast in a positive light by the mainstream media for his role in the Watergate hearings) "knew how to cajole and to threaten," de Mohrenschildt infers that his testimony wasn't recorded honestly, as had several other witnesses, stating, "In reality Jenner spoke much more than I did. The Warren Report, so well doctored, does not show it." He claimed Jenner repeatedly offered him "suggestions" during their breaks, and compared the process to what had happened in the Soviet Union, lamenting "the whole Warren Report and its disastrous effect on the American credibility." Sounding much like the early Warren Report critics, de Mohrenschildt chided the Dallas Police for their inexplicable failure to record Oswald's interrogations, writing, "The City of Dallas was certainly rich enough at the time to have acquired a tape-recorder. And so the tape of Lee's interrogation either did not exist or had mysteriously disappeared." Unlike Ruth Paine, de Mohrenschildt certainly seemed to have recanted whatever role he played in handling and/or setting up Oswald.

Like too many others, George de Mohrenschildt died during the HSCA investigation. He was one of several crucial witnesses whose death prevented them from testifying. His widow Jeanne was adamant that her husband didn't kill himself. "My husband is dead and can't talk," she told reporter Jim Marrs. "That's why I am doing all the talking while I can." Jeanne revealed her own fears that she might be killed as well. "I am the last of the Mohicans, so to speak. They may get me, too, but I'm not afraid. . . . It's about time somebody looked into this thing." Jeanne acknowledged that her husband had been involved in intelligence work dating back to World War II. She stated her belief that Lee Harvey Oswald "was an agent of the United States, possibly the CIA," and did not shoot Kennedy. She described how they'd been victims of "mysterious break-ins and surveillance" dating back to 1962. She claimed that she and her husband had "tried unsuccessfully to get a meaningful investigation into Kennedy's death" starting in 1964. De Mohrenschildt was alleged to have worked as a spy for both the Nazis and Marshal Tito's communist regime in Yugoslavia. Jeanne assured Marrs she would never commit suicide and stated, "The FBI and CIA will be covering up and covering up."[99] It is seldom mentioned, but the de Mohrenschildts actually divorced in 1973. According to researcher Richard Trask, in another of those endless eye-raising connections, before her marriage to George, Jeanne had worked with Abraham Zapruder in his Dallas dress manufacturing business.

De Mohrenschildt sent a letter to then CIA Director George H. W. Bush on September 5, 1976. "Dear George," the letter read, "You will excuse this hand-written letter. Maybe you will be able to bring a solution into the hopeless situation I find myself in. My wife and I find ourselves surrounded by some vigilantes; our phone bugged; and we are being followed everywhere. Either FBI is involved in this or they do not want to accept my complaints. . . . I tried to write, stupidly and unsuccessfully, about Lee H Oswald and must have angered a lot of people I do not know. But to punish an elderly man like myself and my highly nervous and sick wife is really too much. Could you do something to remove the net around us? This will be my last request for help and I will not annoy you anymore." A CIA secretary asked Bush in a note, "Do you know this man?" Bush replied in an internal CIA note, "I do know this man de Mohrenschildt. I first met him in the early 40's. He was an uncle to my Andover roommate. Later he surfaced in Dallas (50's maybe). I don't recall his role in all this. At one time he had/or spent plenty of money. I have not heard from him for many years until the attached letter came in. He got involved in some controversial dealings in Haiti. Then he surfaced when Oswald shot to prominence. He knew Oswald before the assassination of Pres. Kennedy." A few months after writing this letter, de Mohrenschildt was committed to a mental institution. His wife claimed he was suffering from depression. He would undergo shock therapy treatment at Parkland Hospital. When author Willem Oltmans met de Mohrenschildt in early 1977, he was startled by his appearance. "I couldn't believe my eyes. The man had changed drastically . . . he was nervous, trembling. It was a scared, a very, very scared person I saw." Oltmans stated. "I was absolutely shocked, because I knew de Mohrenschildt as a man who wins tennis matches, who is always suntanned, who jogs every morning, who is as healthy as a bull." Oltmans claimed that de Mohrenschildt had confessed to being an intermediary between Oswald and conspirators including Texas oilmen, anti-Castro Cubans, and elements of the FBI and CIA. He quoted de Mohrenschildt as saying, "I am responsible. I feel responsible for the behavior of Lee Harvey Oswald . . . because I guided him. I instructed him to set it up." When Oltmans asked him if he would make a statement, de Mohrenschildt replied, "Yes, but never in America. I am being followed. I find my house all the time searched. So I am scared to death. I first must get out of the country."[100] Interestingly, de Mohrenschildt's second wife, Wynne Sharples, told the FBI George had "enough charm to lie out of anything," and also implied he was a homosexual.[101]

Only a month or so after allegedly making these cryptic remarks, de Mohrenschildt was found dead, allegedly of a self-inflicted gunshot wound, on March 29, 1977. He died in the home of Nancy Tilton, who steadfastly refused to discuss the incident. Supposedly Tilton regularly asked her maid to tape-record her favorite soap operas, and that day the audio of de Mohrenschildt's death was inadvertently recorded in the background. Investigators claimed the sound of footsteps, followed by an explosion, could be heard. Oltmans shared his information with the HSCA, and publicly asked for a meeting with President Jimmy Carter (which never happened).[102] Edward Jay Epstein, author of the wildly overrated early work on the Warren Commission, *Inquest,* and later to write the disinformation piece *Legend: The Secret World of Lee Harvey Oswald,* was the last to interview de Mohrenschildt, less than two hours before he was found shot to death. Bill O'Reilly would make the dramatic claim that he was scheduled to interview de Mohrenschildt that afternoon, and heard the gunshot as he was knocking on the door. This was clearly ridiculous; why would anyone, least of all an ambitious young reporter, not contact the police after hearing gunfire, instead of fleeing the scene? And there is strong evidence that O'Reilly was in Dallas at the time, at the local television station where he worked.[103]

In his autobiography, HSCA investigator Gaeton Fonzi wrote, "About 6:30 that evening I received a call from Bill O'Reilly, a friend who was then a television reporter in Dallas. 'Funny thing happened,' he said. 'We just aired a story that came over the wire about a Dutch journalist saying the Assassinations Committee has finally located de Mohrenschildt in

South Florida. Now de Mohrenschildt's attorney, a guy named Pat Russell, he calls and says de Mohrenschildt committed suicide this afternoon. Is that true?'"[104] In his best-selling Warren Report apologia *Killing Kennedy,* O'Reilly described knocking on the door and hearing the gunshot in detail, claiming he "traced de Mohrenschildt to Palm Beach, Florida and travelled there to confront him." Two of his WFAA colleagues told Media Matters that O'Reilly had been with them in Dallas that day. Fonzi's widow Marie would share the tape with researchers, and it can still be heard online. O'Reilly asks Fonzi *where* it happened and says he's going to "come down there tomorrow," and also mentions wanting to talk with Epstein, because "he knows what happened." Marie Fonzi told Jefferson Morley's JFK Facts website that "Gaet liked O'Reilly and did lots to help him. He hired him in the early '70s when editor of *Miami Magazine* at $25 a month to write movie reviews. He wrote letters of reference for him and was instrumental in getting him his first TV shot." She went on to say, "I always try to do what I think my husband would do, and I sometimes think he would tell me, 'Don't hurt Bill.' But I also know my husband was committed to the truth."[105]

Astonishingly, despite such overt documentation to the contrary, O'Reilly's publisher Henry Holt & Company sprung to his defense. O'Reilly's then WFAA fellow reporter Bob Sirkin stated, in direct contradiction to O'Reilly's recorded words, "Bill and I had found out . . . that de Mohrenschildt, the language professor was missing from his position and on campus apartment at small Bishop College in Dallas. . . . Bill had just learned from his friend and investigator for the House Committee on Assassinations, Gaeton Fonzi, that de Mohrenschildt was in Palm Beach, Florida being interviewed for an article or a book by Edward J. Epstein and that the following day, March 29th, de Mohrenschildt would be served a subpoena to appear before the House Committee on Assassinations. Marty Haag dispatched O'Reilly and me to West Palm Beach late on the night of March 28th." Sirkin laughably described going to the Breakers Motel and knocking on Epstein's door and seeing de Mohrenschildt in the background. He continued, "Epstein becomes furious, calls security." They were escorted off the property, but Sirkin claims, "The footage of de Mohrenschildt that we captured in this incident was included in my and

Bill's WFAA reports from Florida." Footage? There is nothing touching on this anywhere else in the record. Sirkin claimed they split up, and "O'Reilly and I reconnect at the house in Manalpan. That was the story and still is." The Fonzi-O'Reilly tape revealed the young reporter asking more than once about Manalpan, a name he was clearly unfamiliar with. Sirkin, all taped evidence be damned, angrily declared, "It remains preposterous for anyone to claim O'Reilly and I were not in Florida before, during, and following de Mohrenschildt's death."[106] When confronted with the audiotape of O'Reilly being clearly uninformed about de Mohrenschildt's death, Sirkin merely said, "I can't explain it. I'm befuddled by it."[107]

Another underreported conspiratorial tidbit related to de Mohrenschildt is the fact that HSCA investigators discovered some curious activity in his offshore banking account, right after the JFK assassination. As Gaeton Fonzi detailed in a footnote from his book *The Last Investigation*, "Late in 1963, several large deposits popped up in de Mohrenschildt's Haitian bank account including one for two hundred thousand dollars from a Bahamian bank." de Mohrenschildt would maintain the large payout (referred to variously as between $200,000 and $285,000) came from the Haitian government, in return for his geological survey work.

Ironically, some of the few outlets that were open to criticism of the Warren Report in America were adult magazines like *Penthouse.* Col. Fletcher Prouty, whose long, distinguished career had garnered him publication in mainstream giants like *The Nation, New Republic,* and *Air Force Magazine,* was relegated to having his JFK assassination–related work published in other adult magazines like *Genesis* (seven articles) and *Gallery* (fourteen articles). Prouty alleged that the paperback edition of his book *The Secret Team: The CIA and Its Allies in Control of the United States and the World*, published by Ballantine, had been "disappeared" shortly after it was released in February of 1974. A later edition of Prouty's book would be published in 2011 by Skyhorse, my primary publisher. The biggest mainstream organs—*The New York Times, The Washington Post, Time, Life, Newsweek,* and every television network—were (and remain) the most strident defenders of the official story. With the exception of Oliver Stone's seminal 1991 film *JFK,* all modern depictions of the Kennedy assassination in the entertainment world adhere to the same lone assassin fiction every news network promulgates. In 1985, the rebooted *Twilight Zone* series copied an original *Twilight Zone* premise, where a man goes back in time to try to stop the Lincoln assassination, by updating the plot to the JFK assassination. Naturally, of course, the script supported the "Oswald did it" fairy tale. In a February 2016 comment on author Russ Baker's blog, poster J. Neil Schulman stated, "I wrote the 'Profile in Silver' episode of The Twilight Zone and the first-draft script I submitted had a second gunman dressed as a Dallas policeman on the Grassy Knoll. CBS demanded it be removed from the script." As I noted in *Hidden History*, publicly expressing a belief in a JFK assassination conspiracy is not a good career move for anyone working in show business.

Fletcher Prouty, who Oliver Stone used as the basis for the character "Mr. X," played by Donald Sutherland in *JFK*, has been smeared recently as well by the neocons that target conspiracy-friendly witnesses and evidence exclusively. An attack on Prouty's credibility was launched on The Education Forum in a long discussion thread started in October 2020. The primary allegation against Prouty was that he retracted everything he'd ever said before, when he testified before the ARRB. The ARRB, with the sole exception of Doug Horne's devotion to the truth, was just as biased against conspiracy as the Warren Commission and HSCA had been. As Horne wrote in the first volume of his invaluable series of books, *Inside the Assassination Records Review Board*, "*none* of the Board members believed there had been a conspiracy to kill President John F. Kennedy." So they obviously approached the likes of Prouty, who had been a favorite with Warren Commission critics for years, with a decided lack of objectivity. Horne described the attitude of everyone else at the ARRB as one of arrogance and extreme prejudice against anyone questioning the lone assassin narrative. According to Len Osanic, a longtime JFK assassination researcher who hosts the important *Black Op Radio* program, and was a personal friend of Prouty's, after his ARRB testimony, Prouty called him and told him he recognized the spin the board was using and played along with the charade. He didn't trust them and was basically covering himself. I don't agree with Prouty's strategy there, but he didn't honestly retract anything he'd said previously. Prouty summed up the conspiracy and cover up as well as anyone ever has in the following words: "That assassination has demonstrated that most of the major events of world significance are masterfully planned and orchestrated by an elite coterie of enormously powerful people who are not of one nation, one ethnic grouping, or one overridingly important business group. They are a power unto themselves for whom these others work. Neither is the power elite of recent origin. Its roots go deep into the past. Kennedy's assassination has been used as an example of their methodology. Most thinking people of this country, and of the world believe that he was not killed by a lone gunman. Despite that view, the cover story created and thrust upon us by the spokesmen of this High Cabal has existed for three decades. It has come from the lips of every subsequent President and from the pop media representatives and their spokesmen. They are experienced, intelligent people who are aware of the facts. Consider the pressure it must take to require all of them, without exception, to quote the words of that contrived cover story over and over again for nearly three decades."[108]

Two of the JFK assassination witnesses I unsuccessfully tried to contact were Linda and Rosemary Willis, who were young girls watching the motorcade with their parents in Dealey Plaza. Their father Phil Willis took some important photos at the time of the assassination. In a November 1998 interview with *Texas Monthly,* Rosemary said, regarding the suspicious epileptic seizure in front of the Texas School Book Depository building, "so when they make that turn, that's about the time that there was a kid on the corner that had an epileptic seizure. Or appeared to have an epileptic seizure. Which was most interesting because an ambulance came, and if you followed this story, nothing ever became of that. We'll discuss that later. Anyway, no hospital ever received him. Anyway, I always thought at the time that person acted real strangely. Even at age 10, it didn't look like a normal emergency epileptic seizure. There was something strange about it." Her sister Linda, whom along with her mother Marilyn was also at the interview, chimed in, "It seemed staged." Regarding the shots, Rosemary said, "My ears heard four shots. If you ask me how many I think there were, I really think that there were six." She also described seeing smoke coming through the trees on the Grassy Knoll, as did other witnesses. Marilyn Willis was just as forthright, answering the question, "What do you think about this day?" by declaring, "It was a coup." Her daughter Linda echoed, "I agree." Marilyn continued, "The Secret Service interviewed me, at home, and they took Linda and my husband downtown to the old post office building and grilled him and interviewed him. Who was it, Spector? I think it was Spector. He's now a Congressman. My husband disagreed and said (assuming a stern voice), 'You won't let me tell what I saw.' He was just as mad as he could be about it." Rosemary maintained, "I know it was a conspiracy," and stated it had destroyed her faith in America as a democracy. She mentioned that "lots of imposters" were on the scene, and how the authorities "told everybody to stay put. But they really didn't do anything." Rosemary recounted her being interrogated: "When they asked you what happened, you say, 'I heard a shot from over here, I heard a shot and saw smoke from over here,' and they're going (assumes mean voice), 'No, you didn't. Look at me: you didn't. I'm telling you, you didn't.' Very adamantly and depending who they were talking to, they were very strong about it, they did not want you to tell the truth."

On May 17, 2022, I spoke to veteran researcher Gary Shaw, author of perhaps the most underappreciated book about the assassination, *Cover-Up: The Governmental Conspiracy to Conceal the Facts about the Public Execution of John F. Kennedy,* which he wrote with Larry Harris, who as noted later died in a suspicious car crash. I asked him about the Willis family, and he told me he'd known them all very well, and characterized them as very fine people. In 1974, Phil Willis told him "I don't have a theory of the assassination, but I know the Warren version was not right." He related how Willis had purposefully destroyed one of his film slides, which depicted the arrest of a young man in the Dal-Tex Building, wearing black gloves and a leather jacket. Willis explained that he didn't want him to be embarrassed by the picture.

The Willis family, like Roger Craig, Nelson Delgado (Oswald's fellow Marine who told the Warren Commission he was a lousy shot), S. M. Holland, Richard Randolph Carr, Julia Ann Mercer, Jean Hill, and many others, in the JFK assassination case alone, contradict the argument that "someone would have talked." They all "talked," in spite of the fact so many witnesses died unnaturally who knew too much, and had also "talked." It takes a great deal of bravery to come forth and contradict an official narrative, when no one with any authority will listen. Unlike political leaders, or the mainstream media, or most of the Kennedy family itself, these witnesses represented profiles in courage.

It is beyond debate that the Warren Commission was a sham of an investigation; a whitewash, as Harold Weisberg aptly called it. They failed to follow up on countless good leads and didn't call some of the most important witnesses. Meanwhile, they tracked down people like Myrtle Evans, a friend of Marguerite's when Lee was a child. As if she wasn't irrelevant enough, they called her husband Julian as a witness as well. Julian contributed the bombshell information that young Lee "wanted his own way about everything." Julian described Marguerite as "a nice-looking woman," which supports the research of John Armstrong, who has produced information that indicates there were two very different Marguerites, as well as two different Lee Harvey Oswalds (Harvey and Lee).[109] The HSCA was even worse from the standpoint of researchers, as the vast majority of their testimony remains inaccessible to the public. The ARRB was again disappointing, as the only staff member really interested in the truth was Doug Horne. Without a massive awakening on the part of most Americans, the JFK assassination seems consigned to be dishonestly portrayed by the corrupt court historians, to impressionable dumbed-down youngsters and Ivy League graduates alike, as the meaningless act of a demented loner.

There was optimism during the Trump years that the remaining classified JFK assassination documents would be released to the public. Trump himself, in typical style, bragged that he would do this. Trump had tweeted, on October 21, 2017, "Subject to the receipt of further information, I will be allowing, as president, the long blocked and classified JFK FILES to be opened." Some 2,800 documents were released at that time. Under pressure from the CIA and FBI, including then-CIA Director Mike Pompeo, whom Trump would subsequently name as Secretary of State, the blustery president backed down. By April 2018, Trump announced that the threat to national security was "of such gravity that it outweighs the public interest in immediate disclosure."[110] In a 2021 episode of his *Celente and the Judge* Podcast, trends forecaster Gerald Celente spoke with Judge Andrew Napolitano. Napolitano recounted, "I once had a conversation with

President Trump when he was in the White House. He used to call me all the time. And we'd talk about everything under the sun. I said, 'You going to release those documents, or not?' And he said to me, 'If you saw what I saw, you wouldn't release them.' I said, 'I don't know what you saw Mr. President, but you can't treat us like children, as all of your predecessors have. We have a *right* to know. Whatever happened to him, and whoever did it to him, *the public has the right to know.*' He said, 'I entered this job promising, expecting. . .' (And he once promised me personally he would reveal these documents.) He said, 'I've now changed my mind completely after what they showed me.'"[111]

When the remaining classified files next came up for review, in October 2021, President Biden predictably declared, "Temporary continued postponement is necessary to protect against identifiable harm to the military defense, intelligence operations, law enforcement, or the conduct of foreign relations that is of such gravity that it outweighs the public interest in immediate disclosure." Even more laughably, Biden administration officials actually cited COVID-19 as another reason.[112] RFK Jr. blasted the continued concealment of evidence, telling *Politico,* "It's an outrage. It's an outrage against American democracy. We're not supposed to have secret governments within the government. How the hell is it 58 years later, and what in the world could justify not releasing these documents?" Former Rep. Patrick Kennedy, son of Ted Kennedy, supported his cousin, noting the assassination was "something that left such a scar in this nation's soul that lost not only a president but a promise of a brighter future. I think for the good of the country, everything has to be put out there so there's greater understanding of our history." Kennedy also commented, "We're living in a time of a lot of conspiracy theories," but declined to answer whether he believed the official story of the assassination.[113]

In December 2021, the Biden administration reversed course and released over 1,000 files, while leaving an estimated 14,000 still classified. The mainstream media emphasized that a CIA document related that "Kennedy assassin" (there is not even the slightest pretense of doubt, or a qualifying "alleged" any longer) Lee Harvey Oswald visited the Cuban and Russian embassies in Mexico. Researchers debunked "Oswald's" supposed trip to Mexico decades ago. Most feel it represents perhaps the ultimate example of all the Oswald impersonations which took place before the assassination. This CIA document notes that one of the people "Oswald" visited with had connections to the KGB's "assassination department." Reports now were that a "final set" of documents was set for release in December 2022.[114] The memo refers to Oswald entering Mexico City "apparently by car," which contradicts the long-discredited claim that he traveled there by bus. And begs the question: was Oswald behind the wheel? He is alleged not to have known how to drive. If he wasn't driving, who was? Lone nutter Gerald Posner, author of the fanciful 1993 Warren Report apologia *Case Closed,* was front and center, *the* "expert" every television station wanted, to expound upon the file release. Joe Biden issued a bizarre "final certification" on the JFK assassination files in July 2023, even though nearly 5,000 remain either classified or heavily redacted.[115]

One of the most neglected JFK assassination researchers is my friend, former *Real People* creator and host John Barbour. Barbour had a long conversation with Jim Garrison on September 5, 1981. While he would reveal much of what Garrison said in his two important documentaries, *The JFK Assassination: the Jim Garrison Tapes,* and *The American Media & the 2nd Assassination of John F. Kennedy,* he told me privately that Garrison had shared something very significant with him "off the record." Barbour told me that Garrison had called Allen Dulles a mere "hireling," and speculated that the man who gave the orders to assassinate JFK had been Averill Harriman. The son of a railroad baron, Harriman served in the NRA and Business Advisory Council under FDR, as well as ambassador to the Soviet Union. He also served in the Truman administration. Robert F. Kennedy was strongly opposed to Harriman joining the Kennedy administration, but JFK named him an ambassador-at-large, where he came to play a central role in the Vietnam quagmire. Garrison was among those who blamed Harriman for being behind the coup of South Vietnamese president Ngo Dinh Diem, and his subsequent assassination, which took place only three weeks before JFK was murdered in Dallas.

According to author James Douglas, "Even the select few in the State Department whom Kennedy was consulting on Vietnam did not serve him well. In late August, Averill Harriman, who had returned triumphantly from the test ban negotiations in Moscow, and Roger Hilsman, now in charge of the Vietnam desk, precipitated a decision for U.S. support of a coup against Diem. On August 24, during a weekend when Kennedy was in Hyannis Port, Hilsman, working with Harriman and Kennedy's aide Michael Forrestal, drafted an urgent telegram to newly appointed Saigon ambassador Henry Cabot Lodge. The telegram authorized US support of a looming coup by rebel South Vietnamese generals"[116] Close Kennedy friend, Appointments Secretary Kenny O'Donnell, was said to be convinced that National Security Advisor McGeorge Bundy had followed Harriman's orders rather than Kennedy's. As I showed in *Hidden History*, there is evidence to suggest that Bundy was a JFK assassination conspirator inside the Kennedy White House. JFK was reportedly deeply shocked and guilt-ridden after Diem was killed.[117] Garrison told Barbour that RFK was so upset at Harriman over Diem's coup that they almost engaged in fisticuffs. Harriman laughably was dubbed LBJ's "envoy of peace" as the Vietnam War dragged on for years.

Two Key 1968 Assassinations: MLK and RFK

> *Like anybody, I would like to live a long life—longevity has its place . . . I'm not fearing any man. Mine eyes have seen the glory of the coming of the Lord.*
>
> —Martin Luther King Jr., April 3, 1968[118]

> *I did not commit the crime.*
>
> —Sirhan Sirhan[119]

By the Spring of 1968, Martin Luther King Jr. had evolved into a strong advocate for peace and voice for all those mired in poverty, not just Black people. His planned Poor People's March on Washington, D.C., would have shaken the Establishment far more than his earlier "I Have a Dream" speech did. King was shot and killed on April 4, 1968, while standing on a hotel balcony in Memphis, Tennessee. Researchers who were already jaded by the obvious lies and cover-up of the JFK assassination, such as Mark Lane and Harold Weisberg, turned their attention to the King case and found the same holes in the official story.

Like so many other patsies and figures associated with these events, alleged MLK assassin James Earl Ray had some curious connections. Attorney William Pepper, who represented Ray at the barely reported Loyd Jowers trial in 1999, learned from Ron Adkins, the son of Dixie Mafia figure Russell Adkins Sr. that the warden of Missouri State Penitentiary was paid $25,000 to allow Ray to escape in 1967. The money was delivered by none other than J. Edgar Hoover's right-hand man (and rumored lover) Clyde Tolson. Ron knew Tolson well enough to call him "Uncle Clyde." Interestingly, MLK became friends with William Pepper after reading an article about Vietnam that he'd written in *Ramparts.* King was a subscriber to *Ramparts,* which was one of the few media outlets to publish material that exposed the fraudulent Warren Report. Considering this, it is highly probable that MLK was familiar with the work of the Warren Commission critics. King's top aide Ralph Abernathy was troubled by the official narrative of the assassination, and had spoken to James Earl Ray numerous times. It was Abernathy who suggested Pepper visit Ray in prison, and led to him becoming his lawyer.[120] Pepper became a close enough friend that he traveled to Memphis on April 8, 1968, with famous pediatrician and anti-war activist Dr. Benjamin Spock to attend King's memorial march. There had been earlier rumors of a King/Spock Third-Party presidential ticket.

A video on YouTube features Memphis Police Department custodian Lenny B. Curtis, who worked at the Police gun range, claiming to have overheard officer Frank Strausser say that "King is going to get his head blown off." Strausser was spotted practicing with his rifle all day long on the day of the shooting. King's seven-man security detail and three twelve-man tactical units were stripped away the morning of April 4. The person photographed kneeling over the wounded King was Meryll McCollough, who was an undercover operative for both the Memphis Police and the CIA. There were undercover agents everywhere around King; the owner of the Lorraine Motel was a police informer, as was MLK's chauffeur.[121] At the time of the assassination, two witnesses identified a man they saw at a service station located over a mile away from the Lorraine Motel as James Earl Ray, who needed a flat tire repaired. Most people aren't aware that a mock trial televised in 1993 resulted in James Earl Ray being found not guilty.

My friend John Barbour, who has researched all the assassinations of the 1960s, provided me with almost incomprehensible information I was not previously aware of. In an April 12, 2022, Facebook message, Barbour told me, "In his book, Pepper found a woman staff member who claimed she saw 3 men in suits smother King to death with pillows!" Barbour was referring to the aforementioned attorney William Pepper, who represented both accused MLK assassin James Earl Ray and accused RFK assassin Sirhan Sirhan. Indeed, in a *USA Today* story, Pepper was quoted as saying, "He wasn't killed from the bullet that hit him on the balcony. He was taken to the St. Joseph's Hospital, and he was killed in the emergency room of St. Joseph's Hospital by the chief of neurosurgery, Dr. Breen Bland." Differing only slightly from Barbour's recollection, the article goes on to report, "Citing the purported eyewitness account of a surgical nurse named Lula Mae Shelby, Pepper goes on to claim Bland suffocated King with a pillow." The story quotes Dr. Jerry T. Francisco, who conducted the autopsy on King, and was also at Elvis Presley's autopsy, after the iconic star died under suspicious circumstances in 1977, to defend his own conclusion that King's death was from a gunshot wound.[122]

Further details on Pepper's startling accusation were provided in the same *Pressreader* article quoted above. According to nurses present at the time, when King was taken to St. Joseph's Hospital emergency room, he was definitely still alive. The aforementioned Dr. Breen Bland, the ER's chief surgeon, happened to be the family doctor for the Adkins family, who as noted were associated with Clyde Tolson. Ron Adkins, who was a boy at the time, provided intriguing testimony again. He claimed that Bland had visited his family a few weeks before the assassination. Young Ron heard Bland say about King: "Please make sure he is not killed instantly by the shot. Make sure they take him to St. Joseph's, so we can make sure he doesn't leave there alive." Once King arrived at the ER, only Bland and his trusted confidants were allowed in the room. As a surgical nurse was dismissed from the room, she witnessed Bland and company spit on King together, before a pillow was held over King's face until he was dead.[123] As far-fetched as this story sounds, there are multiple witnesses who attested to it. The House Select Committee on Assassinations concluded that "there is a likelihood that James Earl Ray assassinated Dr.

Martin Luther King Jr. as a result of a conspiracy." Unlike the Kennedy family, and in fact the families of most persons killed by political subterfuge, the King family spoke out boldly. MLK's widow Corretta Scott King charged that there was "a major, high-level conspiracy in the assassination of my husband."[124] As Mrs. King explained during questioning by Pepper at the 1999 conspiracy trial of Lloyd Jowers, "We wanted to go on with our lives. We felt the only way we could do it was to really take the position that we did take, because the evidence pointed away from Mr. Ray, not that he might have not had some involvement. but he was not the person we felt that really actually killed him." She testified that their public statements doubting the official story had negatively impacted financial contributions to the King Center. If only more of these families could be such profiles in courage.

I noted in *Hidden History* that only six years after MLK was assassinated, his mother Alberta Williams King was shot and killed while playing the organ in church.[125] This shocking tragedy received surprisingly little coverage when it happened, and has been seemingly forgotten by most researchers. The man who was convicted of shooting her, Marcus Wayne Chenault (another three-namer), would die at only forty-four after suffering a stroke in prison.[126] However, other sources attributed his death to "natural causes." Chenault's motive was said to be a hatred of Christianity. In an interesting aside, MLK's father Martin Luther King Sr. was among the members of Morehouse College's Board of Trustees, who were held hostage by a group of students during a 1969 protest. Among the students was future actor Samuel L. Jackson.

The King assassination also had its list of associated unnatural deaths. Jimmy Hoffa's lawyer, Z. T. Osborn Jr. decided to help James Earl Ray with his case. He abruptly committed "suicide"—which his wife did not believe.[127] *Two* judges considering Ray's request for a retrial—W. Preston Battle and William E. Miller—died of suspicious heart attacks.[128] Just before he died, Battle had received a request for a new trial from one of Ray's new attorneys, Richard J. Ryan, which was refused by Battle's successor, Judge Arthur Faquin Jr., in contradiction to existing Tennessee law.[129] In July 1969, King's brother, the Reverend Alfred Daniel King, was found dead in his home after an apparent swimming pool accident. The emergency responders said upon arrival, "Ain't no water in his lungs, he was dead before he hit the water." King's wife, Naomi said, "Absolutely, he was murdered. He was an excellent swimmer. There was no water in his lungs. He was in the fetal position. He had a bruised forehead. Rings around his neck. And he was in his underwear. He was murdered."[130] Louis Lomax, a Black journalist who was investigating the death of Martin Luther King Jr., and who claimed to have solved the Malcom X assassination, died in a suspicious car accident in New Mexico, shortly after contracting with 20th Century Fox to make a movie exposing the intelligence community's role in the case.[131] William Sartor, a thirty-two-year-old writer for *Life* and *Look* magazine who was investigating the King assassination, was murdered in Waco, Texas, the night before he was to interview a night-club owner linked to Carlos Marcello. Sartor was given a lethal dose of mathaqualone—slipped into his drink.[132] Six years after Sartor's death, former FBI assistant director of intelligence William Sullivan, whom I have listed previously as a victim of the JFK assassination Body Count, was shot and killed by a man (Richard Daniels) who mistook him for a deer while deer-hunting. The killing occurred shortly before he was scheduled to testify before the HSCA about his former boss, J. Edgar Hoover's hatred of King.[133]

On June 5, 1968, only two months after MLK was killed, JFK's brother Sen. Robert F. Kennedy was shot in the pantry of Los Angeles's Ambassador Hotel. The assassination of RFK, in the midst of his own presidential campaign, is inexorably tied to the plot that took the life of his brother five years earlier. I have noted many times that Robert F. Kennedy would never have been assassinated if John F. Kennedy hadn't been.

There are plenty of intriguing, crossover connections between the two Kennedy assassinations. Guy Banister was the Special Agent in Charge of the Chicago FBI office during the 1940s. One of his fellow FBI agents at the time was Robert Maheu, who also had ties to the CIA and became the right-hand man to reclusive billionaire Howard Hughes.[134] It was during this period that Jack Ruby was arrested in connection with the 1939 murder of attorney Leon Cooke. Cooke was actually murdered by union president John Martin, who pleaded self-defense during a fight that erupted between them over missing union money. This particular union had an interesting connection to Al Capone's top henchman Frank Nitti. It is fascinating to consider how this one incident could be tied to Banister, Maheu, and Ruby. More significantly, Maheu and Banister would have been the agents investigating the Cooke case. Maheu, while employed by the CIA, approached Johnny Roselli about killing Fidel Castro. Roselli in turn introduced Maheu to his mobster cohorts Sam Giancana and Santo Trafficante Jr.[135] Roselli happened to be part owner of Santa Anita Racetrack, where Sirhan worked as a stable hand.[136] Extending the bizarre connections even further, one of Sirhan's Santa Anita coworkers was Thomas Bremer, brother of Arthur Bremer, who shot George Wallace in 1972.[137] Interestingly, Bremer was released from prison in 2007, and lives in Cumberland, Maryland, where at last report he was working a regular job at over seventy years old.

Some have speculated that Bremer, like Sirhan Sirhan, was hypnotized and programmed by William Joseph Bryan, who was the great-grandson of William Jennings Bryan. Bryan's secretary later would claim to have received an emergency call from the town of Laurel, Maryland, location of the Wallace assassination attempt, only minutes after the shooting. Bryan supposedly bragged to prostitutes that he'd been Sirhan's programmer. Bryan was a flamboyant character who had also, interestingly enough, been used as a technical advisor on John Frankenheimer's 1962 film *The Manchurian Candidate.* In yet another intriguing connection, RFK would spend his last day alive relaxing at Frankenheimer's Malibu beach house. On March 4, 1977, the fifty-one-year-old Bryan was found dead in a Las Vegas hotel, right after he'd been contacted to testify before the House Select Committee on Assassinations. Bryan has been tied by some to the same Old Catholic Church that David Ferrie belonged to. Bryan also extracted the dubious confessions of Albert DeSalvo, who many now feel was not the Boston Strangler. In belatedly discovered letters, it was revealed that DeSalvo had written "I'm going to drop a bomb!" and recant his confessions to killing thirteen women, two weeks before his November 1973 murder in prison.[138]

Howard Hughes had long-standing ties with Richard Nixon. The eccentric billionaire was known to have given Nixon's brother Donald a huge loan to start a chain of fast-food restaurants.[139] Hughes was so closely allied with the CIA that his nickname there was "the Stockholder." Agency honcho James Angleton spoke at Hughes's funeral, calling him a "great patriot." John H. Meier, considered the second most powerful man in the Hughes organization, has made a variety of explosive allegations in recent years. He mentioned Ace Security guard Thane Eugene Cesar, thought by many to be the second RFK gunman in the pantry, being introduced to him by an associate of Maheu's. Maheu would angrily confront Meier and warn him to stop looking into Cesar. Meier accused the Hughes organization of being involved in RFK's assassination, and even provided a colorful anecdote about a drunk Donald Nixon mentioning his brother being in Dallas when JFK was assassinated, and how Maheu basically took the credit for the murder of RFK.[140] In a June 6, 1968 diary entry, Meier wrote, "5 a.m. Bob Maheu called to ask about the Don Nixon meeting and suggested 8:30 for breakfast at the Desert Inn Country Club. I went to the club. Maheu was all smiles and Don Nixon walks in all smiles. What followed next had to be seen to be believed. They embraced each other and Don Nixon said, 'Well that prick is dead,' and Maheu said, 'Well it looks like your brother is in now.' At the time I did not even know what they were talking about. Maheu joked that they should now be calling Don Nixon 'Mr. Vice President.'"

In another diary entry, Meier stated, "In the aftermath of John F. Kennedy's assassination, Robert Kennedy had amassed a file from many sources, but mostly from the FBI, which indicated that his brother the President had been killed as the result of a plot enacted by a number of leading industrialists in the United States including Howard Hughes. Robert Kennedy had kept the file close to his chest in preparation for the day if, and when, he gained the political power to find out who had ordered his brother's death. According to author and researcher Lisa Pease, Paul Schrade accepted an offer from Howard Hughes to recuperate at his Las Vegas ranch, which was where he met John Meier.[141] Hughes remained grateful to Schrade for his help in organizing autoworkers in a dispute over nuclear testing earlier that year. While Schrade was recovering from the bullet wounds he received when Robert Kennedy was assassinated, he and Meier had discussed what might have happened to that file. Schrade told Meier he would ask Ted Kennedy when the opportunity arose. When he did, the surviving Kennedy brother turned white and told him never to mention the file again."[142] Meier can be seen in a 2008 YouTube video, talking about his family being threatened, and bluntly declared, "The Hughes organization was involved in the assassination of Robert Kennedy in 1968." Meier described communicating closely with Sirhan's then-attorney, Lawrence Teeter, and providing him with evidence. Teeter died at fifty-six years old in Mexico, on July 31, 2005. Meier was unable to retrieve the "documents, tape recordings, and emails" which he'd provided Teeter with. Meier was told that the material had been lost in a home burglary. Teeter was the first attorney for Sirhan who firmly maintained his innocence.

John W. Curington, personal assistant and attorney to oil tycoon H. L. Hunt, also made allegations about *his* boss being involved in the assassination. Curington wrote, "In the late spring of 1968, Mr. Hunt came in and told me that he wanted to go to Los Angeles the next day. I was to get tickets for both of us, along with a room at the Ambassador Hotel in Los Angeles . . . even though we had never stayed at the Ambassador before. Our usual accommodations were at the Beverly Hills Hotel . . . when we arrived, Mr. Hunt told me two things. First, he asked me to contact Wendell Niles. This was a man whose father was Bob Hope's TV announcer, so Wendell was very well connected in L.A. We had him on the payroll so that he would keep us advised as to what was going on in the movie industry and in the Los Angeles area. Mr. Hunt wanted me to find out from Niles exactly what Bobby Kennedy had been doing in California, including where he'd been, where he was going, and who was in his inner circle. . . . I don't know who it was or what they discussed. When I saw Mr. Hunt later, I gave him the information that Wendell Niles had provided. We left to return to Dallas the next day with nothing being said about the business in L.A.—Mr. Hunt never even hinted as to why we made the trip. Within two weeks, Robert F. Kennedy would be dead." Five minutes after hearing that RFK had been assassinated, Curington recalled, "My phone rang, and it was Wendell Niles from LA. with the news. I hung up and immediately called Mr. Hunt, who didn't express any interest one way or the other." Curington went on to describe a curious payoff of $40,000 (about $300,000 in today's dollars), which took place at the Ambassador Hotel, location of the RFK assassination.[143]

Not only did the LAPD destroy the ceiling panels in the Ambassador's pantry, which were said to be full of bullet holes, but in the words of author Lisa Pease, "The LAPD also burned more than two thousand photos relating to Sen. Kennedy's assassination in a hospital incinerator." Some photos that weren't burned, of not only the Ambassador Hotel's pantry, but of RFK's autopsy, were discovered in the safe of Legendary CIA spymaster James Jesus Angleton years after the assassination.[144] Angleton had memorably burned the diary of JFK's rumored lover Mary Pinchot Meyer, wife of CIA official Cord Meyer, after she was mysteriously murdered on October 12, 1964. The bizarre Angleton once noted, "It is inconceivable that a secret intelligence arm of the government has to comply with all the overt orders of the government." Why would any photos related to this important political murder be burned by the police? And why was the CIA involved at all, to the extent that a high-ranking official could simply pilfer crucial evidence?

RFK Jr. "came out" on the subject for real in 2018, on the fiftieth anniversary of his father's assassination, declaring on Instagram, "My father was the chief law enforcement officer in this country. I think it would have disturbed him if somebody was put in jail for a crime they didn't commit." RFK's second-oldest son claimed he was "curious and disturbed by what I had seen in the evidence." Referring to the audiotape analyzed by electrical engineer Philip Van Praag, RFK Jr. stated, "You can't fire 13 shots out of an eight-shot gun."[145] RFK Jr. went on to state, "I had plans to meet Thane Eugene Cesar in the Philippines last June until he demanded a payment of $25,000 through his agent Dan Moldea. Ironically, Moldea penned a meticulous and compelling indictment of Cesar in a 1995 book and then suddenly exculpated him by fiat in a bizarre and nonsensical final chapter. Police have never seriously investigated Cesar's role in my father's killing." In *Hidden History*, I recounted almost exactly the same thing regarding Moldea, author of *The Killing of Robert F. Kennedy*, the book mentioned by Kennedy. Boston.com provided Moldea with a forum to dismiss RFK Jr.'s views. "What Bobby Kennedy Jr. has done, he's launched a whole new generation of conspiracy nuts who are going to believe that Sirhan didn't do it and that somebody else did," Moldea declared.[146] Moldea, who was welcomed with open arms by our state-controlled media in coverage of the fiftieth anniversary of the RFK assassination, even went to the point of preposterously attributing the numerous holes found in the pantry to kitchen carts banging into the wall. Did the carts bang into the ceiling as well? In a September 11, 2019, Instagram post, Robert F. Kennedy Jr. wrote, "Thane Eugene Cesar died today in the Philippines. Compelling evidence suggests that Cesar murdered my father. On June 5, 1968, Cesar, an employee in a classified section of Lockheed's Burbank facility, was moonlighting as a security guard at the Ambassador Hotel. He had landed the job about one week earlier." RFK Jr. is the only member of the Kennedy family who has spoken out about the conspiracies that took his father's and uncle's lives, and the ongoing cover-ups to conceal them.

One unnatural death associated with the RFK assassination was the alleged suicide of researcher Greg Stone. Stone's mentor, former Rep. Allard Lowenstein, had been responsible for first arousing my interest in the RFK assassination when I saw him being interviewed by Tom Snyder on NBC's *Tomorrow* show. Lowenstein would later be assassinated by a supposedly demented follower. Friend Dan Moldea was on hand to helpfully declare that Stone had been "very, very down." The forty-one-year-old Stone sat down under a tree in California's Griffith Park on January 29, 1991, and put a revolver into his mouth.[147] One of Stone's close friends was actor Paul Le Mat, best remembered for his work in the films *American Graffiti* and *Melvin and Howard.* I have communicated off and on with Le Mat, who was actively researching the Kennedy assassinations. When I suggested he write a memoir, Le Mat replied in a November 4, 2021, email thusly: "I can't write a memoir, particularly including the JFK/RFK efforts I made. The bad guys didn't care for me doing radio, newspaper, even TV interviews calling for new investigations, detailing some of the errors in the official 'findings', and lobbying in Wash. (getting in to meet representatives and even one senator, due to my acting notoriety). So, when the RFK book was published, low and behold, poison (arsenic) was put in my food and I nearly died. Maybe you know about that, I've mentioned it to various people, and on FB. Over the years people have asked me what the hell happened to me, my career, etc. Must include that info in any autobiography, explaining how over the years my career went downhill due to being sick . . . so, I don't want to get poisoned again! Simple as that. The bad guys who are now covering up the assassination truth WOULDN'T like me stirring it up."

In August 2019, Sirhan was stabbed in prison by another inmate. He survived with no disabling injuries, and no motive for the attack was ever provided.[148] Two years later, in August 2021, a parole board shockingly recommended that Sirhan be released. In response, the dysfunctional cracks within the Kennedy family broke wide open. RFK Jr. had been the only Kennedy to care enough about his father's assassination to actually examine the evidence, and had pronounced himself satisfied that Sirhan hadn't fired the fatal shot (a conclusion supported by the medical evidence). Of RFK's surviving nine children, only Douglas joined Bobby Jr. in supporting Sirhan's release. RFK Jr. relied on a promise from his siblings not to make a public statement on the subject, but he "got backstabbed," according to an anonymous source quoted in the *New York Post.* Angela Berry, Sirhan's lawyer, explained, "The night before the hearing I got a letter from the parole board via the LAPD. It read, 'On behalf of the Kennedy family, we oppose the release of Sirhan.' [Bobby] had been staying out of it specifically on the assumption that his family was going to stay out of it. . . . I got ahold of him right away letting him know what happened." Responding quickly, RFK Jr. stayed up late to write his own note supporting Sirhan's parole. On August 28, 2021, Kerry Kennedy gave an emotional interview with Ashleigh Banfield on *News Nation,* during which she angrily demanded that they stop airing footage of her father's head being cradled after the shooting. Dropping the family's traditional veneer of privacy, Kerry dismissed her brother Bobby as a "conspiracy theorist," and declared, "Why anyone in the world would take him seriously is beyond comprehension." Banfield had displayed her "morning zoo" type of humor back in 2012, when on the inaugural *Early Start* CNN broadcast, she cold-called Kerry before six a.m., to ask her if she was still haunted by her father's assassination. Kerry handled the intrusive phone call from "journalist" Banfield better than she dealt with her brother having a different opinion.

Paul Schrade, at the time of this writing an almost ninety-seven-year-old Kennedy family friend, was also shot alongside RFK in the Ambassador Hotel pantry. Schrade had tried to broach the subject of the assassination with the Kennedy family over the years, and was disappointed that almost all of RFK's children opposed Sirhan's release. "Some of them listened to what I had to say and got it. But some of them, like Joe, refused." Schrade declared. "The last time I saw [Kerry] and brought all this up she started laughing. It's the attitude they all have, and it's stupid. They ought to learn what really happened."[149] It seems incongruent that Kerry would laugh at the mention of the assassination, and later become so outraged over footage of her wounded father being shown in a television interview. The *New York Times* gave a platform to RFK's youngest child, Rory, to write the September 1, 2021, essay "Robert Kennedy was my Dad. His Assassin Doesn't Deserve Parole." RFK's ninety-three-year-old widow Ethel was brought into the fray, signing a typed statement that concluded with "he should not be paroled." Paul Schrade had contacted me a few years earlier to offer compliments about an article I'd written regarding former California Attorney General and current Vice President Kamala Harris's shameful record in suppressing the truth about the RFK assassination. He was my guest, along with former Sirhan attorney Laurie Dusek, on the September 1, 2021, episode of *The Donald Jeffries Show*.

Another guest on *The Donald Jeffries Show* was Scott Enyart, who appeared on the April 13, 2022, broadcast. Enyart was a fifteen-year-old taking pictures in the Ambassador Hotel for his high school newspaper on the night of the assassination. He is the only known photographer to capture film during the actual shooting of Robert F. Kennedy. The LAPD quickly confiscated his camera and the film, and despite battling for years, including in court, when his property was finally returned to him, twelve key photos (which were captured during the shooting itself) were still missing. Enyart has yet to see those pictures, which may well have shown a second gunman or other crucial information. After being initially promised the photos would be delivered to him by courier, the courier's car tires were slashed, and the property stolen. A 1996 story claimed that "The negatives of some photographs taken in the moments surrounding the assassination of Robert F. Kennedy are missing." It was suggested that Enyart's negatives were among these.[150] Oddly, while Enyart seemed to have believed there was a conspiracy, he largely dismissed any notions of a second gun during our interview. This makes his quote from a 1992 article, "I saw another gun in that pantry. I saw Kennedy fall while I was taking pictures," a bit baffling.[151] Enyart told me of receiving death threats and described obvious surveillance outside his house by some kind of agents. He agreed with me when I responded, "I'm sure you don't think those threats were coming from Sirhan's family." Researcher William Law interviewed Enyart extensively and told me that he'd been driven to sit nervously in a chair holding a gun, fearful of the LAPD's warning that "we have a special cell reserved for you." Podcaster Robbie Robertson told me, in August 2023, that Enyart had vehemently declared to him that "there was no conspiracy" before agreeing to an interview.

The Kennedy-Johnson feud was apparent even at the funeral of Robert F. Kennedy. Lady Bird Johnson would relate, "I found myself in front of Mrs. Jacqueline Kennedy. I called her name and put out my hand. I hardly know how to describe the next few moments of time. She looked at me as though from a great distance, as though I were an aberration. I felt extreme hostility. Was it because I was alive? At last, without a flicker of expression, she extended her hand very slightly. I took it with some murmured words of sorrow and walked on quickly. It was somehow shocking. Never in any contact with her before had I experienced this."[152]

CHAPTER EIGHT

1970s–1990s: THE SLOW DETERIORATION OF AMERICA

Democracy substitutes election by the incompetent many for appointment by the corrupt few.

—George Bernard Shaw[1]

As I have often remarked in interviews, there has always been corruption in the United States. It didn't begin on November 22, 1963. What is so glaring about the mad authoritarian nightmare we confront today is the utter incompetence. Our leaders were often corrupt in the past, but they were not incompetent. The trains ran on time, to use the Mussolini analogy.

Until Donald Trump came along, no one was more despised by the "liberal" Establishment than Richard Nixon. When I was a young man, he was the epitome of evil in my eyes. He played the role of a villain very well, being perhaps even more of an unsympathetic figure than Trump. While Nixon was run out of office because of the overblown and largely irrelevant Watergate burglary, the worst things he did have gone largely overlooked.

The Nixon administration's endorsement of Health Maintenance Organizations (HMOs) in 1971 was the beginning of the putrid medical-industrial complex we have all come to know and love. No more house calls. The explosion of Big Pharma and sinfully profitable insurance companies. Too many Americans died in the ensuing decades because they couldn't afford monstrously expensive medical costs. And probably more died because of the incompetent and insensitive care doled out by the gargantuan medical bureaucracy. Remember, it is readily acknowledged that the medical profession, through its myriad of mistakes and damaging "protocols," is the *third* leading cause of death in this country.[2] I submit that, with all the unrecognized deaths from vaccines and COVID "care" in hospitals, they may very well have taken over the top spot. Yet despite Nixon's generally poor portrayal by our state-controlled media, they never mention his role in the creation of a medical system that is an embarrassment to the entire world.

One of the most astounding allegations against Nixon is that he threatened to assassinate his beleaguered vice president Spiro Agnew. Six years after his forced resignation from office, Agnew wrote a book claiming to have left largely because he feared he might be murdered. Agnew took a comment from Nixon, relayed to him through chief aide General Alexander Haig, as a veiled threat of assassination.[3] In his book, Agnew recounted how "Haig's threat made me realize, with a sickening shock, that I had finally lost the last slim thread of hope that the President would help me in my fight. On the contrary, he had turned against me and became my mortal enemy. Haig insinuated that if I went against the President's wishes and refused to resign, a jail sentence and no assistance with the IRS, finances, placing my staff, or the other carrots Buzhardt had dangled. I would be on my own and the full penalties would be assessed. Stone would withdraw from the Defense Fund. Nixon would publicly blast me, turn the prosecutors loose, and I would go to jail. General Dunn told me that General Haig also reminded him about the great power of the presidency, saying, 'The President has a lot of power—don't forget that.' His remark sent a chill through my body. I interpreted it as an innuendo that anything could happen to me; I might have a convenient 'accident.' What had Haig meant when he said 'anything may be in the offing?' . . . I knew that men in the White House, professing to speak for the President, could order the CIA to carry out missions that were very unhealthy for people who were considered enemies. Since the revelations have come out about the CIA's attempts to assassinate Fidel Castro and other foreign leaders, I realize even more than before that I might have been in great danger. . . . I did not know what might happen to me. But I don't mind admitting I was frightened. . . . I feared for my life. If a decision had been made to eliminate me—through an automobile accident, a fake suicide, or whatever—the order would not have been traced back to the White House any more than the 'get Castro' orders were ever traced to their source. . . . Mr. Nixon did not seem to realize that I was his insurance policy against his own ouster. The left-wingers who despised us both would never push him out of the White House until they were certain I would not be around to take his place."[4] Agnew got the message and resigned from office a week after the disturbing conversation with Haig. Agnew's explosive accusation was so underreported that even a political junkie like me had never heard of it, until Peter Secosh sent it to me.

One significant death that occurred during the Nixon years was that of FBI director J. Edgar Hoover, who'd been a powerful figure in Washington, D.C. for several decades. Hoover's residence was broken into twice in April 1972. Researcher Anthony Summers claimed that the poison thiophosphate was placed on Hoover's personal toiletries during the second break-in. It can purportedly cause a fatal heart seizure, even if only absorbed through the skin. Hoover died in the early morning hours of May 2, 1972. Naturally, as should surprise no reader of my work, there was no autopsy performed. The cause of death was listed as cardiac arrest. Immediately following his death, a slew of government agents descended on Hoover's home, but his secretary destroyed an unknown number of files before they got there. He was lionized and lay in state in the Capitol Building. Nixon called him "a great force for good in our national life."[5]

Since the assassination of President John F. Kennedy, we have crossed what I refer to as lines in the sand too many times. Moral boundaries which altered our civilization for the worse. Waco was a huge moral line in the sand to cross. Our government slaughtered men, women, and children—American citizens—in their own home, using armored tanks and a gas that had been banned by the Geneva Convention. There was virtually no outrage expressed by those with public platforms, outside of some on the far right, and comedian Bill Hicks, who also was the only standup comic who inserted references to the conspiracy that killed JFK into his act. Hicks would die from cancer at a very young age. Highway checkpoints, under the auspices of nabbing drunk drivers, was another unconstitutional breach that solidified the already out-of-control power of law enforcement. During the alleged pandemic and unprecedented lockdown of society, we crossed many lines at once. And these lines in the sand go in only one direction. As Ron Paul has noted, once you give government at any level increased powers, they will never relinquish them. We will cover more of these lines in the sand in detail.

But before we reached that point during the corruption-filled Clinton years in the 1990s, we had Nixon, who clearly held a racist perspective in private, building on Lyndon Johnson's affirmative action program with his 1969 Executive Order 11478, which decreed unilateral affirmative action in all government employment.[6] Nixon also signed the Rehabilitation Act of 1973, which required agencies to submit an affirmative action plan to the EEOC for hiring, placement, and advancement of individuals within government agencies. Affirmative action might have been a noble idea at first, but it has been responsible for far more harm than good. Besides stacking especially government at all levels with a wildly disproportionate number of Black employees, it leads the public to suspect that *all* minority workers were unqualified beneficiaries of politically correct favoritism.

Jimmy Carter failed to use his powerful pulpit to talk about the questions surrounding the JFK assassination. He never raised the issue, even as the House Select Committee on Assassinations was formed during his administration. His bitter battle with Ted Kennedy for the 1980 Democratic nomination became intensely personal. This would culminate in a near fistfight between delegates on the convention floor. Carter and Kennedy shared several stiff and awkward handshakes on stage, but the challenger refused to give Carter what he wanted; a photo of them raising their hands in unison. Carter's press secretary Jody Powell would express the vitriol that the Carter administration felt for Kennedy, in his book *The Other Side of the Story*. "We neglected to take into account one of the most obvious facets of Kennedy's character, an almost childlike self-centeredness," Powell would write.[7] Carter has come to be lionized by much of the Left now, and his drift into "woke" territory as a nonagenarian was made clear by his belief in the absurd "Russiagate" fantasy postulated by the Deep State to cover up the real high crimes exposed by Wikileaks. Donald Trump probably was fairly accurate when he reacted to Carter's comments by calling him a "forgotten president."[8]

Ronald Reagan: No Shining City on a Hill

Jesus—murdered. Martin Luther King—murdered. Gandhi—murdered. Reagan—wounded.

—Bill Hicks[9]

In *Hidden History*, I covered the Reagan presidency, pointing out just how different his record was from his rhetoric. After publication of the book, more research revealed just how deadly the Reagan years were. Many well-intentioned conservatives have deified Ronald Reagan and have credited him with doing things he never did, while ignoring all the awful things that transpired during the Reagan years. Reagan's two terms in office left Americans less free than they'd ever been, increased the disparity of wealth immeasurably, and transformed the conservative movement into an Ayn Rand–inspired religion worshipping a rigged marketplace.

Reagan's war on drugs, and statist proposals like the one that raised the drinking age to twenty-one all across the country, belied the libertarian principles Reagan seemed to espouse. It certainly angered his libertarian supporters. Reagan increased the national debt by 186 percent. His Social Security Reform Act of 1983 increased the fund's payroll tax, raised the retirement age, and required federal employees to join the system. Critics were hoping that he would either offer a private sector alternative to Social Security or revamp it in such a way as to make it economically sustainable. Instead, he kicked the can down the road.

Reagan is the patron saint of modern Republicans. He is revered nearly as much as Abraham Lincoln is. Democrats still invoke the memories of putrid authoritarians like Franklin D. Roosevelt and Harry Truman. Republicans, while paying the mandatory homage to the tyrant Lincoln, idolize Reagan with a religious fervor. This former Hollywood leading man, who epitomized the Stupid Party's methodology of backtracking, apologizing, and compromising, is said to have "never compromised his principles." It's hard to determine what principles, if any, he had, but the legacy of Reagan is darker than just an Israel-centric neocon foreign policy and destructive trickle-down economics.

Civil Asset Forfeiture

It's now possible for a drug dealer to serve time in a forfeiture-financed prison after being arrested by agents driving a forfeiture-provided automobile while working in a forfeiture-funded sting operation.

—Attorney General Richard Thornburgh[10]

In 1969, Richard Nixon declared drugs to be "the number one public enemy of the United States." From 1981 to 2000, the federal drug enforcement budget increased eightfold. By 2003, federal and state governments would spend almost $50 billion on the absurd and utterly failing "drug war." This "war" would provide the impetus for civil asset forfeiture.

Confiscating property, and giving it to the authorities, goes back to medieval England, when swords or other inanimate objects involved in crimes would be forfeited to the Crown. In 1827, in response to an owner's objection to his ship being seized after it was allegedly tied to piracy, the Supreme Court concluded: "The thing is here primarily considered as the offender, or rather the offence is attached primarily to the thing." The Comprehensive Drug Abuse Prevention Act of 1970 first permitted the government to confiscate drugs, anything related to their production, and the means of transporting them. The 1984 Comprehensive Crime Control Act, however, allowed law enforcement agencies to keep the proceeds from asset forfeitures, instead of depositing them with the U.S. Treasury.[11] The Act was written by Strom Thurmond and future President Joe Biden. This diabolical policy—which amounts to state theft—is the heart of the horrific policing-for-profit system that has corrupted law enforcement.

The courts have offered little relief to those whose property has been stolen by the government. In 1996, the Supreme Court, in a shocking 8–1 decision, found that asset forfeiture laws did not constitute double jeopardy. This monstrous decision legalized the government's ability to simply steal a defendant's house, boat, car, cash, or other valuable property. That same year, in a much closer 5–4 vote, the Supreme Court made one of the worst decisions in its history, ruling against Tina Bennis, a Michigan woman who had quite understandably objected to her car being confiscated, after her husband used it to pick up a prostitute. Justifying its lack of logic and fairness, the Court declared, "It has long been settled that statutory forfeitures of property entrusted by the innocent owner or lienor to another who uses it in violation of the revenue laws of the United States is not a violation of the Due Process clause of the Fifth Amendment." Chief Justice William Rehnquist further stated, "An owner's interest in property may be forfeited by reason of the use to which the property is put, even though the owner did not know that it was to be put to such use." *These* are the people Americans entrust as the ultimate arbiters of justice.

Civil asset forfeiture horror stories are endless. In 2014, a Philadelphia couple had their home seized after their son was charged with dealing heroin. Markela and Chris Sourovelis were helpless, as the Supreme Court had already ruled that the state can take away your property even if you're unaware of any criminal activity that is fancifully associated with it. Because their son was accused of selling $40 worth of heroin, without their knowledge, when police showed up to "confiscate" their house, the electric company was with them, to immediately turn off power, and their doors were locked with screws. At the time, 20 percent of the Philadelphia district attorney's office budget came from asset forfeitures. The Fifth Amendment expressly forbids citizens being "deprived of life, liberty, or property, without due process of law." In 2013, James Leonard was stopped by Texas police for speeding. A safe with $201,100 in cash and a bill of sale for a house in Pennsylvania was found during a search of the vehicle. Leonard explained that the money belonged to his mother, Lisa Olivia Leonard, from the recent sale of her house. The report filed by Officer John Shaver, explained, "In my experience, carrying large amounts of U.S. currency is commonly associated with the illegal narcotics trade. In my experience, Highway 59 is a main thoroughfare for the transport of U.S. currency and narcotics in the illegal drug trade." Because this police officer had the power to cavalierly label any such large amount of cash "drug money," it could legally be seized under civil asset forfeiture laws. No drug charges were ever filed against Leonard. Like Tina Bennis, Lisa Olivia Leonard sought redress from the courts to get her property returned. She was just as unsuccessful. Think about that; losing what could very well be an entire net worth because of your child's speeding ticket. While the Supreme Court denied Leonard's writ of certiorari, Justice Clarence Thomas (although oddly agreeing with the denial) wrote, "This petition asks an important question: whether modern civil-forfeiture statutes can be squared with the Due Process Clause and our Nation's history . . . civil forfeiture has in recent decades become widespread and highly profitable. . . . This system—where police can seize property with limited judicial oversight and retain it for their own use—has led to egregious and well-chronicled abuses. . . . These forfeiture operations frequently target the poor and other groups least able to defend their interests in forfeiture proceedings. . . . Whether this Court's treatment of the broad modern forfeiture practice can be justified by the narrow historical one is certainly worthy of consideration in greater detail."

In 2005, Javier Gonzalez was pulled over in Texas. He had $10,000 cash in a briefcase. Officers offered Gonzalez a waiver, which stipulated that if he signed over the money and did not claim it later, he wouldn't be arrested. If he refused to sign the waiver, Gonzalez would be charged with money-laundering. Fearful, and wondering if they were even real law enforcement, Gonzalez signed the waiver. He later sued the county and won. In a rare victory for justice, his cash was returned, along with $110,000 in damages plus attorney's fees.[12] Matt Lee had $2,500 in cash confiscated by police during a traffic stop. As he told the *Washington Post* in 2013, "I just couldn't believe that police could do that to anyone. . . . It's like they are at war with innocent people." A sheriff's deputy was caught on tape suggesting they should "take his money and run, count it as a drug seizure" when they found $50,000 in cash during a traffic stop of Tan Nguyen. In 2008, a federal judge ordered the money to be returned to Nguyen.[13] A particularly egregious case involved officers in Tenaha, Texas, targeting out-of-state drivers, and forcing them to sign "roadside property waivers," which threatened criminal charges unless valuables were handed over. In another instance, a woman was stopped by police, with no charges filed, but a piece of her jewelry was confiscated.[14]

In the worst cases, police don't pull someone over on the road; they break into their homes. In March 2012, in the middle of the night, without a warrant, New York City police burst into Gerald Bryan's home. They ransacked his belongings, ripped out light fixtures, and seized $4,800 in cash. He was arrested, but a year later, the case against him was dropped. When Bryan tried to get his money returned, he was told that it was "too late" since the money had already been placed into the police pension fund.[15] IRS agents have seized money based on suspicions of tax evasion, while the DEA seizes money from airline passengers—$209 million just from 2006 to 2016.[16] The law has been used to confiscate automobiles driven by drunk drivers.[17] Not only have homes been seized because someone other than the owners was suspected of selling drugs on the premises; motel owners can lose their property if someone renting a room is suspected of dealing drugs. A man's sailboat was taken after he was caught with a small amount of marijuana.[18] Those buying vehicles sold at police auctions may very well be purchasing property whose owners were unconnected to any criminal activity. The government can seize money from bank accounts where there have been large deposits. When money is confiscated from individuals or businesses, those victimized have to hire attorneys to fight in the courts. Prosecutors will typically offer a "deal" of returning half the money seized. Police may volunteer to return money, on the promise that they won't be sued. It is routinely acknowledged that victims confront "long legal struggles to get their money back." Incredibly, it's been estimated that only *1 percent* of property taken by federal authorities is ever returned.[19]

The ACLU of Northern California lists several civil asset forfeiture horror stories on their website. In one case, a taco truck owner had $10,000 in his possession taken from him by the Los Angeles Sheriff's Department, even though he was not even suspected of committing any crime. Eighty-one-year-old James Huff of Nevada had the $8,400 in cash he was carrying confiscated from him by police during a routine traffic stop. In February 2015, DEA agents seized the $16,000 young Joseph Rivers was carrying on a train traveling to Los Angeles. It was all the money Rivers had to his name. The DEA rationalized, "We don't have to prove that the person is guilty. It's that the money is presumed to be guilty." Rivers happened to be Black, but there was little coverage in the media, and zero outrage from Al Sharpton or other race hustlers, even though the agents seemed to have clearly targeted Rivers, who was the only Black passenger on the train. Michael Pancer, an attorney representing Rivers, commented, "What this is, is having your money stolen by a federal agent acting under the color of law. It's a national epidemic. If my office got four to five cases just recently, and I'm just one attorney, you know this is happening thousands of times."[20]

Leon and Mary Ames had lived in their Philadelphia home for forty-six years when police seized it, after arresting their son for conducting "a few $20 marijuana deals" with an undercover police informant. Proceeds from the forfeited home would be split between the police and the district attorney's office. The Institute of Justice reported on a 2010 case where Sandra Leino and her three children were forced into homelessness after her husband was accused of selling painkillers, which she insisted was for his own use after being partially disabled in a truck accident. Detailing the horrors that can be inflicted upon people in asset forfeiture cases, the Institute of Justice noted, "Just a few months after his arrest, the Philadelphia District Attorney filed a motion to seize the Leinos' home in May 2010—a year and a half before Sam Leino even went to trial. Later that month, the Leinos were kicked out of their own home. They tried staying at a motel but couldn't afford it for more than one week. With no other options at the time, they were even forced to sleep in the backwoods."[21] In 1992, officers from multiple law enforcement agencies shot and killed Donald Scott during a raid that aimed at seizing his 250-acre Malibu property. No evidence of drugs was found on the property.[22]

Recently, Chicago police officers were caught buying drones with asset forfeiture funds. Former Chicago mayor and wannabe gangster Rahm Emanuel had notoriously pushed hard for legislation to permit drones outfitted with facial-recognition software to monitor protests. Civil asset forfeiture funds were also used by Chicago police to purchase cell phone site simulators. The ACLU's Ed Yohnka remarked, "We should not be surprised. This behavior goes back more than two decades when Chicago first began to place surveillance cameras all across the city. To this day, residents of the city have never seen a privacy policy for the use of those cameras." The emails disclosing the secret drone buying program were leaked by Distributed Denial of Secrets, a nonprofit group comparable to Wikileaks.[23] Harford County, Maryland, was open about the use of drones, purchased with forfeiture money, as Sheriff Jeff Gahler boasted, "This is something we paid for with asset forfeiture meaning the drug dealers paid for the tools that we will then use against them and for other law enforcement operations in the county."[24] In Kentucky, Jeffersontown Police admitted to spending civil asset funds on overtime for officers, body armor, a retirement plaque for a police officer, a submachine gun, a drone, and a sports car for the department.[25]

From 1985 to 1993 alone, law enforcement confiscated $3 billion of cash and property under asset forfeiture. All statistics show that civil asset forfeiture continues to increase. The Department of Justice's Asset Forfeiture Fund grew from $93.7 million in 1986 to $1 billion in 2008, and property seizures overall increased 600 percent from 2002 to 2012. One estimate is that the property owner is never charged with a crime in 85 percent of civil forfeiture cases.[26] So called "civil forfeiture experts" regularly train police officers in how best to steal the property of civilians. After videos of this training were released by the Institute of Justice, Rebel Pundit noted, "In the sessions, officials share tips on maximizing profits, defeating the objections of so-called 'innocent owners' who were not present when the suspected offense occurred, and keeping the proceeds in the hands of law enforcement and out of general fund budgets." According to Rebel Pundit, "Prosecutors estimated that between 50 to 80 percent of the cars seized were driven by someone other than the owner, which sometimes means a parent or grandparent loses their car." One such "expert," Las Cruces, New Mexico City Attorney Pete Connelly, was quoted as saying, "And I thought, boy, what a trap. You liberalize marijuana so somebody can sell it, they sell the marijuana out of the house, then you seize the house, which is like 10 bucks of marijuana and you [the police] get a $300,000 house. What a deal. That's really exciting. They get what they want, and you get what you want." Connelly called confiscated property "little goodies," and, unable to stop his childish bragging, declared, "A guy drives up in a 2008 Mercedes, brand new. Just so beautiful, I mean, the cops were undercover and they were just like 'Ahhhh.' And he gets out and he's just reeking of alcohol. And it's like, 'Oh, my goodness, we can hardly wait.'" Cops even compete with each other on websites devoted to "seizure sizes." One Santa Fe police officer mocked a Hispanic whose car had been confiscated by saying, "Oh, my hijito would never do that" in a feminine voice with an accent.

The Republican Party 2016 platform read, "Civil asset forfeiture was originally intended as a way to cripple organized crime through the seizure of property used in a criminal enterprise. Regrettably, it has become a tool for unscrupulous law enforcement officials, acting without due process, to profit by destroying the livelihood of innocent individuals, many of whom never recover the lawful assets taken from them. When the rights of the innocent can be so easily violated, no one's rights are safe. We call on Congress and state legislatures to enact reforms to protect law-abiding citizens against abusive asset forfeiture tactics." Despite this, Republican President Donald Trump strongly supported law enforcement, including asset forfeiture. His first attorney general, Jeff Sessions, called asset forfeiture a "key tool that helps law enforcement defund organized crime, take back ill-gotten gains, and prevent new crimes from being committed. . . . We will continue to encourage civil-asset forfeiture whenever appropriate." A recent inspector general's report had found that almost $28 billion had been collected in asset forfeiture funds over the past decade, and the *Washington Post* reported that in 2015, civil asset seizures were larger than the collective numbers from all burglaries that year.[27]

In all the furor over "Black Lives Matter," which was supposedly triggered by the abuses of law enforcement, resulting in riots and protests all across the country in the summer of 2020, civil asset forfeiture was never mentioned. Doesn't Black property matter, too? Both the Left and Right seem perfectly fine with what is in effect legalized theft on the part of law enforcement. In all the threats to "defund" police, no one suggested a fair compromise: defunding civil asset forfeiture and abolishing policing-for-profit. Minnesota passed a weak reform effort in 2021, but it merely precluded forfeiture of property under $1,500, essentially prohibiting police from confiscating the least valuable booty. State Auditor Julie Blaha stated that her intention was to make this very small reform without "rocking the system."[28]

There has been a slow but noticeable increase in criticism of this odious practice, even in the mainstream media. In an October 25, 2021, article headlined "New Proof That Police Use Civil Forfeiture to Take from Those who Can't Fight Back," *Forbes* decried "Philadelphia's predatory civil forfeiture scheme that operated from a shady 'courtroom' at City Hall. For years, police and prosecutors seized cash, cars and even homes and then took the property for themselves. Worse still, new data show that the police preyed on people in minority and low-income areas—in other words, people who could least afford to fight back." Evidently, the situation was especially bad in Philadelphia. The story continued, "Property owners were summoned to Courtroom 478 at City Hall, but there was no judge in the room. The show was run by prosecutors, the same people who filed the forfeiture actions and who stood to benefit financially from successful forfeitures." A class-action lawsuit by victims in Philadelphia was filed with Institute for Justice, and the city was pressured by ugly publicity (which included a report on *Last Week Tonight with John Oliver*), into an undisclosed settlement. More than 30,000 people were eligible for compensation.

The explosion of civil asset forfeiture cases in the 1980s led inevitably to one of the Supreme Court's most dangerously wrong decisions. In February 1989, at the very beginning of the George H. W. Bush administration, the Court ruled that, in the words of Chief Justice William Rehnquist, "Nothing in the language of the Due Process Clause itself requires the State to protect the life, liberty, and property of its citizens against invasion by private actors, even where such aid may be necessary to secure life, liberty, or property interests of which the government itself may not deprive the individual" without "due process of the law." While the case was brought by the mother of a child severely damaged by Social Services' failure to stop violent abuse, it set the precedent for Supreme Court rulings to follow, regarding the police specifically. Despite their motto of "Protect and Serve," law enforcement really isn't required to do either. In 2005, the Court ruled that police do not have a constitutional duty to protect a person from harm.[29] Very few Americans realize that this is the case. So, if they aren't there to protect the public, exactly what are we paying them to do? I think this section demonstrates that all too clearly.

Reagan: A Disaster on Immigration

Illegal immigrants in considerable numbers have become productive members of our society and are a basic part of our work force.

—Ronald Reagan[30]

In 1983, an incomprehensible 5–4 Supreme Court decision held that undocumented children were entitled to state-funded primary and secondary education. The Carter administration had been supporting this bizarre position, and the Reagan White House declined to overturn lower court rulings giving children of illegal immigrants the right to an American taxpayer–financed public education. Combined with the border-opening Immigration and Control Act of 1986, which granted amnesty to almost all illegal immigrants who'd arrived in America prior to January 1, 1982, this was a crushing blow to our national sovereignty and cultural cohesiveness. At the time, almost all of Reagan's supporters wanted to do something to stop illegal immigration.

Reagan thumbed his nose at his base by declaring during the November 6, 1986, immigration bill signing ceremony, "The legalization provisions in this act will go far to improve the lives of a class of individuals who now must hide in the shadows, without access to many of the benefits of a free and open society. Very soon many of these men and women will be able to step into the sunlight and, ultimately, if they choose, they may become Americans." In 1987, Reagan signed an Executive Order legalizing the children of parents granted amnesty under the proposal, and announced a blanket deferral on deportments for children under eighteen. The Act impacted an estimated 100,000 families.[31] This act had disastrous consequences for years: the Center for Immigration Studies noted that "by the beginning of 1997 those former illegal aliens had been entirely replaced by new illegal aliens, and that the unauthorized population again stood at more than 5 million, just as before the amnesty."

As with everything about Ronald Reagan, his immigration policy was contrary to the myths propagated by his devoted followers. During the

1980 presidential campaign, Reagan had been asked if "illegal aliens," as they were referred to back in those far-off times, should be allowed to attend US schools. Reagan replied, "Rather than talking about putting up a fence, why don't we work out some recognition of our mutual problems, make it possible for them to come here legally with a work permit. And then while they're working and earning here, they pay taxes here. And when they want to go back they can go back." In a 1984 presidential debate, Reagan said, "I believe in the idea of amnesty for those who have put down roots and who have lived here, even though some time back, they may have entered illegally." President Donald Trump, who wrote the book on "image versus record," tweeted out, "Even President Ronald Reagan tried for 8 years to build a Border Wall, or Fence, and was unable to do so." This was absurd; Reagan never attempted any such thing, and did nothing to stem the endless tide of migrants coming unimpeded across the southern border. "There was not any discussion at the senior policy levels during the Reagan administration about fencing or a wall that I can recall," Doris Meissner, who was executive associate Commissioner of the Immigration and Naturalization Service during the Reagan administration, stated. "He was not anti-immigration." In a perfect illustration of the fake Left-Right paradigm, Meissner would later serve as INS commissioner during the Clinton years. Sounding like a typical "liberal" Democrat, Reagan declared in 1981, "Our nation is a nation of immigrants. More than any other country, our strength comes from our own immigrant heritage and our capacity to welcome those from other lands."[32]

Like the latter-day supporters of Donald Trump, Reagan's disciples had the uncanny ability to ignore all the actions he took that contradicted the rhetoric they loved. Pat Buchanan, who served under Reagan for two years as White House Communications Director, often invoked the Gipper's positive virtues, but seemed not to comprehend how much he'd betrayed his base on immigration, which became one of Buchanan's own core issues during his presidential runs. Buchanan was highly critical of the 1986 prosecution of Cleveland autoworker John Demjanjuk for allegedly being "Ivan the Terrible" in the World War II Nazi concentration camps, even as a member of Reagan's administration. Reagan, needless to say, did nothing to stop the persecution of elderly persons like Demjanjuk under the auspices of the Jimmy Carter–created Office of Special Investigations. Buchanan's classic 2002 book *The Death of the West,* which bemoaned increased immigration and low White birth rates, could not have been written had his seeming hero Ronald Reagan done anything to stop it.

The Reagan cult excuses his abysmal failures on immigration by claiming that Democrats "broke their promise," to step up border security in return for amnesty in 1986. Veteran political strategist Ed Rollins would claim that granting amnesty was Reagan's "biggest regret" in office. Reagan's son Michael disputed this in emails to the *Arizona Republic,* saying his father never regretted the amnesty, but did regret the fact border security wasn't increased. Which, of course, he as president (like Trump), could have taken constitutional measures of his own to ensure, like putting troops at the border. The Immigration Reform Act was supposed to institute severe punishments for employers knowingly hiring illegals, but this was never even half-heartedly enforced. Reagan stated, at the time he signed this legislation, "Our objective is only to establish a reasonable, fair, orderly, and secure system of immigration into this country and not to discriminate in any way against particular nations or people. . . . Future generations of Americans will be thankful for our efforts to humanely regain control of our borders and thereby preserve the value of one of the most sacred possessions of our people: American citizenship." The "humanely" reference was an early example of the kind of lame, virtue-signaling language that has now fully enveloped American political and cultural discourse.[33] Reagan's disastrous "reform" bill led directly to the tsunami of illegal immigrants thereafter, which really exploded in the 1990s.

The open-borders-loving Cato Institute eulogized Reagan in 2004 thusly: "Reagan's vision of an America open to commerce and peaceful, hardworking immigrants contradicts the anti-trade and anti-immigration views espoused by Lou Dobbs, Bill O'Reilly, Pat Buchanan, Rep. Tom Tancredo of Colorado, and many others who claim to speak for the conservative causes Reagan largely defined, Reagan's heart and head were clearly on the side of free trade. While president, he declared in 1986: 'Our trade policy rests firmly on the foundation of free and open markets.

I recognize . . . the inescapable conclusion that all of history has taught: The freer the flow of world trade, the stronger the tides of human progress and peace among nations.'" The Cato Institute approvingly noted that, "More immigrants entered the United States legally under President Reagan's watch than under any previous U.S. president since Teddy Roosevelt. Like President George W. Bush today, Reagan had the good sense and compassion to see illegal immigrants not as criminals but as human beings striving to build better lives through honest work." In a 1977 radio address, Reagan had made one of the first references to what would become a staple of open-borders rhetoric, when he remarked on the apples that were supposedly rotting on New England's trees, declaring, "It makes one wonder about the illegal alien fuss. Are great numbers of our unemployed really victims of the illegal alien invasion or are those illegal tourists actually doing work our own people won't do?" Ah yes, the old "only doing the jobs Americans won't do" line. Like Donald Trump three decades later, Ronald Reagan's slick act fooled millions, and was entirely different from his actual record.

Anthony Fauci

> *For his determined and aggressive efforts to help others live longer and healthier lives, I'm proud to award the Presidential Medal of Freedom to Dr. Anthony S. Fauci.*
>
> —President George W. Bush[34]

Then Texas congressional Rep. George H. W. Bush announced in Congress, on July 29, 1969, that something needed to be done about exploding population numbers, which represented "a growing Third World crisis." Just days earlier, during a hearing before the Subcommittee on Appropriations, the Department of Defense had requested $10 million to develop a "synthetic biological agent, an agent that does not naturally exist and for which no natural immunity could have been acquired." This certainly seems like a strange thing for the United States military to be interested in. Did all this foretell the AIDS explosion a decade later? The conventional narrative is that the AIDS virus came from a monkey biting an African, or something like that. That makes about as much sense as magic bullets, magic fertilizer bombs, and other fantastic fables emanating from state-controlled journalists and court historians.

In 1983, Dr. Robert Strecker of Los Angeles was hired as a consultant by Security Pacific Bank, to work on a healthcare proposal that estimated the coverage costs in the event any of their 30,000 employees contracted AIDS. In tandem with his attorney brother Theodore, their extensive research resulted in *The Strecker Memorandum.* The Streckers' most controversial claim was that the AIDS virus had actually been developed by the National Cancer Institute, in cooperation with the World Health Organization (WHO), in a laboratory at Maryland's notorious Fort Dietrick. In the early seventies, Fort Dietrick's laboratory facility was an integral part of the U.S. Army's germ warfare unit, known as the Army Infectious Disease Unit, or Special Operations Division, and was routinely referred to as the Army's Chemical Biological Warfare Laboratory. This facility, curiously enough, was renamed the National Cancer Institute after 1974. Dr. Strecker also discovered that a group of Japanese scientists captured at the end of World War II were given amnesty in exchange for information on racial and ethnic bio-weaponry, and their research dating back to 1930 was utilized in the program. Expatriated Russian scientists were involved in the project as well. The creation of the virus was overseen by Dr. Robert Gallo, who would later claim to have discovered it. Theodore Strecker wrote a shocking letter on February 26, 1986, which he sent to the editor of *The Annals of Internal Medicine*. In it, he blasted them for their "pious handwringing concerning fraud in science." Another even more provocative letter, dated March 28, 1986, in which the top has been cut off of the versions accessible online, declared, "In the time after you receive this warning, you should decide for yourself whether or not I am correct by consulting the listed references. Make sure that any experts consulted are not working for or supported by grants of the WHO, NIH, CDC, or NCI." The letter (the date must have been at the top) closes with, "All that 14 years of research has done is institutionalize fraud and murder, as national policy." It is unclear who this letter was addressed to. Theodore Strecker "committed suicide" on August 10, 1988, two days before his forty-seventh birthday. The only public official who had been interested in the Streckers's research, Illinois State Rep. Douglas Huff, was found dead in his home on September 12, 1988, from what authorities attributed to an overdose of cocaine and heroin. In an August 8, 1990, interview with John Burns, Robert Strecker was asked if he thought his brother's work had anything to do with his death. "I don't think there's any doubt about it," Strecker replied. Robert Strecker died in an auto accident on April 15, 2018.

I've written quite a bit about eugenics, which many of our leaders openly espouse. In the best-selling 1968 book *The Population Bomb*, by Dr. Paul Ehrlich, the author wrote, 'In summary, the world's population will continue to grow as long as the birth rate exceeds the death rate; it's as simple as that. When it stops growing or starts to shrink, it will mean that either the birth rate has gone down or the death rate has gone up or a combination of the two. Basically, then there are only two kinds of solutions to the population problem. One is a birth rate solution (remember the ZPG—Zero Population Growth—movement?) The other is a death rate solution in which ways to raise the death rate—war, famine, pestilence—find us. The problem could have been avoided by population control, in which mankind consciously adjusted the birth rate so that a 'death rate solution' did not have to occur.'" Ehrlich seems to be pretty clearly saying that such a horrific solution *will* be occurring. William Cooper, author of the conspiracy classic *Behold A Pale Horse,* noted that Ehrlich's wife, Anne, was a member of the Club of Rome, which produced the Global 2000 computer model that proposed a special prophylactic for the ruling class, and advocated that they be given a cure for AIDS, which was to be withheld from the general public until enough people were dead. Cooper claimed that the Global 2000 plan had been presented to President Carter. Cooper, who as I recounted in *Hidden History,* died in a suitably conspiratorial fashion in a shootout with law enforcement on his own property, also wrote about the "Haig-Kissinger depopulation policy which has taken over various levels of government and in fact is determining U.S. Policy. The planning organization operates outside the White House and directs its entire efforts to reduce the world's population by 2 billion people through war, famine and any other means necessary." He also quoted Office of Population Affairs case officer Thomas Ferguson as saying, "There is a single theme behind all of our work: we must reduce population levels. Either they do it our way through nice clean methods or they will get the kind of mess that we have in El Salvador, or in Iran or in Beirut." The 1972 smallpox vaccine, released in Africa under the direction of the WHO, was the subject of an extremely conspiratorial story in a major newspaper fifteen years later, headlined, "Smallpox Vaccine 'Triggered AIDS Virus.'"[35] Then there was that whole 1978 experimental Hepatitis B vaccine experiment, in which the NIH and CDC specifically requested "promiscuous males" as test subjects.

One of the lesser-known aspects of the Reagan years was the role head of the National Institutes of Health Anthony Fauci played in pushing AZT on AIDS patients. Fauci was the first person to sound the alarm about AIDS, with an unscientific, irresponsible article in the May 1983 edition of the Journal of the *American Medical Association* (*JAMA*), in which he recklessly floated "the possibility that routine close contact, as within a family household, can spread the disease." AZT had been rejected as a treatment for cancer, due to its documented fatal toxicity. The FDA's approval of AZT was based on a single study which had already been declared invalid. It was approved faster than any drug in FDA history. The mainstream media predictably promulgated the misinformation that it had "proven to be effective." Fauci and the NIH pushed giving AZT to HIV positive individuals who'd shown no symptoms, declaring that early intervention had "clearly shown" to be effective. Fauci advocated giving AZT to the 1.4 million Americans "assumed" to be HIV positive.[36] AZT was not only more deadly than beneficial, it was also very expensive; it cost what would be $17,000 annually in today's dollars.[37] This, of course, was beyond the means of most Americans. De facto AIDS czar Fauci's love of publicity was such that prominent author Larry Kramer commented that, to meet with Fauci, one didn't call his secretary but his press officers, "who book [his] talks and interviews . . . like movie stars." Kramer wrote "An Open Letter to Dr. Anthony Fauci" published in the *Village Voice* on May 31, 1988, in which he called him "an incompetent idiot" and a "fucking son of a bitch." Kramer charged Fauci with ignoring the gay community's concerns, stating, "You couldn't care less about what we say. You won't answer our phone calls or letters, or listen to anyone in our stricken community. What tragic pomposity!" One of Fauci's harshest critics was Dr.

Joseph Sonnabend, who asked, "Why, in the case of AIDS, was Bactrim, a known preventative measure against PCP, introduced so many years after a need for it had been recognized? To this must be added the question of why this neglect, the consequences of which can be measured in the tens of thousands of lives lost, has received almost no attention."[38] Fauci survived all the criticism, and became lauded as the face of science itself during the COVID "pandemic." In 2019, this at best incompetent and at worst criminal bureaucrat was the highest paid official in the federal government, at $417,608.[39] Still working at eighty-one years of age at the time of this writing, it was estimated that Fauci would receive the largest retirement package in the history of the federal government, at over $350,000 per year.[40]

The aforementioned Robert Gallo, who worked under Fauci, claimed to have identified what caused AIDS—human immunodeficiency virus (HIV). This "discovery" came without the scientific procedures of peer-reviewed studies, and electron microscope analyses. Award-winning Berkeley researcher Prof. Peter H. Duesberg blasted the charade as "science by press conference." Fauci's National Institute of Allergy and Infectious Diseases (NIAID) reaped millions in HIV-AIDS research funds. Alarmist reports in the always compliant media spread fear porn far and wide, portraying AIDS as the greatest public health threat of modern times. Like we would see decades later with COVID-19, the blood test for HIV produced frequent false positives, and looked for active antibodies instead of directly for the virus, violating standard immunology protocols.[41] Robert R. Redfield, appointed by President Trump in 2018 to head the CDC, has an ugly history similar to his associate Anthony Fauci. In a June 7, 1994, letter to Congressman Henry Waxman, Public Citizen's Health Research Group physicians Peter Lurie and Sidney Wolfe demanded an investigation into "accusations of serious irregularities committed by US Department of Defense researchers on AIDS." They specifically charged that there had been "data manipulation." The doctors noted that "The Phase I and Phase II studies, in which this alleged fault occurred, were conducted by researchers at the Walter Reed Army Institute of Research (WRAIR), led by Lt. Col. Robert Redfield, MD, the head of the Department of Retroviral Research. The misleading results of these trials have been reported in various scientific forums, including the New England Journal of Medicine in June 1991, the Journal AIDS Research and Human Retroviruses in June 1992, and the Annual International AIDS Conference in Amsterdam in July 1992. In addition, exaggerated conclusions have been presented twice in hearings before your subcommittee." Redfield's then assistant at the CDC, fellow Army medical officer Deborah Birx, would go on to play a key role in the Trump administration in responding to COVID-19. Robert F. Kennedy Jr. obtained US military documents that showed both Redfield and Birx had knowingly falsified information published in the *New England Journal of Medicine*, which falsely portrayed an HIV vaccine they had helped to develop, as being effective.[42]

As if all this wasn't damning enough, in the later years of the Reagan administration, it became perfectly legal to use foster children for purposes of medical research into AIDS and other diseases. According to Health Impact News, "Once the state takes custody of a child away from the parents, and the child becomes a ward of the state, medical researchers no longer need parental approval to conduct medical research, and they can also bill the U.S. Government directly to fund this research, usually using Medicaid, even if the drugs being used are experimental and have not yet been approved by the FDA." Asserting that children were being *kidnapped* and forced to endure medical experimentation, Medical Kidnap charged,

> The U.S. federal government has mandated drug research with children. The need for children to participate in drug company research is high, and the temptation to overstep parental rights to force children to participate is great. Researchers publicly admit using money and other rewards to obtain participation of children in their drug trials. Organizations that advocate for the rights of parents to make decisions regarding their children's healthcare are finding that foster children in CPS custody are being enrolled in drug experiments without parental approval. State Child Protective Services are enrolling children in drug experiments without parental approval or court orders. However, those who conduct these drug experiments for pharmaceutical companies, and those who are

> charged with monitoring such research, do not see a problem with their recruitment methods.[43]

Children were allegedly subjected to clinical trials for AIDS drugs from the late 1980s until 2001. As Vaccine Impact put it, "The same group of people who have been involved in HIV/AIDS research to develop an HIV vaccine, a vaccine which has never come to market, are the same group of people now working with the U.S. Government to develop a COVID vaccine."

In an article provocatively titled, "What was Fauci's Role in Funding Tuskegee-like AIDS Experiments on Foster Children in Seven U.S. States?," published in July 2020 on her Facebook page and other websites, Faith Dyson pointed out, "In 2004 – investigative journalist, Liam Scheff, exposed the fact that hundreds of Foster children at Incarnation Children's Center [ICC] in NYC were used and abused as lab rats for unsupervised and unrestricted AIDS research and Vaccine studies by Big Pharma and The National Institute of Allergy and Infectious Diseases [NIAID].Years later in separate investigations—13,878 children were discovered to have been made subject of the same fate during the 1980s and 1990s in six other states: Illinois, Louisiana, Maryland, North Carolina, Colorado and Texas." Scheff's book *The House That AIDS Built* detailed some of the horrors these children were subjected to. Here is one chilling excerpt:

> In New York's Washington Heights is a 4-story brick building called Incarnation Children's Center (ICC). This former convent houses a revolving stable of children who've been removed from their own homes by the Agency for Child Services [ACS]. These children are black, Hispanic and poor. Once taken into ICC, the children become subjects of drug trials sponsored by NIAID (National Institute of Allergies and Infectious Disease, a division of the NIH), NICHD (the National Institute of Child Health and Human Development) in conjunction with some of the world's largest pharmaceutical companies—GlaxoSmithKline, Pfizer, Genentech, Chiron/Biocine and others. The drugs being given to the children are toxic—they're known to cause genetic mutation, organ failure,

> bone marrow death, bodily deformations, brain damage and fatal skin disorders. If the children refuse the drugs, they're held down and have them force fed. If the children continue to resist, they're taken to Columbia Presbyterian hospital where a surgeon puts a plastic tube through their abdominal wall into their stomachs. From then on, the drugs are injected directly into their intestines. In 2003, two children, ages 6 and 12, had debilitating strokes due to drug toxicities. The 6-year-old went blind. They both died shortly after. Another 14-year-old died recently. An 8-year-old boy had two plastic surgeries to remove large, fatty, drug-induced lumps from his neck. This isn't science fiction. This is AIDS research. The children at ICC were born to mothers who tested HIV positive, or who themselves tested positive. However, neither parents nor children were told a crucial fact—HIV tests are extremely inaccurate. The HIV test cross-reacts with nearly seventy commonly-occurring conditions, giving false positive results. These conditions include common colds, herpes, hepatitis, tuberculosis, drug abuse, inoculations and most troublingly, current and prior pregnancy. This is a double inaccuracy, because the factors that cause false positives in pregnant mothers can be passed to their children—who are given the same false diagnosis. Most of us have never heard this before. It's undoubtedly the biggest secret in medicine. However, it's well known among HIV researchers that HIV tests are extremely inaccurate—but the researchers don't tell the doctors, and they certainly don't tell the children at ICC, who serve as test animals for the next generation of AIDS drugs. ICC is run by Columbia University's Presbyterian Hospital in affiliation with Catholic Home Charities through the Archdiocese of New York."

Liam Scheff committed suicide at only forty-five on April 6, 2017. No details are available online, but Scheff had left an eerie "Dear Friends—Final Post" on his blog, of which only the first few lines are available on Amazon (and nowhere else). Clicking on the link to the blog from Amazon takes one to a "404" screen, so the exact content of the farewell post is unknown. Amazon only indicates "5 years ago" in terms of when the post was written, putting it somewhere in 2016 at the time of this writing.

The true AIDS story, and especially Fauci's role in it, has been covered up by the mainstream media to a scandalous extent. One of Fauci's many enemies in the medical field, Dr. Robert Wilner, wrote the explosive book, *Deadly Deception: The Proof That Sex and HIV Absolutely Do Not Cause AIDS.* In a video presentation recorded December 7, 1994, Wilner charged,

> We are talking about the most horrible scandal and scam ever perpetrated, not only in the name of 'science,' but in humanity and all history. . . . The great lie of Hitler—it's amazing, I think he would envy the job being done by members of the National Institutes of Health, and even the media, especially in this country. And I will put the lie to the individuals of the NIH, particularly Gallo, Fauci, and Haseltine and Essex and the rest of these scoundrels of the worst order. Criminals guilty of genocide, without a doubt. I invite them to take me to court! I wish Burroughs Wellcome would take me to court! Because they have been putting out a killer drug knowingly. Because in a court of law, I would have the opportunity to provide the absolute proof and evidence, as I have in my book, *Deadly Deception.* Now I'm not alone in what I am doing here today. How does the Press escape such obvious truth? Why would the finest virologist in the world, the most noted virologist, member of our National Academy of Sciences, Peter Duesberg, why would he put his entire career on the line? What did he have to gain? He's already lost his laboratory. And his funding. We can't take away his professorship because he is tenured.

Less than a year after giving this extremely controversial speech, Dr. Wilner died, allegedly from a heart attack. Wilner had already drawn the wrath of the Medical Industrial Complex for his view that "I am convinced you can prevent *all disease with diet,* lifestyle changes, sanitation." The Florida Board of Medicine had suspended his license in 1990.

One of the strongest indications that "outsider" Donald Trump was not sincere in his quest to "drain the swamp" was his appointment of so many swamp creatures to crucial positions. And just as tellingly, his failure to get rid of longtime Deep State veterans like Anthony Fauci. Fauci certainly would never have voted for Trump. His adoration for Hillary Clinton is well-documented. After Clinton gave a speech to the World Health Organization lauding China's healthcare system, Fauci sent her attorney Cheryl Mills an email on June 2, 2012. The email reads more like a fan letter from a starstruck teenager, exclaiming, "Wow! Very rarely does a speech bring me to tears, but this one did it. Talk about telling it like it is. This was a bases-loaded home run. Please tell the Secretary that I love her more than ever . . . you guys too, of course." A year later, Fauci would respond just as fawningly to Hillary's Congressional testimony on Benghazi, during which she pounded the table in defiance, and declared, "At this point, what difference does it make?!" On January 13, 2013, Fauci emailed Mills again, and stated, "Anyone who had any doubts about the Secretary's stamina and capability following her illness had those doubts washed away by today's performance before the Senate and the House. She faced extremely difficult circumstances at the Hearings and still she hit it right out of the park. Please tell her that we all love her and are very proud to know her." Both these emails came from the vast Hillary Clinton archives unearthed by Wikileaks.

The National Childhood Vaccine Injury Act of 1986 was passed in response to the millions of dollars juries had awarded to victims of the Diphtheria Pertussis and Tetanus (DPT) vaccine. This legislation made it very difficult for families to seek damages from vaccine makers. As attorney Robert Moxley wrote, "From the passing of the legislation in 1986, the process has been rigged, one major step at a time, in favor of the vaccine-industrial complex. Policy makers nationwide are yearning, with financial support and lobbying from the pharmaceutical industry, for mandatory vaccination. . . . The VICP creates a classic moral hazard, granting immunity from suit to the vaccine industry while providing insurance against any loss. . . . The so-called vaccine court is not what activist parents thought they had achieved. . . . The injured and their counsel (the latter economically oppressed by the program's prohibition against private attorneys fees) encounter a Kafkaesque system . . . Limits on general damages and death enacted in 1986 are still the same. And the program churns on, taking years to litigate any meaningful issue. The injuries continue, and awards continue to be made, practically in secret."[44] This disastrous legislation was more succinctly described as, "It spares pharmaceutical and device makers from costly liability lawsuits in exchange for taxpayers compensating injured patients."[45] The Supreme Court predictably upheld this onerous law, which is centered around a "no fault" federal vaccine court, in a 6–2 2011 ruling. The ruling prevented what was sure to be a plethora of lawsuits from parents alleging a link between vaccines and autism. The decision was applauded by Big Pharma giant Pfizer and American Academy of Pediatrics President O. Marion Burton ludicrously declared, that it, "protects children by strengthening our national immunization system and ensuring that vaccines will continue to prevent the spread of infectious diseases in this country."[46] Anthony Fauci was right in the center of this statist legislation, but his role seems to have been erased from any results on search engines. I heard the consistently reliable talk show host David Knight specifically addressing Fauci's support for this, but the onerous censorship on every search engine makes it very difficult now to document inconvenient truths.

In October 2021, stories appeared in the mainstream media about the gruesome experiments on dogs that had transpired under Fauci's watch. Fauci's National Institutes of Health apparently provided a grant to a lab in Tunisia, where dozens of beagle puppies were tortured and killed during Frankenstein-style experiments. Rep. Nancy Mace led a group of twenty-four congressional representatives, who expressed "grave concerns about reports of costly, cruel, and unnecessary taxpayer-funded experiments on dogs. According to documents obtained via a Freedom of Information Act request by taxpayer watchdog group White Coat Waste Project, and subsequent media coverage from October 2018 until February 2019, NIAID spent $1.68 million in taxpayer funds on drug tests involving 44 beagle puppies." The letter charged that "The commissioned tests involved injecting and force-feeding the puppies an experimental drug for several weeks, before killing and dissecting them." There were accusations that scientists had slit the dogs' throats during the experiments, to stop them from barking.[47] PETA called on Fauci to resign, but there was little follow-up on this scandalous story, and the nation's highest paid bureaucrat continued to wield power.

Attempted Assassination of Reagan

Jodie Foster may continue to outwardly ignore me for the rest of my life, but I have made her one of the most famous actresses in the world.

—John Hinckley Jr.[48]

When Ronald Reagan was shot and wounded on March 30, 1981, few Americans expected it would be the last high-profile assassination attempt of the twentieth century. As always in this country, authorities attributed the event exclusively to a "lone nut," John Hinckley Jr. Federal agents searching Hinckley's Washington, D.C., hotel room after the Reagan shooting reportedly found a photo of Lee Harvey Oswald. From the description in a news article, "Oswald was holding his rifle in a military pose in an Oak Cliff neighborhood," it certainly sounds like one of the infamous illegitimate "backyard photos." Hinckley's family, coincidentally, lived only a few miles from Oak Cliff.[49] A little-reported death associated with the Reagan assassination attempt was that of Cleveland labor leader Frank J. McNamara, who was one of two men to pounce on John Hinckley following the shooting. McNamara claimed he'd hit Hinckley "so hard I was left with blood on my knuckles." Less than six months after the March 30, 1981, attempt, McNamara died at sixty-two during an operation for a bleeding ulcer.[50] Buried in an otherwise innocuous mainstream story headlined, "John W. Hinckley Jr.: Inside the Mind of Ronald Reagan's Would-Be Assassin," is this reference: "He remained a nonentity even in crime; when he was picked up at the Nashville airport trying to board a plane while carrying three guns, the offense was considered too trivial for him to be fingerprinted." For this October 9, 1980, incident, Hinckley would merely pay a $50 cash bond and forfeit his weapons. In this same article, it is noted that "just two weeks before the assassination attempt, Hinckley Sr. met with officers of one of his favorite charities—World Vision International, a Christian evangelical and humanitarian relief agency—and asked them to 'pray for my son.'"[51] The wealthy Denver oilman had been a previous president of this shadowy outfit, which was largely funded by USAID, long associated with the CIA. John Lennon's alleged assassin, Mark David Chapman, also worked for World Vision.

It hasn't been talked about much, but the mainstream media reported in 1981 that "A Justice Department source late tonight confirmed a report that John W. Hinckley Jr. had written in papers confiscated from his cell in July that he was part of a conspiracy when he shot President Reagan and three other men March 30." Predictably, however, "the source said that after pursuing 'leads' in the confiscated papers, the Federal Bureau of Investigation concluded 'that there was no reliable evidence of any conspiracy.'" The handwritten notes were discovered by guards at Butner Correctional Institution in Butner, N.C., during a routine search of Hinckley's cell. Hinckley reportedly tried to send letters to "fictitious co-conspirators" which were intercepted and read by officials.[52] Hinckley's parents, in their memoir *Breaking Points,* claimed that the notes referred to "an imaginary conspiracy." Very quietly, Hinckley was released from Washington D.C.'s St. Elizabeth's hospital in 2016, transitioning to "home stay," and moved in with his elderly mother in Williamsburg, Virginia. Curiously, one of the conditions of his release was that he never talk to any media. Any contact with the media, even by his family, would violate the terms of his release.[53] A federal judge ruled in 2018 that Hinckley was permitted to live on his own. The logical question here is: why would a deluded, mentally ill "lone nut" be forbidden to talk with the media? Charles Manson, for example, certainly talked to plenty of people. Even at the time of his release, the FBI continued to withhold documents related to Hinckley's associates, organizations, and finances.

Roger Stone, who wrote the Foreword to the paperback edition of my book *Hidden History,* charged that George H. W. Bush was involved in the shooting of President Reagan. In a 2016 interview with WPHT radio, Stone alleged, "There are two shooters in the Reagan assassination attempt, not one. I give you photographic evidence and eye-witness evidence of a second man standing on a balcony holding a gun, who can clearly be seen in the uncropped photos, and I traced many of the connections of the Bushes to the Hinckleys. It's more than you've been told." Stone was referring here to the report that Neil Bush, son of the elder Bush president and brother of Dubya, had been scheduled to have dinner with Scott Hinckley, brother of Reagan's alleged attempted assassin, the day after the shooting. Stone declared, "The Government says five bullets and I traced the trajectory of five bullets and the angle at which the bullet enters Reagan could not have come from the crouching position of Hinckley and if it bounced off a door, where's the chip of paint or evidence that it did? There's none. The government won't release any of these records. They've never released the photos."[54] According to Russ Baker, who wrote the controversial book about the Bushes *Family of Secrets,* George H. W. Bush was close friends with the mysterious Russian "baron" George de Mohrenschildt, seemingly incompatible friend of the much younger Lee Harvey Oswald. As noted earlier, Bush did acknowledge knowing de Mohrenschildt.

The more research I conduct, the more I appreciate the overlooked work of the late Michael Canfield. Canfield's close friend Steven S. Lamb posted the following, fascinating anecdote on Canfield's Facebook page on June 3, 2021: "Ahem. When Hinckley Jr. tried to kill President Reagan, a couple days later it was announced he spent a lot of time in two motels in Hollywood and was delusional thinking he had a relationship with Jodi Foster. At the time my Best Friend Michael Canfield lived a block or so away from one and about 3/4 of a mile from another motel. I drove over to Mike's and we went to interview the motel clerks at each motel. Each one remembered the really odd young Hinckley and that he was with a very attractive young woman who they each claimed was Jodi Foster. One produced a register with what appeared to be both their names on it from a year prior. Did John Hinkley Jr. have a relationship with Jodi Foster? We don't know, but it seems he had a relationship with someone he believed was Jodi Foster. Mike called the FBI to tell them and the Secret Service came to his house a few days later to interview him. They attempted to convince him the Motel Clerks were mistaken. Odd behavior for researchers. Still on the trail of the Assassins."

I questioned Steven Lamb further about this in a December 6, 2021, phone conversation. Lamb recalled that one of the hotel clerks was a Lebanese immigrant who was very adamant about the female being Jodie Foster. Canfield's initial efforts to interest the news media were unsurprisingly not successful. Lamb claimed that when the Secret Service paid Canfield that unexpected visit, they spent three to four hours at his apartment "trying to convince him that he didn't see what he saw." Lamb noted that Hinckley's father was the single largest contributor to George H. W. Bush's presidential campaign. A man of interesting connections, Steven Lamb knew both Sirhan Sirhan and his mother as a child. He used to ride his bike to a health food store where Sirhan worked, and said that he was very nice. Canfield was close friends with not only Bob Dylan, but big 1960s recording artist Johnny Rivers as well. Lamb told me that Canfield and Rivers were with John Belushi at the Chateau Marmont Hotel earlier on the evening that he died. There is no question in my mind that Belushi was deeply interested in the JFK assassination. Veteran NBC Texas affiliate entertainment reporter Bobbie Wygant claimed that every time she interviewed Belushi, he would bring up the fact that Dallas was "the city that killed my president."[55] What are the odds that Freddie Prinze, Sal Mineo, and John Belushi, who all died under questionable circumstances, would just happen to have a keen interest in the same forbidden subject? The always blunt Dick Gregory recounted, "John Belushi called Mark Lane and said 'I have some information to share with you about the Kennedy assassination.' So Mark called me. I couldn't rearrange my schedule. They were supposed to meet in Detroit. The night before they were supposed to meet, John Belushi was murdered, with that overshot of drugs, and that woman from Canada. If you're sitting where I'm sitting, that's a CIA hit. Who's the Canadian woman's lawyer? Robert Shapiro."

In an age of Orwellian online censorship, one of the biggest censors of them all—YouTube—now provides an unfettered platform for John Hinckley, who was given his unconditional release in June 2022. Hinckley's music is growing in popularity; at last count he had over 36,000 subscribers on YouTube. He has also started his own record label. In addition, Hinckley won a lawsuit, and is now permitted to display his paintings on online streaming services. News accounts claimed Hinckley was "freed from the strict conditions of release" that had been previously applied to him, but no mention was made of the gag order not to talk with the media, or whether this had been lifted as well.[56] Particularly strange was Hinckley's promotion of his 2024 concert, to take place in Naugatuck, Connecticut, on March 30, of all dates, the anniversary of the attempted assassination of Reagan.[57]

To almost all conservatives, Ronald Reagan is a secular saint, second only to the first imperial president Abraham Lincoln. This professional actor was all smoke and mirrors, with no substance. His administration has been called the friendliest in history to organized crime. There would be no new undercover operations launched against the Mafia or white-collar crime during his presidency. Instead, the focus shifted to street crime and individual drug possession. Just say no. As reporter Gary Webb showed, before he "killed himself" with *two* gunshots to the head, it was the government itself that brought these drugs into the inner cities.

Why does the Right worship an open-borders advocate like Reagan, who raised taxes on the poor and working class and commingled Social Security with general revenue? Who opened the door to distasteful neo-cons that have converted our dreadful foreign policy into a force for Israeli, not American interests. Lincoln and Reagan are not legitimate alternatives to FDR and Woodrow Wilson. As Huey Long called Democrats and Republicans back in the day, they are the twin towers of disaster. Ronald Reagan was certainly a disaster, no matter how many airports and roads they named after him.

CHAPTER NINE

THE NINETIES: MORE CONSPIRACY CENTRAL

Oklahoma City Bombing—9/11 Dress Rehearsal

McVeigh and Nichols are going to hell regardless. I'm just looking forward to sending them there a little sooner.
—U.S. Attorney Joseph Hartzler[1]

One day you will find out your government was behind this.
—Timothy McVeigh

I covered the Oklahoma City Bombing, which killed 168 people on April 19, 1995, pretty thoroughly in my first *Hidden History* book. There is much additional evidence, which shows even more conclusively that the event was not a simple act of revenge by demented right-wing extremist Timothy McVeigh, who was outraged by the government's actions at Waco.

One of the strangest aspects of this case concerned a GSA employee named Mike Loudenslager. In the weeks leading up to the bombing, Loudenslager became concerned with the alarming amount of explosive material that was being brought into the building by the DEA and the ATF. Information is difficult to come by regarding Loudenslager's story, and limited to alternative websites. Loudenslager's concern over the explosives was shared by the director of the Murrah Building's day care center, Danielle Wise Hunt, and her husband Thomas Hunt, head of security for the building. Thomas Hunt would be fired from his job, and Danielle lost her license for the Stars & Stripes Child Developmental Center, three weeks before the bombing. Loudenslager, who was in court on the morning of April 19, would subsequently be seen by numerous witnesses in the aftermath of the blast, actively helping in rescue efforts. Witnesses also reported seeing him engage in a heated confrontation with an unidentified party or parties. Chillingly, authorities would later report that Loudenslager had died at his desk, one of the official victims of the bombing. These same alternative outlets, without providing any concrete sources, claim that two mysterious deaths connected to Oklahoma City, that of Dr. Don Chumley and police officer Terrence Yeakey, were related to their efforts to prove that Loudenslager was alive and well after the bombing, and that therefore someone must have murdered him.

Terrence Yeakey's bizarre "suicide" was recounted in detail in *Hidden History.* Naturally, there was no autopsy performed. The *New York Times* spoke for the Establishment, as always, with the headline, "A Policeman who Rescued 4 in Bombing Kills Himself."[2] His family, who refused to believe he'd killed himself, was harassed and stalked by Oklahoma City police. His widow Tonia Yeakey's home was broken into, and a balloon was left behind, with a message on it in black marker proclaiming, "we know where you are." Tonia was forced to move her two small children four times in one year alone. In a truly frightening incident, she found that her front door had been removed from its hinges, and a "Get Well" card was attached to her bedroom's closet door. Yeakey's 91-year-old grandmother, Mary declared, "From my heart I want something to happen to show he had no right to be killed. His life was taken away for nothing." Terrence's sister, Vikki Yeakey stated that as soon as she was told by the police that Yeakey had committed suicide, "I screamed out He didn't take his life. Someone murdered him." Family members reported they were told to "keep our mouths shut." Yeakey's mother later declared that for fourteen years she had been "going over and over something I don't believe to be true. I believe it to be murder. I don't know who did it. [That's] why we need answers . . . you need to put your child to rest and without knowing what happened [we can't] . . . I vowed I will never give up. I need answers. If there's ANYONE who could help I would appreciate it."[3] Oklahoma City police sergeant Don Browning courageously blasted the fact there hadn't been an autopsy performed, and accused OKC police Chief Sam Gonzales and the FBI of covering up Yeakey's murder. Browning was incensed that the FBI and police tried to smear Yeakey by claiming he was unstable and dealing with marital problems. According to online journalist Patrick Briley, who did great work on the case, "Yeakey even was pounding the desk and yelling at the OKC Councilman Mark Schwartz shortly before Yeakey was found murdered. Yeakey was demanding answers from Schwartz about the members of the City council, the Governor, the fire chief, the police chief and the FBI who had advance warning and met about the warning on Monday before the bombing." Mark Schwartz would be subsequently promoted to a cushy job in Bill Clinton's Department of Energy.

Patrick Briley wrote about the FBI threatening and harassing injured bombing victim Leah Moore. They warned her not to talk to reporters about what she'd seen, especially the photos she'd taken of the Ryder truck. Another person injured in the blast, Army recruiter Larry Martin, committed suicide in a bizarre way, by flying his plane into the ground near his church. Martin knew that his Army colleague Arlene Blanchard had been threatened by the FBI. In fact, all the Army recruiters were ordered not to talk about the "John Doe #2" they'd seen McVeigh with around the Murrah Building. Briley recounted how witnesses at the Travelers Aid were "brow beat and traumatized" for months, to intimidate them into forgetting the fact they'd seen three "John Doe" FBI informants with McVeigh's car. The FBI hounded and tried to trick dying snack shop owner Danny Wilkerson into changing his story about seeing a "John Doe #2" in the Ryder truck just prior to the bombing. Briley had a personal stake in this as well. Mike Carpenter of KWTV News in OKC advised him that he had better be worried because he'd "pissed off" the FBI over his complaints that they'd been harassing his wife. Briley's conclusion that the OKC Bombing was a failed sting operation remains the most logical explanation.[4] His friend and fellow researcher Devvy Kidd told me, in a June 3, 2022, email, "The last contact I had with Patrick was probably 15 years ago. For his mental health sake and his family, he was done."

An April 30, 1995, FBI report concerns Danielle Hunt's encounter with a clean-cut man wearing camouflage fatigues. The report states: "HUNT stated between 5:00 and 5:30 p.m. approximately two weeks prior to losing the contract, around March 10, 1995, she observed an individual who she believes to be TIMOTHY McVEIGH at the door on the east end of the day care center. This individual was wearing camouflage fatigues, fatigue hat and black boots with the pants bloused. HUNT later observed there were no name or service strips, unit badges or rank insignia on his uniform. HUNT admitted this individual into the day care center when he indicated he was being transferred to Oklahoma City and would be working on the fourth floor of the Murrah Building. HUNT stated that when asked he did not know when he would be transferred to Oklahoma City. He did not answer HUNT when asked where he lived or was being transferred from." Hunt went on to relate, "This individual stated he had an infant and a preschooler that he wanted to enroll in the day care center. HUNT thought it was strange that he did not provide ages, sex or talk about his children. When asked about the sexes of his children he told HUNT he had a boy and a girl. HUNT advised this individual they had a waiting list for infants and asked for a name and telephone number so she could put him on the list. This individual did not provide a name or number, stating he would wait for his wife. HUNT stated that based on his behavior she wondered if this individual had any children. HUNT provided this individual with a tour of the day care center and noticed he seemed to be looking at the lay out." Hunt thought it strange that he paid no attention to the children and never asked about the cost involved for the day care center. During this approximately ten-minute tour, what stood out to Hunt was his questioning about the security there, but he suddenly appeared nervous and hurriedly left when she mentioned that her husband was a federal agent. Earlier in the memo, George Hunt is described as an officer with the Federal Protective Services. Does this correlate to being the "head of security" for the Murrah Building? Hunt describes "McVeigh" as being 5'9" in height, while the real person was 6'2". Shades of Lee Harvey Oswald's wildly varying heights. Strangely, a newspaper report touching on Hunt's encounter stated that she had spoken to the FBI on December 16, some eight months later.[5]

There were other encounters with "McVeigh" leading up to the OKC bombing, much as Lee Harvey Oswald was clearly being impersonated in the time period just before the JFK assassination. Dr. Paul Heath, a VA psychologist who worked in the Murrah Building, reported speaking to someone named "McVeigh" late one Friday afternoon, a week and a half before the bombing. In an interview with David Hoffman, author of the definitive book on the subject, *The Oklahoma City Bombing and the Politics of Terror,* Heath described his encounter with "McVeigh" and two other men, one of whom strongly resembled the elusive John Doe #2: "I've narrowed this to probably a Friday [April 7], at around three o'clock," Heath told Hoffman. "A bell rang in the outer office of room 522. No one answered, so I went out to the waiting room. . . . A man came in with two others to apply for a job. One other was American Indian looking, the other was Caucasian. A male individual was standing there, and I introduced myself as Dr. Heath, 'how can I help you?' and this individual said 'my name is *somethin*' and I don't remember what his first name was, but he told me his last name was McVeigh. So I said 'can I help you?' and he said 'well, we're here looking for work.' and I said 'what kind of work are we looking for?' He said '*we* are looking for construction work.'" After offering to help them find some job leads, which they appeared uninterested in, Heath recalled, "I . . . continued to talk to Mr. McVeigh . . . And he said, 'Well, I've been living in Kansas.' So then I said, 'Do you happen to be a member of the McVay family from Cussing, Oklahoma?' . . . he said, 'Well Dr. Heath, how do they spell their name?' 'Well I assume, M-c-V-a-y.' And he took his finger, and he kind of put it in my face and said, 'Well Dr. Heath,' in kind of a boisterous way, 'Dr. Heath, you remember this. My name is McVeigh, but you don't spell it M-c-V-a-y."

This "McVeigh" seemed careful to stress his name, like those impersonating Oswald invariably did. On Saturday, April 8, 1995, McVeigh was seen, along with friends Andreas Strassmeir and Michael Brescia, at Lady Godiva's topless bar in Tulsa, Oklahoma. Security footage obtained by J. D. Cash of the *McCurtain Gazette,* and Trish Wood of CBC, recorded the dancers discussing McVeigh's boasting. A dancer named Tara can be heard recounting to another girl in the dressing room, "He goes, 'I'm a very smart man.' I said, 'you are?' And he goes, 'Yes, you're going to find an (inaudible) and they're going to hurt you real bad.' I was like, 'Oh really?' And he goes, 'Yes, and you're going to remember me on April 19, 1995. You're going to remember me for the rest of your life.'" Laughing, she replies, "Oh, really?" "Yes you will," McVeigh says.[6] Like Oswald, McVeigh was seen and encountered in places where documentation shows him to have been somewhere else at the time, often accompanied by a person matching the description of the mysterious "John Doe #2." Barbara Whittenberg, owner of the Santa Fe Trail Diner, shared her experience serving breakfast to Terry Nichols, McVeigh, and "John Doe #2"early on a Saturday morning. "I asked them why they had a Ryder truck outside," Whittenberg related. "I wasn't being nosy, I just wondered if Terry Nichols was moving. My sister was moving here, and she needed to find a place. Well, the guy who they haven't arrested yet—John Doe #2—he blurted out that they were going to Oklahoma. When that happened, it was like someone threw ice water on the conversation. . . . McVeigh and Nichols just stared at the guy."[7]

The FBI would admit that McVeigh's fingerprints were not found in many of the places where they should have been, during his supposed construction of the bomb. FBI fingerprint expert Louis G. Hupp testified during McVeigh's trial, that he found no prints belonging to McVeigh on the rental contract for the Ryder truck that prosecutors claim carried the bomb, in the truck rental office itself, or in the Kansas motel room where McVeigh was staying at the time the truck was rented. He also acknowledged that no prints belonging to McVeigh were found in any of the storage lockers in which he supposedly kept explosives prior to the blast, or in the pickup truck that the government claimed codefendant Terry L. Nichols drove to Oklahoma City three days before the bombing to meet McVeigh.[8] During McVeigh's trial, two defense witnesses testified to seeing a large Ryder truck at the Kansas motel where the prosecution maintained that McVeigh had stayed at the weekend before the bombing. However, this sighting occurred a day before McVeigh's supposed alias Robert Kling rented the truck that purportedly was used in the blast. Prosecutors had McVeigh checking into the motel on Friday, April 14, which was Good Friday. Herta King, a longtime friend of Lea McGown, owner and manager of the Dreamland Motel in Junction City, Kansas, remembered how she took an Easter basket to her son David, who was then living at the motel, on Easter Sunday. That was one day before the truck that supposedly carried the bomb was rented by a man calling himself Robert Kling. King recounted noticing a large Ryder truck on that Easter Sunday, in the parking lot. High school student Renda Truong, who ate dinner with the McGown family on Easter Sunday, also noticed the Ryder truck in the parking lot, and even asked Mrs. McGown whether someone was moving. The defense also called Jeff Davis, who had delivered Chinese food to McVeigh's motel room some four days before the bombing. The man who had placed the order for that food had identified himself as Kling. Davis testified that the individual who accepted the food and paid for it was not McVeigh. Even with the half-hearted defense McVeigh received from Stephen Jones, there were enough witnesses to raise reasonable doubt in the minds of reasonable people. Vicki Beemer, who handled the paperwork for the Ryder truck rental at Elliott's Body Shop in Junction City on the afternoon of Monday, April 17, told the jury that she couldn't remember what either of the two men who came in to pick up the truck that day looked like.[9] Beemer, her boss Eldon Elliott, and shop mechanic Tom Kessinger, all initially reported having interacted with "Robert Kling" and "John Doe #2," but like others were intimidated by the authorities into changing their description of "McVeigh" and dropping any mention of "John Doe #2."

As should be expected from anyone who is awake to the systemic corruption, the press coverage of McVeigh's sham trial was worthless. In a January 30, 1996, story in *The Denver Post,* headlined, "John Doe 2 not a suspect," it was breathlessly reported that authorities had now confidently identified the enigmatic figure, seen in the company of McVeigh by multiple witnesses. "John Doe #2" was "identified" as Army private Todd Bunting, who had supposedly rented a Ryder truck in Junction City, Kansas, a day after McVeigh did. The article reports, "The sketch of John Doe No. 2 was based on descriptions from a rental-truck mechanic, Tom Kessinger, who now admits he was mistaken. . . . Kessinger is now confident he had Todd Bunting in mind when he provided the description for the John Doe No. 2 composite. Prosecutors said Kessinger realized he had made a mistake when meeting with a prosecutor and two FBI agents Nov. 22, 1996." Yes, many witnesses have realized their "mistake" when meeting with law enforcement. The authorities can provide great enlightenment. The story notes that "the government says it is still looking for a second man who accompanied McVeigh on April 17, 1995. Two employees of Elliott's Body Shop in Junction City, Kan.—Eldon Elliott and Vicki Beemer—told the FBI of the second man." Presumably, they have stopped looking. Elliott alone stood firm, and as late as 2003 was maintaining the man with McVeigh was not Nichols. He described how FBI agents "wanted me to change my mind that there was a second person there. And I wouldn't change my mind."[10]

Alec McNaughton, in describing his former law partner, McVeigh's attorney Stephen Jones, stated, "He is the most dishonest person I've ever met, including all the criminals I've defended."[11] Jones began his career working for Richard Nixon, and would represent Establishment figures such as Oklahoma Governor Frank Keating. As the intrepid Nebraska State Senator John DeCamp wrote in his book *The Franklin Cover-Up*: "Only hours before I was to file the legal papers for a civil action to keep the building standing, I was contacted by Timothy McVeigh's attorneys, who presented me with two major requests. First, they asked that I allow them to file the motions to keep the building standing so that the investigation could be conducted. . . . It was clear that if McVeigh's attorneys believed, or even suspected government cover-up, they would definitely want the building examined. Their second request was that I release from retainer the bomb investigation team I had assembled—John A. Kennedy and Associates—which, they claimed, they wanted to hire. I granted these requests to McVeigh's attorneys. A few hours later, I watched in horror as CNN and all the national news channels reported that McVeigh's attorneys had no intent to file any motions to keep the Federal Building standing. They had 'just reached agreement with the government,' the reporters explained, to permit the building to be destroyed almost immediately. Angry beyond belief, I called McVeigh's attorney and asked what they were doing. . . . McVeigh's attorney told me, 'Oh yes, we are going to allow the building to be destroyed.' 'Why?'

I demanded. 'Because we could not afford to pay the retainer fee that the Kennedy and Associates firm wanted,' he answered. . . .'For God's sake!' I screamed at him. 'I will raise the money! I will pay the fee! There's too much at stake for America. How . . . can McVeigh go along with wanting that building destroyed, when that building is the one thing that can tell America the story of what really happened?'My protests were futile. Within hours of my call, by mutual agreement between McVeigh's attorneys and the government prosecutors, the building was destroyed, and any evidence was destroyed with it."[12] Among other obvious derelictions of duty, Jones failed to call key witnesses like General Ben Partin, one of the most preeminent bomb experts in the country, who had been very critical of the official story. Jones had called McVeigh "the boy next door" and proclaimed "he's innocent." McVeigh would grow deeply disenchanted with his lawyer.

Timothy McVeigh, in a late June 1995 interview published in *Newsweek*, said, "For two days, in the cell, we could hear news reports; and of course everyone, including myself, was horrified at the deaths of the children. And you know, that was the No. 1 focal point of the media at the time, too, obviously—the deaths of the children. It's a very tragic thing." McVeigh adamantly denied media reports that he'd refused to give out any information other than name, rank, and serial number upon being arrested. "I never, never called myself a prisoner of war," McVeigh declared, and also claimed his alleged "confession" in jail, as reported by the *New York Times*, was a concoction of the media. But enigmatic as always, when *Newsweek* asked, "Did you do it?" the alleged bomber gave the cryptic reply, "The only way we can really answer that, is that we are going to plead not guilty." He evaded, rather than rebutted, questions from the magazine about evidence against him, and chuckled while stating, "Yeah, here comes John Doe 2 for the 18th time." He declined to say whether or not he had read William Pierce's *The Turner Diaries*, which was actually used as "evidence" against him.[13] Keep in mind, of course, that *Newsweek* is a big mainstream media organ, and has misrepresented the truth about every notable historical event. McVeigh was also recorded as telling *The London Sunday Times* on April 21, the day after the bombing that he'd been "set up" by the FBI because of his political views. How do we reconcile these statements with his purported later comments about "collateral damage," and his curious refusal to testify in his own defense?

I had a pleasant conversation with Edye Smith on April 29, 2022. Edye lost her twins in the OKC blast, and the media milked all the drama it could out of the situation, until she questioned the narrative during a live CNN interview. Edye referred me to her mother, Kathy Sanders, who continues to actively investigate the cover-up. Sanders has done extensive research and wrote the book *After Oklahoma City: A Grieving Grandmother Uncovers Shocking Truths about the Bombing . . . And Herself.* Sanders told me she was unavailable to talk because she'd signed an exclusive agreement with a documentary filmmaker. When I asked her about Mike Loudenslager and Danielle Hunt, two figures that particularly interest me, she stated that she hadn't really looked into them, and was concentrating on John Doe #2.

I interviewed former Oklahoma State Rep. Charles Key, who'd been one of the few lawmakers to push for the truth about this case, on May 20, 2022. When I asked about author David Hoffman, Key informed me that he'd "passed away a long time ago, in Europe—I think it was Poland, or maybe Czechoslovakia. It's a little sketchy just why he died, but he got, I think he was taken into custody into a local jail or something and he died there." He characterized Jayna Davis, former Oklahoma local TV reporter who had done extensive work on the case, as being "all about me, me, me," and said he had the impression she had "kind of walked away from all of that stuff a long time ago." He said, regarding Danielle Hunt, that "they would not respond, they were very afraid" and had only talked to "some people" in the "very beginning." He said the Loudenslager case was "a really hard one," and that they had "tried, tried—a bunch of people . . . trying to get some kind of facts related to that. . . . It's one of those I've had to put over into the category—I don't think we're ever going to find out." Key recalled, "There were so many people we talked to that wouldn't give us an affidavit . . . there were probably a half dozen or so I would describe like this; they were so scared even talking to us. . . . I remember one lady in a small southern Oklahoma City, we went and hunted her down, and she was shaking visibly like a leaf . . . these people are scared that 'they' are going to come and get them." He related how a contact at the jail told him how Terry Nichols just "jabbered" away, talking nonstop, while McVeigh kept up his stoic silence. He surprisingly stated that James Nichols, brother of Terry, who wrote a book strongly questioning the official narrative, wouldn't talk to him. Key felt at that point, James was trying to stay out of jail himself. He also let me know that Kathy Sanders had been communicating with Terry Nichols for a long time.

Terry Nichols filed a declaration in a Salt Lake City District Court in 2007, in connection with attorney Jesse Trentadue's wrongful death lawsuit regarding the death of his brother Kenneth in an Oklahoma City federal corrections facility. As detailed in *Hidden History,* Trentadue claimed his brother was killed by FBI agents who mistook him for a suspect in the bombing. Nichols shockingly alleged in his declaration that McVeigh had let it slip that the bombing was an FBI operation, and that he was taking orders from former FBI official Larry Potts. Potts had been the lead FBI agent during the mindless "siege" at Ruby Ridge, Idaho, which resulted in the death of Randy Weaver's wife and son, and was also involved in the disastrous massacre of American civilians at Waco. Nichols asserted that McVeigh had revealed to him in 1992 that "while he was serving in the U.S. Army, he had been recruited to carry out undercover missions." Nichols stated, "McVeigh said he believed Potts was manipulating him and forcing him to 'go off script,' which I understood meant to change the target of the bombing," Nichols claimed not to know anything about the target for any bombing. Nichols has declared he has more information, which he offered to then Attorney General John Ashcroft in 2004, but would only divulge it under sworn video deposition.[14]

As noted in my Introduction, during the course of researching this book, I attempted to phone many witnesses. One of the few people I was able to speak with was Timothy's father William McVeigh, on May 25, 2021. The elder McVeigh wanted to know how I'd gotten his number, said "I better not" in response to my attempts to converse with him, and stated he was tired of answering the same questions. Interestingly, in a 2020 newspaper article, it was revealed that William McVeigh had no idea where his son's ashes had been scattered, as the secrecy was his son's wishes.[15]

JFK Jr. Revisited—Another Kennedy Assassination

My family is used to all manner of controversy.

—John F. Kennedy Jr.[16]

In my previous book, *Hidden History: An Exposé of Modern Crimes, Conspiracies, and Cover Ups in American Politics,* I conducted the first independent investigation into the 1999 death of President Kennedy's son John F. Kennedy Jr. I exposed the absurdity of the official narrative, which held that a "reckless" Kennedy had died in a plane crash due to pilot error. In fact, the evidence shows that JFK Jr. was a cautious pilot who was experienced and more than capable enough to make the flight in question. An overlooked story published after his plane disappeared, but before the bodies were found, emphasized this theme. Students at Vero Beach's Flight Safety Academy, where Kennedy got his pilot's license in April 1998, maintained that he "took safety seriously."[17]

It wasn't until 2007 that transcripts of JFK Jr.'s last alleged radio communication with air traffic control were publicly released. That often mentioned 9:39 p.m. phone call from Kennedy, reporting everything was fine and awaiting landing instructions, had been conveniently thrust down the memory hole. 9:39 p.m. was exactly the moment that officials would claim Kennedy's plane went down into the water in a death spiral.[18] In 2017, HLN's "How it Really Happened" attempted to further delve into the crash. They reported that some people claimed to have spoken to Kennedy, although this didn't involve that elusive 9:39 pm call. Steven Lagudi, an employee at Republic Airport in Farmingdale, New York, claimed he heard a pilot attempting to contact "someone at Martha's Vineyard" on the night Kennedy's plane went down. Lagudi stated that the pilot's voice sounded "increasingly anxious and frustrated" and at the end of the transmission said, "Well, if there is nobody on the ground, we're not going to make Martha's Vineyard." A 2002 story quoted Lagudi as saying, "His voice still haunts me. I'll never forget it."[19] Another employee at the same airport, Richard Perez, also heard a pilot trying to contact Martha's Vineyard during the same time, somewhere between 9:00 and 9:30 p.m. On June 13, 2022, Steven Lagudi answered my text request for an interview with, "Nope. I'm good." When I asked if he'd been threatened, he replied, "Threatened?!?! My 'testimony?' Not sure what kind of book you are writing but there is nothing I can add that was not already said. And have zero interest in talking w you or the countless other people who reach out to me trying to get some hidden info which does not exist so you can sell books, movies, tv shows or whatever to make money." He didn't deny or verify hearing a conversation that nineteen years earlier he had described as "haunting" him.

The 2020 multi-episode podcast *Fatal Voyage: The Death of JFK Jr.*, resorted to predictable disinformation. Adopting the cherished "blame the Kennedys" line, it was alleged that the family—not the government—had "instigated an immediate cover-up of the truth." Calling the coroner's report "full of holes" that "looks like a cover-up," the podcast noted that it was only a page long, and "confirms he's dead, but says nothing more," to quote journalist James Robertson. Podcast host, ex-homicide detective Colin McLaren added, "If this flimsy excuse for a coroner's report on JFK Jr.'s body sounds like a rush job, that's because it was." Well-known pathologist Cyril Wecht declared, "My recollection is that the family tried not even to have autopsies done." As I noted in *Hidden History*, there was a rushed cremation, which contradicted the family history (and as was shown earlier in this book, flies in the face of what RFK Jr. wrote about in his journal), which led to obviously incomplete autopsies. As Wecht suggested, JFK Jr. certainly "would not be the first Kennedy to have his coroner's report adjusted" to fit an implausible narrative. In a shocking indication of his ignorance, McLaren proclaimed that Kennedy "was not qualified or competent enough to fly his plane that night, in those conditions, and with his injured ankle . . . but he did so anyway." Those "conditions" were just fine, as Edward Meyer, who wrote the official weather report on the accident for the FAA, declared while attacking the media for their inaccurate reporting. The host of this ridiculous program went on to say, "It seems that the Kennedys themselves instigated an immediate cover-up of the truth—simply to preserve the mythology of the family name."[20]

In another episode of this deceptive podcast, McLaren declared that JFK Jr. wasn't in contact with air traffic control at all during that "fateful" flight. McLaren didn't bother to mention that now memory holed 9:39

p.m. call, or explain why the Coast Guard sent someone to be interviewed about it. Ludicrously, the podcast claimed that Kennedy would have been unable to communicate anyway, as his radio was "a digit off the proper frequency." Bringing to mind all those JFK assassination documentaries and their laughably inaccurate "re-creations," the podcast reconstructed JFK Jr.'s final flight. "This is very uncomfortable stuff," McLaren claimed. "I don't like this. This is like being in the washing machine. Up, down, left, right. And now the right bend is at a 45-degree angle and I don't like it." Maybe they should have checked with a genuine expert like Edward Meyer, who could have set them straight. The great detective concluded that the crash was "terrible and preventable," and said, "[It was] brought about by a number of factors that include, in no small part, John Jr.'s own recklessness, overconfidence and sense of immortality."[21] The series did address what I first exposed in *Hidden History*: JFK Jr. was obsessed with finding out the truth about his father's assassination. Reporter Leon Wagner was quoted as saying, "When he was 17 years old . . . He's doing his own research. He reads the books written at that time . . . there's an article about there being three assassins. He was well-versed in the research on it." Wagner also touched on a truly fascinating rumor that JFK Jr. once wrote a threatening letter to then Senator Joe Biden. McLaren claimed the FBI investigated the 1994 letter, explaining, "Yeah, it says it was postmarked in Worcester, Massachusetts, to Joe Biden." The note supposedly read, "Dear Senator Biden, you are a traitor. You must die." The show speculated that Kennedy's anger at Biden might have stemmed from his support for the disastrous 1994 crime bill that helped create the world's largest prison population.[22] It is impossible to imagine Kennedy threatening a US senator with death, and it's highly likely that the story originated from one of the typical anti-Kennedys sources.

Reporter Maureen Callahan, who would later write the earlier referenced attack piece on RFK Jr., blasted the ABC special *The Last Days of JFK Jr.*, which supported every tenet of the impossible official narrative. Despite this, Callahan felt ABC hadn't been tough enough on JFK Jr. In the spirit of every "Oswald did it" apologist, Callahan wrote, "Not only did the program soft-pedal Kennedy's complete and utter fault for the crash but it got crucial details wrong—claiming that the FAA said flying conditions that night were 'excellent' (according to the National Transportation Safety Board review of the crash, they were extremely poor, and JFK Jr. would have known it), and that his flight instructor was unavailable that night to fly with him. In fact, the NTSB report said one of Kennedy's instructors did offer to fly with him, but Kennedy said no, that 'he wanted to do it alone.'" In reality, neither that ABC special or any other has ever even hinted that the weather that night was anything but terrible, as noted by the FAA's Edward Meyer, who called the media out on all their misreporting. There is much controversy swirling around the flight instructor, and good reason to think that one might have been scheduled to fly with Kennedy, or even actually on board. The "he wanted to fly alone" fairy tale comes from an extremely dubious source, as I detailed in *Hidden History.* This supposed "journalist" continues grinding her axe, writing, "Philosophically, though, there's a much more malignant problem here: the continued idolatry of all things Kennedy, the media's reluctance or outright refusal to acknowledge the clan's dark and sometimes criminal side, and—when she's not been villainized as the cause of all John's woes, if not the fatal accident—the perfunctory treatment of Carolyn in this narrative." What media outlet idolizes the Kennedys? As I've documented over the years, the mainstream media despises the Kennedy family, and continues to lie about the unnatural deaths that have befallen so many of them. Callahan can commiserate with an unlimited number of fellow "journalists" who also irrationally hate the Kennedy family. This article is as full of vicious hatred for the Kennedys as her later story on RFK Jr. would be. She writes like a spurned lover.[23]

In another *New York Post* story, dubious excerpts from sleazy writer C. David Heymann's book *American Legacy: The Story of John and Caroline Kennedy* were published. Heymann, relying upon "new information from National Transportation Safety Board and Federal Aviation Association investigations, recounted Kennedy's final terrifying moments." Of course, how he or the NTSB, or the FAA, knew anything about those last moments is impossible to determine. After all, according to these agencies, there was no communication between JFK Jr. and ground officials after he took off that night. There are lurid inferences that JFK Jr. and his wife were sleeping apart, and argued on the night of the crash. Heymann alleged that

Kennedy was taking Vicodin for the pain from his broken ankle, Ritalin for attention deficit disorder, and another medication for a thyroid condition. Heymann also repeats the lie that JFK Jr. opted not to have a copilot on board with him. Heymann quotes the recollections of "business executive" Roy Stoppard, who had just flown in from the Cape and warned JFK Jr. about flying in the worsening weather conditions. Stoppard allegedly encountered JFK Jr. at a service station, and observed him holding what looked like a bottle of white wine. So, the "reckless" Kennedy was hopped up on prescriptions, and probably drunk, too. He pretty much deserved it, just like his father. Stoppard's account can be rejected solely on his claim of ominous weather. As bears repeating, Edward Meyer, who wrote the official account of the weather that night for the FAA, found that the weather was not bad at all that night, and he was incensed at the media for suggesting it was. On top of his other scurrilous slander, Heymann accused JFK Jr. of almost colliding with an American Airlines flight.[24] Another laughable claim was made by Michael Pangia, "a leading aviation attorney," who supposedly studied the crash report. While Pangia portrayed JFK Jr. as remaining calm and bravely fighting to the end, he could not have heard what he claimed were his last alleged words of "We're not going to make it" over the cockpit recorder. As CNN reported on July 30, 1999: "A cockpit recording device was recovered from the high-performance plane, but it had been destroyed on impact." And yet, according to an account on The Free Library, "Air experts investigating the tragedy have told how a radio operator picked up his last words: 'We're not going to make it.'"

On January 8, 2019, I emailed former WCVB-TV, Boston reporter Steve Sbraccia, whose skepticism about the official story had helped to fuel my efforts at finding the truth about the death of John F. Kennedy Jr. I asked him for his thoughts on the ABC special. Later that day, he wrote back: "They did NOT contact me and I did not know anything about the show till after it aired when I read the NY POST story about how inaccurate it was." Sbraccia provided a link to the very same attack piece from Margaret Callahan, and said, "After reading it I thought they made many good points. . . . Sorry I can't give you my personal opinion of the show since I didn't watch it." This seemed like a startling departure from

Sbraccia's earlier position, when he had reiterated in an email to me that he'd swear in court to the reality of the still unidentified reporter from the *Martha's Vineyard Gazette* whose account of seeing an explosion in the sky at the time of the crash was widely reported in the Establishment press.

I was finally able to contact Todd Burgun, who as a Coast Guard petty officer gave a live interview with WCVB-TV's Susan Wornick during the search for JFK Jr.'s missing aircraft. The subject of the interview was that 9:39 radio call from Kennedy, in which he had calmly awaited landing instructions. The 9:39 communication was widely reported early on, including by UPI and other mainstream outlets. In the live videotaped coverage I was sent by researcher Scott Myers, this call is mentioned numerous times on WCVB-TV. To my shock, Burgun actually responded to me, in a May 10, 2021, email. Alas, it was not a polite response. "Hello Mr. Jeffries, I do not buy into your conspiracy theory BS. I am not for your brand of crazy. Please leave me alone. Thank you," Burgun wrote. Later that day, I replied thusly: "I promise I will not bother you further. But you have called me 'crazy,' which I think requires a response. First, I have no 'theory' about anything. I ask questions, and seek the truth. Which is what professional journalists should do, but don't. I've written a critically acclaimed book about economics, and another about bullying. I have a book coming out this year about showbiz. So I don't write exclusively about government corruption and cover ups. You were the one the Coast Guard sent to give a television interview about the widely reported 9:39 p.m. phone call from JFK Jr. As I'm sure you realize, such a phone call alone contradicts the official narrative. Since the government subsequently declared no such phone call was made, why did the Coast Guard assign you to be interviewed about it? Do you now not believe there was such a phone call, either? If so, where did you get the information you discussed during the interview? Certainly, it must have been based on some intelligence. The call was reported by UPI, ABC and other mainstream outlets. Again, I won't keep bugging you, but you're connected to an important historical event, to simply label legitimate questions as 'conspiracy theories' or 'crazy.' Thanks." Burgun dismissed me for good in a reply later on May 10, by stating, "No, I looked you up. I read some of your blog on the 'plandemic.' You read like a typical Trumper. JFK Jr.

crashed his plane. He owned a magazine. Not really an 'important historical' event. A tragic, untimely death, but not historically important. It's only important to conspiracy nuts with nothing better to do than spread misinformation. Look for the 'Jewish Space Lasers.' Maybe he was shot down by one of them. I asked you to leave me alone, you couldn't. I will not read any response. Good day."

What stands out about Burgun's angry responses is his complete avoidance of that 9:39 p.m. phone call, and the interview he gave specifically about it. This was in the same vein as Steven Lagudi's texts not addressing what he'd claimed to have overheard. My question was not only reasonable, it was at the heart of exactly what happened that night. Burgun's refusal to address the subject, and predictable ridicule of the messenger, only breeds suspicion that he was warned not to talk about it by someone. The government would, almost as soon as the bodies were allegedly recovered, refute any suggestion that JFK Jr. had attempted to contact anyone after takeoff. Burgun's Trump Derangement Syndrome was at least interesting; exactly what did Donald Trump have to do with this? Since Susan Wornick never replied to my several email attempts, it seems we will never have an explanation from either of those who participated in an interview detailing a radio communication that now officially never happened.

I interviewed John Hankey and John A. Quinn, on separate broadcasts of my weekly radio show *I Protest*. Hankey and Quinn, along with John DiNardo (who has been impossible to contact and may well no longer be with us), had done much of the investigating in the immediate aftermath of JFK Jr.'s death. Certainly, no mainstream journalist was interested in the case. Hankey had started a correspondence with Utah health food store owner True Ott in 2007. Ott claimed to have sent JFK Jr. information that was going to result in George H. W. Bush being indicted for the murder of his father. After JFK Jr.'s death, Ott claimed to have spoken with an editor at *George* magazine, who told him that the magazine was folding, and that their offices had been burglarized, so that "all evidence went with John." As I learned from a few people who'd been close to JFK Jr., this editor told Ott that regarding the JFK assassination, "It is one of his major goals in life to find out the Truth!" Ott supposedly received a phone call from JFK Jr. on July 5, 1999, only a few weeks before he died, in which he was told about this file that was going to bring down Bush the Elder and make it impossible for Dubya to "run for dogcatcher after this grand jury convenes." Kennedy then told Ott that "I feel my Father's spirit beside me on this, and finally, I can exorcise a few demons from my life."

Regarding the strange, rapid cremation and spreading of ashes at sea, even some mainstream journalists were skeptical. Supposedly, JFK Jr. had told "friends" of his request to be buried at sea, and perhaps it might be reasonable for his wife to be buried with him, but they weren't exactly buried at sea. They were cremated. And what about Lauren Bessette? As RFK Jr.'s journal reveals, Caroline Kennedy's husband Edwin Schlossberg bullied the Bessette family, who had their own plans for their daughters' burial. Cindy Adams of the *New York Post* reported, on July 23, 1999, that "Calls to and from Greenwich, CT (where the Bessettes live) influenced decisions regarding the final resting place of John Kennedy and the Bessette sisters. Voices out of Boston say these were 'strong' phone calls." Getting the new narrative in order, the nation's newspaper of record reported, "Similar requests (for a sea burial) were made by the families of Mr. Kennedy's wife Carolyn Bessette Kennedy and her sister Lauren G. Bessette and also approved immediately, the Pentagon said."[25] In yet another attempt to "blame the Kennedys," on July 22, the *Cape Cod Times* claimed that "the Kennedy family had asked that the Barnstable Medical Examiner's office refrain from photographing JFK Jr.'s body, a procedural omission which may be against the law. It is unclear whether the same request covered the Bessette sisters and, if so, whether their parents were consulted." The *New York Daily News* quoted Cape and Islands District Attorney Michael O'Keefe as saying, "The wishes of the family were appropriately expressed. Where it was possible, they were followed." However, Fox News' Shepard Smith reported that autopsy photos *were* taken. Nailing down the lid of secrecy, a spokeswoman for Barnstable, Massachusetts Medical Examiner Dr. Richard Evans stated merely, "Out of respect for the family, we are not answering any questions."

Adding to the intrigue was a July 20, 1999, article in the *New York Post,* headlined "He might lie alongside parents." The article began, "The heir to Camelot is likely to be buried with his parents by the eternal flame at Arlington National Cemetery, a source close to the family said yesterday."

Solidifying this was the statement, "Yesterday, Arlington officials were spotted measuring the area where the eternal flame burns for President Kennedy, who was assassinated in 1963." A July 22 story in the *New York Post* reported, "A conventional burial is expected for the sisters, even as the Kennedy family contemplates a burial at sea for John Kennedy Jr. It was unclear whether the Bessettes and the Kennedys have discussed a joint ocean burial." Combined with the clear inferences in RFK Jr.'s journal that both the Kennedys and Bessettes wanted their loved ones buried, the rushed and secretive cremation and ash spreading ceremony at sea become all the more mysterious.

Young Martha's Vineyard Airport intern Adam Budd had made a call to the FAA on behalf of some friends waiting for JFK Jr.'s aircraft on the night it went down. Budd described feeling "put off" by the FAA official he spoke to and didn't press further. In an article about the incident, it was noted, "Budd, meanwhile, was wondering whether he'd still have a job to return to after his scheduled days off Tuesday and Wednesday. The operations manager at the Vineyard airport refused to discuss him. 'It sounds like they're going to fire me,' Budd said, 'but I'll find out.'"[26] I spoke to Adam Budd's mother during the course of researching *Hidden History,* as I recounted in that book. I tried again to contact Adam while writing this book, but he never replied to my email.

Reporter Pat Shannan visited the air traffic control room at Martha's Vineyard Airport. Shannan wrote, "two men in the office were both adamant that Kennedy had never called the tower. Earlier in town that day we had received a tip and asked the older ATC man, 'Was Buddy Wyatt in the tower that night?' He first responded with, 'Are you guys still beating that dead horse?!' Then he reluctantly confirmed that Wyatt had been the man on duty on the night July 16th. We asked to speak to him, but were informed that Wyatt had left town for a long weekend." Shannan persisted, and "We reached Buddy Wyatt, on duty in the tower, by telephone a week later. He denied that Kennedy had ever talked with him or anyone else in the tower that night, at 9:39 p.m. or any other time. It was easy to notice that his response was much like that of John McColgan two weeks earlier. Short, curt, clipped, quickly to the point, and offering no additional information. It made me wonder if these two had been schooled by the same teacher." In a July 20, 1999, *Boston Globe* story headlined "Plane Fell Fast, Probe Finds," Marvin (Buddy) Wyatt was mentioned. The story notes, "Wyatt declined comment on whether he had radio contact with Kennedy's plane." Researcher Chris Graves exchanged emails with Buddy Wyatt in February 2019. On February 17, 2019, Wyatt wrote, "No problem Chris. That one article did jog a memory cell, what few I have left, and that guy Adam Budd that the article says was in the ATC tower might have been an Airfield Operations clerk on duty that night. Aircraft would sometimes notify ops miles out prior to the tower generally 15 or more miles out. I do remember getting a phone call late that night asking if I heard from NXXXXX (don't remember call sign) and I said no. That was the extent of that. I heard nothing more about it until my morning controller called me at 6:30 a.m. Every time someone hears I was a controller on MVY the first thing they ask is was I there when JFK Jr. went down. I just shake my head and chuckle under my breath. A lot of things on that tape recording vindicate my innocence but there are some comments not related to the accident that the FAA was not at all happy with. I'll leave it at that! LOL." Wyatt followed up on February 20 with, "Hey Chris that last article like told you jogged a brain cell and I did some checking. I found out that Adam Budd did work at airfield operations and had absolutely nothing to do with the air traffic control tower and a lot of people didn't have a whole Lotta nice things to say about him but beside the point he may have got a radio call from junior when he was well outside my area. The thing about it is when he called and asked if I had heard from that particular aircraft and I said no that was the only thing that was said." In a subsequent conversation with Graves on Facebook Messenger, Wyatt would declare, "He never contacted MVY tower and I have the tapes to prove it!!!!! Yes. . . . FAA told me to destroy the tape after 5 years but I kept it. I have original!!!" To Graves's questions about the 9:39 p.m. communication, Wyatt stated, "I have never heard of Todd Burgun or Susan Wornick. I don't know what to tell you except it never happened is the reason Susan Wornick won't talk about it." Except that I have a videotape of the interview she did with Burgun on television. About a communication that "never happened." Wyatt, incidentally, was one of those quoted early on who said that visibility was actually great the night

Kennedy's plane went down. And what did Wyatt mean about "vindicate my innocence?" Why would he keep the original tape, and why would the FAA order him to destroy it?

John McColgan was JFK Jr.'s flight instructor who'd described him as an experienced and capable pilot, not "reckless" in any sense. McColgan had talked with Seattle radio show host Mike Webb on July 26, 1999. According to Shannan, "Webb says McColgan was reluctant to talk at first, notably suspicious and generally paranoid in his initial responses to questions, stating that he had 'answered everything already' (in a newspaper interview the previous week). But then, according to Webb, McColgan 'loosened up' and went on to make highly positive assessments of Kennedy's flying skills and also said that Kennedy had many hundreds of hours of flying experience under his belt. McColgan then admitted that this was much more than what he had been aware of when he was interviewed by the Orlando Sentinel on July 18th. He further stated that JFK Jr. was about to receive his instrument flight rating. But by August 30th, John McColgan had reverted to his 'suspicious and generally paranoid' self when this reporter was in Vero Beach and talked ever so briefly with him. He didn't know anything about Kennedy 'flying since 1982' or how many hours he had logged. 'Mike Webb? Who is he?' was McColgan's response, about to terminate the conversation. When informed that Webb was a talk show host in Washington State with whom he had had a telephone interview a month earlier, McColgan quickly retorted, 'Never heard of him,' and our interview was abruptly over." Putting a suitably conspiratorial exclamation point on all this, Mike Webb was viciously murdered with an axe in 2007. Oddly, the mentally ill supposed killer was sentenced to only twenty years in prison.[27]

An absurd bit of disinformation appeared in the immediate wake of JFK Jr.'s death. *George* columnist Lauren Lawrence declared, "There was a death wish that allowed the reckless behavior that led to the tragedy. There is a reckless, explosive sense to his nature, due to assassination trauma. He definitely had a subtle wish to join his father." Completely on board with the freshly minted official narrative, Lawrence continued, "Flying in hazy weather, when another pilot had already decided not to because it was too risky, shows that kind of reckless behavior on the part of John Kennedy

Jr." They really do like that "reckless" adjective when writing about the Kennedys. Lawrence, in one of those disturbing examples of predictive programming with which we are all too familiar, had published a book, *Dream Keys,* just a week before Kennedy's crash. The book included an eerie profile of her boss, in which she uses a Fawn Brodie style of pop psychology to conclude that he had a fear of assassination as well as a desire to be assassinated. Lawrence was led to this remarkable conclusion by a photo shoot of JFK Jr. which had appeared in *Esquire.* What makes this article truly astonishing is the fact it was published, in the *New York Post,* on July 18, 1999, *three days before* the recovery of the bodies of JFK Jr. and the Bessettes.

The most ridiculously inaccurate contention made about JFK Jr. came from the earlier mentioned Steven Gillon. In his 2019 book, *America's Reluctant Prince,* the resident historian at the History Channel, and Kennedy's purported close friend, made numerous pathologically false statements. Gillon claimed that JFK Jr. "rarely spoke of his father's assassination." The assassination was, Gillon declared, "the only topic that was absolutely off-limits." As I discovered while researching *Hidden History,* JFK Jr. in fact had a real obsession with his father's murder, as two different people who were close to him assured me. Sounding much like countless other Warren Commission apologists over the past fifty-plus years, Gillon stated, "John said, 'I don't understand why people are so fascinated with my father's death.' He couldn't understand why people focused so much energy on it. He wanted to remember his father for the life that he lived, and that's how he wanted others to remember him." This has also been the mantra of the Kennedy family (outside of JFK Jr. and RFK Jr.). To ignore his death, and focus on his life; something very convenient for those who conspired to kill him. Gillon did quote JFK Jr. once cryptically mentioning that "Bobby knew everything" about the JFK assassination. Gillon also claimed that JFK Jr. basically had decided not to use *George* magazine to investigate his father's assassination.[28] This is directly contradicted by journalist Wayne Madsen's disclosure to me, during the writing of *Hidden History,* that he was about to be hired by *George* magazine at the time of JFK Jr.'s death. His first assignment was to be the JFK assassination.

Because no honest investigation of JFK Jr.'s death ever took place, just as with the assassination of his father, the events of 9/11, and a host of other significant events, speculation and sometimes irresponsible theories have arisen. QAnon claimed that JFK Jr. had faked his death, and there were many breathless predictions about him emerging from the shadows to help Donald Trump finally defeat the Deep State. There were numerous photographs online alleged to be an aged JFK Jr. and Carolyn Bessette, in attendance at Trump rallies. This theory was first proposed in an October 7, 1999, story headlined, "JFK Jr. May Have Faked Own Death" on the conspiracy-friendly website The Konformist. During many interviews I've given on QAnon-friendly podcasts over the past few years, I've been met with outrage over any suggestion that JFK Jr. was actually dead. I adopted the talking point that whatever happened, the official story is impossible.

Caroline Kennedy's reaction to her brother's death was decidedly strange. Unlike her brother, the intensely private Caroline had, without explanation, not planned to attend the wedding of her cousin Rory at Martha's Vineyard. Upon hearing that her brother's plane was missing, Caroline did not gather at the Kennedy compound with other family members, but instead retreated to her Long Island summer home with her husband and three children.[29] Meanwhile, Ted Kennedy, who had requested that he and his sons be present when the bodies were recovered,[30] and supervised his nephew's remains being whisked out to sea, in one report was surprisingly said to have been hopeful that JFK Jr. would run for Governor of New York in 2002, and eventually return to the White House.[31]

As my experience with Todd Burgun demonstrated, those connected to this case are extremely reluctant to talk. First and foremost here, as we find in most politically charged events, are the family members. Lisa Bessette is the sole surviving Bessette sister. After the tragedy, Lisa went off the grid, moving to Ann Arbor, Michigan, and interacting with only a few trusted friends. A 2019 story quoted an unidentified "acquaintance" as saying, "Today, she lives a quiet existence in the college town, occasionally working part-time at the University of Michigan Art Museum as a contract editor. She had a really hard time when they passed away and was strong for her mother and her family and has since decided that she doesn't want to be in any way public." As her then eighty-eight-year-old stepfather Richard Freeman told the *New York Post,* "We never cooperate with the media, no interviews, no questions, and that is still our position." The *Post* story mentions the Bessette parents as both being alive, with neither responding to the *Post's* attempts to contact them.[32] That policy seems all too oddly common among families impacted by these events. However, they must not have fact checked thoroughly, as William Bessette died at age 85 in 2014. In a story that appeared five years after Kennedy's plane went down, Carolyn and Lauren's mother Ann Freeman was said to have wished her daughter had never met the heir to Camelot. From the article: "Neighbours say Carolyn's mother Ann Freeman refuses to speak John Junior's name in the house, only referring to the president's son as 'him' and blames Kennedy for being a reckless daredevil. A pal said: 'Ann is still mad at John—she blames him for her daughters' deaths. I also think Ann regrets that her daughters weren't buried in a cemetery. She doesn't have a place to visit them and grieve.'" Freeman was referred to as a recluse, and was said to have remained permanently indoors after attending the memorial service in Greenwich, Connecticut. Her surviving daughter Lisa was said to have moved to Europe, because America "held too many painful reminders" of her sisters' deaths. This seems to contradict the above 2019 article about her "going off the grid" in Michigan. The girls' father William Bessette was described as "living in awful grief" and "He won't talk about his daughters' deaths." JFK Jr.'s friend Robert Littell recounted how Lauren Bessette's best friend had cornered him at her memorial service and raged: "Your friend killed my friend. If John weren't so reckless Lauren would still be alive."[33]

There were two suspicious deaths which connect in some way to John F. Kennedy Jr. Thirty-three-year-old Giovanni Agnelli, heir to the Fiat fortune, died in 1997 of an extremely rare, fast-spreading intestinal cancer. My friend, researcher and historian Vince Agnelli, who has an understandable interest in the Agnelli family, told me that Giovanni and JFK Jr. used to be close friends, partying together regularly. Agnelli in fact was dubbed the "JFK Jr. of Italy."[34] While his death occurred two years before JFK Jr.'s, there is a precedent for such potential "warning" shots; for instance, Marilyn Monroe's murder a year before the assassination of John F. Kennedy. Perhaps more intriguingly, yet another young member of the wealthy Agnelli clan, forty-six-year-old Edoardo Agnelli, was found under a bridge in Turin, Italy, on November 15, 2000. It was ruled a suicide, but there was no autopsy performed, and there was a strange absence of witnesses on the busy adjoining road.[35] It is more than likely that JFK Jr. was friends with Edoardo. If so, he probably talked about his keen interest in his father's assassination, like he must have done with his brother Giovanni, as he routinely did with friends. There were other ties between the two families: for instance, rumors of an affair between family patriarch Gianni Agnelli and then First Lady Jacqueline Kennedy.

Todd Burgun's name appeared in a story published on July 18, 1999, in regards to the emergency beacon signal received from off Montauk, New York at around 2:15 a.m., over five hours after Kennedy's plane had taken off. Independent researchers found it suspicious that a search wasn't immediately launched in the area where the beacon had signaled, but Burgun helpfully explained here that "it is standard procedure to wait for additional beacon 'hits' to pinpoint the location of a downed airplane." After a second signal was received a little over an hour later, the Air Force's Air Rescue Coordination Center opened a "case," but it wasn't until around 4:30 a.m. that the Coast Guard began searching the area. Why the two-hour wait? As should be readily apparent by his emails to me, Todd Burgun would probably have an innocent explanation. In the same article, it was noted that Minir Hussain, who sold the Piper Saratoga to JFK Jr., conveniently happened to be at the Essex County Airport that night. Hussain was quoted as saying, "It was a risky situation for him to be flying without an instructor because he was not instrument-rated to fly on his own. I know that John was a very good pilot. Everyone knew that. But I immediately began to worry because the conditions were not that good."[36] Once again, the best evidence indicates that weather conditions were actually fine that night. The question that should be asked is: why were so many people saying otherwise? In another helpful article, NTSB spokesman Ted Atkiewicz said it was unclear whether any sort of recording device in the cockpit had been recovered, and he noted he was unsure that the device—after being in salt water for five days—would be any good to investigators. Atkiewicz stated that black boxes on commercial flights are waterproof, but the type of recording device in Kennedy's Piper Saratoga "is not meant to survive a crash, it's meant to assist the pilot."[37]

Not meant to survive a crash? Isn't that the primary purpose of a black box? Confusion also surrounds the voice box recorder, which according to the NTSB was found crushed, with the backup battery missing, and had retained no data. Some alternative researchers find sinister implications behind the absence of a battery.

John F. Kennedy Jr. was about to enter politics—there is no doubt about that. And he had one underlying quest; to find out who really had killed his father. As journalist Wayne Madsen recounted, "In a few weeks, I was scheduled to meet with Kennedy at his magazine's offices in Washington, DC to discuss hiring on as one of a few investigative journalists Kennedy wanted to dig deep into a number of cases, but most importantly that of his father's assassination. Kennedy had made initial contact with me via a colleague with *The Village Voice*." Madsen also reported how JFK Jr.'s seemingly rather harmless sister Caroline "would see her own hopes to be appointed to the Senate seat dashed when, according to John F. Kennedy Jr.'s friend, Senator Charles Schumer and Barack Obama chief of staff Rahm Emanuel conspired to have New York Governor David Paterson appoint a virtual unknown, Kirsten Gillibrand, to the seat. Caroline Kennedy was instead offered a consolation prize of the post of U.S. ambassador to the Vatican, a position that Schumer and Emanuel knew in advance she would never accept."[38]

Predictably, the only investigative reporting on this case has come from citizen journalists like me and others, primarily on the internet. *The National Enquirer* ran several interesting stories, which revolved around their patently lurid, sensationalist themes. In one story, they alleged that Ted Kennedy led the "cover-up" to conceal dark secrets regarding rumors Carolyn was on drugs and/or pregnant. The paper claimed to have spoken with Gwen Kopechne, elderly mother of Mary Jo, and quoted her as saying, "Ted Kennedy is covering up the plane crash the same way he covered up the death of my daughter Mary Jo."[39] Stories appeared in the mainstream media in 2000, about a Kennedy biopic tentatively titled *Like Father, Like Son.* George Clooney was set to star as JFK Jr. The script, incomprehensibly enough, revolved around the "lovechild" of Lee Harvey Oswald going on to kill JFK Jr. According to one article, "The script of the tragic tale is currently in pre-production stage, and posits that Oswald had an affair with a waitress later leaving his illegitimate offspring hellbent on seeking revenge on the Kennedy clan and fanatical in his belief of his father's innocence in the killing." The film, from Miramax, depicted the illegitimate Oswald offspring as launching a missile, with the help of "Arab terrorists," while "crack CIA operatives" tried to stop him.[40] No, it wasn't an *Onion* story, but it appears the movie was never produced. The elites know that blood is thicker than water. They understand that, behind the scenes, the Kennedy family is obviously aware that someone is very interested in silencing them. No one in the family was more open about his doubts about the official narrative of his father's assassination than JFK Jr. Like so many in his family have, he paid the ultimate price.

CHAPTER TEN

9/11: A TRANSFORMATIVE INSIDE JOB

September 11 is clearly an inside job, there's massive evidence that suggests that it was either allowed to happen or even worse, deliberately made to happen.

—Matthew Bellamy, lead guitarist for Muse[1]

As I write this, it is the twentieth-year anniversary of the unprecedented events of September 11, 2001. 9/11 changed America forever, and not for the better. I have referred to the pre-9/11 United States as America 1.0. Since 9/11, we have been in a different, far worse America 2.0. The Patriot Act, and the draconian rollback of civil liberties set the template for the nightmarish, Orwellian world we live in today. Without an endless "war" on "terror," would we have ever been subject to "cancel culture," blatant double standards, and the rest of the "woke" agenda?

As with all significant historical events, it is important to examine the early news accounts and eyewitness testimony. Before an official narrative becomes established, an amazing amount of contradictory information seeps through initially, until it's unceremoniously flushed down the memory hole. On September 11, 2001, there were many early interesting tidbits coming from mainstream media. *USA Today* foreign correspondent Jack Kelley reported, "Apparently what appears to happen, that at the same time two planes hit the buildings, that the FBI most likely thinks that there was a car or truck packed with explosives underneath the buildings which also exploded at the same time and brought both of them down." MSNBC's Rick Sanchez appeared to corroborate this by stating, "I spoke with some police officials moments ago . . . and they told me they have reason to believe that one of the explosions at the World Trade Center may have been caused by a van that was parked in the building that may have had some type of explosive device in it." A WNYW Fox 5 anchor continued this theme with, "There is an explosion at the base of the building, white smoke from the bottom. Something happened at the base of the building. Then another explosion." MSNBC's Pat Dawson declared, "Just moments ago I spoke to the chief of safety for the New York City fire department, he received word of the possibility of a secondary device—that is another bomb going off . . . according to his theory he thinks that there were actually devices that were planted in the building."

Even the unflappable Establishment voice Peter Jennings noted, "Anybody who has ever watched a building being demolished on purpose knows, that if you're going to do this, you have to get at the under infrastructure of a building and bring it down," during live ABC News coverage on September 11. Jennings also stated, "Well, there's Building 7 coming down. . . . It's a very careful operation in order to make sure a building comes down safely. I think the last one we saw was when they brought down one of the old casinos in Las Vegas. It's just stunning to see these buildings come down. . . and now, number seven World Trade Center which is 47-stories tall." This loyal Establishment mouthpiece certainly seemed to be saying that Building 7 was deliberately imploded. Fellow incredibly wealthy talking head Dan Rather described Building 7 going down as, "For the third time today, it's reminiscent of those pictures we've all seen too much . . . when a building was deliberately destroyed by well-placed dynamite to knock it down."

"It just descended like a timed explosion—like when they are deliberately bringing a building down . . . It was coming down so perfectly that in one part of my brain I was thinking, 'They got everyone out, and they're bringing the building down because they have to,'" declared Berth Fertig on WNYC Radio. New York Fire Department Assistant Fire Commissioner

Stephen Gregory testified, "When I looked in the direction of the Trade Center before it came down, before No. 2 came down, . . . I saw low-level flashes . . . *I saw a flash flash flash and then it looked like the building came down* . . . You know like when they demolish a building, how when they blow up a building, when it falls down? That's what I thought I saw." His NYFD colleague Captain Dennis Tardio backed this up with, "It was as if as if they had detonated . . . *as if they had planned to take down a building, boom-boom-boom-boom-boom-boom-boom-boom.*" Outspoken NYFD firefighter Louie Cacchioli declared, "I was taking firefighters up in the elevator to the 24th floor to get in position to evacuate workers. On the last trip up a bomb went off. We think there were bombs set in the building." Fellow firefighter Richard Banaciski had a similar recollection: "There was just an explosion in the south tower. It seemed like on television when they blow up these buildings. It seemed like it was going all the way around like a belt, all these explosions." Other NYFD firefighters echoed these reports. "It almost sounded like bombs going off, like boom, boom, boom, like seven or eight," said Thomas Turilli. "Heard explosions coming from . . . the south tower . . . There were about ten explosions. . . . We then realized the building started to come down," stated Craig Carlsen. "It actually gave at a lower floor, not the floor where the plane hit. . . . We originally had thought there was like an internal detonation, explosives, because it went in succession, boom, boom, boom, boom, and then the tower came down," noted Edward Cachia.[2]

Firefighters seeing and hearing the same things was so common that, according to Christopher Fenyou, "A debate began to rage because . . . many people had felt that possibly explosives had taken out 2 World Trade." "Somewhere around the middle . . . there was this orange and red flash coming out. Initially it was just one flash. Then this flash just kept popping all the way around the building and that building had started to explode. . . . With each popping sound it was initially an orange and then a red flash came out of the building and then it would just go all around the building on both sides as far as I could see. These popping sounds and the explosions were getting bigger, going both up and down and then all around the building," NYFD Captain Karin Deshore reported. William Rodriguez, who went on to save many lives that day, reported that there were twenty-two others on the B2 subbasement level who also felt and heard the first explosion he reported, which seemed to come from between that level and subbasement B3. "When I heard the sound of the explosion, the floor beneath my feet vibrated, the walls started cracking and everything started shaking," Rodriguez recalled.[3] Sue Keane, a sergeant with the Port Authority Police Department, described hearing several explosions that "sounded like bombs going off." As she made her way down the stairs of the North Tower, she remembered, "I can't tell you how many times I got banged around. Each one of those explosions picked me up and threw me."[4] Teresa Veliz, who worked on the 47th floor, experienced the same thing going down the stairs, declaring, "There were explosions going off everywhere. I was convinced that there were bombs planted all over the place and someone was sitting at a control panel pushing detonator buttons."[5]

Stories even appeared in the mainstream media early on, such as a September 12 piece in *The Los Angeles Times,* which noted, "There were reports of an explosion right before the tower fell, then a strange sucking sound, and finally the sound of floors collapsing." The same day, *The Guardian* reported, "Some eyewitnesses reported hearing another explosion just before the structure crumbled. Police said that it looked almost like a 'planned implosion.'" *Wall Street Journal* reporter John Bussey was a close eyewitness to the collapse, from his newspaper's office building. Bussey recalled, "I . . . looked up out of the office window to see what seemed like perfectly synchronized explosions coming from each floor. . . . One after the other, from top to bottom, with a fraction of a second between, the floors blew to pieces."[6] An anonymous fellow *Wall Street Journal* reporter declared, "'My God, they're going to bring the building down.' And they, whoever they are, HAD SET CHARGES. . . . I saw the explosions."[7]

Many witnesses reported anomalies that contradicted the official version of events. Kim White was an administrative assistant working on the 80th floor of 1 World Trade Center. She recalled that after the "the building shook, then it started to sway," someone was joking, "I hope it wasn't another bomb." Firefighter Louie Cacchioli testified, "We were the first ones in the second tower after the plane struck. I was taking firefighters up in the elevator to the 24th floor to get in position to evacuate workers. On the last trip up a bomb went off. We think there was bombs set in the building."[8] Dariah Coard was a WTC 1 security officer. She reported that the security detail had been working twelve-hour shifts for the past two weeks because of numerous phone threats. However, less than a week before 9/11, their bomb-sniffing dogs were abruptly removed. In the same article, fellow security guard Hermina Jones recounted how bulletproof windows and fireproof doors had recently been installed in the 22nd-floor computer command center.[9] Lane Core Jr. stated that, after he had evacuated the building, "We still heard the secondary explosions consistently, so I continued to look back at the WTC and noticed that people were jumping out of both towers from above the fire lines!" I continue to question the curious phenomenon of so many people jumping to their deaths that day, before anyone could have reasonably expected the Twin Towers to literally collapse. Notice here the reference to "above the fire lines." Why was anyone committing suicide when they clearly weren't being overwhelmed by fire and smoke, as has been suggested? NBC's Pat Lawson reported on September 11, "Shortly after 9 o'clock [. . .] [Albert Turi the Chief of Safety for the New York Fire Department] received word of the possibility of a secondary device, that is another bomb going off. He tried to get his men out as quickly as he could, but he said there was another explosion which took place, and then an hour after the first hit, the first crash that took place, he said there was another explosion that took place in one of the towers here, so obviously according to his theory he thinks that there were actually devices that were planted in the building. One of the secondary devices he thinks that took place after the initial impact he thinks may have been on the plane that crashed into one of the towers. The second device, he thinks, he speculates, was probably planted in the building."

Engineer Dr. Thomas Eagar told PBS that steel high-rises are built around redundancy principles, making the collapse of the WTC buildings unexplainable. "If one component breaks, the whole thing will not come crashing down," Eagar said. "Some people were concerned the building would fall down. The structural engineers knew it wouldn't, because the whole thing had an egg-crate-like construction. Or you can think of it as a net. If you lose one string on a net, yes, the net is weakened but the rest of the net still works." Stephen Evans reported live from inside the WTC for the BBC, and mentioned "two or three similar huge explosions" He went on to state "then when we were outside, the second explosion happened and then there was a series of explosions." Neighborhood resident Geronimo Jones called out the media for their "creative" reporting "But one thing the reporters left out was something I witnessed firsthand. A very important omission at that! Seconds before the South Tower crumbled to its doom, I heard/felt a series of explosions. Same with the North Tower. There was no denying it, I could FEEL the vibrations of them like a small earthquake. Yet when I turned on the news none of the other eyewitnesses commented on this." Jones said. "Indeed, in the days that followed, like many Americans, I remained glued to the news networks to keep myself informed of any developments and confirm what I had witnessed. But despite the numerous eyewitness accounts, there was still no mention of the explosions." WTC construction worker Phillip Morelli was interviewed by NY1 News. He recalled being thrown to the ground by two explosions while in the fourth subbasement of the North Tower. The first, which threw him to the ground and seemed to coincide with the plane crash, was followed by a larger blast that again threw him to the ground and this time blew out walls. He then made his way to the South Tower and was in the subbasement there when the second plane hit, where he described a similar underground explosion. North Tower stationary engineer Mike Pecoraro heard at least one explosion while he was in subbasement *six.* He and a coworker went up to C level, where "There was nothing there but rubble." Further up, on B level, they found that a three-hundred-pound steel and concrete fire door had been left wrinkled "like a piece of aluminum foil."[10] Jose Sanchez, working on the fourth sub-level, heard an explosion that "sounded like a bomb," and recalled that "a huge ball of fire went through the freight elevator."[11]

Emergency medical technician Mercedes Rivera provided some fascinating testimony. From their vantage point across the street from the WTC, Rivera and her partner raced to the scene and immediately began treating people. "I just remember the fear, the constant sounds of things falling, and the flying paper and debris. . . . I saw a burned woman in a sitting position in the lobby, as if she was still typing behind a desk.

. . . She was already dead." Inside WTC Building 7, they heard "A big, thunderous, crash that sounded just like an engine." Most interestingly, she recounted, "Explosions everywhere, and then once again, complete silence."[12] A woman burned to death in the lobby? From a plane that had crashed more than eighty floors above her? Recalling the valiant efforts of citizen investigators wading through the huge 26 volumes of mostly irrelevant material compiled by the Warren Commission, Retired professor Graeme MacQueen pored through 12,000 pages of oral accounts given by New York Fire Department employees to the Port Authority of New York. MacQueen determined that using the most conservative estimate, 118 people described hearing explosions. In true Warren Report style, the NIST claimed in its report that "there were no witness reports" of explosions in Building 7. NY1 reporter Gigi Stone Woods was only one of those who suggested otherwise, as she described hearing "a loud, incredibly loud explosion." Like the late Barry Jennings, whose story was recounted in *Hidden History*, attorney Michael Hess described witnessing an explosion in Building 7. Hess was one of many witnesses I tried to contact without success.

EMT Jason Charles described the collapse of the North Tower: "I heard a ground level explosion and I'm like holy s___, and then you heard that twisting metal wreckage again. Then I said s___ and everybody started running and I started running behind them, and we get to the door."[13] A ground-level explosion? Citywide Tour Commander FDNY Chief Frank Cruthers witnessed the collapse of the South Tower, declaring, "And while I was still in that immediate area, the South Tower, 2 World Trade Center, there was what appeared to be at first an explosion. It appeared at the very top, simultaneously from all four sides, materials shot out horizontally. And then there seemed to be a momentary delay before you could see the beginning of the collapse."[14] Paramedic Kevin Darnowski reported, "I heard three explosions, and then we heard like groaning and grinding, and tower two started to come down."[15] Battalion Chief Dominick Derubbio said, "It looked like it was a timed explosion."[16] EMS Captain Karin Deshore talked about "These popping sounds and the explosions were getting bigger, going both up and down and then all around the building."[17] Battalion Chief Brian Dixon testified, "The lowest floor of fire in the South Tower actually looked like someone had planted explosives around it because the whole bottom I could see—I could see two sides of it and the other side—it just looked like that floor blew out. I looked up and you could actually see everything blew out on the one floor. I thought, geez, this looks like an explosion up there, it blew out."[18] Dixon, like his fellow Battalion Chief Derubbio, both noted after their initial impressions that the floors must in reality just have been collapsing, as explained by the official story. FDNY Assistant Commissioner James Drury stated, "I should say that people in the street and myself included thought that the roar was so loud that the explosive bombs were going off inside the building." Correcting himself like the others, he continued, "Obviously we were later proved wrong."[19] FDNY Deputy Commissioner Thomas Fitzpatrick said, "My initial reaction was that this was exactly the way it looks when they show you those implosions on TV."[20]

FDNY Assistant Commissioner Stephen Gregory noted, "We both for whatever reason—again, I don't know how valid this is with everything that was going on at that particular point in time, but for some reason I thought that when I looked in the direction of the Trade Center before it came down, before No. 2 came down, that I saw low-level flashes. In my conversation with Lieutenant Evangelista, never mentioning this to him, he questioned me and asked me if I saw low-level flashes in front of the building, and I agreed with him because I thought—at that time I didn't know what it was. I mean, it could have been as a result of the building collapsing, things exploding, but I saw a flash flash flash and then it looked like the building came down."[21] EMT Michael Ober stated, "It looked to me just like an explosion. It didn't look like the building was coming down, it looked like just one floor had blown completely outside of it. I was sitting there looking at it. I just never thought they would ever come down."[22] Paramedic Daniel Rivera recalled, "At first I thought it was—do you ever see professional demolition where they set the charges on certain floors and then you hear 'Pop, pop, pop, pop, pop?' That's exactly what—because I thought it was that."[23] Firefighter Kenneth Rogers saw the same thing; "There was an explosion in the South Tower. . . . Floor after floor after floor. One floor under another after another and when it hit about the fifth floor, I figured it was a bomb, because it looked like a synchronized deliberate kind of thing."[24] Firefighter Thomas Turilli testified that, "It almost actually that day sounded like bombs going off, like boom, boom, boom, like seven or eight. . . . It just seemed like a huge explosion."[25]

A recognizable pattern emerged, especially in all the fire department accounts. Clearly, most witnesses at first thought there were bombs going off in the buildings, and many compared the towers going down to the controlled demolition of buildings we've all seen in movies and television. That was my first impression as well, watching the television coverage from home. But virtually all of them learned the error of their ways, and tacitly supported the conventional narrative, that the collapse was caused by that magical jet fuel cocktail. In another of the many similarities to the JFK assassination, the majority of witnesses reported shots from the front of the limousine, not the rear where Oswald was allegedly located. Almost all those witnesses "corrected" themselves, too. Who are you going to believe, the authorities or your lying eyes (and ears)? As Lieutenant Paul Isaac of the NYFD told Randy Lavello of Prison Planet, "many other firemen know there were bombs in the buildings, but they're afraid for their jobs to admit it because the 'higher-ups' forbid discussion of this fact."[26] Regarding Paul Isaac, reporter Greg Szymanski elaborated, "Over the last four years he's compiled information and names of civilians and firefighters, whose identities he keeps anonymous for their safety, who all claim to have either witnessed explosions in the towers or have information that a controlled demolition took place. Szymanski quoted Isaac as saying, in reference to the FBI gag order, "It's just amazing how many people are afraid to talk for fear of retaliation or losing their jobs."[27]

One witness who wouldn't be intimidated was Lou Cacchioli. He stuck to his story of hearing three distinct "huge explosions," while rescuing people on the 23rd and 24th floors in the North Tower. Frustrated and depressed after 9/11, Cacchioli even contemplated suicide. In an interview four years after that tragic day, Cacchioli remembered, "I somehow got into the stairwell and there were more people there, who I began to try and direct down, when another huge explosion like the first one hits. This one hits about two minutes later, although it's hard to tell, but I'm thinking, 'Oh. My God, these bastards put bombs in here like they did in

1993!'" Like everyone else, the veteran firefighter said, "it never crossed my mind the building was going to collapse." Cacchioli was called to testify before the 9/11 Commission, but quickly realized they were conducting a whitewash, not an investigation. "My story was never mentioned in the final report and I felt like I was being put on trial in a court room," Cacchioli stated. "I finally walked out. They were trying to twist my words and make the story fit only what they wanted to hear. All I wanted to do was tell the truth and when they wouldn't let me do that, I walked out. It was a disgrace to everyone, the victims and the family members who lost loved ones. I don't agree with the 9/11 Commission. The whole experience was terrible." Vowing that he would not be silenced, Cacchioli proclaimed, "I know what happened that day and I know the whole truth hasn't come out yet. I have my own conscience, my own mind and no one, I mean no one, is going to force Lou Cacchioli to say something that didn't happen and wasn't the truth."[28]

The aforementioned William Rodriguez is one of the most interesting characters associated with the events of 9/11. Rodriguez certainly appeared to be a genuine hero, but for unclear reasons, many "truther" researchers soured on him and accused him of being a fraud. Rodriguez was the last witness before the 9/11 Commission, and the only one to testify behind closed doors. "Every other testimony was shown on TV. Everyone else had a public hearing," Rodriguez noted. Rodriguez's account would be left out of the Commission's Report, and they didn't call any of his twenty expert witnesses. "My allegations were never investigated and the perpetrators never caught. The people they did question—the chiefs of the fire and police departments—weren't even in the building. It was a complete whitewash," Rodriguez charged. Rodriguez reported to the FBI that he'd seen a mysterious man—"possibly one of the hijackers," asking questions about the layout of the WTC a few months before 9/11, but they had no interest. Rodriguez filed a RICO lawsuit against the Bush administration in 2004, alleging they "had knowledge that the attacks were impending but failed to take countermeasures because they desired such attacks to occur." Predictably, the lawsuit was thrown out by the New York courts in 2005. Rodriguez reported that his apartment had been broken into, and his laptop stolen. He was also punitively placed on the no-fly list. "Do I fear for my life? Of course."

Rodriguez declared. "Several experts in the intelligence and security fields have told me to be careful, and say an attack could come from anywhere at any time."[29] The former janitor has become a noted lecturer on the subject. Much as Warren Commission witnesses like courageous Deputy Roger Craig would be accused by some in the research community of changing or embellishing their testimony, Rodriguez was accused of altering his testimony. However, in 2009, Rodriguez gave 911Truth.org the original notes taken by the 9/11 Commission investigators who questioned him. The notes showed clearly that he'd mentioned "explosions" from the very beginning, and his testimony had remained consistent.

The most intense criticism of Rodriguez came from Phil Jayhan, admin of the often fascinating Let's Roll Forums. Poring over the threads on the "Unofficial William Rodriguez UnFan Club" —the "Free Willy" section of the Let's Roll Forums, it is difficult to determine the reason for the intense hostility. One thread asks, "Should 9/11 Traitors like William Rodriguez be Executed & put to Death?" In another poll on whether or not Rodriguez is a "fraud," 69 percent said "yes," and another 20 percent said, "it sure doesn't look good for William Rodriguez." As far as I can figure, Jayhan and most of those who post there believe in the "hollow towers" theory, that there were no people in the WTC buildings, and thus Rodriguez's claims to have witnessed bombs, and rescued people, cannot possibly be true. I think. I have no theory about 9/11 or anything else, except that the evidence shows clearly the official narrative is impossible. Where the most basic questions aren't answered, theories will emerge. In the case of 9/11, this means hollow towers, no planes, holograms, energized laser weapons, crisis actors and much more. As Mark Lane once said about the JFK assassination, when those tasked to investigate these things don't honestly do so, they provide "fertile ground for speculation." I asked Richard Gage, founder of Architects and Engineers for 9/11 Truth, about Rodriguez, and he replied in a June 26, 2021, email, "I am not aware of any wrath or other negative issues re: Willy. R." I asked Rodriguez to come on my talk show, but he replied in a July 20, 2021, Facebook message that "at this time I am not interested in doing radio interviews."

One of the most disquieting and little discussed elements of 9/11 are the memorial funds and charities established in its wake. In a rare example of mainstream investigative journalism, the Associated Press scrutinized an astounding 325 9/11 charities in 2011, many of them still active, and found rampant fraud and waste. In one example, Kevin Held of Arizona reportedly raised $713,000 for a 9/11 memorial quilt "big enough to cover 25 football fields." According to AP, Held "gave himself a $175,000 salary, a $200 weekly car allowance, 'rent reimbursement,' and unreported 'loans.' He paid his family members 'consulting fees.' He apparently said a Catholic priest was the chairman of his charity's board, but the Catholic priest wasn't even aware of it. He told lies about the origin of his charity. He will soon move into a $660,000 five-bedroom home overlooking a lake." The quilt never emerged. Another project sold flags with 9/11 victims' names on them that cost $5 to be made in China, for $25 each. The AP discovered none of the profits had been donated to charity. Urban Life Ministries, a church based near Ground Zero in New York, raised $4 million "to help victims and first responders," but the Rev. Carl Keyes could only account for $670,000 of the funds.[30] As an indication of just how much money was raised collectively by all these funds, Howard Lutnick, chairman of Cantor Fitzgerald, has disbursed more than $250 million to 9/11 victim families over the years, although this number also includes payments to others impacted by terrorism and disasters.[31]

The story of French filmmaker brothers Jules and Gedeon Naudet raises a number of questions. The brothers claimed that, as soon as they entered Building 1, they saw "two people engulfed in flames and dying," which they refused to film out of respect. How anyone in the lobby could have been impacted by a collision some eighty floors above is fancifully attributed to fuel from the airliner gushing down the elevator shaft. The brothers caught the only live shot of the first plane to strike the towers. They were "out with New York's fire fighters on a routine call following a suspected gas leak in downtown New York when the first plane hit." They were being led by battalion chief Joseph Pfeifer, who strangely "made the deduction very quickly" that the plane hadn't struck the WTC by accident. Pfeifer, apparently immune from normal human curiosity, also turned his back on the plane crashing into the building and instead looked at the camera. Pfeifer would subsequently be promoted to deputy assistant chief, while his brother Kevin was one of the 343 fatalities among firefighters. What is the explanation for why one of the Naudet brothers can be heard to exclaim "Yes" as they capture the first plane crashing into the WTC? The brothers shopped their tape around to the highest bidder, and it turned out to be CNN, which admitted they'd never spent so much on amateur footage before. Researcher Leslie Raphael thoroughly investigated the Naudet film and raised many troubling questions. He noted that, in the film at street level, there appears to be no moving traffic in the street at 8:45 a.m. on a workday. All the vehicles look to be parked. The mother of one of the firefighters at the local firehouse, Tony Benetatos, Rev. Patricia Ray Moore, told Raphael she thought the Naudet film was scripted.

The Naudets' film became incorporated into the award-winning 2002 documentary *9/11*. It was codirected by former New York City firefighter James Hanlon, whose curious résumé includes a background in acting and directing. Those acting backgrounds pop up far too frequently in these events to be purely coincidental. Hanlon had convinced the Fire Commissioner to let him shoot a documentary about a probationary firefighter, and the September 11 attacks took place during this filming. Hanlon had become friends with the Naudet brothers in the 1990s. Unlike Abraham Zapruder, whose reaction to gunfire in Dealey Plaza caused a noticeable jiggling, young Jules Naudet's camera never wavered as he zoomed in on the plane hitting the North Tower. The Naudets should seemingly have become celebrated figures in the wake of their remarkable film—which captured the only images of the first plane striking the North Tower, but instead they seem to have faded back into anonymity. The brothers also described hearing the "huge sound" of bodies hitting the ground. They made the remarkable claim that people were jumping at the rate of "every 40 to 50 seconds."[32] I don't know that we can do the math on that, but it seems to me that would add up to an incredible number of people. As for the loud sound, is there testimony from other instances, where humans fell or jumped from great heights, which alluded to this? If so, I've never heard it. I broached this subject in *Hidden History,* and as I noted earlier, it really seems incomprehensible that so many people would turn suicidal that quickly. Why wouldn't they have held some hope of being rescued? Many researchers, like the late, great Jack White, analyzed film of the Twin Towers, and demonstrated that the figures gathering at windows, and eventually falling/jumping, were often in areas where no visible flames could be seen. There didn't seem to be much visible smoke in those areas, either. Human nature being what it is, again I am seriously baffled by the number of those who plummeted to their deaths that day. Why should this particular aspect of the official 9/11 story be accepted, when no other part of the narrative is true? In the official report on these jumpers conducted by the National Institute for Standards and Technology, it is noted that the first documented jumper plunged from the North Tower's 93rd floor just over *four minutes* after the building was struck. Really? Someone lost all hope within four minutes? In another instance, nine people jumped/fell from five adjacent windows within five seconds. Fireman Danny Suhr was supposedly killed by the falling body of a jumper. There was an emotional response to the falling bodies that bordered on the irrational; film of the bodies was quickly banned from television reports, and the public seemed outraged at the very mention of it. Was this really because of sensitivity to human tragedy, or did someone not want any close analysis of the subject?[33]

One witness who has disappeared down the memory hole is Detective Timothy Morley. Morley was one of the police officers who were making their way out of the North Tower following the first plane strike. As they approached the 21st floor, they encountered a suspicious Middle Eastern–appearing man, who had been ignoring orders from firefighters and was "talking gibberish" on his cell phone. The officers noticed that he appeared to be sneaking back *into* the building as everyone else was evacuating. The man refused to answer any of Morley's questions, then suddenly took a white stuffed rabbit from the valise he was carrying, and shoved it into Morley's face. Other employees in the building verified that the Middle Eastern man didn't work on the 21st floor. After fighting with police, eventually the man was handcuffed and led down the stairs by Morley. He made sporadic cryptic comments like "I was a soldier in my country," and claimed to come from Ukraine. As they emerged from the tower, the man commented, "Look at the fire. Nice, nice fire." After police turned him over to the FBI, a man in a dark suit instructed Morley to keep quiet about the incident. The toy rabbit was strangely left behind in the North Tower and never recovered. The unidentified man was subsequently released and his arrest isn't on the record. I found a story on Morley being honored as part of then- New York Jets' quarterback Geno Smith's annual "Sunday Heroes" program in 2016. There was no mention in the story about the mysterious man Morley encountered. It was noted that Morley retired in 2006 for health reasons.[34]

Flight 77, which allegedly struck the Pentagon, remains mired in controversy as well. Not only was the hole left by the impact far too small to accommodate a plane of its size, not only was there little to no debris from the plane visible anywhere, but the myriad of security cameras that littered the world's most powerful military center evidently failed to capture whatever it was that struck the Pentagon. Or at least the public has never been shown such a video. One underreported and decidedly bizarre tidbit concerned a "secret note" that was found inside the stomach of one of the Flight 77 victims. The unidentified passenger wrote the note for unknown reasons and then inexplicably swallowed it. Of course, authorities were unwilling to share anything about what the note said. While Establishment stalwart, "conspiracy" author Brad Meltzer was researching a novel years later, he claimed to have talked to a mortician about a plot device where "if you're on a plane that's going down, if you handwrite a note and eat it, the human stomach has enough liquids to protect the note from burning." The mortician called it the "ultimate message in a bottle." Soothsayer Meltzer divined that the writer must have been in the military, because "Who else would know that the liquid in your belly could preserve a piece of paper?"[35]

Witnesses at the Pentagon provided similar unwelcome testimony of explosions. Over 100 of these accounts were compiled by researcher Eric Bart. Navy Captain Charles Fowler described, "You could feel the building shake. You knew it was a major explosion." Ex-Marine aviator Terry Morin, who was in the nearby old Navy Annex, likened it to "a 2,000 lb. bomb going off 1/2 mile in front of you." James S. Robbins, watching from his office a little over a mile away, described seeing "a dark, mushroom shaped cloud rose over the building. I froze, gaping for a second until the sound of the detonation, a sharp pop at that distance, shook me out of it." Peter M. Murphy, inside the Pentagon, termed it "a tremendous explosion." Don Perkal remarked, "I could smell the cordite. Then I knew explosives had been set off somewhere."[36] As has been pointed out repeatedly by researchers, there was little or no debris from the huge jetliner that allegedly struck the Pentagon. However, authorities claimed to have retrieved the remains of all but one of the sixty-four passengers on board. So all that metal was obliterated completely, but human bodies weren't?

Of all those who have contended that it must have been a missile that struck the Pentagon, none had more impressive credentials than retired Major General Albert Stubblebine III. Stubblebine was the commanding general of the United States Army Intelligence and Security Command from 1981 to 1984. "How easy is it for you to shift your belief system from 'I totally believe in my government' to 'Oh My God! What's going on?'" Stubblebine declared. "That's exactly where I went in all of this." When Stubblebine first saw the picture of the impact point at the Pentagon, he stated, "Well there was something wrong. And, so I analyzed it not just photographically, I did measurements. . . . I checked the plane, the length of the nose, where the wings were. . . . I took measurements of the Pentagon—the depth of the destruction in the Pentagon. . . . I went public at the time. I am the highest-ranking officer, I believe, that has ever gone public. . . . The official story was not true." A man after my own heart, Stubblebine didn't turn his speculation into a conclusion. "I was very careful to not say what it was because I couldn't prove it. I was careful to say that it was not the airplane that did that, because I can prove that it was not the airplane."[37] Stubblebine also pointed out the curious fact that all of the Pentagon sensors except one had been turned off that day. This was verified in a largely ignored 2006 interview with the Pentagon's maintenance team chief Brian Austin and Steve Pennington, a private consultant responsible for the Pentagon's security cameras, where it was quietly revealed, "Many security cameras at the Pentagon that could have captured the building being hit were switched off or had been taken down due to construction work that was taking place and therefore do not film the attack." Pennington stated, "Because that area was being renovated, a lot of the connectivity of these cameras and the infrastructure that allowed those cameras to be connected back to the building had been removed or destroyed, so they weren't capturing images and offering fields of view." Nonfunctioning security cameras would become one of the most glaring aspects in so many of the mass casualty shootings in years to come.

Pentagon employee April Gallop described what seemed like a bomb, and a YouTube video recorded her as saying that, as she was waiting outside on the Pentagon lawn to be transported to a hospital, "I didn't see any evidence of metal, airplane seats, luggage, nothing that would give me any indication that it was a plane that had hit the building." She also declared that she saw no evidence of jet fuel, and "There was nothing on the inside that would give me any indication that there was a plane on that particular day that hit the building." She spoke to everyone in her section and reported that they all had the same impression—there was nothing to indicate a plane had hit the Pentagon. Gallop boldly stated that this was "part of something more sinister," which included "going out of your way to fabricate an official story." Gallop claimed to have been visited by "men in suits" in the hospital more than once. "They never identified themselves or even said which agency they worked for. But I know they were not newsmen because I learned that the Pentagon told news reporters not to cover survivors' stories or they would not get any more stories out of there." Gallop recounted. "The men who visited all said they couldn't tell me what to say, they only wanted to make suggestions. But then they told me what to do, which was to take the (Victim Compensation Fund) money and shut up. They also kept insisting that a plane hit the building. They repeated this over and over. But I was there, and I never saw a plane or even debris from a plane. I figure the plane story is there to brainwash people."

April Gallop launched a lawsuit against members of the Bush administration, alleging that they knew about the attacks in advance. Predictably, a federal judge dismissed the case, declaring Gallop had "failed to present anything beyond vague and conclusory allegations of conspiracy." In April 2011, a three-judge appeals panel upheld the dismissal, and ordered her attorneys to be sanctioned and fined for filing a "frivolous" appeal. The judges ordered Gallop and her legal team to show cause as to why they should not be sanctioned for forcing the court "to consider, and the government to defend, a frivolous and vexatious appeal." Her lawyers responded by demanding the panel be disqualified for "evident severe bias, based in active personal emotions arising from the 9/11 attack." Their demand was justified; one of the three judges, John Walker, was

George W. Bush's first cousin! The court ominously and arrogantly warned against any "future frivolous filings, either as a *pro se* litigant or one represented by counsel."[38]

The affidavits that Gallop's team obtained from genuine experts David Lee Griffin and Steven Jones were brushed off by judge Denny Chin in his ruling to dismiss, as "conclusory statements and personal opinions without evidentiary support." They quoted former Secretary of Transportation Norman Mineta, who reported that a young man in the White House kept coming into the room where Vice-President Dick Cheney was, to tell him how close the plane was getting, and asked if his orders *not* to shoot had been changed. Cheney replied that they hadn't. In the words of Gallop's attorney William Veale, of the Center for 9/11 Justice in California: "Cheney knew for 71 minutes that a plane was coming towards Washington, there should have been an alarm sounded within the Pentagon building so employees could run for safety. Indeed such alarms, complete with evacuation of the building, had been so common in the past that employees found them annoying. Second, the jets that should have been scrambled were capable of going from their hangars to a height of 29,000 feet in three minutes, and were very capable of dealing with an attacker plane. Again, that was common practice: 67 times in the 9 months prior to 9/11, when aircraft went astray in the US, Air Force jets went aloft in response."[39]

One of the strangest elements of Flight 77 was the fact that partial remains of some passengers (along with some from Flight 93 in Pennsylvania) were incinerated by a military contractor, and disposed of in a landfill, according to a government report released in 2012. An independent panel studying flaws at Dover Air Force Base in Delaware followed up on a 2011 investigation that discovered "gross mismanagement" there. Military officials would plead ignorance regarding this suspicious and certainly unusual disposal of important historical remains. "This is new information to me," Air Force Secretary Michael Donley claimed. George Little, press secretary for Secretary of Defense Leon Panetta, maintained his boss "never would have supported" such a shocking breach of protocol. "He understands why families would have serious concerns about such a policy," Little said. Debra Burlingame, sister of Flight 77 pilot

Charles Burlingame spoke of attending an Arlington National Cemetery burial ceremony where unidentified 9/11 remains were treated with such reverence, and reacted to this puzzling report by stating, "I would want to know more." Somerset County, Pennsylvania coroner Wallace Miller, who as readers will see made other intriguing comments about the events of 9/11, reacted to some remains from Flight 93 being mixed in with those from Flight 77 by declaring, "I wouldn't know how there would be any possibility how any remains would get to Dover." Rep. Rush Holt from New Jersey, charged, "The Pentagon must provide absolute clarity and accountability as to what human remains were dishonored in this manner." More than 1.6 million tons of debris from the World Trade Center were sent to the Fresh Kills landfill on Staten Island, and included a significant amount of human remains. Families understandably launched a lawsuit over this disrespectful treatment of their loved ones, but as usually happens, it was dismissed, and their appeal to the Supreme Court was unsuccessful.[40]

9/11 Body Count

David F. Wherley Jr., the head of the Washington National Guard who scrambled jets over the nation's capital on September 11, 2001, was killed in a 2009 commuter train crash. Wherley was reported to have mobilized aircraft with orders to protect the White House and the Capitol, according to the 9/11 Commission report.[41] Louisiana dentist David Graham met two of the alleged 19 crazed hijackers, some ten months before September 11. He tried to warn the FBI that the men seemed to be planning to target an air force base, but they ignored him. Graham would write the "9/11 Graham Report," which he shared online. He would complain about being threatened and abused by the FBI, and claimed for two years prior to his September 2006 death that someone had poisoned him with antifreeze. Graham reportedly suffered with paralysis and organ failure for twenty-seven months before dying in a Shreveport nursing home. A year later, a complaint seeking to determine who killed Graham was filed with the Inspector General's office at the Department of Justice. The complaint was filed by 9/11 researcher Sander Hicks and others. Hicks claimed Graham's family was so fearful they didn't even request an autopsy. The FBI was quoted as saying they didn't investigate Graham's death because there was no connection between it and his writings.[42] Firefighter Sal Princiotta was credited with rescuing many people from the burning towers on 9/11. Later, he developed the health problems so many at Ground Zero would, and was forced to retire to Arizona. On May 14, 2007, his decomposed body was found riddled with bullet holes in his apartment. His alleged murderer would be cornered by police in California, and supposedly killed himself. As a news account put it, "Police are saying little about the suspect and nothing about why he may have killed Princiotta, only adding to the mystery surrounding the former firefighter's final days." His brother was quoted as saying, "You could say Sal was a victim of 9/11. He would never have moved to Arizona if 9/11 hadn't happened."[43]

Other 9/11-related unnatural deaths include Michael H. Doran, killed in an April 28, 2009, airplane crash. Doran was working for free to help relatives of 9/11 victims who'd refused to accept anything from the 9/11 Compensation Fund. [44] Then there was journalist Hiroshi Hasegawa, chief commentator and news analyst for Japan's only public television station. Among the early stories Hasewaga broke was the revelation that Israeli nationals were warned shortly before the attacks via a text message sent out in Hebrew through Odio, an Israeli telecommunication company.[45] It was reported on October 17 that Hasewaga had committed suicide, although he actually died on October 15. Few other details were provided. No suicide note was found, and as is certainly typical of controversial American deaths, no autopsy was performed. Hasewaga was a vocal skeptic of the Bush administration's "terrorist" 9/11 theory and is considered one of the first real "Truthers" looking into the case.

Wendy Burlingame, daughter of aforementioned Flight 77 pilot Charles "Chic" Burlingame, died in a fire in December 2006. The Hudson County, New Jersey prosecutor labeled the fire "suspicious," an uncharacteristic move in these cases. The fire broke out in the bedroom she shared with her longtime boyfriend, but he "escaped unscathed." Hudson County Prosecutor Edward De Fazio declared that "drinking might have been involved" but failed to elaborate. Neighbors reported hearing a mysterious "thump" and stated that "it was louder than usual" in Burlingame's apartment.[46] I could find no further updates on this curious fire, after a

December 19 story that reported the authorities still were unsure of the cause. Sandy Dahl, wife of Flight 93 pilot Jason Dahl, died in her sleep while staying at a friend's house on May 25, 2012. She was just fifty-two years old. Months later, it was reported that she had died from heart failure brought on by an accidental drug and alcohol overdose. A heart condition and antianxiety drugs were also cited. She had spoken of still waking up from nightmares and declared, "Normally, people have a memorial, and it's behind them. This is never going away."[47]

Minnesota Sen. Paul Wellstone would die in a highly suspicious plane crash, on October 25, 2002, along with his wife and one of his children. Wellstone was a maverick Democrat and was rumored to be keenly interested in 9/11. His close friend Pat O'Reilly recounted, "I asked him how his week had been. He said, 'it's been tough. Vice President Cheney called me in and told me to get on their bandwagon or there would be serious ramifications in Minnesota. 'And stop sticking your nose into 9/11; there are some rumors going around, but we are going to get to the bottom of this.' When Paul made this statement, there were about 10 military veterans standing around us, and he spoke to them about 9/11. . . .' There are so many things going on about 9/11 that just don't make sense. . . .' Wellstone knew 9/11 was staged. Wellstone was after 9/11." Some 9/11 researchers claim that writer Kurt Vonnegut was "seriously considering" becoming a part of the 9/11 Truth movement before his death in 2007. 9/11 "truther" John Patrick Bedell was killed at the Pentagon Metro station by police officers on March 4, 2010. Police alleged that Bedell fired first. Stories focused on Bedell's "deep-seated anger" at the government, and his "often rambling" posts and lectures on the "totalitarian federal government."[48] Australian Gerard Holmgren, originator of the "no planes" theory, died of "an aggressive brain tumor" at just fifty-one in 2010. Some conspiratorial sources claim the circumstances around his death are "unclear." Holmgren went through information on the Bureau of Transportation Statistics website, and concluded that two of the 9/11 flights, Flight 11 and Flight 77, had never existed.

One of the most interesting personalities associated with the events of 9/11 is Kurt Sonnenfeld. Sonnenfeld was a videographer employed by the Federal Emergency Management Agency (FEMA) who filmed the rubble at

Ground Zero. In all, Sonnenfeld produced twenty-nine videos, but didn't turn them all over to FEMA. He alleged, among other things, that the gold vaults at World Trade Center 6 had already been emptied prior to the attacks. Then–New York Mayor Rudy Giuliani would publicly confirm that most of the $200 million in gold from the Toronto-based Bank of Nova Scotia's vault had been recovered from the WTC rubble.[49] However, it was estimated that some $650 million in gold was in the Building 6 vaults. Sonnenfeld's wife Nancy would be found dead from a gunshot to the head on December 31, 2001. The authorities quickly arrested Sonnenfeld for the murder, even though his fingerprints weren't on the gun, and he tested negative for gunpowder residue.[50] In 2002, the murder charge was dropped due to lack of evidence. However, the prosecutor seemed intent on perhaps recharging Sonnenfeld, so he fled to Argentina, where he remarried and had children. The US government made several attempts to extradite him back to this country for the murder of his wife. Sonnenfeld maintained that the government was targeting him for his outspoken opposition to the official story. On her last day in office in 2015, Argentine president Cristina Kirchner reversed an Argentine Supreme Court decision and granted Sonnenfeld permanent political asylum.[51] WTC Building 6 is not often scrutinized, even by critics of the official narrative. It was seemingly damaged before either of the Twin Towers fell, which left an inexplicable crater that extended to the lowest level of its subbasements.[52] There were rumored to be nearly $1 billion in precious metals stored in the vault under WTC Building 4. The door to the vault was found intact, but it appeared as if someone had tried to gain entry.[53] A September 13, 2001, Reuters report seemed to contradict this somewhat. The story reported, "Nearly 12 tonnes of gold appears to be buried under mountains of debris from New York City's destroyed Twin Towers, where experts said it was securely out of reach of treasure hunters, looters and, for now, even the bullion trading community. The bars, worth about $106 million, were stored in an underground warehouse near the World Trade Center and held on behalf of the COMEX metals trading division of the New York Mercantile Exchange." Why would the vaults be emptied, only to leave the precious metals loose somewhere?

On May 8, 2009, Sonnenfeld gave a remarkable presentation at the Buenos Aires Book Fair, for his book *El Perseguido (Persecuted)*. Sonnenfeld declared, "There has never been an independent commission officially assigned to investigate the horrible events that occurred on September 11, 2001. . . . And now almost all of the evidence has been destroyed. Does anyone believe the official version offered as to what happened on September 11, 2001? There are many who say that the wildest conspiracy theory of all is the theory offered by the United States Government. Do you know that on the weekend prior to the attacks on the WTC, all electricity was cut off for approximately 36 hours, including the security cameras and control systems in a highly irregular 'maintenance operation?' Do you know that in the weeks leading up to the attacks there were several unusual evacuations of both towers? Do you know that the company in charge of security at the World Trade Center was directed by Marvin Bush, George Bush's younger brother, and Wirt Walker III, George Bush's cousin? . . . Do you know that hundreds of government personnel were pre-positioned in New York City on September 10, preparing to do a large-scale simulation of a terrorist attack to be carried out on September 12? FEMA officials had already set up their command post at Pier 92 near the World Trade Center one day before the attacks." Clearly, Sonnenfeld had done his research.

Sonnenfeld went on to say, "Do you know that the 47-story Salomon Smith Barney Building, officially known as Seven World Trade Center, imploded at 5:20 in the afternoon of September 11, 2001, some nine hours after American Airlines Flight 11 struck the North Tower? It took only about 6.5 seconds for the entire structure to fall straight down into itself. . . . The collapse of Building Seven left a curiously small and tidy rubble pile, and the buildings to either side of it were relatively undamaged. It had not been hit by an airplane and had suffered only minor injuries to its structure when the Twin Towers collapsed. The Secret Service, the Department of Defense, the Federal Bureau of Investigation, the Internal Revenue Service, the Securities and Exchange Commission and the Office of Emergency Management's 'Crisis Center' occupied huge amounts of space there, spanning several floors of the building. . . . After September 11, it was discovered that concealed within Building Seven was the largest clandestine domestic station of the Central Intelligence Agency outside of Washington, DC. . . . But the 9/11 Commission Report, supposed to investigate thoroughly all aspects and consequences of the attacks for devising public safety and national security recommendations, does not even mention Building Seven, its collapse, nor the bizarre specifics of that collapse. Nor did NIST, the government agency assigned to investigate the collapse of the Twin Towers. . . . Again the media was manipulated, and some willingly played the role of accomplice. US news crews signed contracts with the military that limited what they were allowed to report, and a few reporters were even paid by the government to write stories favorable to the administration."

Detailing his own personal involvement, Sonnenfeld continued, "I was at the world Trade Center. I was part of the official investigation. Previously I had been an official videographer for the US government in critical or catastrophic situations. I've done work characterized as confidential at many classified and maximum security locations related to the storage, development and transportation of nuclear, biological and chemical weapons or their components and participated in simulations and training for disasters, catastrophic accidents and terrorist incidents for many different agencies. Immediately after the attacks on the World Trade Center, the entire area in lower Manhattan was sealed off to the public and to the news media. All cameras were prohibited inside the secured perimeter. . . . I was given total and absolute access, however, and was instructed to document for the investigation and to provide some 'sanitized' pool video to virtually every news network in the world. But I never handed my tapes over to the authorities. Since then, over the course of the past seven years, I have been falsely accused, imprisoned twice in two different countries, tortured, put in solitary confinement, followed across two continents and slandered relentlessly in a campaign to dehumanize me so that no one will protest and to discredit me so that when I talk, no one will listen. Four years ago, the US embassy sent a note to Argentine officials to confiscate all of my possessions and documents and to remit them to the United States. To this day, my wife, my twin daughters and I live in a closed world surrounded by threat and harassment."

In a February 10, 2006, interview with the website Killtown, EMT Patricia Ondrovic recalled seeing explosions in Building 6. Ondrovic recounted, "I tried to run into the lobby of 6 World Trade, but there were federal police—maybe 4 to 6 of them—standing in the open doorways. As I tried to run in, they wouldn't let me, waving me out, telling me 'you can't come in here, keep running.' As I turned to start running west again, I saw a series of flashes around the ceiling of the lobby all going off one-by-one like the X-mas lights that 'chase' in pattern. I think I started running faster at that point." She volunteered, "I did find it very odd that they wouldn't let me in to get cover." Regarding the flashes and pops she witnessed from the doorway of Building 6, Ondrovic stated, "I immediately got the impression they were timed explosives. I have never thought they were anything else, not then, not now." Ondrovic was questioned only by the WTC Task Force, and her published testimony contained redactions. She was unaware of this, having never read her testimony or seen a copy. She told them about seeing the apparent explosions in Building 6, but that wasn't in her official transcript. She also described Building 5 as "the building that blew up on me." Ondrovic had stumbled upon the Killtown site, which revived her interest in the subject. CNN aired the explosion of Building 6 live, which happened just after the South tower was struck, but literally ignored it even as viewers could see the high rising plumes of smoke in the background.

There are so many unexplained elements of 9/11 that remain largely unscrutinized. What happened to the White Plains federal grand jury that was reportedly being convened to investigate the 9/11 attacks? New York City Police Commissioner Bernard Kerik was quoted as saying, "You're going to see things like the grand jury in White Plains. You're going to see grand juries around the country, perhaps, looking into matters pertaining to this investigation."[54] The following month, it was being reported that "The federal grand jury investigating the Sept. 11 terrorist attacks is casting a wide net, seeking information from witnesses about their contacts with the 19 hijackers as well as other suspected terrorists."[55] And there the story ends. There are no follow-ups about this. In a February 7, 2007, article that otherwise attempted to smear "conspiracy theorists" in the customary manner, the BBC inadvertently disclosed that "We no longer have the original tapes of our 9/11 coverage (for reasons of cock-up, not conspiracy)." Hmm. While I'm not familiar with the British term "cock-up," it sounds as implausible as every other excuse our own best and brightest use. For instance, NASA admitting the original Apollo 11 moon landing footage had been lost. Our leaders are astonishingly careless with such precious material. The BBC was responding to the fact that reporter Jane Standley had memorably described Building 7 collapsing over twenty minutes before it actually did. The building could clearly be seen standing in the background during her report. The BBC article explained, "Unsurprisingly, she doesn't remember minute-by-minute what she said or did." Contradicting the BBC's contention that Standley's premature report was due to a "miscommunication," was anchorman Philip Hayton's detailed description. "We're now being told," Hayton said, "that yet another enormous building has collapsed. It's the 47-story Salomon Brothers Building." Hayton would continue, "WTC 7 collapsed not as a result of an attack, but because the building had been weakened from this morning's attacks. Presumably, there were very few people in the Salomon Building when it collapsed."[56] Remember, this report was *before* the building came down.

Mohamed el-Amir Awad el-Sayed Atta, father of alleged 9/11 hijacker Mohamed Atta, publicly said that his son called him the day *after* the attacks and claimed he'd been framed by the Mossad. The father, a retired lawyer living in Egypt, was interviewed by the German news magazine *Bild am Sonntag* in late 2002 and reported that his son was in hiding. "He is hiding in a secret place so as not to be murdered by the US secret services," the elder man, referred to as Mohamed el-Amir Atta here, declared. He vehemently denied the accusation that his son flew the first plane into the World Trade Center, and blamed the attacks this time not on the Mossad, but on "American Christians."[57] Prof. David Ray Griffin looked closely at the widely disseminated report that Atta had left his luggage behind at Boston's Logan Airport, filled with incriminating evidence, à la James Earl Ray's deposit of evidence helpful to the prosecution in the doorway of the roominghouse from where authorities claimed he killed Martin Luther King Jr. Atta and an associate were said to have inexplicably traveled from Boston to a Comfort Inn in Portland, Maine, on September 10, only to return the next morning in time to hijack Flight 11. As Deep State Hall of Famer Robert Mueller told a Joint Intelligence Committee on September 26, "Their reason for going there, to date, remains unclear." Even the 9/11 Commission Report admitted, "No physical, documentary, or analytical evidence provides a convincing explanation of why Atta and Omari drove to Portland, Maine, from Boston on the morning of September 10, only to return to Logan on Flight 5930 on the morning of September 11."[58]

One witness who recounted horribly graphic details was Dave Donovan, who appeared in the seldom-seen British documentary *9/11: A Tale of Two Towers*. Donovan described seeing planes and body parts strewn everywhere, as he exited the North Tower into the plaza between the Twin Towers. Near where the "globe" was at, Donovan recalled, "I remember seeing plane seats with bodies still in them." He also declared, "I remember seeing a pregnant woman hitting the ground, when she jumped from about a hundred floors up." He made the fantastic claim that "you could see the baby come out with the cord." No other witness, to my knowledge, described seeing significant plane debris, let alone seats with passengers in them. Ron DiFrancesco, who also appeared in the documentary, had the notable distinction of being perhaps the only person in the Twin Towers who decided to go *up* instead of down after the building was hit. Overcome by smoke on the eighty-fourth floor, DiFrancesco inexplicably decided to climb the stairs. He found every floor locked, after going up to the ninety-first level, before finally heading back down. He claimed to see people "lying down, trying to get a bit of air, and going to sleep" on a landing near the eightieth floor. DiFrancesco decided to lie down as well. He attributed his exit to safety to a "miracle," wherein "someone" helped him up and he found the strength to traverse all those stairs. I found his rather undetailed reference to a person who saved his life to be quite curious. I also found it shocking that people would be lying down to sleep in such a situation, instead of doing everything possible to escape.

Why did more than 350 people cancel their reservations or not show up for the doomed 9/11 flights? The ratio of celebrities involved is certainly attention-grabbing. Among these was Seth MacFarlane, the creator of the cartoons *Family Guy* and *American Dad*, who apparently obfuscated the truth about the timing, for dramatic purposes, but was scheduled to fly on American Airlines Flight 11. Others who narrowly avoided tragedy included actors Mark Wahlberg (who was criticized for initially boasting, "If I was on that plane with my kids, it wouldn't have went down like it did. . . . There would have been a lot of blood in that first-class cabin and then me saying, 'OK, we're going to land somewhere safely, don't worry,'"[59]) and Edward James Olmos, actress Jaime Pressly, Bobby Farrelly, writer and director of comedies like *Dumb & Dumber* and *There's Something About Mary*, comedian Sacha Baron Cohen, and celebrity chef Julia Child. Sam Mendes, the director of *American Beauty* and the James Bond movie *Skyfall*, among others, was originally scheduled to be on American Airlines Flight 77. And Robert Redford, the world-famous actor and director, narrowly avoided being on United Airlines Flight 93. These aren't even all the figures associated with the entertainment world that were originally scheduled to be on one of the flights. Other notables who were originally scheduled to be on one of the hijacked flights included NHL coach Bruce Boudreau and longtime Georgetown University basketball coach John Thompson. Is it common to have so many celebrities on board the same plane? And why were so many celebrities in the Boston and Washington, D.C. areas at that time? Were some of these narrow misses invented by publicists? I think it's fair to question the inordinate number of public figures who signed up for (but didn't board) these flights. Some celebrities also just missed out on being in the Twin Towers that day. Michael Jackson was scheduled to have a meeting in the WTC on September 11, but overslept. So was British royal Sarah "Fergie" Ferguson, whose *Today* show interview fortuitously overran, interfering with a WTC meeting for her children's charity.

The FBI was initially suspicious of all these cancellations and no-shows. They interviewed a number of them but limited their investigation into any possible connection with the alleged hijackers. It's appropriate to ask whether any of these people had some kind of foreknowledge of the events. "A particularly urgent warning" was supposedly received on the night of September 10, resulting in some senior Pentagon officials canceling a trip scheduled for the morning of September 11.[60] Although the 9/11 Commission assured us that there was nothing unusual about all the flights being so under capacity in terms of passengers, those half empty or less (Flight 77 and Flight 175 were only one third full, Flight 93 only 20 percent full) airplanes seem all the stranger in light of the huge numbers of cancellations. As if this wasn't suspicious enough, a good number of pilots, flight attendants, and passengers were only booked on the doomed flights at the last minute. In fact, half of the pilots and copilots were assigned to those flights with very little notice. Steve Scheibner was bumped from Flight 11 by Thomas McGuinness. As Scheibner would recount, "I can count three times in 20 years at American Airlines that I've been bumped from a trip the night before."[61] John Ognowski, pilot of Flight 11, invoked his seniority to bump Walter Sorenson. Another red flag were the seven cancellations that had all been booked by the same Pakistani travel agency. The FBI's investigation into this concluded there was a need for "further inquiry," which, naturally, seems not to have happened. One particular oddity was that none of the seven people gave their first names, in violation of American Airlines policy, and none of the names were Pakistani.

Another celebrity, actor James Woods, attempted to alert the FBI to what he considered suspicious activity. Woods had noticed some Middle Eastern–looking men acting strangely, one week before 9/11, during a flight from Boston to Los Angeles (the same route scheduled for Flight 11). According to Woods, none of the men ate, drank, or slept during the flight. When they spoke to each other, it was in low hushed voices. Woods reported his concerns to the flight attendants, and ground authorities after landing. Later, he shared his encounter with the FBI, but they seem not to have taken it seriously. The FBI never confirmed whether any of the men had been identified as the alleged 9/11 hijackers. Woods, who would later become a vocal critic of the "woke" Left in Hollywood and the political world, stated through his publicist, "I think it prudent not to comment on this and let the FBI continue to do their job."[62]

When there is no adequate investigation into such a cataclysmic event, the questions left unanswered are endless. Citizen researchers—certainly no professional journalists—have calculated that some 1,400 automobiles caught fire or exploded in New York City on 9/11. Several of these vehicles were on FDR Drive, several blocks away from the World Trade Center. Some of these fires were exceedingly curious, with unique features that brought to mind spontaneous human combustion comparisons. There is no indication that any authorities even acknowledged this, let alone investigated it. Then there was the internal FAA memo, time stamped at 5:30 p.m. on September 11, which included this gem: "The American Airlines FAA Principal Security Inspector (PSI) was notified by Suzanne Clark of

American Airlines Corporate Headquarters, that an on-board flight attendant contacted American Airlines Operations Center and informed that a passenger located in seat 10B shot and killed a passenger in seat 9B at 9:20 a.m. The passenger killed was Daniel Lewin, shot by passenger Satam Al Suqami. One bullet was reported to have been fired." FAA spokeswoman Laura Brown told World Net Daily that, "It was a first draft. There was no gun." Brown declared that the "corrected" version of the memo, which contained no reference to a shooting, couldn't be released because it was "protected information."[63] Beyond the reference to a gun, which can be found nowhere else in the record, it is exceedingly curious that Suzanne Clark would have been focused enough to identify both victim and shooter in such a grave situation. An anonymous FAA official would rebut the agency, declaring, "The document was reviewed for accuracy by a number of people in the room, including myself and a couple of managers of the operations center. Nobody disputed it before I left work for the day."[64] Also of interest is the background of the supposed shooting victim here, Daniel Lewin, who just happened to be an elite commando in a top-secret unit of the Israeli army.[65]

Why were so many 9/11 victim family members so willing to accept the laughable official narrative? The *Arctic Beacon* attempted to contact "at least 10 airline family members," but their phone calls and emails were ignored. One who did answer, Julie Sweeney, seemed "apprehensive," and suspicious about how the reporter had found her number. Why do so many associated with these tragedies exhibit so little skepticism? The parents of purported Flight 11 passenger Waleed Iskandar were contacted a year after the 9/11 flights and informed that his unscathed ATM card had miraculously been found amid the rubble. His parents never publicly questioned this anomaly, perhaps because Waleed wasn't listed on either the original manifest for Flight 11 or the official list provided by American Airlines. These kinds of baffling discrepancies in the record—and there are many—should have caught the attention of any real enterprising reporter. In a similar, "magic bullet" fashion, Flight 77 victim Suzanne Calley's California ID card, driver's license, and wedding ring were all found in perfect condition at the Pentagon crash site. In an underreported incident, RFK's accused assassin Sirhan Sirhan was interrogated by the

FBI after 9/11. Sirhan had shaved his head two days before the attacks, something he'd never done in thirty-three years in prison, and traded with another inmate for a television. Sirhan's lawyer Lawrence Teeter stated, "He [Sirhan] had no knowledge or involvement at all, and he's absolutely outraged by this attack. He's opposed to terrorism and he hopes these people [responsible] are burning in hell." Regarding his suddenly shaved head, Teeter said, "People sometimes change their hairstyles. I have no idea why he shaved his head. This was just a random event, and there should be no significance attached to it."[66]

By 2002, Robert Shaler, head of New York City's Department of Forensic Biology, whose staff oversaw the daunting efforts to find testable remains among the WTC rubble, had yet to find a trace of any of the hijackers. All told, nearly half of the 2,751 victims of the 9/11 attacks in New York had yet to be identified. However, by 2009, "Through a combination of innovative DNA-mapping techniques, help from the FBI's crime lab and dumb luck, the scientists have now ID'ed four of the 10 New York hijackers. The remains of the nine hijackers from the Pentagon and Pennsylvania crash sites have also been confirmed; six other hijackers have yet to be identified." Interestingly, "What's left of the terrorists—which, all told, likely amounts to less than 24 pounds of flesh and bone fragments—are sequestered at undisclosed locations in New York and Virginia." A mainstream article reported that they are "stored as evidence in a refrigerated locker in sealed containers and test tubes," according to FBI spokesman Richard Kolko. Oddly, it was stated that none of the families of the hijackers had requested their remains. The same article makes some fanciful claims: "In Pennsylvania, Somerset County coroner Wallace E. Miller and his team scoured the "halo"—the field and woods surrounding the crater left when United Airlines Flight 93 plunged into the ground. The debris was everywhere. Trees were draped with scraps of luggage, clothing, bits of the fuselage and human remains. Walking through the crash site in the days after the attacks, Miller's eye caught a flash of light 20 feet up in the branches of a hemlock tree. 'I only noticed it because the sun happened to hit it at just the right angle,' he says. A tree climber brought it down. It was a single tooth with a silver filling. Eventually it was matched to one of the passengers."[67] Now, that's some sharp eyesight. And really shiny silver.

This incident is all the more astounding in light of other comments Miller would make, which will be discussed later in this chapter.

I wasn't alone in wondering, at the time, why there were no rooftop rescues attempted, or any helicopters with water hoses utilized on September 11, 2001. ABC News ran a November 8, 2001, story headlined, "Why No Rooftop Rescues on Sept. 11?" The article was basically an apologia, with officials rationalizing the lack of effort in this regard. NYPD aviation unit pilot Officer Timothy Hayes, was in the first helicopter to reach the tragic scene. "The smoke had covered 90 percent of the entire roof, so I couldn't even see the roof to make an evaluation of where we could go," Hayes said. "We were looking at probably 15 to 20 stories burning simultaneously. Probably well over 1,000 degrees, you know, if not more." ABC explained, "Though helicopter rescues have flown hundreds of people to safety in other instances, aerial rescues would not have worked on Sept. 11, according to authorities." Yes, those "authorities" always have the final word. Lt. Glen Daley, another aviation unit pilot, stated, "Well, there's high-rise fires and then there's the 11th . . . add to that scenario hundreds of thousands of pounds of jet fuel as an accelerant to the fire. Multiply the heat factor . . . now you've got the worst of all possible situations playing themselves out." The story went on to defend the "authorities," as all mainstream press accounts invariably do. Left unasked was why none of the helicopters attempted to throw down a rope ladder to the people they could see gathered in the windows. People would tell alternative media about witnesses claiming to have seen military helicopters circling around the WTC. Several witnesses would describe seeing a mysterious helicopter flying around the Pentagon just before it was struck, and then briefly landing on the helipad. A senior Air Force officer told CNN's Chris Plante that he'd seen "a helicopter circle the building."[68] Jennifer Reichert reported that "a helicopter (took) off from the heliport at the Pentagon," as she sat in traffic, and only "minutes—maybe seconds—later," something hit the Pentagon.[69] In a December 13, 2002, interview with the U.S. Naval Historical Center, Jeffrey Mark Parsons, an assistant chief patrol agent with the United States Border Patrol, described seeing a helicopter, too. From a window on the 17th floor of the Marriott Residence Inn in Arlington, a few minutes before the building was hit, Parsons noticed a blue and white helicopter flying at "a weird angle" and circling "between the hotel and the Pentagon, going toward the landing pad [at the Pentagon] where that airliner ultimately hit." He thought the helicopter "landed on the pad."

Combining a strange death with helicopters, Paul M. Smith piloted the helicopter which shot the first footage of Flight 175 striking the second tower of the WTC. On 7th October 2007, Smith was killed when he was run over by a cabdriver who'd been cut off by a "black car" that was never identified. "The black car left the accident. You don't run away from an accident. You just don't do that," the cabdriver claimed.[70] Cameraman John Del Giorno was in the helicopter with Paul Smith on 9/11. Del Giorno has refused to talk about 9/11 and doesn't respond to reporters. A CIA "secret office" was destroyed in the collapse of Building 7. An anonymous government official stated that" immediately after the attack, a special CIA team scoured the rubble in search of secret documents and intelligence reports stored in the station, either on paper or in computers. It was not known whether the efforts were successful."[71]

Then Senator Joe Biden appeared to forecast the 9/11 attacks in a speech the day before, on September 10, 2001, as he stressed the dangers of a terrorist attack that could come, among other ways, "in the belly of a plane." Biden, after being confronted by the feisty We Are Change organization, admitted that he'd met with Mahmoud Ahmad, the alleged chief financier of the 9/11 hijackers, two days after the attacks. Ahmad notably had breakfast on the morning of September 11, 2001, with Sen. Bob Graham, and then Rep. Porter Goss, later to become director of the CIA. "We asked him the question—what was he doing with the head of the Pakistani ISI General Mahmoud Ahmad," Luke Rudkowski of We are Change recounted. "He told me—he admitted that he met with him—he met with the head of the Pakistani ISI—he said I told them not to do it, I told them not to wire the money—I told them to stop supporting the Taliban, which shows he had foreknowledge of them supporting him." Rudkowski replied, "Sir, he funded the hijackers, you did business with him, you let him go—he's free." Biden dismissed him with a curt "Get a life kid," and Rudkowski was ushered away by Biden's security staff. In a similar vein, Bill Clinton told a group of businessmen in Australia he was being paid $150,000 to speak to, ten hours *before* the 9/11 attacks began, that he could have killed Osama Bin Laden, but refrained from doing so because, according to belatedly released audio, "I would have to destroy a little town called Kandahar in Afghanistan and kill 300 innocent women and children, and then I would have been no better than him."[72] That's the Bill Clinton we've come to know and love.

The massive rubble at the WTC site was carted away, in the manner that authorities now confiscate, conceal, or destroy (as in the Sandy Hook case) the crime scenes of all high-profile incidents. The public was told, "More than 2,600 artifacts collected from the site were housed inside Hangar 17 at John F. Kennedy International Airport in New York, under the purview of the Port Authority of New York & New Jersey . . . the items were given out to 1,585 fire and police departments, museums, municipalities and organizations in an effort to remember the nearly 3,000 people who died that day."[73] Author/researcher Christopher Bollyn was sent an email about a mysterious "final load" removed from Ground Zero, which he forwarded to Lawyers Committee for 9/11 Truth. Bollyn's March 24, 2019, email noted, "I spoke to you about this matter briefly and want to give you more information about the 'final load' that was taken from the clean-up site of the World Trade Center in the summer of 2002. I have tried many times to reach the two people involved in this operation without luck. The tip for this story came from a truck driver who worked for Logano Trucking at the time. At the end of the clean-up operation at the WTC, the office of Logano Trucking was asked to bring a special container (50 cu. yards) for a hazardous material load to be taken to the CWMC hazardous material disposal site near Model City, NY. This was an unusual load because a young executive from Logano Trucking went with to NYC and back with the load. Her name is Lindsay Kelly, and she still works with the company, which is now known as RED Technologies. . . . It was very unusual that she went with to get this 'live load' to be taken to upstate New York. The driver for this load was Richard Gamberale from East Hampton, Conn. who has a listed phone number, but has not answered at that number. According to the driver, Gamberale and Kelly stayed in NYC. . . . What was the nature of this load and why was it taken to a hazardous disposal site? . . . I have tried to reach Lindsay Kelly many times at RED Tech. LLC, but she has never come to the phone and seems to be avoiding me. Richard Gamberale seems to be out-of-town and is probably engaged in NASCAR racing with the Logano family, which is involved in the sport."

Exceedingly strange was the fact that no relatives of those on board the doomed Flight 93, which supposedly crashed in Pennsylvania, were waiting at San Francisco International Airport for its arrival. A counseling center was set up for any relatives that might show up, and dozens of clergy members gathered in the VIP lounge to talk with them. San Francisco Mayor Willie Brown had arranged to meet grieving family members at the airport, but when none had shown up an hour after the scheduled landing time, he canceled the trip. Knight Ridder Newspapers helpfully suggested that this seemingly unexplainable anomaly could be attributed to United Airlines contacting many of the families at home.[74] In keeping with the theme about last-minute changes, it is beyond mind-boggling that nearly half—16 of 33—of Flight 93's passengers were not originally scheduled for the flight, and many signed up at the very last minute, on the morning of September 11.[75] At Los Angeles International Airport, it was reported that "a few grieving relatives" of those on the other three crashed flights were there.[76] One story recounted how, "In Los Angeles, several dozen relatives met grief counselors at an airport hotel."[77]

Even the mainstream media found the discernable calm in Flight 11 attendant Betty Ong's voice to be noteworthy. Ong's "amazingly calm" voice informed an American Airlines reservation specialist (is that who would answer this kind of call?), "The cockpit is not answering the phone. . . . Someone's coming. . . . Another one [passenger] got stabbed. . . . Our First Class gal's stabbed, our purser has been stabbed. . . . We can't get inside the cockpit." One presumes these stabbings were inflicted with the box cutters the hijackers were "armed" with. 9/11 Commission investigators developed a theory that the hijackers "probably sprayed Mace around the cockpit area on all four flights, apparently to keep passengers away." This is based solely on Ong's remark that "Somebody's been stabbed in Business Class, and, um, I think there's Mace and we can't breathe and I don't know, I think we're getting hijacked." "I believe that the tape belongs to the people," Ong's sister Cathie said. "She and the crew did the best they could. They were our first soldiers."[78] During the twentieth anniversary coverage of 9/11, Ong's dubious phone call (see *Hidden History* for an in-depth look at why all the reported calls were implausible to put it kindly) fit perfectly with the emotion-driven "journalism" displayed throughout the mainstream media. In a story lauding her as a "hero," it was noted how Ong had the presence of mind to identify the hijackers by their seat numbers, as if that stopped them or was responsible for bringing them to justice. The article emphasized Ong's Asian heritage, while mentioning the totally unrelated recent deluge of alleged "hate crimes" against Asian Americans. Her sister Cathie declared, "My sister gave her life for her country on Sept. 11, and it's very hurtful when you think about what's going on today."[79]

Local television reporter Joe Collum revealed, on the afternoon of September 11, how he'd been told by several police and firefighters that people had been seen "planting bombs" in the aftermath of the airplanes hitting the Twin Towers, and they suspected this is what caused them to fall. Much as witnesses described encountering Secret Service agents on the Grassy Knoll after the JFK assassination, when all agents were known to have proceeded to Parkland Hospital with the limousine, there have been allegations of imposters on 9/11 as well. On September 11, an Arlington County, Virginia firefighter at the Pentagon witnessed a crew of supposed firefighters walking past burning fires, in violation of protocol. The following day, The Defense Protective Service arrested three people at the Pentagon who were dressed as firefighters, but weren't. DPS officer Lt. Robbie Turner saw people stealing plane debris from the road in front of the Pentagon. Turner recollected, "We had to try to stop other people from pilfering the wreckage because, believe it or not, there were people—military personnel involved—you know, included, rather, that was picking up the wreckage of the plane from off the highway." Another DPS officer, Roosevelt Roberts Jr., reported that, "We had a lot of people vandalizing, stealing evidence."[80] A large part of the Pentagon mystery, of course, is the seeming absence of wreckage outside of the building, as seen in photographs.

Flight 93, which allegedly crashed in Shanksville, Pennsylvania, left as many questions as the flights involving the World Trade Center and the Pentagon. There are theories that the plane was shot down by the government, or didn't crash there at all. As one mainstream news account noted,

"Of course, in 2001, Internet conspiracy theories are hardly shocking. What is surprising is this: Go to Shanksville and the surrounding farm fields where people actually saw or heard the jetliner go down at roughly 10:06 that morning and there are a number of people—including witnesses—who also think that Flight 93 was shot down, or at least aren't ruling it out."[81] In an early, September 13 story, Reuters disclosed that "FBI Does Not Rule Out Shootdown of Pennsylvania Plane." The report referred to FBI agent Bill Crowley's remarks during a news conference in writing, "Federal investigators said on Thursday they could not rule out the possibility that a United Airlines jetliner that crashed in rural Pennsylvania during this week's attacks on New York and the Pentagon was shot down." Within a few days, Crowley would say, "There was no military involvement here. I hope that ends that speculation."[82] Vice President Dick Cheney was widely quoted in the mainstream media as having initially believed his orders to shoot down the hijacked airliners had been carried out. A transcript of a phone call between Cheney and Secretary of Defense Donald Rumsfeld revealed the vice president saying, "It's my understanding that they've already taken a couple of aircraft out."[83]

Shanksville Mayor Ernie Stull would reveal his knowledge that F-16 fighter jets were "very, very close." Stull even more importantly stated on camera that "Everybody was dumbfounded because they were called to an aircraft crash, and there is no airplane!" He went on to reiterate, "No! There was nothing! Only this hole." As was the case at the Pentagon, there seemed to be no real wreckage from the plane itself. Warren County Sheriff Brian Zeybel remarked, "I was surprised, still am surprised, (about) the lack of evidence of a plane hitting the earth. In the way of debris fields and all that, the earth absorbed that pretty well, almost sucked it up." Zeybel went on to state, "The trees themselves looked like someone had painted half with fire retardant. That was odd for me. That to me looked odd. I've never seen anything like that—that hot, that fast, (that) could burn the side of a tree."[84] Witness Dennis Roddy, editor in chief of the *Pittsburgh Post-Gazette*, corroborated Stull, stating, "Airplane debris? Nothing that I could have recognized." Roddy also noted that law enforcement on the scene "were very, very secretive" while "United Airlines was not cooperative at all." Photographer Scott Spangler reported, "I was looking for anything that said tail, wing, plane, metal. There was nothing." Pennsylvania State Police Commander Patrick Madigan commented, "I was amazed because it did not, in any way, shape, or form, look like a plane crash."[85] Assistant Fire Chief Rick King reacted to the site by asking, "Where is this plane? And where are the people?" King recounted seeing "thousands of tiny pieces scattered around—bits of metal, insulation, wiring—but no fuselage, no wings, only a smoking crater and charred earth." King ordered his men into the woods to search for the fuselage, but they came back, reporting, "Rick, there's nothing."[86] Witness Homer Barron testified that "It didn't look like a plane crash, because there was nothing that looked like a plane" and he had "never seen anything like it. Just a big pile of charcoal."[87] Jon Meyer, the first reporter to arrive at the scene, reported, "All I saw was a crater filled with small, charred plane parts. Nothing that would even tell you that it was the plane. . . . There were no suitcases, no recognizable plane parts, no body parts."[88] Frank Monaco of the Pennsylvania State Police described what all the others did: "nothing but tiny pieces of debris. It didn't look like a plane crash." Crash site commander FBI agent Wells Morrison's first thought was "Where is the plane?"[89]

Lyle Szupinka, an area commander of the Pennsylvania State Police, also spoke of just "small pieces of debris," and stated, "There was actually nothing to tell you that that was an aircraft. Had you not known that that was an aircraft crash, you would've looked at that and you would've said something happened here, but I don't know what."[90] In his official Oral History of the incident, Szupinka elaborated even further, declaring, "If you've ever been to a bad airplane crash, they're nasty with the human remains and what have you. When I was going to that site, I was preparing myself that basically this wasn't going to be a pretty scene. This was going to [be] nasty. When I got there, I was surprised to find that I saw no human remains. None whatsoever." William Baker, of the Somerset County Emergency Management Agency, recalled: "When they said it was a 757, I looked out across the debris field. I said, 'There is no way there is a 757 scattered here. The biggest piece of debris I saw would have probably fit in my pocket." Paramedic Paul Bomboy remarked, "It was a very strange thing that there weren't normal things going on that you would have expected. When a plane crashes, there is a plane and there are patients."[91] FBI agent Michael Soohy, a veteran of numerous plane crash sites, talked about expecting to see "chaos, bodies, [and] a hulking wreck of a jet." Instead, he darkly noted, "I don't think anyone expected to see what they didn't see."[92] The senior Pennsylvania State Trooper at the scene, Bob Weaver, said, "I was totally amazed that this big plane was just swallowed up in the ground. . . . It took a while for it to sink in that there was an airplane in there."[93] And in another parallel to the Pentagon, where the hole left by whatever struck it was obviously too small for it to have been Flight 77, the "gouge" in the earth left in Shanksville measured only about eight to ten feet deep and fifteen to twenty feet long. A huge jetliner should have made a much greater impact.

John Carlin reported that "air-traffic controllers in Cleveland who tracked the last minutes of Flight 93 on radar have been forbidden by the authorities to speak publicly about what they saw on their screens." Carlin also noted that the last phone call received from Flight 93 was from a panicked passenger in the toilet, who spoke of hearing an explosion on board. The FBI confiscated the tape of this conversation, and ordered the operator, Glen Cramer, not to speak to the media.[94] One of the elite insiders in corporate America, Oracle CEO Larry Ellison, sent an email to his employees, praising the heroic efforts of Todd Beamer and the "Let's Roll" passengers, on the afternoon of September 13, a full twenty four hours before Beamer's own wife learned about it.[95] Both Beamer and his wife Lisa worked for Oracle; Ellison had started his company as a project building a database for the CIA. Another odd connection here is that Lisa Jefferson, the operator whom Todd Beamer strangely chose to spend his final moments chatting with rather than his wife, was associated with World Vision, the purportedly Christian group connected to both Mark David Chapman and John Hinckley. Lisa Beamer was quoted as understandably wondering about her husband's decidedly odd last call; as *Newsweek* reported, "Why had her husband, a man so attached to his cell phone that [she] had to confiscate it when they went on vacation, not called her from the plane? Other passengers had called home from Flight 93 to say goodbye and talk to their loved ones. Why not Todd?"[96]

Lisa Beamer made some two hundred public appearances in the first six months after the attacks. She set up a foundation in her husband's memory as well, and wrote the inevitable book, *Let's Roll! Ordinary People, Extraordinary Courage*. As one story put it, "donations dwindled, and Beamer receded from public view."[97] In her book, Lisa wrote that she was "so glad" her husband hadn't contacted her from the plane. It doesn't take a "conspiracy theorist" to wonder about *that.*

That phone call from Todd Beamer deserves closer scrutiny. His last words, "Let's roll!" became "Embraced and promoted by President Bush as a patriotic battle cry," with the iconic words "now emblazoned on Air Force fighter planes, city fire trucks, school athletic jerseys, and countless T-shirts, baseball caps and souvenir buttons. It's also commemorated in popular songs."[98] Leaving aside the incomprehensible aspect of someone wanting to spend their final moments talking to an anonymous operator rather than their spouse, Lisa Jefferson herself had some questions. In her book, Lisa Beamer wrote that Jefferson had told her "It was a miracle that Todd's call hadn't been disconnected." The call lasted for thirteen uninterrupted minutes, while the GTE systems had been overloaded, with calls being disconnected all around her. Jefferson produced her own book in 2006, *Called,* in which she described how unusually calm Todd Beamer was, in the midst of such a stressful situation. She told Lisa Beamer, "If I hadn't known it was a real hijacking, I'd have thought it was a crank call, because Todd was so rational and methodical about what he was doing."[99] Beamer's odd explanation to Jefferson that he didn't want to upset his pregnant wife is contradicted by the fact, which was revealed at the 2006 trial of Zacarias Moussaoui, that he *had* initially tried to phone his wife, but the call was "terminated upon connection." And Lisa Beamer reported getting two phone calls that morning, recalling that, "When I picked it up, it was dead air. I feel fairly confident that it was Todd. It would be on his mind to call me, to protect me."[100] This seems to be in stark contrast to what she would write in her book, about not being surprised (and happy) that he hadn't opted to call her. Because Jefferson didn't record the phone call, in the words of British reporter Rowland Morgan, the seminal "Let's Roll!" legend was "single-sourced, unsubstantiated hearsay of which there was no record."[101] As is maddeningly routine in these narratives, a week after 9/11, it was reported that the call *had* been tape recorded.[102] Such a recording, if it ever existed, has never been produced. And, going deep down the rabbit hole, alternative researchers claimed to have searched the Social Security death index, and found that the only Todd Beamer with his birth date had died on June 10, 1997! They further searched the marriage records and found nothing for a May 14, 1994, wedding between Beamer and Lisa Brosious. A search of the same Social Security Death Index also discovered that shockingly low percentages—ranging from 13 to 28 percent, of the passengers and crew names from the four 9/11 flights can be found there. With all the witness accounts of there being little or no identifiable wreckage at the Flight 93 crash site, it is beyond suspicious that two items that were recovered just happened to be Todd Beamer's business card and watch. Researchers found that, as of 2010, only 446 names out of the official 2,970 9/11 victims appear in the Social Security Death Index.[103]

Some witnesses in Shanksville reported seeing a small white plane flying in the area, while others reported it was a missile, just before the Flight 93 crash. Joe Wilt described hearing a "whistling like a missile, then a loud boom. The first thing I thought it was, was a missile."[104] Mayor Ernie Stull said, "I know of two people—I will not mention names—that heard a missile. . . . This one fellow's served in Vietnam and he says he's heard them, and he heard one that day."[105] Susan McElwain testified, "There's no way I imagined this plane—it was so low it was virtually on top of me. It was white with no markings but it was definitely military, it just had that look. . . . The FBI came and talked to me and said there was no plane around. . . . But I saw it and it was there before the crash. . . . They did not want my story—nobody here did."[106] While some believe Flight 93 was shot down by the government, others believe there either was no crash at all, or it was something else entirely which landed there. The comments of the aforementioned Somerset County coroner Wallace Miller, who had fancifully claimed to have spotted a *tooth* with a silver lining in a tree, were particularly interesting. Miller declared that it looked like the airliner had "stopped and let the passengers off before it crashed," and also recounted that he hadn't seen a "single drop of blood" there. "I stopped being coroner after about 20 minutes," Miller said, "because there were no bodies there."[107] However, despite there being no evidence of human remains or even mid-sized pieces of aircraft, evidently a significant amount of paper—especially mail—was discovered at the scene. One of the first witnesses to arrive, Lee Purbaugh, thought at first that it "was just a cargo plane carrying some mail," because that's all he could see.[108] According to Jere Longman of the *New York Times,* Purbaugh recounted seeing "envelopes with California addresses, magazines, [and] paper on the ground and in the trees." Some of the envelopes were incomprehensibly undamaged. More significantly, incriminating evidence like passports, identification cards, and pages from the Koran were left unscathed by an inferno that obliterated all evidence of the plane and its passengers.[109] People reported finding paper, mostly mail, as far as eight miles away from the crash site.[110]

Reporter Christopher Bollyn visited the Shanksville scene numerous times, and stated that "many of the people were noticeably afraid to talk about the things they had seen and noticed around Shanksville on September 11, 2001. Several of them apologized and told me that they had been told by the F.B.I. or other agents of the U.S. government not to talk. From others I got the clear impression that they had been warned not to talk about what they knew. Then there are those who had obviously been told to tell lies." Bollyn alleged that there was a hidden debris field hundreds of meters away in the woods, near the cottage of Barry Hoover. Rev. Larry Hoover would claim that body parts had been found there. The supposed crash site was heavily guarded; reporters were not allowed within three hundred yards of the scene. "We haven't seen anything bigger than a phone book, certainly nothing that would resemble a part of a plane," Capt. Frank Monaco of the Pennsylvania State Police observed. Barry Hoover, meanwhile, witnessed debris scattered over an area of at least a mile, and said, "There was stuff everywhere back there. It made you want to drop to your knees and cry for those people."[111] The *Pittsburgh Post-Gazette* talked about "the shock waves set off by the impact of that crash heavily damaged Hoover's home." Hoover compared his house to having gone through a hurricane or tornado, and called it "a total ruin." If indeed a diversionary fake crash scene was created, was it related to the reports that Flight 93 had actually landed safely in Cleveland? On the morning of September 11, 2001, the Associated Press, for instance, had reported that Flight 93 had made an emergency landing at Cleveland Hopkins International Airport. This was quite a detailed "mistake," as Cleveland's Mayor Michael R. White was quoted as saying that the landing was related to suspicion that it had a bomb aboard.

Bollyn followed up on the Cleveland story. Bollyn noted, "The Akron Beacon Journal reported that the mayor had stated that 200 passengers had been released from the plane at 11:15 a.m. The airport in Cleveland had been evacuated at 10 a.m." The *Journal* had included the details, "Airline passengers and crew members were walking onto the highway to find their rides as no cars were allowed into the passenger drop off and pick up areas." The next day, September 12, the *Journal* disclosed that seventy-eight passengers "were taken to NASA Glenn Research Center to be interviewed by FBI agents." Bollyn tried to speak with former Mayor Michael R. White, but the conversation was very brief, with White telling him, "I'm out of the interview business." Bollyn continued, "I called the NASA Glenn Research Center to ask about the passengers that were taken to the facility on 9/11. 'No one was brought here,' said a puzzled NASA spokesperson." Mary Ethridge of the *Akron Beacon Journal*, however, stood by the paper's report, which alone raised a number of very troubling questions. An October 19, 2001, FBI report describes an interview with Newark International Airport fueler Anthony F. Mazza. On 9/11, Mazza entered the cockpit of Flight 93 to inform the pilot the plane was fully fueled. The next month, Mazza saw memorial pictures of the Flight 93 crew and saw that the listed copilot, Leroy Homer, who was Black, was definitely not the White copilot he encountered that day. Especially given the unexplained indications of a Cleveland landing, the FBI should have thoroughly investigated this situation.

Four shipping containers purporting to hold the remaining wreckage from Flight 93 were quietly buried in the woods near the Flight 93 Memorial's Wall of Names in a private July 2018 ceremony. The wreckage lies in a highly restricted zone, which is off limits to the media and the public. One story reported that "about 95 percent" of the wreckage had been recovered, which certainly doesn't seem to jibe with all those witnesses who claimed that basically nothing was there except for a giant crater.[112] By September 2021, the narrative had changed so that the reason there was virtually no wreckage found was attributed to the fact the airliner crashed upside down into the ground, leaving debris as deep as thirty-five feet below. Stories spoke of airplane parts being entangled in trees, something no witness reported seeing. Apparently, a lot less than "95 percent" of the victims were found; it was now reported that *five* human bones were among the debris in those four containers.[113] However, a variation of this had been reported by local KOMO 4 News on May 31, 2007. At that time, the narrative went that "files and material" were buried deep underground at a facility called Iron Mountain in Pittsburgh, including the wreckage of Flight 93, "which is now under armed guard." Was this material moved from this underground location to another near the Wall of Names, eleven years later? A spokeswoman for United Airlines had indicated early on that the FBI was giving the wreckage back to United to use as they saw fit. She mentioned that a memorial was being planned at United headquarters. As always, there shouldn't be this many inconsistencies in the story.

In a twenty-year anniversary story, WITF's Tim Lambert described going back to the "sacred ground," of the Flight 93 Memorial, run by the National Park Service. Lambert reported finding a foot-long piece of metal at the base of a tree. In the article, Lambert recalled first seeing the Flight 93 crash scene at the invitation of county coroner Wallace Miller. Alone among all the witnesses whose accounts I could find, Lambert was immediately struck by the overpowering stench of jet fuel. He recounted seeing tiny bits of debris everywhere. Compare this to all the accounts cited earlier, where virtually no evidence of the plane could be found. Lambert even found a heart-tugging, charred wedding invitation.[114] Lambert didn't mention questioning Miller about his shocking comments about there being no blood anywhere, or even the minutest trace of the passengers. Lambert's testimony about smelling jet fuel contradicted not only all other eyewitness accounts, but also the Pennsylvania Department of Environmental Protection tests which found no evidence of jet fuel. DEP spokeswoman Betsy Mallison remarked that, "whether it burned away or evaporated," any jet fuel "seems to have dissipated."[115] DEP hydrologist David Bomba had, in fact, informed local residents that initial test samples of soil and water had proven to be perfectly clean. I found Lambert's Facebook page, and it was filled with predictably Establishment posts, some displaying clear signs of Trump Derangement Syndrome. In one, he castigated those who ridicule the "mainstream media." His antipathy for any "conspiracy theories" was pretty obvious.

Devvy Kidd has been a prominent figure in alternative media for decades. She visited Shanksville in 2005, and reported on her website, "There is something not right about the county coroner, Wallace Miller, never filing a single report as the coroner of record. During my testy interview with him, he denies making any reports to his client, the FBI. Miller was acting in his official capacity as the county coroner and he didn't file one single report after doing months of work at that crash site? No photos? Nothing but some documentation on DNA testing? I'm afraid I don't believe this for a second." Kidd interviewed Miller on August 2, 2005, and related how "the minute we walked into Miller's office, he jumped right down my throat. Miller knew exactly who we were before I could say a word. Few times in my life have I ever been treated so rudely by a perfect stranger in a business environment. Miller's attitude and speech was belligerent and I found quite disturbing." Kidd was shocked that "the county coroner on such a highly publicized aviation disaster had prepared no reports. Miller stated emphatically that he had no reports and made it clear that even if he did, he would refuse to make them available. Having done a number of investigations on site, I have never run across this problem. Sure, you have to buy the autopsy and toxicology reports, and they aren't cheap, believe me, but they are a matter of public record unless sealed by the court. For the county coroner who did the Flight 93 crash site for recovery of remains, any autopsies and DNA, not to have prepared a single report defies credibility. It also makes you wonder why?" Adding to all the confusion over the debris, Kidd learned that "Only 8 percent of the human remains have ever been recovered, Miller said, and three caskets full of those have yet to be identified and are in an undisclosed mausoleum." Wallace Miller is front and center in several stories, and as one can easily see, his testimony was all over the place.

Kidd described how Mayor Ernie Stull was still angry that his bombshell comments to German television in March 2003 had been taken out of context. Stull had declared, "There was no plane. My sister and a good friend of mine were the first ones there. They were standing on a street corner in Shanksville talking. Their car was nearby, so they were the first here—and the fire department came. Everyone was puzzled, because the call had been that a plane had crashed. But there was no plane." When questioned later by American Free Press, Stull disputed the time frame, saying he had visited the site "a day or two later," but reiterated that there was little evidence of a plane crash. Stull had been quoted in a September 12 news story about his house shaking, as if from some explosion, and then seeing "a cloud that looked like a mushroom cloud from an A-bomb," in the area of the alleged crash.[116] Witness Bob Blair had also described seeing "a mushroom cloud." Another anomaly not reported elsewhere was witness and reporter Bob Leverknight's comment to Christopher Bollyn about one of Flight 93's massive engines being found in the woods. Figuring out what happened with Flight 93 is a nearly impossible task. Eyewitness testimony is stunningly inconsistent. Even figuring out how much of the wreckage was recovered, and where it was stored, is difficult to do. And, of course, there are those disturbing indications that the plane actually landed in Cleveland.

One thing that had long intrigued me was the rumor that the Logan Airport employee who'd checked in the hijackers had later committed suicide. Researcher Chris Graves tracked down a September 10, 2021, article in *Muskogee Phoenix* on retired Logan Airport employee Kay Elliott. On September 11, 2001, Elliott wasn't in her customary position, or otherwise she would have checked the hijackers in. As she explained, "The girl that was in the position that I would have been in had I stayed, she did check in the terrorists, and she ended up committing suicide. She was 21 years old." I had a telephone conversation on June 2, 2022, with Kay Elliott. When I asked her the name of the girl who'd committed suicide, she said she couldn't remember. She said, "I can see her face," but just didn't recall the name. She wasn't sure if the girl took her own life before or after Elliott had retired, which was in 2002. I wondered if she'd seen anything suspicious that day, or had any questions about what happened, but she seemed perfectly satisfied with the official story.

In a precursor to what would be associated with all the widely reported mass casualty events over the next few decades, there were some curious exercise "drills" going on right before September 11, 2001. NORAD's Northeast Air Defense Sector simulated a scenario where a plane was hijacked by terrorists, who intended to blow it up over New York City. This was only two days before 9/11. On September 10, NORAD's Southeast Air Defense Sector practiced a situation where "Cuban" hijackers demanded a plane be taken to New York. Needless to say, it seems a bit too coincidental that NORAD would have such concerns in mind on the two days preceding a real, nearly identical event that shook this country. In fact, when NORAD employees first learned of the hijacked planes on 9/11, they quite reasonably assumed it was all part of the exercise. This "Vigilant Guardian" drill was supposed to continue on the morning of September 11, when the Northeast Air Defense Sector was scheduled to practice another similar hijacking scenario.[117] NORAD learned about planes being hijacked about a half-hour before the second hit on the South Tower of the WTC. And yet survivors recalled being told by their superiors to "go back to work" and that they were in no danger, following the first plane hitting the North Tower. Why didn't NORAD contact WTC officials and have the South Tower evacuated? Why, in fact, didn't NORAD do anything during the hour or so between the first plane hitting the WTC, and the Pentagon being struck? Were they still under the impression this was an exercise? An online report from a witness referred to only as Sabrina, quoted her as saying, "a few minutes later we heard the radio announcer say that a second plane was heading straight for 2 WTC. A few seconds later our building once again swayed back and forth as the as result of the second plane crashing into 2 WTC. I hear now that it was 18 minutes between crashes. In those 18 minutes we heard no sirens, only the ones in the building when there's a fire, there was not one announcement from authorities at the WTC alerting us that there was an emergency situation and that we should evacuate, nothing. If we hadn't turned the radio on, we would not have known what the hell had happened. I was in such a rage."

Just as a "blue ribbon" commission had been formed by President Lyndon B. Johnson following the assassination of JFK, the 9/11 Commission was packed full of the usual Deep State suspects, guaranteeing an imprimatur for the absurd official story. It was chaired by trusted RINO ex-governor of

New Jersey Thomas Kean. Other members included veteran congressional "representatives" Lee Hamilton, Slade Gorton, and Bob Kerrey, former Clinton Deputy Attorney General Jamie Gorelick, and former Watergate chief prosecutor Richard Ben-Veniste, to name just some. The executive director of the 9/11 Commission was Philip Zelikow, who replaced the original choice, Deep State Hall of Famer Henry Kissinger. Even the *New York Times* reacted by editorializing, "It is tempting to wonder if the choice of Mr. Kissinger is not a clever maneuver by the White House to contain an investigation it long opposed."[118] Indeed, it took President George W. Bush an incredible 441 days to finally appoint a commission. Zelikow proved his worth to the corrupt elite to such an extent that he would be named director of the strangely named COVID Commission Planning Group, which was intended to develop into a National COVID Commission.[119] Even Thomas Kean would later admit, "We think the Commission in many ways was set up to fail."[120] As I detailed in *Hidden History,* the 9/11 Commission ignored witnesses with crucial information, like Scott Forbes, who worked in the Twin Towers and wanted to notify them of all the suspicious circumstances he and his group had noticed in the immediate period before September 11, 2001. The 9/11 Commission, like the Warren Commission, relied on an extremely inadequate inquiry by the FBI. Incredibly, the Bureau spent a grand total of *five days* on site at the Pentagon, after initially estimating it would take a month to investigate the crime scene.

In its final report, the National Institute of Standards and Technology (NIST) ludicrously declared that it found "no corroborating evidence for alternative hypotheses suggesting that the WTC towers were brought down by controlled demolition using explosives planted prior to September 11, 2001." Much as the Warren Report "answered" powerful evidence contradicting its lone assassin conclusion by dismissing it as "rumors and speculation," the NIST addressed contradictory evidence in their "frequently asked questions" section. With a presumably straight face, they declared, "There was no evidence (collected by NIST or by . . . the Fire Department of New York) of any blast or explosions in the region below the impact and fire floors as the top building sections began their downward movement upon collapse initiation." A real investigator, retired professor Graeme MacQueen, chronicled the accounts of some *one hundred fifty-six* witnesses reporting exactly such evidence, one hundred thirty-five of them first responders. A 2019 Channel 5 documentary in England reported that more than 118 accounts from firefighters citing explosions were "left out" of the official 9/11 report.[121] In 2007, a group of scientists, an architect, and two 9/11 family members filed a "Request for Correction" with the NIST report, arguing that the plethora of eyewitness testimony regarding explosions had been ignored. The NIST replied by stating, "Taken as a whole, the interviews did not support the contention that explosives played a role in the collapse of the WTC Towers." This, of course, differed significantly from their FAQ response that "There was no evidence (collected by . . . the Fire Department of New York) of any blast or explosions."

In 2014, another one of those sham Establishment commissions was established to "review" the FBI evidence related to the events of 9/11. It was chaired by former Reagan Attorney General Edwin Meese. Even our state-controlled media didn't take the predictable whitewash they produced, in their embarrassingly small 127-page report, seriously. The title of their report, "The FBI: Protecting the Homeland in the 21st Century," revealed their agenda quite clearly. The Review Commission's secrecy extended to the compensation paid to its members. The feisty *Florida Bulldog* fought to obtain access to the commission's records under the Freedom of Information Act, and also sued for the release of some 80,000 pages of classified FBI information.[122] This commission, which appears to have done no investigating at all, was the diluted remnant of a proposed congressional investigation in 2011. To no one's surprise, the commission was generally full of praise for the FBI.

In 2019, a board of fire commissioners from the Franklin Square and Munson Fire District, near Queens, New York, unanimously passed a resolution calling for a new investigation into 9/11, citing "overwhelming evidence" that explosives were planted in all three buildings that collapsed. "It was a mass murder," declared Commissioner Christopher Gioia. "Three thousand people were murdered in cold blood." A few months prior to this little publicized story, a federal lawsuit against the FBI was launched jointly by Architects and Engineers for 9/11 Truth, the Lawyers'

Committee, and 9/11 victims' family members. In clear reference to the bogus "Review" Commission, the suit charged that the Bureau failed to look at evidence not known to the 9/11 Commission, as mandated by Congress. Around the same time, the results of the Building 7 Study (A Structural Reevaluation of the Collapse of World Trade Center 7) by the University of Alaska Fairbanks (UAF) were made public. The study concluded, "fires could not have caused weakening or displacement of structural members capable of initiating any of the hypothetical local failures alleged to have triggered the total collapse of the building, nor could any local failures, even if they had occurred, have triggered a sequence of failures that would have resulted in the observed total collapse."[123]

While most family members of 9/11 victims swallowed the nonsensical official fairy tale, there were some outspoken exceptions. Perhaps the most vocal of these were the so-called "Jersey Girls," widows who asked the kind of questions professional journalists refused to. I tried contacting them while writing this book and spoke twice to the father of 9/11 widow Kristy Breitweiser. Our first conversation, on May 25, 2021, seemed promising; he indicated that he thought she'd be interested in talking with me. When I contacted him again on June 29, 2021, he explained that his daughter was a very private person and suggested that I read her book. I was a bit confounded then, to find Kristy speaking out again on the twentieth anniversary. She and her fellow "Jersey Girls" seemed to have directed most of their skepticism toward Saudi Arabia, which in my view has always been a fallback option for 9/11, like the Mafia was in the JFK assassination. Referring to the remarkable fact that no "terrorist" has been held legally accountable, Breitweiser declared, "Obviously, it's not comforting to know that my government has not prosecuted one co-conspirator of the terrorists. Yes, we have detainees in Guantanamo, some of whom have made self-admissions as to planning the 9/11 attacks, like [Khalid Sheikh Mohammed], and yet, we will never be able to hold them accountable in an open court of law. And so, at the end of the day, what you have is 3,000 homicides in broad daylight, and this country really letting them go unanswered. And that's not something I would have ever thought to see in my country."[124] The British family of 9/11 victim Geoff Campbell has been very vocal recently, publicly stating that the Twin Towers were brought down by explosions. The family submitted a 3,000-page dossier to England's Attorney General Michael Ellis. Older brother Matt Campbell charged, "I believe there has been a cover-up. We have scientifically and forensically backed evidence that the official narrative surrounding the Twin Towers collapse on 9/11 is wrong."[125] A New York circuit court predictably dismissed a lawsuit alleging that Dick Cheney, Donald Rumsfeld, and other Bush administration officials had orchestrated the 9/11 events. The lawyers and their client were charged with "rank, dishonest wielding of power," and fined $15,000 for filing a "frivolous" appeal.[126]

Perhaps the most vocal family member was Ellen Mariani, widow of 9/11 victim Louis Neil Mariani. She launched the Ellen Mariani Legal Defense Fund, and fought for years to find the truth about what happened that day. Mariani refused the money offered to her by the Victims' Compensation Fund created by Congress, and as late as 2012 was still trying to petition the Supreme Court to hear her case. Her former attorney Bruce Leichty revealed, in May 2017, that the outspoken activist had died on October 31, 2015. For unclear reasons, her family had opted to keep her death a secret; there wasn't even an obituary published. "The reasons for Ellen's illness and death remain somewhat mysterious, but neither of the family members I have spoken with suggested that Ellen was the victim of foul play," Leichty stated. Mariani "guarded her age closely," so it isn't known how old she was. One of her last actions was to challenge sanctions imposed on her and Leichty for disclosing the Israeli connections of New York judge Alvin Hellerstein and others she was suing. "Ellen was a hero to many in the 9/11 truth movement for holding out, not taking the easy money from the victims' fund, not accepting the government's narrative, not wanting to settle, continuing to ask questions, and trying to find out what actually happened on 9/11 and why," Leichty stated, and bemoaned "The level of opposition, legal illogic, willful blindness and sophistry she and I encountered from 9/11 defendants and from the media and from the judges we dealt with."[127]

The attitude of the mainstream media toward 9/11 Truth was exemplified by the inexcusable treatment Mariani received at the hands of MSNBC's Joe Scarborough. During a December 2005 appearance on his program *Scarborough Country*, Mariani was asked what she thought of the 9/11 Commission Report. She replied, "1) 9/11 Report is nothing more than obstruction of justice and a continuous cover-up by the Bush administration, 2) 9/11 commissioners were all handpicked by Mr. Bush to obstruct justice and maintain a cover-up of the facts and the evidence, 3) The Bush crime family was behind the attack on America. 4) Let's talk about *Able Danger*, the scripted 9/11 attack on America, the Oklahoma City Bombing, with direct ties to the Philippines and Wachovia Bank and then, let's connect the dots: Oklahoma City, 9/11 & *Able Danger*." At this point, Scarborough cut off Mariani's mike, took the camera off her and refused to permit her to complete her comments. Mariani expressed her feelings about the interview to intrepid internet journalists Stew Webb and Tom Flocco. Webb and Flocco wrote, "An NBC insider told U.S. intelligence yesterday that Scarbororgh was drinking heavily in the afternoon while complaints came in to MSNBC questioning his treatment of Mariani and his reasons for shutting off the widow's microphone just as she was discussing 9/11 evidence never heard before during a national news broadcast in the United States." Mariani went on to tell Webb and Flocco: "I was interviewed in May of 2002 by FOX News Network and their top spin doctor, Bill O'Reilly. O'Reilly and Joe Scarborough are nothing more than little boys doing an adult job as spin doctors for the Bushes; and Americans know this. I finally realize that the major media in America is nothing but a cover-up machine for the Bush-Clinton crime families. On September 11, I not only lost my husband Neil, but I lost my country as well—especially my freedom of speech and my rights in the federal judicial system."

Donald Trump's administration was no more open than Dubya's and Obama's had been. Many had hopes that Trump would say something explosive about 9/11, given his initial comments right after the Twin Towers were hit, in which he expressed his belief that bombs were involved. In 2020, Trump's swampish Attorney General William Barr and intelligence director Richard Grenell blocked the release of documents to victims' families for use in their civil lawsuit against Saudi Arabia. Barr went so far as to claim that merely discussing the justification for keeping the material secret could cause "serious damage" to national security.[128] Alleged 9/11 conspirator Zacarias Moussaoui sued President Donald

Trump, former New York City Mayor Rudy Giuliani and Attorney General William Barr in a series of lawsuits alleging they were covering up the truth about the attacks, which he claimed involved the royal family of Saudi Arabia. Moussaoui was sentenced to life and has complained of abuse and mistreatment by the authorities, including "psychological torture." He remains the only person convicted in connection with the events of 9/11, and one of his complaints was that the ACLU had refused to represent him.[129] Trump's Justice Department was merely following the lead of Obama's which suppressed the same documents, using what the World Socialist Web Site called "extraordinary measures" to side with the government of Saudi Arabia against the families of victims in 2009.[130]

As the twenty-year anniversary of the event approached, filmmaker Spike Lee, for the first time in his career stepping outside a racially obsessed cocoon, was the source of brief controversy over his HBO series *New York Epicenters: 9/11–2021 ½*. Lee initially had the audacity to include a smattering of comments from "conspiracy theorists," but the normally proud and arrogant director quickly backed down in the wake of headlines like Breitbart's "HBO, Spike Lee Spread Debunked 9/11 Conspiracy Theories" and the Washington Examiner's "Spike Lee and HBO Spread Disinformation." The most ridiculous story of all came from the *New York Post,* and was headlined, "Spike Lee's Disgraceful Conspiracy Theories About 9/11—And How Liberal Media Promotes It." Yes, that "liberal" media has certainly always embraced "conspiracy theories." Lee had particularly come under attack for telling the *New York Times* that he doubted the "official explanations" of 9/11. "I mean, I got questions—and I hope that maybe the legacy of this documentary is that Congress holds a hearing, a congressional hearing about 9/11," Lee declared to the nation's newspaper of record. "The amount of heat that it takes to make steel melt, that temperature's not reached. And then the juxtaposition of the way Building 7 fell to the ground—when you put it next to other building collapses that were demolitions, it's like you're looking at the same thing." Lee explained that he was simply trying to "put the information in the movie and let people decide for themselves. I respect the intelligence of the audience." After feeling the familiar Establishment heat, a humbled and contrite Lee explained in a statement, "I'm Back In The Editing Room

And Looking At The Eighth And Final Chapter Of NYC EPICENTERS 9/11➔2021½. I Respectfully Ask You To Hold Your Judgement Until You See The FINAL CUT. I Thank You, Spike Lee."[131]

Salon, which was founded by seeming open-minded skeptic David Talbot, ran an article that smeared all 9/11 researchers as "Truthers," much as all those questioning Barack Obama's very dubious history have been blasted as "Birthers." Talbot was one of the higher-profile figures who deleted me as a friend on Facebook, in a clear response to my many posts questioning the COVID narrative and criticizing the lockdown. Talbot has gone further than most mainstream journalists with his work on the JFK assassination, but like many in the dysfunctional research community, obviously feels the assassinations of the '60s happened in a vacuum, and were not part of any systemic corruption. Lee had initially talked to members of Architects and Engineers for 9/11 Truth. Salon dismissed them by saying, "This group pushes the debunked theory that the World Trade Center towers were destroyed not by al-Qaeda, but a controlled demolition." This Snopes-centric reliance on summarily declaring something has been "debunked" never includes any evidence of the supposed debunking. It basically boils down to: the state-controlled media says it's a "conspiracy theory," and thus it's been "debunked." As Salon notes, "Media critics who received the docuseries to screen in advance have objected to how the final episode (which has now been pulled from review consideration) features extensive interviews with conspiracy theorists alongside interviews with experts who have researched 9/11 and its impacts for years including Shyam Sunder, who researched the attacks for the National Institute of Standards and Technology." So apologist lackeys are respectable "researchers," but the genuinely expert architects and engineers, who most assuredly have done extensive research, are crudely banished from polite society. The article goes on to declare, "Conspiracy theories about the truth about 9/11, some of which wrong-headedly assert the terror attack was an 'inside job' carried out by the Bush administration, are often given the meme treatment or laughed off on social media. But experts have concerningly linked the success of 9/11 theories through the years to the success of some of the most dangerous conspiracy theories that have poisoned our politics, today." Catch the reference to "experts," which is all that's needed to persuade most people, just as quotes from anonymous "authorities" serve as "journalism" in local and national news. The story then makes the predictable link between 9/11 "Truthers" and advocates of QAnon.[132] Slate's Jeremy Stahl went even further, stating that Lee including alternative views in his documentary was tantamount to "presenting Covid-19 vaccine skeptics in a debate alongside Anthony Fauci, or Holocaust deniers alongside the Simon Wiesenthal Center, or a clique of climate change skeptics alongside the authors of the United Nations IPCC report."[133]

With that particular small speed bump out of the way, the twentieth anniversary of 9/11 was left free to revolve around the standard emotional disinformation that has become the trademark of American "journalism." As has been the case since September 11, 2001, not a single hint that there are any doubts about the official narrative was permitted to be broadcast over any television network. As unified as the Oswald-did-it mantra has always been in the mainstream media, critics like Mark Lane at least appeared occasionally on television talk shows and documentaries about the assassination. No "inside job" advocate, however, has ever been allowed to play in our state–controlled media's reindeer games. People like me made the rounds of the alternative circuits that were interested, and advocated for the truth on the platforms that were available to us. The "woke" forces in total control of America succeeded in "canceling" any dissenting views about 9/11, as they have done with political dissent in general. "Building 7" had long been a dirty word to all network executives. In a hit piece on Jesse Ventura's assertions that the Bush administration was complicit in some way for the events of 9/11, Jeffrey Scott Shapiro of Fox News inadvertently provided "Truthers" with more solid evidence of that "inside job." Shapiro stated, "Governor Ventura and many 9/11 'Truthers' allege that government explosives caused the afternoon collapse of Building 7. This is false. I know this because I remember watching all 47 stories of Building 7 suddenly and silently crumble before my eyes. Shortly before the building collapsed, several NYPD officers and Con-Edison workers told me that Larry Silverstein, the property developer of One World Financial Center was on the phone with his insurance carrier to see if they would authorize the controlled demolition of the building—since its foundation was already unstable and expected to fall." In a monumental display of delusion, Shapiro contended this was evidence that Silverstein, who also was notably quoted as urging they "pull" Building 7 ("pull" is industry parlance for controlled demolition), was not complicit here.[134] It was certainly a fortuitous turn of events for Silverstein (still alive at age ninety at the time of this writing), who would be awarded some $4.6 billion in insurance payments for the lost structure.[135] It was largely ignored, and never explained, why officers trying to enter Building 7, which was on fire, found the entrance door locked.[136]

The man who was nominally in charge that day, George W. Bush, continued the restoration of his character and reputation among the court historians, which began with his criticism of Donald Trump. In a speech that was received to universal Establishment acclaim, delivered from Shanksville, Pennsylvania, site of the Flight 93 crash, Bush declared, "There is little cultural overlap between violent extremists abroad and violent extremists at home. But in their disdain for pluralism, in their disregard for human life, in their determination to defile national symbols, they are children of the same foul spirit." Bush had joined in the mob attack on protesters gathered in Washington, D.C. to "stop the fraud" in the 2020 election on January 6, 2021, which the Establishment laughably mischaracterized as an "insurrection," when he said in March that it made him "sick to my stomach . . . to see our nation's Capitol being stormed by hostile forces."[137] President Joe Biden was among the many Establishment voices who praised Dubya's speech. "George W. Bush is right—we must always remain vigilant against terrorist extremists both at home and abroad. And we cannot rest until all of Trump's traitorous, insurrectionist foot soldiers face justice," tweeted the Democratic Coalition. Certified lunatic "journalist" Keith Olbermann tweeted, "Even George W. Bush now recognizes Trump, his supporters and those who directly participated in the 1/6 Coup attempt are terrorists—surely as the 9/11 ones were."[138]

On the ten-year anniversary of 9/11, the *Empire Strikes Black* blog provided more pertinent comments than we were likely to ever find from any professional "journalist." "'Never Question' is the true underlying meaning of this emotive, Orwellian motto that has been seared into the

American psyche like brands on the hides of cattle," the editor of the blog wrote.

> Rational thought has been obliterated by emotion, fear, and pseudo-patriotic jingoism. The 'Never Forget' mantra, and the flags and plaques in Manhattan attest to the exceptionalism of 'American suffering', a concept so disingenuous it makes any honest, aware person sick to their stomach. Every shade of human life, from America to Afghanistan, and from Iraq to Libya, is precious. But the tears shed at Ground Zero are not rooted in universal compassion; they are rooted in a grotesque sense of false victimhood and superiority, and a resounding ignorance of the most important event of this generation. . . . Alas, it is important that Americans be distracted. They must be kept in an emotional haze, deterred from questioning the official account, because even the most cursory inspection exposes it for the monstrous lie that it is. The official narrative is so bizarre and fantastical, it is an absolute wonder that so many fail to question it. The most basic, central elements of the story stretch even the most childish imagination. The laws of physics, immutable as they are, are the arch-enemy of this fantasy. . . . Aside from the inexplicable failure of America's air defenses and the Pentagon's unrivalled military defense system, what are the chances of these inept and inexperienced amateurs stepping into the cockpits of gargantuan, advanced commercial jet aircraft for the *first time*, only to slam at high speed into their respective targets with clinical precision? . . . Ten years on and millions are dead, maimed, orphaned, displaced, tortured, humiliated, and subjugated as a direct result of the Zionist 'War on Terror.' We all must stand up and be counted, there really are no excuses for continuing to buy this abominable lie."

On the fifteenth anniversary of 9/11, the conclusions of a study done by physicists were published in the *European Scientific Journal*. "It bears repeating that fires have never caused the total collapse of a steel-framed high-rise before or since 9/11. Did we witness an unprecedented event three separate times on September 11, 2001? The NIST reports, which attempted to support that unlikely conclusion, fail to persuade a growing number of architects, engineers, and scientists. Instead, the evidence points overwhelmingly to the conclusion that all three buildings were destroyed by controlled demolition. Given the far-reaching implications, it is morally imperative that this hypothesis be the subject of a truly scientific and impartial investigation by responsible authorities." The report stated, and went on to note, "Videos show that the upper section of each tower disintegrated within the first four seconds of collapse. After that point, not a single video shows the upper sections that purportedly descended all the way to the ground before being crushed. Videos and photographs also show numerous high-velocity bursts of debris being ejected from point-like sources. . . . NIST also provides no explanation for the midair pulverization of most of the towers' concrete, the near-total dismemberment of their steel frames, or the ejection of those materials up to 150 meters in all directions. NIST sidesteps the well-documented presence of molten metal throughout the debris field and asserts that the orange molten metal seen pouring out of WTC 2 for the seven minutes before its collapse was aluminum from the aircraft combined with organic materials. Yet experiments have shown that molten aluminum, even when mixed with organic materials, has a silvery appearance—thus suggesting that the orange molten metal was instead emanating from a thermite reaction being used to weaken the structure. Meanwhile, unreacted nano-thermitic material has since been discovered in multiple independent WTC dust samples."

Even in alternative media, there are curious cases like Abby Martin, the former Russia Today host who has done some good work. Martin started her own 9/11 "Truther" group in San Diego in 2008, but on March 22, 2014, she told the Associated Press that she no longer believed 9/11 was an "inside job." As I have told many converts to lone nutterism in the JFK assassination, this is simply not believable. It is not possible to be aware of the truth, and the extent of the corruption and cover-up, and somehow revert back to such a naïve state. It is tantamount to regaining one's virginity. Martin deleted me as a friend on Facebook in the aftermath of the Sandy Hook event, obviously offended by my questions. Seemingly the most rational voice in the mainstream media, Tucker Carlson, has no patience for anyone doubting the official 9/11 story. At least he's not as bad as his psychotic predecessor on Fox News, Bill O'Reilly, who angrily attacked Jeremy Glick, whose father died in the 9/11 attacks, during a 2003 on-air interview. When Glick expressed skepticism about the official narrative, O'Reilly called his views "a load of crap," became increasingly unhinged and yelled at him to "Shut up!" Losing all control, O'Reilly screamed, "Cut his mic. I'm not going to dress you down anymore, out of respect for your father." Glick would claim that "The executive producer and the assistant encouraged me to leave the building because they were, quote, concerned that if O'Reilly ran into me in the hallway, he would end up in jail." O'Reilly would continue to assail Glick's character on subsequent shows, telling his audience a year later, that Glick was "a coward as well as a propagandist" for refusing to "come on the [*O'Reilly Factor*] program."[139]

The record is a bit confusing regarding Jeremy Glick. Evidently, one of the heroes of Flight 93, which crashed or was shot down in Pennsylvania, was also named Jeremy Glick. Jeremy Glick is not the most common name, so this is just another strange tidbit in the record. This Glick was a former national judo champion. In one of those dubious, emotional phone calls that don't appear to have been possible at the time, Glick's mother-in-law is supposed to have urged his wife Lyz to, "Make him, make him brave." Glick told them the men had voted to overpower the hijackers, something the men on the other flights incomprehensibly had never thought to do. "I think you need to do it," said Lyz. "You're strong, you're brave. I love you." Lyz Glick is purported to have kept the phone connection with her husband on for over two hours, with the most fantastic claim being, "The hijackers that were outside the cockpit, they took them down. They broke through the cockpit door. Jeremy dispatched one of the hijackers with a judo chop to the neck, you could hear his windpipe being destroyed," in the words of his uncle, Tom Crowley.[140] This was less believable than the claims made that the hijackers on Flight 93 can be heard yelling "Allah is the greatest!" on the cockpit recorder.

With the endless "War on Terror" that was triggered by the factually incorrect narrative of 9/11, America crossed yet another moral line in the sand. And the primary target of that "war" was chosen cavalierly. Bush's former head of counterterrorism Richard Clarke told ABC News,

"Well, Don Rumsfeld said—when we talked about bombing the al-Qaeda infrastructure in Afghanistan, he said, 'There are no good targets in Afghanistan; let's bomb Iraq.' And we said, 'But Iraq had nothing to do with this,' and that didn't seem to make much difference."[141] The CIA and American military engaged in gleeful torture of dubiously termed "terrorist" suspects at Cuba's Guantanamo Bay facility. Waterboarding was common there, along with the horrific sounding "rectal feeding," and plenty of conventional beatings. Established in 2002, "Gitmo" is contained within a US naval base. It routinely holds at least dozens of prisoners who haven't been charged with any crime and aren't scheduled to be brought to trial. Barack Obama famously promised to close the prison, but like every other politician quickly forgot about it once he entered office. Less well known are similar, secret sites around the world, in places like Iraq, Lithuania, Afghanistan, Thailand, Romania, and Poland, where the United States treats uncharged detainees in a similarly brutal manner. In 2014, a heavily redacted report was released, detailing egregious abuses. Afghanistan's "Detention Site Cobalt" was described as a medieval-style "dungeon," which remained dark twenty-four hours a day. Blasting music to keep detainees awake was common (something we saw at both Ruby Ridge and Waco), and again those ghastly "rectal feedings" were cited.[142] The shameful abuse at Iraq's Abu Ghraib was briefly a source of controversy for most Americans, but evidently the naked males with various objects stuck up their rectums continue to suffer at the hands of our government. As they say, freedom isn't free.

I seem to be one of the few who remember journalist Seymour Hersh's contention that there are videos that exist of US soldiers raping young Iraqi boys in front of their screaming mothers. Hersh acted as if these tapes would become public, but they have yet to be produced. I had a brief phone conversation with Seymour Hersh on May 26, 2021. He told me he "better not talk," and referred me to his upcoming book. Quoted in some big media outlets was the testimony of Abu Ghraib detainee Kasim Hilas, who told military investigators, "I saw [blacked out], who was wearing the military uniform putting his dick in the little kid's ass. I couldn't see the face of the kid because his face wasn't in front of the door. And the female soldier was taking pictures." The United

States contends that military prisons in Afghanistan are not subject to Geneva Convention jurisdiction because those they define as terrorists are "unlawful combatants."[143] The US military had very little regard for children well before 9/11 precipitated such terrible abuses at these facilities; UNICEF estimated that over 500,000 children died during the Gulf "War." As Hersh stated publicly in 2004, "The women were passing messages out saying 'Please come and kill me, because of what's happened' and basically what happened is that those women who were arrested with young boys, children in cases that have been recorded. The boys were sodomized with the cameras rolling. And the worst above all of that is the soundtrack of the boys shrieking that your government has. They are in total terror. It's going to come out."[144]

The unconstitutional monstrosity that is the Department of Homeland Security was created in the wake of 9/11, with only nine Democratic Senators, including Edward Kennedy and Russ Feingold (the only Senator to vote against implementing the Patriot Act) opposing it. In the House, the measure passed by a 295–132 vote. Nancy Pelosi reacted in her typically nonsensical way, remarking, "I have some concerns about the bill. That doesn't mean I have concerns about the idea. We all know we want a Department of Homeland Security."[145] When the House voted to reauthorize Homeland Security in 2017, the vote was even more lopsided, at 386–41.[146] Homeland Security also begot the awful Transportation Security Administration (TSA), which has harassed the elderly, small children, and other innocent travelers, without apprehending a single "terrorist." Just as the CIA, FBI, and other law enforcement agencies had long infiltrated "extremist" organizations on both ends of the political spectrum, Homeland Security quickly followed suit. Their Red Cell office hired "people from outside their insular bureaucracies to arrive at fresh insights." Those "fresh insights" are state propaganda in non-Orwellian terms, designed to manipulate any potential opposition. One of those who provided "terrorism ideas" to Homeland Security was widely publicized "conspiracy" author Brad Meltzer, who as I noted in my book *Hidden History,* in reality serves to debunk any and all "conspiracy theories." Meltzer explained, "Sometimes I was paired with a psychologist or a philosopher. Sometimes I was contacted alone, via email, and given a target to attack. I'm not allowed to tell you what the targets were. Or where they were. But I can say that we'd destroy major cities like my hometown, New York. In minutes. And when I went home at night, I felt horrified, because I saw how easy it was to kill us."[147] Was the aforementioned fanciful note found in the stomach of a Flight 77 victim part of his work with Homeland Security?

The "fact-checkers" who control debate now on all large social media platforms will reflexively "correct" any attempt at spreading the truth about the very clear "inside job" that took place on September 11, 2001. An early, extreme example of this Orwellian censorship took place in 2012. A former Marine wrote some comments about 9/11 on Facebook and made reference to a "revolution." In typical 'Murrican overkill, agents from the FBI, Secret Service, and local Chesterfield County Police visited Brandon Raub's home, and questioned him about the posts. He was summarily handcuffed and taken to John Randolph Psychiatric Hospital in Hopewell, Virginia. Officers told his mother the arrest was for "assaulting an officer," and for making "terrorist" threats. Both the FBI and local police blamed the other for the arrest. Raub had also, quite reasonably, called our government "evil."[148] Fortunately, a Virginia judge ordered Raub to be released from the institution, and in 2013 the former Marine sued the agencies involved for violating his constitutional rights.[149]

As the JFK assassination was to Baby Boomers, 9/11 was to Millennials and Gen-Xers. Sources report varying numbers in terms of how the public feels about the 9/11 official narrative. The most encouraging poll I've found, from 2016, showed that 54.3 percent of Americans believe the government is concealing information about the attacks on 9/11. In reporting what were clearly unwelcome results, "experts" claimed that those most likely to believe "conspiracy theories" are White Christian Republicans.[150] In other words, the very people that are most persistently demonized by the same media. One would think that a perspective shared by a majority of Americans ought to be represented in the news coverage of 9/11. But present-day Americans receive about as much "representation" from television networks as they do from their elected officials. While 9/11 caused many people, especially the young, to become "awake," clearly it didn't wake up enough Americans.

The Body Count Marches On

No, I'm not planning to commit suicide. I'm planning on going into court and defending myself vigorously and exposing the government."

—"DC Madam" Deborah Jeane Palfrey[151]

Deborah Jeane Palfrey was hardly the only witness touched by the corrupt criminals who misrule us, to publicly vow that they wouldn't kill themselves, and then have their deaths attributed to suicide. The building manager of the Florida condo where Palfrey lived (who requested anonymity) told a local news channel that "Jean Palfrey was a class act. She wore very good clothes. She was well educated. Her way out of this world certainly would not have been in an aluminum shed attached to a mobile home in Tarpon Springs, Florida. She insinuated that there is a contract out for her and I fully believe they succeeded." On at least four occasions, including twice on the Alex Jones Show, Palfrey declared that she would never kill herself. Yet mainstream media accounts invariably reported that she'd been suicidal, despite her own mother refuting that notion. Our old friend Dan Moldea was on hand to state, "She wasn't going to jail, she told me that very clearly. She told me she would commit suicide."[152] She had unwisely contracted with Moldea to help her write a book. Palfrey was facing the prospect of as much as fifty-five years behind bars, for her part in running a prostitution ring that serviced some of Washington, D.C.'s most powerful figures. None of those powerful figures would have been in danger of facing time behind bars, even if Palfrey hadn't died on May 1, 2008. These unnatural deaths serve to send a clear message, a warning to others.

It sometimes really does appear as if there is some kind of Naysayer Hit Squad, perhaps run out of one of our intelligence agencies (whose budgets, after all, remain top secret), to eliminate whistleblowers and inconvenient witnesses. In 2009, investigative journalist Seymour Hersh spoke about a covert operation he termed an "executive assassination ring."[153] We know that organized crime has put out "hits" on their mob opponents for at least a century. Most of us don't want to face the reality that our leaders are also engaged in organized crime, except their enemies aren't rival gang leaders. They are often average citizens, who "know too much." And unlike mafia dons, our leaders don't even have any twisted principles.

Maverick politician Dennis Kucinich, the onetime "Boy Mayor" of Cleveland who became an Ohio congressman frequently clashing with the Democratic Party hierarchy, lost two family members under strange circumstances. Dennis's brother Perry, who had notably robbed a bank decades earlier, was found dead in his apartment on December 19, 2007. Authorities helpfully concluded that there were no signs of foul play. Remarkably, a year later, Kucinich's forty-eight-year-old sister Beth Ann died in a Cleveland Veterans Hospital from "acute respiratory distress syndrome."[154] The timing here is more than interesting. Dennis Kucinich had participated in a conference call with 911Truth.org a few months before his sister's death, on the same day he introduced an article of impeachment against George W. Bush.[155] In 2007, Kucinich told New Mexico US Senate candidate Leland Lehrman and others that he was in favor of a new "full investigation" of 9/11.[156] Kucinich, one of the most populist-minded representatives this country has had in the past seventy-five years, notably introduced a House Resolution on July 1, 2001, to establish a new federal Department of Peace. Robert F. Kennedy Jr. selected Kucinich as his campaign manager when he announced his presidential run.

Jeremy Crocker was looking deeply into the TWA Flight 800 incident. The sixty-two-year-old mysteriously vanished on December 9, 1996, five days after giving an explosive interview on *The Peter Ford Show*. He was last seen, in fitting fashion, conducting research at the downtown, central branch of the Los Angeles Library. Crocker's grown sons strongly suspected that his disappearance was connected to his research. Ford was quoted as saying, "The dark side theory would be that he was taken out. That someone, somewhere felt he was a threat."[157] Among the firsthand research Crocker conducted were interviews with baggage handlers at Los Angeles International Airport and Ontario Airport. A right-wing talk show host claimed to have received mail from Crocker, which was postmarked December 10, after he vanished. In 2000, then–Palm Springs Police Chief Lee Weigel informed the City Council that Crocker's missing-persons case had been closed. According to Weigel, the Los Angeles

County Sheriff's Department had contacted Crocker and found he left voluntarily. However, the Los Angeles County Sheriff's Department would subsequently claim to have no record of any contact with Crocker. In what appears to have been the last update on the case in the press, we learned that Crocker was a bit of an eccentric, eating raw liver and once arrested for protesting in Palm Springs during a visit from President Reagan.[158]

Much as I recounted the series of suspicious deaths of scientists in my book *Hidden History*, there was a similar series of strange deaths of holistic doctors. An incredible eight such deaths took place between June 19 and July 23, 2015, alone. Dr. Jeff Bradstreet, a prominent researcher into autism, was shot and killed shortly after the FDA raided his clinic. His body was found in a river, and his death was predictably ruled a suicide. The Bradstreet family promised on their Facebook page to "get to the bottom of this."[159] Thirty-three-year-old, physically fit Dr. Baron Holt died "while on a trip to Jacksonville, Florida," on Father's Day, June 21, 2015. There don't seem to be any further details on how he died, nor was there a cause of death listed. Incredibly, on that same Father's Day, sixty-seven-year-old Bruce Hedendal was found dead in his car in Boca Raton, Florida. He held a PhD from Harvard in nutrition, and friends described him as being "very healthy." Forty-six-year-old holistic doctor Teresa Ann Sievers was murdered on June 29, 2015, again in Florida. Sievers had been visiting her sister in Connecticut, along with her husband and children, but for undisclosed reasons had flown home alone, and let her husband know she'd arrived safely.[160] The crime was eventually attributed to a Hollywoodish plot by her husband to hire his friend and lookalike to murder his wife.[161] Holistic oncologist Dr. Mitch Gaynor's body was found, Clinton-style, in the woods near his home.[162] All told, Health Nut News tabulated the deaths of more than 100 holistic physicians. A more recent example was the November 2021 murder-suicide of chiropractor John Kolonich, who was accused of shooting himself after stabbing his wife, Melissa.[163] I have detailed some of the many raids on health stores and holistic clinics in the past by an out-of-control FDA in previous books.

One belated victim of the Obama Body Count was Department of Homeland Security whistleblower Philip Haney. Haney was found shot to death near his vehicle in California, on February 21, 2020. He was the author of the 2016 book *See Something, Say Nothing: A Homeland Security Officer Exposes the Government's Submission to Jihad.* Haney's gunshot wound was unsurprisingly declared to be self-inflicted. "My friend Phil Haney was found shot yesterday in CA. I had lunch with him a month ago. He warned something could happen to him. He was to get married in a month. It will be falsely called a suicide." Declared Haney's close friend, radio host and author Jan Markell.[164]

The BP oil spill, which I covered in detail in *Hidden History,* would spawn a series of suspicious deaths. It is shocking that not a single "climate change activist" even mentions BP, the greatest ecological disaster in modern history. James Patrick Black, an incident commander for BP's Gulf of Mexico oil spill response team, died on November 23, 2010, in a small plane crash. That same month, Dr. Jeffrey Gardner, who'd been investigating unexplained bird deaths associated with the oil spill, closed his practice and disappeared. Other than a video covering his work that aired on a local Fox station, the only references to him are on blogs. There is no updated information about him. Dr. Thomas B. Manton, former President and CEO of the International Oil Spill Control Corporation, was highly critical of the lack of accountability for the Gulf oil spill. He was imprisoned on unknown charges and died on January 19, 2011, after being assaulted at Florida's Liberty Correctional Facility.[165] Roger Grooters, bicycling cross country to raise awareness about the Gulf oil disaster, was struck and killed by a truck on October 6, 2010. Matthew Simmons, member of the National Petroleum Council and the Council on Foreign Relations, was the only real "insider" to speak out publicly against the officials responsible for the oil spill. On August 8, 2010, he was found dead in his hot tub, of "accidental drowning."[166] On October 23, 2011, BP pilot George Wainwright was killed in a freak shark attack. Gulf truth activist Tucker Mendoza was shot four times through the door of his home on April 2, 2011, but survived. These are just a sampling of silenced Gulf oil spill whistleblowers.

Michael Ruppert was a former LAPD officer who became a well-known personality in the conspiracy world. He claimed that his work as a police officer had left him with "combat fatigue." Ruppert focused on things like CIA involvement in drug trafficking, the Bush administration's complicity in 9/11, and his speculation regarding the upcoming collapse of the human race. During a heated community conference held to address the charges of journalist Gary Webb, who alleged that the CIA was behind the shipment of crack cocaine into the inner cities, Ruppert told CIA director John Deutch, during the Q and A session, "I will tell you, Director Deutch, emphatically and without equivocation that the agency has dealt drugs throughout this country for a long time." On April 13, 2014, Ruppert, like Gary Webb before him, allegedly shot himself in the head.

One death in the endless Clinton Body Count that I inadvertently left out of *Hidden History* was that of Clinton's former business partner Jim McDougal, a central figure in the Whitewater scandal. McDougal was serving a three-and-a-half-year sentence for fraud charges and had purportedly proclaimed he was "sick and tired of lying" and admitted he was "trying to protect" Bill Clinton. As a newspaper report noted at the time of McDougal's death in prison on March 8, 1998, his dying was "a blow" to independent counsel Kenneth Starr's case against the Clintons. The fifty-eight-year-old McDougal supposedly suffered from heart disease and had predicted he wouldn't live to make it out of prison.[167] McDougal's wife Susan remained loyal to the Clintons, and was rewarded with a full pardon on Clinton's last day in office.

I recounted the tragic and highly suspicious death of journalist Danny Casolaro in *Hidden History.* Casolaro was one of the most notable entries in the Bush Body Count; he was found dead in a West Virginia hotel bathroom on August 10, 1991. Casolaro had famously been investigating what he called "the Octopus" of crimes and scandals associated with the administration of George H. W. Bush. Researcher Chris Graves alerted me to the fact that Casolaro's cousin Dominic Orlando had written a play provocatively titled "Danny Casolaro Died for You." I contacted his representative, Adam Peck, about interviewing him. To my shock, Peck replied in a June 4, 2022, email that, "I'm saddened to report that Dominic passed away several months ago after a short illness. He would have been extremely interested in participating as this project was near and dear to him and we were in the process of shopping the play as a feature film.

Just LMK if there's anything further I can do for you." When I responded incredulously and mentioned my "Spidey-sense" being activated, Peck wrote back, "It was cancer actually but Dominic 100% would very much appreciate your suspicion given the subject matter at hand!"

CHAPTER ELEVEN

CONCLUSION BUT NOT THE END: PAVING THE WAY FOR THE NEXT VOLUME OF HIDDEN HISTORY

I am reluctant to criticize authorities. My interpretation of when they need to be [criticized] and somebody else's might be different . . . how easy it is to take potshots from the outside. . . .

—CBS correspondent and former FBI and NYPD official John Miller[1]

During the course of writing this book, thanks largely to the efforts of researchers Chris Graves and Peter Secosh, whom I mentioned in the Introduction and several times throughout this book, I accumulated so much information that it soon became apparent it would have to be divided into two separate books. Thus, while Donald Trump and a few more current events were touched upon in this work, the events beginning in 2015 or so will be covered in detail in the next volume in what has become a series of books chronicling what I call "hidden history." I even considered doing an entire volume on Trump, using the clever title *Right on Q,* which was suggested by my good friend and producer Tony Arterburn, but opted to use him as a key foundation for the next book.

I spoke with a woman who has become a friend on December 7, 2021. She requested to remain anonymous. Her story illustrated just how bad our political "representatives" really are. She worked in Congress for twenty-three years. She described Senator Arlen Spector, whose parking space was across from hers in the lot, as being such a drunk that he routinely vomited in the morning when he arrived at work. She said he was "not a nice person, belligerent" and noted "I always suspected Spector was an alcoholic because he'd sold himself out." Bob Dole came off perhaps even worse, as "one of the meanest, nastiest, rottenest people I have met—he'd have to be in the top five." She said she'd periodically hear "screaming, like someone was being hurt" coming from Dole's office. She once witnessed him twisting his secretary's arm behind her back and then shoving her against the wall, over a minor mistake. Dole actually broke her arm in two places. She declared, "Nobody liked Bob Dole—not even his family." She specified that his second wife Elizabeth hated him, and daughter Robin wouldn't speak to him. Of great interest was what she called the nefarious "Good Old Boys Club," and she recounted how they would leave an ominous brown bag on the desk of someone who'd crossed them. This "Brown Bag" ritual was reserved exclusively for members of Congress. She claimed that Paul Wellstone was "brown bagged" before his fatal plane crash. According to her, Sonny Bono got a "brown bag" too, before his highly suspicious January 5, 1998, death while skiing. She called Bono's wife "a piece of work." She said, "the Brown Bag is universally known among staff," but it never left Capitol Hill, so no one else knew about it. She worked for John Glenn and Peter Rodino, both of whom she "dearly loved." She described Ted Kennedy as "going after anything with a pulse," and characterized him as very entitled. She was "friends, bordering on good friends" with Rosey Grier. She met Grier while working on the presidential campaign of Edmund Muskie, whom she also loved. She depicted George McGovern as a very nice man, and said he tried to recruit her to his staff while eating dinner with her. She recalled one dinner out with Grier, when two men approached the table and one asked, "Why did you let them kill Robert F. Kennedy?" Grier got up, and beat both men to a bloody pulp. She didn't paint a pretty picture of Ethel Kennedy, claiming that she'd bring her dogs into the Capitol, where they'd predictably relieve themselves. She'd then snarl at the closest Capitol employee to "get on your hands and knees and clean it up." She stated that you could always get a job with Strom Thurmond or John McCain because of the high turnover—they treated people terribly and were nasty people. She reinforced my prejudices about Congress.

Hidden History is everywhere. I know I haven't come close to covering it adequately in what is presently three, and will eventually be at least four, volumes. Especially now with a great volunteer research staff, I discover previously unknown facts every day. Bits of history that have been shoved down the memory hole. Peter Secosh alone was responsible for most of the research about the hidden history from the 1800s in this book, as well as the sections on Theodore Roosevelt, Woodrow Wilson, Franklin Roosevelt, and Joe McCarthy. Chris Graves was prolific in ferreting out information, particularly about 9/11, the death of JFK Jr., and Oklahoma City. I've been researching these subjects for close to fifty years now, and I learned plenty of things I didn't know before while writing this book. I'm sure readers who haven't done such extensive research will find lots of new information here.

It's more important now than ever to know the truth about our past. As Shakespeare observed, what's past is prologue. We didn't arrive at the disastrous state we find ourselves in today by accident. The wrong people have seemingly almost always been in charge, since the second revolution of the 1860s, which transformed this country into something quite different than that envisioned by the Founders. The Consent of the Governed was the primary principle for which the War of Independence was fought. Abraham Lincoln, by waging a bloody war to keep those who no longer consented in what was supposed to be a voluntary union, demolished all that. The message then, and ever since, has been: *your consent is not necessary.*

The Union Army's "total war" strategy set the precedent for the horrors to come in the Philippines, Haiti, Dresden, Hiroshima, Nagasaki, Vietnam, Afghanistan, Iraq, and other places. Our troops have been "scorching the earth" ever since Sherman terrorized the women and children of Georgia. Not enough good people spoke up when the Supreme Court upheld Woodrow Wilson's unconstitutional jailing of World War I protesters. As a result, we were rewarded with the first asterisk on free speech; the "yelling fire in a crowded theater" exception. As I've noted many times, the World War I protesters were not yelling fire in a crowded theater. Lincoln's unconstitutional imprisonment of Northern citizens who opposed him, without trial or even charges, paved the way for FDR's forced incarceration of Japanese, German, and Italian Americans in this nation. And even though the writ of habeas corpus was never suspended, as it was under Lincoln, the January 6 political prisoners who've been held unconstitutionally behind bars for well over two years might as well have been northern protesters during the Civil War. Unconstitutional roadblocks led inexorably to the contact tracers of the COVID narrative. No-knock police SWAT raids violate the Fourth Amendment if anything does, yet again no one protests. Sinning by silence, I think they call it.

I've been ranting about the abuses of authorities since I was a teenager in the mid-1970s. Few listened then, and few listen now. If you don't object to the concept of "hate speech," or "misinformation," then you've allowed tyrants to subvert the First Amendment. These Orwellian terms are incompatible with free speech. They are becoming institutionalized because most Americans just rolled over, as they have each and every time our civil liberties have been curtailed. Thomas Jefferson, George Mason, Patrick Henry, Thomas Paine, and the other Founders would be appalled at the dangerous, draconian mess we've allowed horrific leaders to construct. It happened gradually, like the well-known boiling frog analogy. The Patriot Act, passed in response to the absurd 9/11 fairy tale, has no place in a free society. We are obviously no longer a free society.

"Many people, especially ignorant people, want to punish you for speaking the truth," Mahatma Gandhi said. Jefferson reminded us, "No people can be both ignorant and free." It is absolutely undeniable that most of present-day America is woefully ignorant. In his classic book *The Devil's Dictionary*, Ambrose Bierce defined history as "An account, mostly false, of events, mostly unimportant, which are brought about by rulers, mostly knaves, and soldiers, mostly fools." He certainly got the "mostly false" part right. And no one can deny that soldiers are doing fool's work, however noble may be their intentions. Denying that makes senseless wars possible. More people need to have the perspective of my friend Cindy Sheehan, who won't be swayed by medals or heroic proclamations regarding her late son Casey.

As I noted earlier, if the court historians were doing their job, there would be no market for books like this, and no reason to write them in the first place. As long as they continue their fables, of Oswald and crazed Arab terrorists and weapons of mass destruction and live shooter drills, someone has to expose the lies. The role of a historian should be, to quote the German historian Ranke, "to present the past as it was." The court historians that control all educational discourse in this country do exactly the opposite. They frame historical events and personalities through the prism of today's increasingly mad "woke" world.

My Hidden History books are an attempt to counter the myths and propaganda of the court historians, who have the same agenda every television network has. Every person I can wake up, to the corruption all around them, represents another tiny ripple of hope. As Robert F. Kennedy reminded us in his greatest speech, "Each time a man stands up for an ideal, or acts to improve the lot of others, or strikes out against injustice, he sends forth a tiny ripple of hope, and crossing each other from a million different centers of energy and daring those ripples build a current which can sweep down the mightiest walls of oppression and resistance."

SELECTED BIBLIOGRAPHY

Allen, Gary, with Abraham, Larry, *None Dare Call It Conspiracy,* California, Concord Press, 1972.

Beito, David T., *The New Deal's War on the Bill of Rights,* Oakland, Independent Institute, 2023.

Butler, Smedley, *War Is a Racket,* New York, Round Table Press Inc., 1935.

Canfield, Michael, and Weberman, Alan J., *Coup D'etat: The CIA and the Assassination of John F. Kennedy,* University of Michigan, 1975.

Carr, William Guy, *Pawns in the Game*, Hollywood, Angriff Press, 1958.

DeCamp, John, *The Franklin Cover-Up*, Lincoln, NE: AWT, Inc., 1996.

DiLorenzo, Thomas J., *The Real Lincoln, A New Look at Abraham Lincoln, His Agenda, and an Unnecessary War,* New York, Crown Forum, 2002.

Evans, Medford, *The Assassination of Joe McCarthy,* Massachusetts, Western Islands, 1970.

Farrell, Joseph P., *McCarthy, Monmouth, and the Deep State,* Lulu Books, 2019.

Farrell, Joseph P., *McCarthy, Marshall, and the Other International: Roosevelt, Trotsky, Stalin, and America's Progressivist Deep State,* Lulu Books, 2020.

Griffin, G. Edward, *The Creature from Jekyll Island,* New York, American Media, Inc., 1994.

Herman, Arthur, *Joseph McCarthy: Reexamining the Life and Legacy of America's Most Hated Senator,* New York, Free Press, 1999.

Hoffman, David, *The Oklahoma City Bombing and the Politics of Terror,* Washington, Feral House, 1998.

Jeffries, Donald, *Hidden History: An Expose of Modern Crimes, Conspiracies, and Cover-Ups in American Politics,* New York, Skyhorse Publishing, 2014.

Jeffries, Donald, *Crimes and Cover-Ups in American Politics: 1776–1963*, New York, Skyhorse Publishing, 2019.

Law, William Matson, *In the Eye of History: Disclosures in the JFK Assassination Medical Evidence,* Oregon, Trine Day, 2015.

Lowen, James W., *Lies My Teacher Told Me: Everything Your American History Textbook Got Wrong,* New York, The New Press, 1995.

Marrs, Jim, *Crossfire: The Plot That Killed Kennedy,* New York, Carroll & Graf, 1989.

Marrs, Jim, *Rule by Secrecy: The Hidden History That Connects the Trilateral Commission, the Freemasons, and the Great Pyramids*, New York, HarperCollins, 2001.

McCarthy, Joseph R., *America's Retreat from Victory: The Story of George Catlett Marshall,* New York, Devin-Adair, 1951.

Nelson, Phillip F., *LBJ: The Mastermind of the JFK Assassination,* New York, Skyhorse Publishing, 2011.

Olsen, Jack, *Aphrodite: Desperate Mission,* New York, Putnam, 1970.

Oshinsky, David M., *A Conspiracy So Immense,* New York, Simon & Schuster, 1983.

Palamara, Vince, *Survivor's Guilt: The Secret Service and the Failure to Protect President Kennedy,* Oregon, Trine Day, 2013.

Schivelbusch, Wolfgang, *Three New Deals: Reflections on Roosevelt's America, Mussolini's Italy, and Hitler's Germany, 1933–1939*, London, Picador Publishing, 2007.

Schoultz, Lars, *Beneath the United States: A History of U.S. Policy toward Latin America* Cambridge: Harvard University Press, 1998.

Seagrave, Sterling, and Peggy Seagrave, *Gold Warriors,* Verso Books, 2003.

Shaw, J. Gary, and Harris, Larry R., *Cover-up: The Governmental Conspiracy to Conceal the Facts about the Public Execution of John Kennedy,* Texas, 1976.

Stone, Oliver, and Kuznick, Peter, *The Untold History of the United States,* New York, Simon & Schuster, 2012.

Sutton, Antony, *Wall Street and the Bolshevik Revolution,* New York, Arlington House, 1974.

Sutton, Antony, *Wall Street and FDR: The True Story of How Franklin D. Roosevelt Colluded with Corporate America,* New York, Arlington House, 1975.

Thomas, Evan, *The War Lovers, Roosevelt, Lodge, Hearst, and the Rush to Empire, 1898,* New York, Little, Brown and Company.

Transcripts of Army Signal Corps—Subversion and Espionage, Senate Committee on Government Operations, Senate Permanent Subcommittee on Investigations, Senator Joseph R. McCarthy, Chairman, 1953.

Zinn, Howard, *A People's History of the United States, 1492–Present,* New York, Harper & Row, 1980.

NOTES

Introduction

1. George Orwell, *All Art is Propaganda: Critical Essays* (Boston: Mariner Books, 2009), p. 26.
2. *VOA News,* January 19, 2016.
3. *History News Network,* February 26, 2008.
4. *CBS News,* March 19, 2004.
5. Lipstadt, Deborah (1993) *Denying the Holocaust: The Growing Assault on Truth and Memory* (New York: Plume, 1994), p. 67.
6. Annika Mombauer, *The Origins of the First World War* (London: Pearson, 2002), p. 87.
7. Lipstadt, p. 81.
8. *National Geographic,* January 8, 2021.
9. Speech in the House of Commons, July 14, 1856. Reproduced in *Hansard's Parliamentary Debates. Vol. CXLIII, London: Longmans, 1856,* pp. 773–774.
10. *MSN,* May 19, 2020.
11. *The Blaze,* February 2, 2016.
12. *Daily Mail,* February 21, 2021.
13. George Orwell, *1984,* p. 80.

Chapter One

1. Speech by Patrick Henry to the Second Virginia Revolutionary Convention meeting at St. John's Church, Richmond, March 23, 1775.
2. Kenneth C. Davis, *America's Hidden History* (New York: HarperCollins Publishers, 2002), pp. 87–118.
3. Howard Zinn, *A People's History of the United States, 1492–Present* (New York: Harper & Row, 1980), pp. 68, 74, 79.
4. *Diary of David Zeisberger, a Moravian missionary among the Indians of Ohio* (Cincinnati, R. Clarke & Company, 1885), pp. 80–81, 83.
5. Max Farrand, ed., *The Records of the Federal Convention of 1787,* vol. 3 (New Haven: Yale University Press, 1911), CCLXVII: Jared Sparks: Journal.

6. Cited in Washington Irving, *Life of George Washington,* vol. 1 (1856), p. 656.
7. *Philadelphia Independent Gazetteer*, February 5, 1788.
8. Cited in *Life, Correspondence and Speeches,* vol.1 (New York: Charles Scribner's Sons, 1891), p. 496.
9. Letter from Thomas Jefferson to Spencer Roane, 9 March, 1821 https://founders.archives.gov/documents/Jefferson/03–17-02–0025.
10. Letter from Thomas Jefferson to Nathaniel Macon, 19 August, 1821 https://founders.archives.gov/documents/Jefferson/03–17-02–0384.
11. *The Atlantic,* February 9, 2017.
12. Andrew Jackson, Bank Veto Message, 10 July, 1832. https://millercenter.org/the-presidency/presidential-speeches/july-10–1832-bank-veto.
13. *Yahoo News,* May 17, 2021.
14. https://www.monticello.org/thomas-jefferson-foundation/monticello-a-unesco-world-heritage-site/.
15. *Washington Post,* June 15, 2018.
16. "A Civil Action: Sally Hemings v. Thomas Jefferson," *American Journal of Trial Advocacy,* vol. 31: 1, 2007.
17. *The Atlantic,* August 19, 2015.
18. *Daily Mail,* October 13, 2021.
19. *Democracy Now!,* July 24, 2017.
20. *New York Times,* July 3, 2015.
21. Thomas Jefferson, *The Writings of Thomas Jefferson,* vol. 2, p. 130.
22. https://www.history.com/this-day-in-history/tyler-is-burned-in-effigy-outside-white-house.
23. John Tyler, Veto Message Regarding the Bank of the United States, August 16, 1841. https://millercenter.org/the-presidency/presidential-speeches/august-16–1841-veto-message-regarding-bank-united-states.
24. https://fee.org/articles/the-most-violent-demonstration-to-ever-occur-at-the-white-house/.
25. Gary May, *John Tyler (The American President's Series: The 10th President, 1841–1845),* p. 71.
26. Ibid, pp. 73–74.
27. John T. Hubbell, *John Tyler, World Book Encyclopedia*, p. 534.
28. James K. Polk Inaugural Address, March 4, 1845.
29. Zinn, *A People's History of the United States, 1492–Present,* pp. 149–152.
30. Ibid, p. 156.
31. Ibid, pp. 160–161.
32. Daniel A. Sjursen, *A True History of the United States: Racialized Slavery, Hyper-Capitalism, Militarist Imperialism and Other Overlooked Aspects of American Exceptionalism* (New Hampshire: Steerforth Press, 2021), p. 186.
33. Jolie Anderson Gallagher, *Colorado Forts: Historic Outposts on the Wild Frontier* (South Carolina: The History Press, 2013), pp. 98–99.

34. *Future of Freedom Foundation,* July 1, 2020.
35. Zinn, *A People's History of the United States, 1492–Present,* pp. 165–168.
36. Ibid, pp. 168–169.
37. Frederick Merk, *Proceedings of the Massachusetts Historical Society*, Third Series, vol. 81 (1969), p. 123.
38. *Washington Post,* December 5, 1998.

Chapter Two

1. Murray Rothbard, "America's Two Just Wars: 1776 and 1861," in *The Costs of War: America's Pyrrhic Victories*, p. 131.
2. Alexis de Tocqueville, *Democracy in America*, p. 359.
3. Lincoln, "Speech at Peoria, Illinois, in Reply to Senator Douglas, Oct. 16, 1854," in *Abraham Lincoln: His Speeches and Writings*, Roy P. Basler, ed., p. 306.
4. Thomas J. DiLorenzo, *The Real Lincoln, A New Look at Abraham Lincoln, His Agenda, and an Unnecessary War* (New York: Crown Forum, 2002), p. 18.
5. Lincoln, "Address at Cooper Institute, New York, Feb. 27, 1860," in *The Collected Works of Abraham Lincoln,* Roy Basler, ed., p. 541.
6. Lysander Spooner, "*No Treason: The Constitution of No Authority*", in *the Lysander Spooner Reader,* p. 121.
7. Webb Garrison, *The Lincoln No One Knows* (Nashville, Tenn.: Rutledge Hill Press, 1993), p. 36
8. Zinn, p. 188.
9. Abraham Lincoln's reply to Stephen Douglas, First Debate at Ottawa, Illinois, August 21, 1858, in *Abraham Lincoln: His Speeches and Writings*, Roy P. Basler, ed., p. 444.
10. Thomas J. DiLorenzo, *The Real Lincoln, A New Look at Abraham Lincoln, His Agenda, and an Unnecessary War* (Roseville: Prima Publishing, 2002), p. 29.
11. Stanley W. Campbell, *The Slavecatchers,* p. 188. Campbell writes, "In Cincinnati, a Negro named George Lee was arrested by United States Marshall and taken before a United States commissioner without opposition. Following the hearing, he was remanded to the custody of his claimant, and taken across the river to Covington, Kentucky to await return of his owner in Clarksburg, Virginia—despite the fact that the Deep South had seceded from the Union, the Fugitive Slave Law was still being enforced by Federal Marshalls." Campbell cites *National Intelligencer,* April 10, 1861.
12. Jackson, Helen, *A Century of Dishonor* (United States: Indian Head Books, 1994), p. 344.
13. Sides, Hampton, *Blood and Thunder: An Epic of the American West* (New York: Doubleday, 2006), p. 379.

14. Cited in David Donald, *Lincoln Reconsidered* (New York: Open Road Media, 2016), pp. 105–106.
15. Cited in *Abraham Lincoln, Selections from His Speeches and Writings,* J.G. de Roulhac Hamilto, ed. (Birmingham: Palladium Press, 2003), pp. 259–260.
16. Ibid, p. 255.
17. James M. McPherson, *Battle Cry of Freedom: The Civil War Era* (New York: Oxford University Press, 1988), p. 558.
18. Derek Wilson, *Rothschild: The Wealth and Power of a Dynasty* (New York: Scribner, 1988), p. 178.
19. Niall Ferguson, *The House of Rothschild* (New York: Penguin, 2000), p. 28.
20. Jim Marrs, *Rule by Secrecy: The Hidden History That Connects the Trilateral Commission, the Freemasons, and the Great Pyramids* (New York: HarperCollins, 2001), pp. 215–216.
21. G. Edward Griffin, *The Creature From Jekyll Island* (New York: American Media, Inc., 1994), p. 395.
22. "Evidence for The Unpopular Mr. Lincoln, The People at the Polls 1860–1864", *American Battlefield Trust,* https://www.battlefields.org/learn/articles/evidence-unpopular-mr-lincoln.
23. Donald Jeffries, *Crimes and Cover-Ups in American Politics, 1776–1963* (New York: Skyhorse Publishing, 2019) , p. 71.
24. *Washington Times,* October 29, 2004.
25. Cited in Elizabeth Keckley, *Behind the Scenes, Or, Thirty Years a Slave, and Four Years in the White House* (Eastford, CT: Martino Fine Books, 2017), p. 59.
26. *Civil War Times,* April 2011.
27. Ibid.
28. Ethan Rafuse, "Still a Mystery? General Grant and the Historians, 1981–2006" *The Journal of Military History* #71, no.3 (2007).
29. Lance Janda, "Shutting the Gates of Mercy: The American Origins of Total War, 1860–1880," *Journal of Military History* #59, no. 1 (1995).
30. Donald E. Sutherland, "Abraham Lincoln, John Pope, and the Origins of Total War," *The Journal of Military History*, no 4 (October 1992), p. 581.
31. Janda, p. 13.
32. Janna, p. 12.
33. Mildred Rutherford, *Truths of History* (Dahlonega, Georgia: Crown Rights Book Company, reprint of original 1920 edition), p. 21.
34. Michael R. Bradley *With Blood and Fire: Life Behind Union Lines in Middle Tennessee, 1863–65* (Pennsylvania: Burd Street Press, 2003), pp. 78–80.
35. *Official Records, Series 1, Vol. 38* pp. 39, 76–77.
36. *Official Records, Series 1, Vol.43, part 2,* p. 308.

37. Thomas J. DiLorenzo, *The Real Lincoln, A New Look at Abraham Lincoln, His Agenda, and an Unnecessary War* (New York: Crown Forum, 2002), pp. 219–220.
38. Ibid, p. 226.
39. *The National Interest,* April 22, 2021. One of the motivations appears to have been to use American warships and Marines to negotiate a trade treaty by force-of-arms, with the then-isolationist Korean government, similar to the treaty Commodore Perry had pushed Japan into adopting in 1853.
40. *Native American Words,* June 12, 2018. https://web.archive.org/web/20180612211000/http://spirit_cherokee.webs.com/nativeamericanwords.htm.
41. *Smithsonian,* November 2016.
42. Sjursen, *A True History of the United States,* p. 246.
43. Michael Fellman, *Citizen Sherman: A Life of William Tecumseh Sherman* (New York: Random House, 1995), p. 264.
44. *New York Times,* December 18, 1890.
45. Fellman, op. cit., p. 264.
46. Stephen Kinzer, *The True Flag: Theodore Roosevelt, Mark Twain, and the Birth of American Empire* (New York: MacMillan Publishers, 2017), p. 37.
47. Ibid, p. 29.
48. The September 2000, *Rebuilding America's Defenses,* states "Further, the process of transformation . . . is likely to be a long one, absent some catastrophic and catalyzing event—like a new Pearl Harbor."
49. Point 3 of this document states, "A 'Remember the Maine' incident could be arranged in several forms: a. We could blow up a US ship in Guantanamo Bay and blame Cuba." https://publicintelligence.net/operation-northwoods-documents/.
50. Zinn, p. 318.
51. Truth Dig, November 10, 2018.
52. Zinn, p. 300.
53. Evan Thomas, *The War Lovers, Roosevelt, Lodge, Hearst, and the Rush to Empire, 1898* (New York: Little, Brown and Company, 2010), p. 59.
54. Noel Maurer and Carlos Yu, *What T.R. Took: The Economic Impact of the Panama Canal, 1903–1907* (Cambridge University Press, 2008), pp. 711–713.
55. Lars Schoultz, *Beneath the United States: a History of U.S. Policy toward Latin America* (Cambridge: Harvard University Press, 1998), p. 191.
56. Thomas, p. 28.
57. *Dan Carlin's Hardcore History,* Episode 49: *The American Peril* (3:07 mark).
58. Truth Dig, November 10, 2018.
59. Thomas, pp. 404–405.
60. Woodrow Wilson, "Democracy and Efficiency," *Atlantic Monthly* #87 (March 1901), pp. 289–299.
61. *Philippine Daily Inquirer,* July 1, 2019.

62. *The Nation,* December 5, 2002.
63. Richard E. Welch Jr., "American Atrocities in the Philippines: The Indictment and the Response," *Pacific Historical Review,* vol. 43, no. 2, May 1974.
64. Zinn, pp. 313–317.
65. Ibid.
66. Ibid, p. 316.
67. Truth Dig, November 10, 2018.
68. Ibid.

Chapter Three

1. Wilson, Speech of October 11, 1915, in *The Foreign Policy of Woodrow Wilson* (New York: The Macmillan Company, 1917), eds. Edgar E. Robinson & Victor J. West, pp. 283–284.
2. *Washington Post,* March 8, 2017.
3. *Jewish Telegraphic Agency,* July 18, 1947. Additionally, one should consult Edwin Black, *War against the Weak, Eugenics and America's Campaign to Create a Master Race,* pp. 319–324. Katzen-Ellenbogen would be accused of murdering a thousand prisoners by injection. (-Editor)
4. *The Heritage Foundation,* July 31, 2012.
5. *Los Angeles Times,* December 1, 2013.
6. *Publishers Weekly,* February 15, 1919.
7. Dr. Stanley Montieth, *Brotherhood of Darkness* (Oklahoma City: Bible Belt Publishing, 2000), p 65.
8. William Jennings Bryan & Mary Baird Bryan, *The Memoirs of William Jennings Bryan,* Vol. II (1925), pp. 404–405.
9. Robert Ferrell, *Woodrow Wilson and World War I, 1917–1921* (New York: HarperCollins, 1986), p. 88.
10. Charles Seymore, *The Intimate Papers of Colonel House,* Vol. I, p. 432.
11. William G. McAdoo, *Crowded Years* (New York: Houghton Mifflin, 1931), p. 333.
12. As a pertinent aside, Lord Mersey would also head up the inquiry into the earlier 1912 sinking of the RMS Titanic, on behalf of the British Board of Trade. While the subject is not dealt with in this work, the interested reader should consult Robin Gardiner, *Titanic: the Ship that Never Sank?* (Ian Allan Publishing, 1998) and *The Great Titanic Conspiracy* (Ian Allan Publishing, 2010).
13. (The papers of Lord Mersey) Colin Simpson, *The Lusitania,* pp. 190, 241.
14. H. L. Mencken, *Prejudices: A Selection,* James T. Farrell, ed. (New York: Vintage Books, 1958), pp. 180–82.
15. *Smithsonian,* February 1998.
16. *Inquiry,* June 1980.

17. James W. Lowen, *Lies My Teacher Told Me: Everything Your American History Textbook Got Wrong* (New York: The New Press, 1995), pp. 18–19.
18. *New York Times,* October 14, 1920.
19. Nancy J. Weiss, *Farewell to the Party of Lincoln: Black Politics in the Age of FDR* (New York: Princeton University Press, 1983), p. 20.
20. Hans Schmidt, *The United States Occupation of Haiti, 1915–1934* (New York: Rutgers University Press, 1995), pp. 108–111.
21. Lowen, pp. 15–17.
22. Cited in A. Scott Berg, *Wilson* (New York: G.P. Putnam's Sons, 2013), p. 5.
23. Oliver Stone and Peter Kuznick, *The Untold History of the United States* (New York: Simon & Schuster, 2012), pp. 2–3.
24. *Denver Post,* March 14, 2014.
25. H. C. Peterson, *Propaganda for War. The Campaign against American Neutrality, 1914–1917* (Norman, Okla.: University of Oklahoma Press, 1939), p. 83.
26. *Forbes,* April 6, 2017.
27. Smedley Butler, *War is a Racket* (New York: Round Table Press Inc., 1935), pp. 31–32.
28. *New York Times,* February 14, 1917.
29. *New York Times,* March 24, 1917.
30. *Forbes,* April 6, 2017.
31. William Guy Carr, *Pawns in the Game* (Hollywood: Angriff Press, 1958), p. 104.
32. *Atlantic,* December 2009.
33. *New York Times,* July 11, 1935.
34. Marrs, *Rule by Secrecy*, pp. 31–32.
35. *The Crisis,* September 1913.
36. *Friday's Labor Folklore: The Force Feeding of Alice Paul* https://myemail.constantcontact.com/Friday-s-Labor-Folklore—The-force-feeding-of-Alice-Paul.html?soid=1110406756984&aid=bt5w2Be0oA8.
37. George Donelson Moss, *America in the Twentieth Century*, Fourth Ed. (New York: Prentice Hall, 2000), pp. 55–56.
38. Zinn, pp. 370–371.
39. *New York Times,* March 24, 1917.
40. UPI, February 4, 1924.
41. *Atlantic,* March 2005.
42. Griffin, *The Creature From Jekyll Island,* p. 263.
43. Antony Sutton, *Wall Street and the Bolshevik Revolution* (West Hoathly, England: Clairview Books, 2011 edition), p. 23.
44. Ibid, p. 26.

45. Jennings C. Wise, *Empire and Armament: The Evolution of American Imperialism and the Problem of National Defense* (New York: G.P. Putnam's Sons, 1915), p. 647.
46. Gary Allen with Larry Abraham, *None Dare Call it Conspiracy* (California: Concord Press, 1972), p. 73.
47. *New York Journal-American,* February 3, 1949.
48. Interesting to note is Jacob Schiff's involvement in the overthrow of the Russian Czar, actually beginning as early as the Russo-Japanese War of 1904. Kuhn, Loeb, & Company, had raised the capital for large war loans to Japan. Due to this funding, the Japanese were able to launch a stunning attack against the Russians at Port Arthur and virtually decimate the Russian fleet. In 1905, the Emperor awarded Schiff a medal for his help, the Second Order of the Treasure of Japan. During the two years of hostilities, thousands of Russian soldiers and sailors were taken prisoner. Schiff would finance the printing of Marxist propaganda and have it delivered to prison camps. Russian-speaking revolutionaries were then trained in New York to distribute the pamphlets among the prisoners and to indoctrinate them into rebellion against the Czarist government. When the war was ended, the officers and enlisted men returned home to become virtual seeds of treason against the Czar. They were to play a major role a few years later in creating mutiny among the military during the Communist takeover of Russia. See G. Edward Griffin, *The Creature from Jekyll Island,* pp. 263–264. Additionally, one should consult "Mayor Calls Pacifists Traitors," *New York Times,* March 24, 1917, pp. 1–2.
49. David Icke, *And the Truth Shall Set You Free* (United Kingdom: David Icke Books, 1996), p. 78.
50. Allen, *None Dare Call it Conspiracy,* p. 72.
51. Icke, *And the Truth Shall Set You Free,* pp. 77–78.
52. Antony Sutton, *Wall Street and FDR: The True Story of How Franklin D. Roosevelt Colluded With Corporate America* (New York: Arlington House, 1975), p. 162.
53. Antony Sutton, *Wall Street and the Bolshevik Revolution* (New York: Arlington House, 1974), p. 89.
54. Ibid, p. 174.
55. William Reswick, *I Dreamt Revolution* (Chicago: Henry Regnery, 1952), p. 78.
56. John P. Diggins, *Mussolini and Fascism: The View From America* (Princeton, NJ: Princeton University Press, 1972), p. 147.
57. Griffin, pp. 292–293.
58. Ibid.

Chapter Four

1. Cited in Alan Brinkley, *Voices of Protest: Huey Long, Father Coughlin & The Great Depression* (New York: Vintage Books, 1983), p. 64.
2. Sutton, *Wall Street and FDR* (West Hoathly, England: Clairview Books, 2011 edition), pp. 17–18.
3. *New York Times,* June 28, 1997.
4. Sutton, *Wall Street and FDR,* p. 37.
5. Sutton, *Wall Street and FDR,* pp. 42–43. Sutton cites a press release marked "From Hon. Franklin D. Roosevelt" in the FDR files.
6. Ibid, p. 42–43.
7. Ibid, p. 43.
8. Sutton, *Wall Street and FDR,* p. 25.
9. There is strong evidence to indicate that the Great Depression was deliberately brought on in an effort to rescue the failing, postwar British economy. G. Edward Griffin notes, "Benjamin Strong was a Morgan man and was appointed as the first Governor of the Federal Reserve Bank of New York which rapidly assumed dominance over the System. Strong immediately entered into close alliance with Montagu Norman, Governor of the Bank of England, to save the English economy from depression. This was accomplished by deliberately creating inflation in the U.S. which caused an outflow of gold, a loss of foreign markets, unemployment, and speculation in the stock market, all of which were factors that propelled America into the crash of 1929 and the great depression of the 30s." G. Edward Griffin, *The Creature from Jekyll Island* (West Lake, CA: American Media, Fourth ed., 2010), pp. 423, 427–428; additionally one should consult John Kenneth Galbraith, *Money: Whence It Came, Where It Went* (Boston: Houghton Mifflin, 1975), pp. 174–175.
10. Ibid, pp. 15–16, 116, 175.
11. Ibid, p. 41.
12. *Washington Post,* June 3, 2013. Additionally, one should consult George Donelson Moss, *America in the Twentieth Century,* Fourth Ed. (New York: Prentice Hall, 2000) pp. 214–215.
13. Moss, p. 207.
14. *American Heritage,* December 1984.
15. Sutton, *Wall Street and FDR,* pp. 161–162.
16. Wolfgang Schivelbusch, *Three New Deals: Reflections on Roosevelt's America, Mussolini's Italy, and Hitler's Germany, 1933–1939* (London: Picador Publishing, 2007), pp. 86–94.
17. Sutton, *Wall Street and FDR,* p. 128.
18. Schivelbusch, p. 88.
19. Ibid, p. 88.
20. Ibid, cited on p. 127.

21. John T. Flynn, *The Roosevelt Myth* (New York: Devin-Adair Co., 1948), p. 44.
22. Schivelbusch, pp. 80.
23. Amity Shlaes, *The Forgotten Man, A New History of the Great Depression* (New York: HarperCollins, 2007), p. 202.
24. Ibid, p. 6.
25. Ibid, p. 208.
26. Ibid, p. 227.
27. Flynn, p. 45.
28. Flynn, pp. 136–137.
29. Shlaes, p. 221.
30. Ibid. p. 225.
31. Ibid, p. 339.
32. Ibid, p. 344.
33. For the unfamiliar reader, Andrew Mellon was perhaps the richest man in America at the time. Former treasury secretary under Harding, Coolidge, and Hoover, Mellon was a "caricature" of capitalism; a figure to be widely demonized by FDR and his new policies for political purposes. Mellon hadn't broken any laws in the old tax loopholes he had used previously, but the FDR administration created new laws to retroactively prosecute him.
34. Ibid, p. 312.
35. Ibid, p. 234.
36. Kenneth S. Davis, *FDR: The Beckoning of Destiny, 1882–1928: A History* (New York: G.P. Putnam's Sons, 1972), p. 512.
37. David T. Beito, *The New Deal's War on the Bill of Rights: The Untold Story of FDR's Concentration Camps, Censorship, and Mass Surveillance* (Oakland: Independent Institute, 2023), pp. 248–249.
38. Ibid, p. 208.
39. Ibid, p. 15–35.
40. Ibid, p. 59.
41. Ibid, pp. 60–68.
42. Ibid, pp. 120–121.
43. Ibid, pp. 127–128.
44. *National Review,* September 28, 2023.
45. Beito, pp. 231–232.
46. *New York Daily News,* March 30, 1942.
47. Nicholson Baker, *Human Smoke, The Beginnings of World War II, the End of Civilization* (New York: Simon & Schuster, 2009), p. 210. Baker cites U.S. Senate Committee on Military Affairs, *Compulsory Military Training and Service,* pp. 21, 25, 148, 255.
48. Ibid, p. 222. Baker cites *New York Times,* August 20, 1940.

49. Ibid, p. 232. Baker cites the text of the Selective Service Measure reprinted in the *New York Times,* September 15, 1940.
50. Franklin D. Roosevelt campaign speech, Philadelphia, October 23, 1940.
51. *New York Times,* November 14, 1940.
52. *New York Times,* January 7, 1941.
53. Baker, p. 287. Baker cites *New York Times,* February 12, 1941.
54. *New York Times,* June 17, 1941.
55. Baker, p. 434. Baker cites *New York Times,* November 27, 1941.
56. Ibid. p. 312. Baker cites Howard Schoenfeld, "The Danbury Story" in Holley Cantine and Dachine Rainer, eds. *Prison Etiquette*, pp. 12 et seq.
57. Ibid, p. 351.
58. *National Review,* September 28, 2023
59. Beito, *The New Deal's War on the Bill of Rights,* pp. 236–237.
60. Ibid. p. 253.
61. Ibid.p. 257.
62. *Politico,* December 22, 2016. See also *Today in Civil Liberties History* "Truman Pardons 1,523 WW II Draft Resisters," (https://todayinclh.com/?event=truman-pardons-1523-ww-ii-draft-resisters)
63. Baker, pp. 335, 338–339.
64. Gus Russo, *Supermob: How Sidney Korshak and his Criminal Associates Became America's Hidden Power Brokers* (London: Bloomsbury Publishing, 2008), p. 114.
65. *Nichi Bei Times,* April 27, 1999.
66. See for example, "Roosevelt Says," *Macon Telegraph* (Macon, GA), April 30, 1925, p. 4: "Anyone who has travelled in the Far East knows that the mingling of Asiatic blood with European or American blood produces, in nine cases out of ten, the most unfortunate results . . . Californians have properly objected on the sound basic grounds that Japanese immigrants are not capable of assimilation into the American population." See also Greg Robinson, *By Order of the President: FDR and the Internment of Japanese Americans* (Cambridge, MA: Harvard University Press, 2001), pp. 93–94, 120: "Later that month, Roosevelt told journalist Quentin Reynolds that the Japanese were 'treacherous people' and 'hissed through his teeth,' imitating stereotypical speech patterns." Additionally, Robinson, *By Order of the President*, p. 120 & Richard Reeves, *Infamy* (New York: Henry Holt and Co., 2015), p. 34: "Roosevelt's assistant, William D. Hassett, recounted that in August 1942, 'the President related an old Chinese myth about the origin of the Japanese. A wayward daughter of an ancient Chinese emperor left her native land in a sampan and finally reached Japan, then inhabited by baboons. The inevitable happened and in due course the Japanese made their appearance.' In private conversations with friends during the same period, Roosevelt speculated that the Japanese were inferior to whites because their

less developed skulls had accentuated 'devious and treacherous' traits. That idea so fascinated him that he asked his friend, the eminent anthropologist Aleš Hrdlička, 'Could that be dealt with surgically?'"

67. Roger Daniels, *Prisoners without Trial* (New York: Hill & Wang, 2004), p. 55; Richard Reeves, *Infamy*, p. 48; and Greg Robinson, *By Order of the President: FDR and the Internment of Japanese Americans* (Cambridge, MA: Harvard University Press, 2001), p. 144.
68. Beito, pp. 181–182.
69. It is worth noting the US federal government actively promoted forced sterilization in Puerto Rico at the time. The 1937 Law 116 implemented eugenics boards to inflict sterilizations amongst the perceived "insane", "feeble minded", "diseased", and "dependent". The purpose of the Eugenics Board was to regulate the reproductive capacities of "socially inferior" and perceived undesirable Puerto Ricans, and to incite economic growth through population reduction. Clinics were set up for this purpose, and doctors financially incentivized. A survey in 1949 indicated that 21 percent of Puerto Rican women had been sterilized. By August of 1975, close to one-third of Puerto Rican women of child-bearing age had, in fact, been sterilized. See Bonnie Mass, *Latin American Perspectives* (Autumn, 1977), vol. 4, no. 4, pp. 71; https://en.wikipedia.org/wiki/Sterilization_of_Latinas; additionally one should consult, Beito, *New Deal's War,* pp. 264, 457.
70. Congressional Record, August 5, 1939.
71. Denis, Nelson, *War Against all Puerto Ricans: Revolution and Terror in America's Colony* (New York: Bold Type Books, 2015), pp. 241–245.
72. Robert Freeman Smith, "Good Neighbor Policy," *Watershed of Empire, Essays on New Deal Foreign Policy* (Colorado Springs: Ralph Myles, Publisher, 1976), pp. 75–76.
73. Nelson A. Denis, *War Against all Puerto Ricans: Revolution and Terror in America's Colony* (New York: Nation Books, 2015), p. 49.
74. Schivelbusch, p. 91.
75. *Newsweek,* December 9, 2008.
76. *History is Now Magazine,* January 7, 2015.
77. Letter from Secretary of War Stimson to the President, September 15, 1944.
78. Michael Beschloss, *The Conquerors: Roosevelt, Truman and the Destruction of Hitler's Germany 1941–1945* (New York: Simon & Schuster, 2003), p. 104.
79. Ibid, pp. 158–159.
80. Ibid, p. 144.
81. William L. Hitchcock, *The Bitter Road to Freedom: The Human Cost of Allied Victory in World War II Europe* (New York: Free Press, 2008), p. 171.
82. Time, August 11, 1947.
83. *Harvard Gazette,* January 9, 1997.

Chapter Five

1. Speech delivered by Senator Joseph McCarthy before the Senate on June 14, 1951. *The Congressional Record: Proceedings and Debates of the 82nd Congress, First Session,* Volume 97, Part 5 (May 28, 1951–June 27, 1951), pp. 6556–6603.
2. M. Stanton Evans, *Blacklisted by History* (New York: Crown Forum, 2007), pp. 179–194.
3. Transcript of Army Signal Corps—Subversion and Espionage, Tuesday November 3, 1953, Senate Committee on Government Operations, Senate Permanent subcommittee on Investigations, Senator Joseph R. McCarthy, Chairman, Testimony of Abraham Chasanow, p. 2920. (Vol. 4), https://archive.org/details/McCarthy-Hearing-Transcripts/McCarthy-Vol4/page/n197/mode/2up.
4. Ibid, Testimony of Harry J. Donohue, pp. 2366–2367. (Vol. 3). https://archive.org/details/McCarthy-Hearing-Transcripts/McCarthy-Vol3/page/n565/mode/2up.
5. Ibid, Testimony of Harry J. Donohue, p. 2368. (Vol. 3). https://archive.org/details/McCarthy-Hearing-Transcripts/McCarthy-Vol3/page/n565/mode/2up.
6. See for example, October 27, 1953, statement of Peter Rosmovsky, p. 2845 (Vol. 4). https://archive.org/details/McCarthy-Hearing-Transcripts/McCarthy-Vol3/page/n565/mode/2up.
7. Ibid, Testimony of Alan Sterling Gross, p. 2222. (Vol. 3). https://archive.org/details/McCarthy-Hearing-Transcripts/McCarthy-Vol3/page/n565/mode/2up.
8. See for example, see October 27, 1953, Statement of Peter Rosmovsky, p. 2845 (Vol. 4). https://archive.org/details/McCarthy-Hearing-Transcripts/McCarthy-Vol3/page/n565/mode/2up.
9. Ibid. See October 16, 1953 Testimony of Major General Kirke B. Lawton, Commandant, Fort Monmouth, New Jersey; Major General George I. Back, Chief Signal Officer, Major Jennistra, Security Officer, Office of Chief Signal Officer; Colonel Ferry; John Pernice, Chief Legal Division, Fort Monmouth; and Karl Gerhard, Chief, Special Projects Analysis Branch, Fort Monmouth, pp. 2570–2571 (Vol. 3). (https://archive.org/details/McCarthy-Hearing-Transcripts/McCarthy-Vol3/page/n565/mode/2up).
10. Years later in an interview, physicist John G. Trump would explain what it was he was sent to Tesla's residence to look for: *"something which would be evidence of a secret weapon, which I was reminded by the . . . two [FBI] Agents who were present during the entire time, was a matter of concern to the United States. . . . I spent a great deal of time looking through these papers, trying to find out what the nature of this secret weapon was. I think I had . . . an idea of what its properties were. It had the capability of*

acting at a great distance, of being destructive to flying objects and things of that kind, at a place which was remote from the source." https://m.youtube.com/watch?si=CJxqV-VFGbqp8mrq&v=7w3TAbsSzHY&feature=youtu.be Physicist John Trump worked in MIT's secretive Radiation Laboratory, and was a protégé of Dr. Vannevar Bush. In a November 29, 1983 reply letter written to author William Steinman, Dr. Robert Sarbacher states, *"1. Relating to my own experience regarding recovered flying saucers, I had no association with any of the people involved in the recovery and have no knowledge regarding the dates of the recoveries. If I had I would send it to you. 2. Regarding verification that persons you list were involved, I can only say this: John von Neuman was definitely involved. Dr. Vannevar Bush was definitely involved, and I think Dr. Robert Oppenheimer also."* (https://medium.com/@richgel99/letter-from-dr-robert-sarbacher-to-author-william-steinman-on-recovered-flying-saucers-cb31195828b2).

11. *The New Yorker,* April 8, 2016.
12. Ibid, Testimony of Dr. Fred D. Daniels, p. 2225–2226. (Vol. 3). (https://archive.org/details/McCarthy-Hearing-Transcripts/McCarthy-Vol3/page/n565/mode/2up).
13. Joseph P. Farrell, *McCarthy, Monmouth, and the Deep State* (Lulu Publishing, 2019), pp. 159–160.
14. Sean McMeekin, *Stalin's War* (New York: Basic Books, 2021), pp. 532–533. McMeekin cites George Racey Jordan and Richard L. Stokes, *From Major Jordan's Diaries,* pp. 93–95, 117.
15. Joseph Farrell, *The Third Way: The Nazi International, European Union, and Corporate Fascism* (Illinois: Adventures Unlimited Press, 2016), p. 299. Farrell cites George Racey Jordan and Richard L. Stokes, *From Major Jordan's Diaries,* pp. 229–230.
16. Transfer of Occupation Currency Plates—Espionage Phase, Monday, October 19, 1953, Senate Committee on Government Operations, Senate Permanent Subcommittee on Investigations, Senator Joseph R. McCarthy, Chairman, Testimony of William H. Taylor (Accompanied by his Counsel, Byron Scott), pp. 3406–3407 (Vol. 4). (https://archive.org/details/McCarthy-Hearing-Transcripts/McCarthy-Vol4/page/n679/mode/2up)
17. Transfer of Occupation Currency Plates – Espionage Phase, Monday, October 19, 1953, Senate Committee on Government Operations, Senate Permanent Subcommittee on Investigations, Senator Joseph R. McCarthy, Chairman, Testimony of Alvin W. Hall, Director of the Bureau of Engraving and Printing, p. 3422 (Vol. 4). (https://archive.org/details/McCarthy-Hearing-Transcripts/McCarthy-Vol4/page/n699/mode/2up?q=Forbes)
18. Farrell, *McCarthy, Monmouth, and the Deep State,* pp. 156–171.
19. M. Stanton Evans, *Blacklisted by* History (New York: Crown Forum, 2007), pp. 319–320.

20. David M. Oshinsky, *A Conspiracy So Immense* (New York: Simon & Schuster, 1983), pp. 74, 75–79
21. *Smithsonian,* July, 2020.
22. Ibid.
23. Thomas C. Reeves, "The Search for Joe McCarthy," *The Wisconsin Magazine of History,* vol. 60, no. 3 (Spring, 1977), pp. 185–196.
24. *Los Angeles Times,* January 24, 2002.
25. Medford Evans, *The Assassination of Joe McCarthy* (Massachusetts: Western Islands, 1970), pp. 261–265.
26. Arthur Herman, *Joseph McCarthy: Reexamining the Life and Legacy of America's Most Hated Senator* (New York: Free Press, 1999), p. 279.
27. Joseph P. Farrell, *McCarthy, Monmouth, and the Deep State,* pp. 70–71.
28. Burton Hersh, *Bobby and J. Edgar: The Historic Face-Off Between the Kennedys and J. Edgar Hoover That Transformed America* (New York: Carroll & Graf, 2007), p. 88.
29. Farrell, *The Third Way* (Illinois: Adventures Unlimited Press, 2015), p. 333. Additionally, one should consult M. Stanton Evans, *Blacklisted by History* (New York: Crown Forum, 2007), p.106. See also Sterling and Peggy Seagrave, *Gold Warriors: America's Secret Recovery of Yamashita's Gold* (New York: Verso, 2005), p. 251.
30. Sterling and Peggy Seagrave, *Gold Warriors: America's Secret Recovery of Yamashita's Gold* (New York: Verso, 2005), pp. 1, 3.
31. Ibid, p. 16.
32. Ibid, p. 12, 115.
33. John Foster Dulles's Speech at the San Francisco Peace Conference, September 5, 1951. Cited in The Department of State Bulletin, Vol. 25, Part 1, p. 457.
34. Seagrave, p. 12.
35. Wehler, Hans-Ulrich, *Deutsche Gesellschaftsgeschichte* [*German civil history*] (in German). Vol. 4. Munich, 1987.
36. Joseph R. McCarthy, *America's Retreat from Victory: The Story of George Catlett Marshall* (New York: Devin-Adair, 1951), pp. 13–16.
37. Joseph P. Farrell, *McCarthy, Marshall, and the Other International* (Lulu Publishing, 2020), p. 57.
38. Ibid, pp. 16–17.
39. Kennedy worked as a foreign correspondent for Hearst Newspapers, reporting on the 1945 Potsdam Conference in Berlin.
40. Cited in *Time,* May 14, 1951.
41. *Insurge Intelligence*, February 20, 2018.
42. Associated Press, September 29, 1999.
43. *CBS News,* June 6, 2000.
44. *Chicago Daily Law Bulletin,* March 26, 2001.

Chapter Six

1. Speech delivered by US Senator Ted Kennedy during the 1980 Democratic National Convention at Madison Square Garden, New York City.
2. *Chicago Magazine,* August 12, 2010.
3. *Daily Beast,* April 17, 2017.
4. *People,* May 7, 2014.
5. *Time,* October 31, 2017.
6. *New York Post,* July 13, 2019.
7. *New York Post,* November 3, 2013.
8. *Vanity Fair,* November 4, 2013.
9. *Daily Mail,* June 20, 2012.
10. *National Enquirer,* October 29, 2013.
11. *New York Post,* September 25, 1999.
12. *Daily Mail,* July 5, 2019.
13. *New York Post,* September 9, 2013.
14. *Time,* June 5, 2018.
15. *Daily Mail,* June 16, 2016.
16. *Daily Beast,* April 14, 2017.
17. *Politico,* May 8, 2019.
18. Ibid.
19. *New York Post,* August 28, 2021.
20. Cited in *New York Times,* January 21, 1964.
21. *Chicago Tribune,* November 11, 1986.
22. Hansen, Chris, *Enfant Terrible: The Times and Schemes of General Elliott Roosevelt* (Tucson: Able Baker, 2012).
23. Edward J. Renehan Jr., *The Kennedys at War, 1937–1945* (New York: Doubleday, 2002), p. 304.
24. Richard Dolan, *UFOs and the National Security State, Chronology of a Cover-up 1941–1973.* (Charlottesville: Hampton Roads Publishing Company, 2002), p. 9.
25. *New York Times,* March 28, 1970.
26. Olsen, Jack, *Aphrodite: Desperate Mission* (New York: Putnam, 1970), p. 223.
27. Ibid, p. 316.
28. Ibid, p. 317.
29. *New York Times,* October 4, 1973.
30. *Irish Central,* November 7, 2021.
31. *UK Telegraph,* May 20, 2016.
32. Cited in A. J. Langguth, *Our Vietnam: The War 1954–1975* (New York: Simon & Schuster, 2000), p. 297.
33. Hoover and Johnson were actually neighbors in Washington, D.C., and often dined privately together. See Jim Marrs, *Crossfire: The Plot That Killed Kennedy,* p. 223.

34. *ABC News,* September 8, 2011.
35. *New York Times,* October 26, 1997.
36. *Los Angeles Times,* September 18, 1996.
37. *CBS News,* November 23, 2013.
38. *United Press International,* August 14, 1985. Additionally, one should consult Jim Marrs, *Crossfire: The Plot that Killed Kennedy,* p. 275.
39. Reymond, William, and Billie Sol Estes, *JFK le Dernier Témoin: Assassinat de Kennedy, enfin la vérité.* (Paris: Flammarion, 2003), pp. 282–283.
40. Townsend Hoopes & Douglas Brinkley. *Driven Patriot: The Life and Times of James Forrestal* (Naval Institute Press, 2000), pp. 462, 543.
41. Craig Zirbel, *The Texas Connection: The Assassination of President John F. Kennedy* (New York: Time-Warner, 2001), p. 232.
42. Edward M. Kennedy, *True Compass: A Memoir* (New York: Twelve, 2009), p. 1262.
43. *People,* July 18, 2019.
44. *Breitbart,* July 18, 2019.
45. *Daily Mail,* August 2, 2011.
46. *Politico,* January 12, 2020.

Chapter Seven

1. Rolling Stones, lyrics to "Sympathy for the Devil," Track 1 on the album, *"Beggars Banquet"* (1968)
2. Cited in Kenneth P. O'Donnell & David F. Powers, *Johnny, We Hardly Knew Ye: Memories of John Fitzgerald Kennedy* (New York: Open Road Media, 2018), p.25.
3. *Smithsonian,* October 2013.
4. *Kennedy Assassination Chronicles,* Vol. 4, Issue 4, Winter 1998.
5. Kenn Thomas, *NASA, Nazis & JFK, The Torbitt Document and the JFK Assassination* (Illinois: Adventures Unlimited Press, 1996), p. 142.
6. William Davy, *Let Justice Be Done: New Light on the Jim Garrison Investigation* (Reston, Virginia: Jordan Publishing, 1999), pp. 59–60. Additionally, one should consult the Wikipedia article for more on the space plane (https://en.wikipedia.org/wiki/Boeing_X-20_Dyna-Soar). It is worth noting, Dornberger played a major role in the creation of another space plane, the X-15. In 1967, the X-15 would set the world record for highest speed ever recorded by a crewed, powered aircraft. Incredibly, the speed record remains unbroken to this day. (https://en.wikipedia.org/wiki/North_American_X-15). Pilot Joe Walker would claim that the purpose of the X-15 was to "hunt for UFOs during high altitude flights." See Philip J. Corso, *The Day after Roswell* (Gallery Books, 1997), p. 136.
7. *New Dawn,* September 2011.
8. *The Continuing Inquiry,* January 22, 1978, p. 4.

9. *Dallas Morning News,* September 20, 1978.
10. *Raleigh Spectator,* July 17, 1980.
11. *Raleigh News and Observer,* July 17, 1980.
12. *Dallas Morning News,* March 18, 1978.
13. *Dallas Morning News,* April 2, 1977.
14. *Dallas Morning News,* April 21, 1977.
15. *Inside the ARRB Journal,* December 8, 2009.
16. *Richmond Times-Dispatch,* November 17, 2013.
17. Warren Commission Hearings and Exhibits, Testimony of Patrick Dean. Vol. V, p. 254.
18. Sylvia Meagher, *Accessories After the Fact* (New York: Vintage Books, 1976), p. 24.
19. *Dallas Morning News,* March 25, 1979.
20. *Dallas Morning News,* November 21, 1993.
21. *Warren Commission Hearings & Exhibits,* Vol. 1, pp. 145–152.
22. *Dallas Morning News,* November 21, 2017.
23. *New York Post,* October 27, 2017.
24. *WC Hearings & Exhibits,* Vol. 3, p. 428.
25. *Vanity Fair,* September 9, 2023.
26. *Powell Tribune,* November 21, 2013.
27. *The Continuing Inquiry,* November 22, 1982.
28. Fonzi cited in *The Assassinations: Probe Magazine on JFK, MLK, RFK and Malcolm X,* James Di Eugenio & Lisa Pease, eds. (U.S.: Feral House, 2003), p. 56.
29. *The Continuing Inquiry,* February 22, 1981.
30. *New York Times,* March 27, 1978.
31. *New York Times,* October 16, 2019.
32. *Coverups!,* May 1984.
33. NBC, August 18, 1975.
34. *The Free-Lance Star,* January 23, 1992.
35. *New Orleans States Item,* February 21, 1969.
36. William Matson Law, *In the Eye of History: Disclosures in the JFK Assassination Medical Evidence* (Oregon: Trine Day, 2015), pp. 165–166.
37. *Reuters,* May 28, 1992.
38. Charles A. Crenshaw, with Jens Hansen and J. Gary Shaw, *JFK: Conspiracy of Silence* (New York: Signet, 1992), pp. 153–54.
39. William Matson Law, *In the Eye of History: Disclosures in the JFK Assassination Medical Evidence* (Oregon: Trine Day, 2015), pp. 430–431.
40. *People,* November 22, 2019.
41. Jefferson Morley, *Our Man in Mexico; Winston Scott and the Hidden History of the CIA* (Kansas: University Press of 2008), p. 292.

42. "White House Communications Agency," Signal Corps Regimental History (http://signal150.army.mil/white_house_communications_agency.html).
43. Peter Dale Scott, *Dallas '63, The First Deep State Revolt against the White House* (Forbidden Bookshelf, 2015), p. 193.
44. Larry Jordan, *Jim Reeves: His Untold Story* (Washington: Page Turner Books International, 2011), p. 627.
45. Craig Roberts, *JFK: The Dead Witnesses,* pp. 3–4.
46. *The Federalist Papers,* February 9, 2018.
47. *World Tribune,* February 19, 2021.
48. *Warren Commission Hearings & Exhibits,* Vol. 1, p. 153.
49. *Los Angeles Times,* March 11, 1964.
50. *The Daily Beast,* November 14, 2013.
51. *Fort Worth Star-Telegram,* January 19, 1981.
52. *Smithsonian Magazine,* November 20, 2014.
53. *The Daily Beast,* April 17, 2017.
54. *American Heritage,* October 1992.
55. UPI, January 18, 1981.
56. *The Daily Beast,* November 17, 2013.
57. *Washington Post,* August 15, 2014.
58. *Life,* October 24, 2013.
59. *Washington Post,* August 3, 1999.
60. David Harold Byrd, *I'm an Endangered Species: The Autobiography of a Free Enterpriser* (Texas: Pacesetter Press, Houston, 1978), pp. 3, 97–98.
61. *JFK CounterCoup2,* October 30, 2015, "OSS X-2 Report on Werner von Alvensleben," (http://jfkcountercoup2.blogspot.com/2015/10/oss-x-2-report-on-werner-von-alvensleben.html).
62. *Assassination Archives and Research Center,* 17 August, 2023, "Update: AARC v. CIA Opposition to Motion for Summary Affirmance as Filed," (https://aarclibrary.org/17-august-2023-update-aarc3-v-cia-opposition-to-motion-for-summary-affirmance-asfiled/).
63. *The Leopard's Trail—Christian von Alvensleben* (https://alensleben.com/stories/cva_leopards_trail.html).
64. Stan Deyo, *The Cosmic Conspiracy,* p. 25. Deyo writes, *"Some of the major contractors and suppliers for the Pine Gap facility have been Collins Radio, Ling-Tempco-Vought (L.T.V.)—both of Texas . . .* " Curiously, not only was LTV owned by DH Byrd, but *Collins Radio* was owned by Lyndon Baines Johnson. One of the last areas investigated by Danny Casolaro before his death was the Nugan Hand Bank (closely linked to Pine Gap). (Cheri Seymore, *The Last Circle,* New York: Trine Day, 2010, pp. 207–208).
65. *New York Times,* September 16, 1986.
66. The University of Texas at Dallas, "University's Precursor was to be Featured in Undelivered JFK Speech," November 22, 2013 (https://news.utdallas

.edu/campus-community/universitys-precursor-was-to-be-featured-in-undeli/). See also, *UT Dallas Magazine,* "The JFK Connection" (https://magazine.utdallas.edu/the-jfk-connection/). One of the proposals for the event involved Berkner being presented a flag that had previously flown over the nation's capitol.

67. Richard M. Dolan, *UFOs and the National Security State: Chronology of a Cover-Up, 1941–1973* (Massachusetts: Hampton Roads Publishing Company, 2002), pp. 123–124.
68. Engineering and Technology History Wiki, article: "Lloyd V. Berkner" (https://ethw.org/Lloyd_V._Berkner).
69. James E. MacDonald, *Firestorm: Dr. James E. MacDonald's Fight for UFO Science,* p. 382.
70. Dolan, pp. 380–381.
71. Dr. Berkner was an interesting figure indeed. An associate of Dr. Vannevar Bush, several of Berkner's accomplishments include: setting up long-range radio communications in Little America (as part of the Byrd expedition); proposing the 1957–1958 International Geophysical Year (during which time, several low-yield nukes were set off in the upper regions of the Earth's atmosphere); delivering the initial announcement to the public of the Russian satellite Sputnik's flight in 1957; and chairing the National Academy of Sciences' Space Science Board, which would go on to form NASA. (-Editor)
72. *Washington Post,* September 3, 1988.
73. See for example Josiah Thompson, *Last Second in Dallas* (University Press of Kansas, 2021), pp.129–130, 193 and passim; *"There is reason to believe that Alvarez saw his work on the Kennedy Assassination as an act of patriotism that would cleanse the public arena of the confusion introduced by a 'bunch of nuts' criticizing the Warren Report."* op cit., p. 349.
74. Dr. Alvarez may have actually acquired the fuses from a captured German scientist during the war, one Dr. Heinz Schlicke. Jim Marrs reports, " . . . There is evidence to support the idea that the necessary fuses were obtained from U-234 passenger Dr. Schlicke. A message from the chief of Naval Operations to the authorities in Portsmouth, where the U-234 was taken after its surrender, indicated that Dr. Schlicke along with his fuses were to be taken to Washington accompanied by naval officers. Once there, the doctor was scheduled to present a lecture on his fuses in the presence of a 'Mr. Alvarez,' apparently meaning Dr. Luis Walter Alvarez, the man who is credited with producing fuses for the plutonium bomb. Alvarez and his student Lawrence Johnson are credited with designing the exploding-bridgewire detonators for the spherical implosives used in the Trinity bomb test as well as the Nagasaki bomb." See Jim Marrs, *Rise of the Fourth Reich* (New York: HarperCollins Publishers, 2008), pp. 69–70.

75. *Slate,* July 16, 2014.
76. Richard Dolan, *UFOs and the National Security State, Chronology of a Cover-up 1941–1973* (Charlottesville: Hampton Roads Publishing Company, 2002), p. 125.
77. Jim Marrs, *Alien Agenda* (New York: HarperCollins Publishers, 1997), p. 80. One should also consult Luis Alvarez, *Alvarez: Adventures of a Physicist,* pp. 232–236.
78. *Washington Post,* September 3, 1988.
79. Robert J. Groden & Harrison Edward Livingstone, *High Treason: The Assassination of President John F. Kennedy and the New Evidence of Conspiracy* (New York: Berkeley Books, 1990), pp. 154–155. Groden and Livingstone are citing Colonel Fletcher Prouty.
80. Larry Sneed, *No More Silence: An Oral History of the Assassination of President Kennedy* (University of North Texas Press, 2002), p. 148.
81. *Salon,* September 10, 2017.
82. Albert A. Harrison, *Starstruck: Cosmic Visions in Science, Religion, and Folklore* (New York: Berghahn Books, 2007), p. 40.
83. *Vanity Fair,* October 17, 2014.
84. William Manchester, *Death of a President* (New York: Harper & Row, 1967), p. 290.
85. Ibid.
86. Militarycorruption.com, March 15, 2020.
87. *Time,* November 29, 1963.
88. *Warren Commission Hearings & Exhibits,* Vol. 21, p. 217.
89. Vincent Palamara, *The Not-So-Secret Service,* p. 9.
90. Craig Roberts and John Armstrong, *JFK: The Dead Witnesses* (Tulsa: Consolidated Press International, 1995), p. 3.
91. Associated Press, November 21, 1993.
92. Militarycorruption.com, March 15, 2020.
93. *Dallas Morning News,* March 23, 1971.
94. *New York Journal American,* November 15, 1965.
95. *New York Post,* September 2, 2017.
96. *Politico,* February 4, 2016.
97. *Cleburne Times-Review,* June 20, 2011.
98. George de Morenschildt, *I Am a Patsy!* (manuscript), p. 3.
99. *Fort Worth Star-Telegram,* May 11, 1978.
100. *Washington Star,* March 31, 1977.
101. *USA Today,* October 27, 2017.
102. *South Florida Sun-Sentinel,* November 21, 1993.
103. *Newsweek,* March 9, 2015.
104. *Politico,* February 24, 2015.
105. CNN, March 1, 2015.

106. *Deadline,* March 9, 2015.
107. *Washington Post,* March 10, 2015.
108. Fletcher Prouty, *JFK: The CIA, Vietnam, and the Plot to Assassinate John F. Kennedy* (New York: Skyhorse, 2011), p. 302.
109. Warren Commission Hearings & Exhibits, Vol. VII, p. 68.
110. Associated Press, April 26, 2018.
111. Gerald Celente Twitter post of November 8, 2021.
112. *New York Post,* October 23, 2021.
113. *Politico,* October 24, 2021.
114. *NBC News,* December 15, 2021.
115. *New York Times,* July 16, 2023.
116. James Douglas, *JFK and the Unspeakable: Why he Died and Why it Matters* (New York: Touchstone, 2008), p. 163.
117. *Washington Post,* November 25, 1998.
118. Martin Luther King Jr. "I've Been to the Mountaintop" speech, Memphis, Tennessee, April 3, 1968.
119. Sirhan Sirhan, February 10, 2016 parole hearing.
120. *Pressreader,* April 1, 2018.
121. *Who Killed Martin Luther King?* Documentary (Clarendon Entertainment) (25:00–32:20 mark)
122. *USA Today,* January 20, 2022. Additionally, one should consult *Covert Action Information Bulletin,* No. 34, Summer, 1990.
123. *Pressreader,* April 1, 2018.
124. *Washington Post,* March 30, 2018.
125. *The Guardian,* July 1, 1974.
126. *New York Times,* August 22, 1995.
127. John Larry Ray & Lyndon Barsten, *Truth at Last: The Untold Story behind James Earl Ray and the Assassination of Martin Luther King Jr.,* p. 136.
128. James Earl Ray, *Who Killed Martin Luther King Jr.?* (De Capo Press, 1997), pp. 138–140, 163. Additionally, one should consult Ray and Barnstein, *Truth at Last,* p. 168.
129. James Earl Ray's new attorney, Richard J. Ryan attributed Judge Faquin's decision to an FBI-CIA conspiracy.
130. *Buffalo News,* January 20, 2014. See also *Rielpolitik,* January 22, 2022. The week after his brother's death, Alfred King had given a powerful sermon at the Ebenezer Baptist Church in Atlanta entitled "Why America Can Go to Hell."
131. Louis Lomax, *To Kill a Black Man: Shocking Parallel of the Lives of Malcolm X and Martin Luther King Jr.* (Los Angeles: Holloway House Publishing, 1968).

132. William Pepper, *Orders to Kill* (New York: Carroll & Graf Publishers, 1995), p. 239. See also Jesse Ventura, *American Conspiracies* (New York: Skyhorse Publishing, 2010), p. 58.

Sartor, who was on the staff of the *Birmingham News*, had reported on an alleged meeting between Ray and an associate Charles Stein with members of the Carlos Marcello crime family in New Orleans before King's assassination. Sartor's original death certificate was evasive, stating that the cause of death was undetermined. After 21 years, it was acknowledged that he died from an overdose when Sartor was not known to use drugs of any kind. The Waco district attorney had characterized his death as a homicide.

133. Philip F. Nelson, *Who REALLY Killed Martin Luther King Jr.? The Case against Lyndon B. Johnson and J. Edgar Hoover* (New York: Skyhorse Publishing, 2018), p. 400. Gary Revel, who worked on the HSCA investigation, wrote to author Phillip Nelson that his "brother and cousin's husband, Ivan Riley, as well as Sullivan and five other FBI officials who could have been valuable to my investigation died mysteriously or were simply killed during 1977."
134. Crossfire by Jim Marrs, p. 220.
135. Memorandum for the Director of Central Intelligence, Subject: Roselli, Johnny, November 19, 1970
136. American Mafia.com, June, 2002.
137. Lisa Pease, *A Lie Too Big To Fail; the Real History of the Assassination of Robert F. Kennedy*, p. 409.
138. *Daily Mail*, May 25, 2021.
139. *New York Times*, January 4, 1976.
140. Gerald Bellett, "John Meier's Diary, October 25, 1969," *Age of Secrets, The Conspiracy that Toppled Richard Nixon and the Hidden Death of Howard Hughes* (Las Vegas Free Press LLC, 2015), p. 348.
141. Lisa Pease, *A Lie Too Big to Fail* (Washington: Feral House, 2018), p. 64.
142. Ibid, pp. 248–249.
143. *H. L. Hunt, Motive & Opportunity*, pp. 134–142.
144. Pease, *A Lie Too Big to Fail*, pp. 194–195.
145. *Washington Post*, June 5, 2018.
146. Boston.com, May 31, 2018.
147. *Los Angeles Times*, February 17, 1991.
148. *The Guardian*, August 31, 2019.
149. *New York Post*, September 11, 2021.
150. *Los Angeles Times*, January 18, 1996.
151. *Chicago Tribune*, March 31, 1992.
152. *Texas Monthly*, April 2021.

Chapter Eight

1. George Bernard Shaw, "Maxims for Revolutionists," *Man and Superman* (New York: Bretano's, 1905).
2. CNBC, February 22, 2018.
3. *Washington Post,* April 20, 1980.
4. Spiro T. Agnew, *Go Quietly . . . Or Else* (New York: Morrow, 1980), pp. 189–190.
5. Richard M. Dolan, *UFOs and the National Security State: Chronology of a Cover-Up, 1941–1973* (Massachusetts: Hampton Roads Publishing Company, 2002), pp. 373–374.
6. *Smithsonian,* June 22, 2016.
7. *Politico,* January 21, 2019.
8. *Politico,* June 28, 2019.
9. Bill Hicks, *"It's Just a Ride"* Comedy Special (1992).
10. Cited in *The New Yorker,* August 5, 2013.
11. *Wall Street Journal,* August 22, 2011.
12. NPR, June 16, 2008.
13. *Wall Street Journal,* August 22, 2011.
14. *The New Yorker,* August 12, 2013.
15. *Washington Post,* January 15, 2014.
16. *Washington Post,* January 15, 2020.
17. *New York Times,* February 24, 1999.
18. Associated Press, April 18, 1993.
19. *San Francisco Chronicle,* May 26, 2013.
20. *Huffington Post,* May 8, 2015.
21. *Institute for Justice,* September 9, 2013.
22. *Los Angeles Times,* October 11, 1992.
23. *Chicago Sun-Times,* May 12, 2021.
24. *CBS Baltimore,* June 17, 2021.
25. *Kentucky Center for Investigative Reporting,* March 4, 2019.
26. *Washington Post,* January 15, 2014.
27. *The Atlantic,* July 19, 2017.
28. *Minneapolis Star-Tribune,* July 3, 2021.
29. *New York Times,* June 28, 2005.
30. Cited in *New York Times,* July 31, 1981.
31. *Politifact,* September 8, 2017.
32. *Washington Post,* December 21, 2018.
33. *Arizona Republic,* February 11, 2018.
34. The White House, "President Bush Honors Presidential Medal of Freedom Recipients," (June 2008)
35. *London Times,* May 11, 1987.
36. *Spin,* November 1989.

37. *Time,* March 19, 2017.
38. *Huffington Post,* February 21, 2014.
39. *Forbes,* January 25, 2021.
40. *Forbes,* December 28, 2021.
41. *State of the Nation,* April 22, 2020.
42. *Children's Health Defense,* April 22, 2020.
43. *Medical Kidnap,* May 16, 2015.
44. *The American Conservative,* March 30, 2017.
45. *Insurance Journal,* August 14, 2020.
46. NPR, February 22, 2011.
47. *New York Post,* October 24, 2021.
48. Cited in *New York Times,* July 9, 1982.
49. *Dallas Morning News,* April 1, 1981.
50. UPI, September 18, 1981.
51. *Newsweek,* April 13, 1981.
52. *New York Times,* October 21, 1981.
53. *CBS News,* July 27, 2016.
54. *CBS Philly,* January 28, 2016.
55. NBCDFW, April 19, 2019.
56. CNN, June 1, 2022.
57. https:///www.youtube.com/watch?v=UtFcna4z1AQ.

Chapter Nine

1. Cited in David Hoffman, *The Oklahoma City Bombing and the Politics of Terror* (Washington: Feral House, 1998), p. 163.
2. *New York Times,* May 11, 1996.
3. Wendy Bird's Blog, October 2, 2009.
4. Newswithviews.com, September 30, 2005.
5. *Dallas Morning News,* October 8, 1995.
6. *McCurtain Daily Gazette,* September 25, 1996.
7. *McCurtain Daily Gazette,* July 14, 1996.
8. *New York Times,* May 16, 1997.
9. *New York Times,* May 23, 1997.
10. *The Oklahoman,* May 8, 2003.
11. *People,* March 31, 1997.
12. John DeCamp, *The Franklin Cover-Up* (Lincoln, NE: AWT, Inc., 1996), pp. 345–46.
13. *Newsweek,* July 2, 1997.
14. *Deseret News,* February 22, 2007.
15. *Buffalo News,* April 17, 2020.
16. Interview on Oprah, 1996.
17. *Orlando Sentinel,* July 19, 1999.

18. Associated Press, February 8, 2007.
19. *London Sunday Mirror,* July 7, 2002.
20. *In Touch Weekly,* March 25, 2020.
21. *US Magazine,* March 18, 2020.
22. *Star Magazine,* February 6, 2020.
23. *New York Post,* January 5, 2019.
24. *New York Post,* June 17, 2007.
25. *New York Times,* July 23, 1999.
26. Associated Press, July 21, 1999.
27. *Seattle Times,* July 10, 2009.
28. *People,* July 3, 2019.
29. *Hartford Courant,* July 20, 1999.
30. *Cape Cod Times,* July 25, 1999.
31. *Inside Scene,* August 28, 2016.
32. *New York Post,* July 13, 2019.
33. *London Sunday Mirror,* July 11, 2004.
34. *Chicago Tribune,* December 14, 1997.
35. *Daily Telegraph,* June 19, 2001.
36. *Tampa Bay Times,* July 18, 1999.
37. *Cape Cod Times,* July 25, 1999.
38. *Wayne Madsen Report,* August 12, 2009.
39. *National Enquirer,* July 18, 2014.
40. *The Guardian,* May 29, 2000.

Chapter Ten

1. *Drowned in Sound,* October 13, 2006.
2. The People's Voice.tv, "156 Eyewitnesses say 9/11 Twin Towers Collapsed due to Explosives," January 1, 2016.
3. *News With Views, September 2, 2005.*
4. Susan Hagen and Mary Carouba, *Women at Ground Zero: Stories of Courage and Compassion* (Indianapolis: Alpha Books, 2002), 65–66, 68.
5. Dean E. Murphy, *September 11: An Oral History* (New York: Doubleday, 2002), pp. 9–1–15.
6. *Wall Street Journal,* September 12, 2001.
7. Alicia Shepard, Cathy Trost, and Newseum, *Running Toward Danger: Stories Behind the Breaking News of 9/11* (Lanham, Md.: Rowman & Littlefield, 2002), p. 87.
8. *People,* September 24, 2001.
9. *NY Newsday,* September 12, 2001.
10. *The Chief Engineer,* July, 2002.
11. *Arctic Beacon,* July 12, 2005.

12. Susan Hagen and Mary Carouba, *Women at Ground Zero: Stories of Courage and Compassion* (Indianapolis: Alpha Books, 2002), pp. 21–30.
13. *New York Times,* January 23, 2002.
14. *New York Times,* October 31, 2001.
15. *New York Times,* November 9, 2001.
16. *New York Times,* October 12, 2001.
17. *New York Times,* November 7, 2001.
18. *New York Times,* October 25, 2001.
19. *New York Times,* October 16, 2001.
20. Ibid.
21. *New York Times,* October 3, 2001.
22. *New York Times,* October 16, 2001.
23. *New York Times,* October 10, 2001.
24. *New York Times,* December 10, 2001.
25. *New York Times,* January 17, 2002.
26. *The Rutherford Institute,* February 6, 2007.
27. *Arctic Beacon,* July 21, 2005.
28. *The Arctic Beacon,* July 19, 2005.
29. *911Blogger.com,* February 26, 2007.
30. Associated Press, August 25, 2011.
31. Associated Press, September 12, 2021.
32. *The Guardian,* September 12, 2002.
33. *Daily Mail,* September 11, 2011.
34. *The Jet Press,* September 14, 2016.
35. *Washington Post,* March 4, 2018.
36. Barbara Honneger, "Eyewitness for and Evidence of Explosives at the Pentagon," *The 9/11 Toronto Report,* 2012, Chapter 13.
37. *CS Globe,* February 4, 2017.
38. *Courthouse News Service,* October 19, 2011.
39. *Gumshoe News,* September 23, 2019.
40. Associated Press, February 29, 2012.
41. *Bloomberg,* June 26, 2009.
42. *KSLA 12 News,* October 18, 2007.
43. Associated Press, May 27, 2007.
44. *Buffalo News,* May 1, 2009.
45. *Haaretz,* September 26, 2001.
46. *New York Post,* December 6, 2006.
47. *Denver Post,* September 14, 2012.
48. *New York Times,* March 5, 2010.
49. UPI, October 31, 2001.
50. *Denver Post,* November 17, 2009.
51. *GQ,* June 28, 2016.

52. *The Millennium Report,* July 10, 2014.
53. *New York Times,* November 1, 2001.
54. Associated Press, September 18, 2001.
55. *Wall Street Journal,* October 22, 2001.
56. *American Free Press,* April 6, 2015.
57. *The Guardian,* September 2, 2002.
58. *9/11 Commission Report,* note 451 for Chapter 1.
59. *Fox News,* January 18, 2012.
60. *Newsweek,* September 13, 2001.
61. *WYFF 4,* September 10, 2011.
62. *ABC News,* January 6, 2006.
63. *World Net Daily,* February 27, 2002.
64. *World Net Daily,* March 7, 2002.
65. Ibid.
66. *New York Post,* November 4, 2001.
67. *Newsweek,* January 2, 2009.
68. CNN, September 11, 2001.
69. *Washington Post,* September 5, 2002.
70. *New York Daily News,* October 9, 2007.
71. *CBS News,* November 5, 2001.
72. MSNBC, July 31, 2014.
73. *PBS,* September 10, 2016.
74. Knight Ridder, September 12, 2001.
75. *San Francisco Chronicle,* September 17, 2001.
76. *New York Times,* September 12, 2001.
77. Associated Press, September 11, 2001.
78. *Baltimore Sun,* January 28, 2004.
79. *New York Post,* September 10, 2021.
80. *Shoestring 911 Blog,* October 8, 2008.
81. *Philadelphia Daily News,* November 15, 2001.
82. *Pittsburgh Post-Gazette,* September 14, 2001.
83. *New York Post,* June 18, 2004.
84. *Times Observer,* September 11, 2021.
85. Glenn J. Kashurba, *Courage After the Crash: Flight 93 Aftermath—An Oral and Pictorial Chronicle* (Somerset, PA: SAJ Publishing, 2002), p. 60.
86. Jere Longman, *Among the Heroes: United Flight 93 and the Passengers and Crew Who Fought Back* (New York: HarperCollins, 2002), p. 216.
87. *Pittsburgh Post-Gazette,* September 12, 2001.
88. Newseum, Cathy Trost and Alicia C. Shepard, *Running Toward Danger: Stories behind the Breaking News of 9/11* (Rowman & Littlefield Publishers, 2002), p. 148.
89. Glenn J. Kashurba, *Courage After the Crash: Flight 93 Aftermath—An Oral and Pictoral Chronicle* (Saj Publishing, 2002), p. 110.

90. *Pittsburgh Tribune-Review,* September 14, 2001.
91. David McCall, *From Tragedy to Triumph*, p. 25.
92. Associated Press, September 3, 2006.
93. *Pittsburgh Post-Gazette,* March 30, 2012.
94. *The UK Independent,* August 13, 2002.
95. Lisa Beamer and Ken Abraham, *Let's Roll: Ordinary People, Extraordinary Courage* (Wheaton, IL: Tyndale House Publishers, 2002), pp. 184–185.
96. *Newsweek,* December 3, 2001.
97. Ibid.
98. *Washington Post,* May 12, 2002.
99. Lisa Beamer and Ken Abraham, *Let's Roll!: Ordinary People, Extraordinary Courage* (Wheaton, IL: Tyndale House Publishers, 2002), p. 211.
100. *San Francisco Chronicle,* September 17, 2001.
101. *Daily Mail,* December 27, 2019.
102. *Pittsburgh Post-Gazette,* September 19, 2001.
103. Salem-News.com, September 12, 2010.
104. *Boston Globe,* September 12, 2001.
105. *Philadelphia News,* November 18, 2001.
106. *Mirror,* September 12, 2002.
107. *Pittsburgh Post-Gazette,* October 15, 2001.
108. *Daily American,* September 12, 2001.
109. *Pittsburgh Tribune-Review,* September 4, 2011.
110. *Dayton Daily News,* September 14, 2001.
111. *Dayton Daily News,* September 12, 2001.
112. Associated Press, July 9, 2018.
113. *Johnstown Tribune-Democrat,* September 6, 2021.
114. *NPR News,* September 3, 2021.
115. *Pittsburgh Post-Gazette,* September 17, 2001.
116. *Tribune Democrat,* September 12, 2001.
117. *Vanity Fair,* August 1, 2006.
118. *The New York Times,* November 29, 2002.
119. *New York Times,* June 16, 2021.
120. C-SPAN, September 11, 2006.
121. *UK Express,* September 11, 2019.
122. *Sarasota Herald-Tribune,* December 12, 2016.
123. *Common Ground,* May 9, 2019.
124. *Yahoo,* September 11, 2021.
125. *Daily Mail,* August 26, 2021.
126. *New York Law Journal,* October 17, 2011.
127. *From the Trenches World Report,* May 10, 2017.
128. *Independent,* April 16, 2020.
129. *Denver Post,* October 5, 2020.

130. *New York Times,* June 24, 2009.
131. *New York Post,* August 25, 2021.
132. *Salon,* August 25, 2021.
133. *Slate,* August 24, 2021.
134. *Fox News,* April 22, 2010.
135. *New York Times,* March 27, 2008.
136. *Tactical Edge,* December 6, 2002.
137. *USA Today,* September 11, 2021.
138. *Newsweek,* September 11, 2021.
139. *Media Matters,* July 21, 2004.
140. *11Alive Atlanta,* September 10, 2021.
141. *ABC News,* January 7, 2006.
142. *International Business Times,* December 10, 2014.
143. *The Guardian,* May 21, 2004.
144. *Salon,* July 15, 2004.
145. *Los Angeles Times,* July 27, 2002.
146. *The Hill,* July 20, 2017.
147. *Washington Post,* June 18, 2004.
148. *Business Insider,* August 18, 2012.
149. *Reason,* May 24, 2013.
150. *Live Science,* October 13, 2016.
151. The *Alex Jones Show,* Sunday, 4 May 2008 (14:40 mark).
152. *Time,* May 1, 2008.
153. *Minneapolis Post,* March 11, 2009.
154. *Cleveland.com,* November 11, 2008.
155. *911Truth.org,* July 11, 2008.
156. *Rense.com,* October 10, 2007.
157. *Hard Copy,* November 27, 1997.
158. *Press-Enterprise,* December 9, 2006.
159. *Health Nut News,* June 23, 2015.
160. *News-Press,* June 29, 2015.
161. *CBS News,* August 22, 2020.
162. *Health Nut News,* July 14, 2015.
163. *Cherry Hill Courier-Post,* November 12, 2021.
164. *Gateway Pundit,* February 22, 2020.
165. *Natural News,* January 26, 2011.
166. *Washington Post,* August 10, 2010.
167. *Baltimore Sun,* March 9, 1998.

Chapter Eleven

1. Cited in *CBS Crime News,* April 29, 2013.

INDEX

H